YORK COUNTY

CONTENTS

Chapter I
Out of the Wilderness   9

Chapter II
The Founding of York Town   21

Chapter III
Capital of Revolutionary America   35

Chapter IV
Center of Trade and Commerce   55

Chapter V
Railroads Above and Below the Ground   75

Chapter VI
Post-Civil War Prosperity   95

Chapter VII
Word War I and the "Roaring Twenties"   117

Chapter VIII
The Depression Years   135

Chapter IX
The Rise of the Greater York Area   145

Chapter X
Into A New Millennium   177

Chapter XI
Chronicles of Leadership   195

A Timeline of York County's History   268

Acknowledgments   276

Bibiliography   277

Index   279

Facing page

Top
Salem Square, west of down-town York, was a restful, inviting place when this photo was taken after the turn of the century. The Civil War monument seen below the American flag was refurbished after standing guard for decades at this spot and can still be seen today. Note the statuary and flower urns, now gone from the scene. Postcard published by Fair and Square Bargain House, York, courtesy, The Schintz Studio

Bottom
This watercolor by William Wagner shows Smyser's Black Bear Hotel on the Gettysburg Turnpike, just beyond what was later West York Borough. Courtesy, The York County Heritage Trust

This painting by William Wagner shows a view from the southeast corner of Beaver and Market streets. The building on the left is the old White Hall or National Hotel. The full three-storied house to the east still stands. Courtesy, The York County Heritage Trust

THE PORTRAICTUER OF CAPTAYNE IOHN SMITH ADMIRALL OF NEW ENGLAND.

One of the first white men to meet the Susquehannock Indians was Captain John Smith. He wrote of the natives, "Such great and well proportioned men are seldome seene. . . ." Courtesy, The Historical Society of York County.

CHAPTER I

OUT OF THE WILDERNESS

The history of York is a richly colored mosaic stretching over three centuries. It takes its tone and rhythm from great and quiet moments, and its texture and breadth from inhabitants and visitors as varied as human nature itself. Once an Indian hunting ground, then a frontier village, the town of York was destined to serve for nine months as the capital of the New Republic and would further distinguish itself throughout its development from a planned pioneer settlement of thrifty, energetic, and religious individuals to a highly diversified community of more than 300,000 people. York's heritage and modern-day story are both marked by bountiful contributions to the American spirit.

The story of York weaves together the tales of powerful Indians, passionate soldiers, anxious Congressmen, skilled craftsmen, artists, inventors, industrialists, Confederate generals, bold schoolgirls, peaceful churchgoers, self-proclaimed witches, eccentric businessmen, and thousands of other men, women, and children.

Located in southcentral Pennsylvania, York is 50 miles north of Baltimore, 200 miles southwest of New York City, 90 miles west of Philadelphia, and about 10 miles west of the Susquehanna River. The Maryland border, surveyed by Mason and Dixon, lies south of York about 18 miles from center city.

The Susquehanna—450 miles long—flows from New York State's Otsego Lake southeast through Pennsylvania, then empties into the Chesapeake Bay at Havre de Grace, Maryland. The river was the region's single most important factor in attracting people—first Indians, then the early explorers and settlers.

The Indians' story begins millenia before York's three centuries of recorded history, when nomadic hunters migrated across the land bridge of the Bering Sea (through what is now Alaska) and followed Ice Age animals over North America.

During the 15th century, tribes classified by archaeologists as Late Woodland arrived in New York State. This group of Indians spoke the Iroquois language. Intertribal conflicts apparently caused a splinter group to move away from the main body and migrate southward into southern New York and northern Pennsylvania. This group began to increase in size but further conflicts with the main group forced its members to move southward again.

About the year 1575, Indians reached the area of the Susquehanna and built a stockaded town on the east side of the river in Washington Borough. The Susquehannocks, as they were called, built "long houses" made of two parallel rows of posts 20 feet apart. Each post was tied to the one facing it in the opposite row. The pole frame, 60 to 80 feet long, was then covered with slabs of bark. Beds were built inside along the walls, and storage pits were dug beneath them. Like the Iroquois from whom their culture derived, the Susquehannocks were a matriarchal society and female members of the same family shared the long house. The only other clues to the nature of their life in the Susquehanna Valley are hidden in the shards of pottery, projectile points and other artifacts buried by the centuries.

Captain John Smith was one of the first Europeans to describe these people. Smith, who had had considerable experience with other Indians, was impressed by their size, their cleanliness, and their independence. The English explorer, in 1608, wrote: "Sixty of those Sasquehanocks came to us with Skins, Bowes, Arrows, Targets, Beads, Swords and Tobacco pipes for presents. Such great and well proportioned men are seldome seene, for they seemed like Giants to the English yea and to the neighbours, yet seemed of an honest and simple disposition with much adoes restrained from adoring us as Gods. These ar the strangest people of all those Countries, both in language and attire; for their language it may well beseeme their proportions, sounding from them as a voyce in a vault." He wrote that the Indians' proportions made them seem to the English "the godliest men we ever beheld."

The Indians used the river as a trade route, as a battleground, and as a source of food and transportation. A few of them made settlements along its banks and used the interior land for another source of food—game and plants—both of which were abundant in the forests and fields. They roamed the land freely, and sometimes a small group or a family would break away from the main tribe and settle in distant places, so it is not unlikely that a few of them lived on the banks of the Codorus in what is now York.

About 1665 the Susquehannocks, still engaged in wars with their northern neighbors, erected one town and perhaps two in York County directly across the river from their Washington Borough site. The Indians along the river developed extensive trade with the Europeans, who brought guns, powder, kettles, iron knives, axes, glass beads, and liquor. Furs were the Indians' chief trading commodity and these animal pelts became much in demand at European and Indian markets.

Soon the Indians stopped producing their own pottery and tools, relying on European substitutes that proved to be more durable. The Susquehannock culture, also weakened by increasing alcoholism, deteriorated.

The Indians' lands near the Susquehanna River had an enormous variety of flora and fauna. According to Bruce B. Smith, a biology professor known for his work along the Susquehanna and the Codorus Creek, the plant and wildlife has remained largely unchanged through the years. There were, and still are, rhododendrons, azaleas, violets, honeysuckles, bulrushes, skunk cabbage, rushes, onion, jonquils, pussy willows, buckwheat, star grass, amaryllis, blueberries, and cranberries. Remnants remain of the huge forests of poplar, cottonwood, walnut, oak, beech, elm, silver maple, sugar maple, red maple, and dogwood—where the Indians hunted deer, bear, rabbits, and squirrels. The plants and animals were similar along Codorus Creek, the Susquehanna's tributary that cuts right through present-day York, passing at one point within a block of City Hall before leaving town and joining the Susquehanna for that river's journey to Havre de Grace, Maryland and the Chesapeake Bay.

But in 1608, when John Smith had encountered the Indians, the Susquehanna River Valley was Indian country, a kind of buffer area between southern and northern Indian groups. A steady influx of explorers and settlers would soon change that.

In 1609 the British explorer Henry Hudson sailed into Delaware Bay, searching for a trade route to the Far East. He left the region, which lay less than 100 miles from the future York townsite, but the reports he sent back to Europe encouraged the Dutch sea captain, Cornelius Hendrickson, to sail up the Delaware River in 1615 to what is now Philadelphia. His travels would later have far-reaching implications to the history of the York area, but it was another explorer, Etienne Brule (then working as an interpreter for

Excavation of burial sites for Susquehannock Indians have revealed these people were what we might consider of average height, not "giants," as some explorers described them in early days. These native Americans, however, would have been impressive in other ways as this rendering suggests, especially to men like John Smith who was shorter than most men who lived in his time period. Courtesy, *Sunday News*

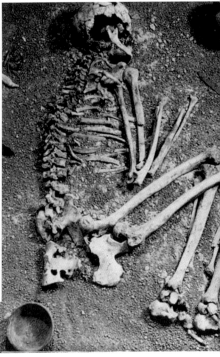

Samuel de Champlain), who became the first white man actually to set foot in the future Commonwealth of Pennsylvania.

Brule had been sent to the tribes of the Susquehanna in 1616 to ask for reinforcements in a proposed attack against Onondaga Fort, one of the strongholds of the Five Nations of the Iroquois Indians in what is now New York State. While waiting for the Indians to prepare themselves, he "busied himself in exploring the country." He followed the Susquehanna "to the sea," which probably meant "to the Chesapeake Bay," a journey that must have included areas of what is now York County.

At the same time Swedish settlers were following Captain Hendrickson's route up the Delaware and in 1643 became Pennsylvania's (although not York's) first permanent settlers. The lands passed from Swedish hands to Dutch in 1655, and to the English in 1664.

The Swedes, English, and Dutch put down settlements among the area's "aboriginal" natives. The Susquehannocks were still using lands along the river and they were continually occupied by disputes with their neighbors to the north, the Five Nations. Even though Brule reported meeting, in 1618, "a large number of [Susquehannock] people who are of good natural disposition," their friendliness was not extended toward the Five Nations (consisting of the Senecas, Cayugas, Onondagas, Oneidas, and Mohawks).

A priest working in the Susquehannock territory told of how 60 Susquehannock boys, about 15 to 16 years old, surprised and killed two northern warriors, and "following up their advantage pursued the rest of the war party in canoes and killed fourteen more and wounded many others."

The Five Nations treated the Susquehannocks with equal cruelty. John de Lamberville, a missionary, wrote this account of how Susquehannocks were tortured: "The hot irons were applied [to their bodies]. One of whom having been burnt during the night from his feet to his knees in a cabin, still prayed to God with me the next day, being fastened to a stake in the square of the town. . . . It is impossible to behold without horror their flesh roasting and men who make a vile meal of them like hungry dogs." Even though some accounts of early Indian activities are known to be exaggerated, archaeologists have found evidence that cannibalism among the early Indian inhabitants and hunters of the Susquehanna Valley was not unknown. (The word "Mohawk," for instance, came from the Algonquin term meaning "man-eaters.")

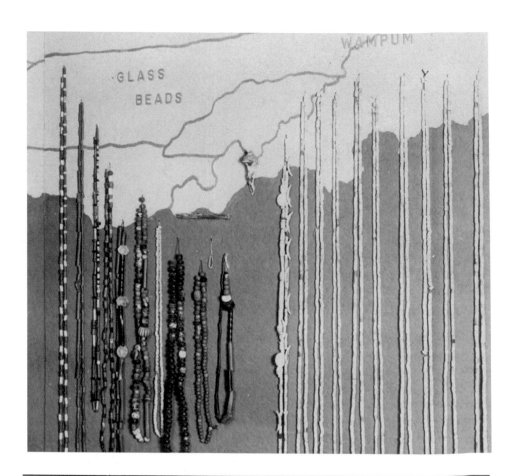

Despite the tactics used against them, the Susquehannocks managed to beat the Five Nations back, reaching the height of their own power between 1660 and 1667. A publication of the Pennsylvania Historical Commission asserts: "Had they taken full advantage of their strength they might have changed our history considerably. As a result of their rise the warlike activities of the Five Nations were curtailed."

Meanwhile the English were still arriving in Pennsylvania. English mercenaries had captured the land around the Susquehanna in 1664 and given it to the Duke of York, but King Charles II transferred the land to William Penn, in 1681, to pay a debt that he owed to Penn's father. William Penn was a devout Quaker with a firm belief in religious freedom, for which he had been thrown out of school and sent to prison at least three times— once in the Tower of London. Penn was anxious to reach his newly acquired lands, which promised not only religious freedom but also personal rights, property privileges, and self-government. He had decided to call the lands "Sylvania," but King Charles II added the name "Penn" to honor William's father. William Penn set sail for "Pencilvania" (as it was spelled on early documents), arriving there in 1682.

But Penn "the Proprietor" immediately encountered problems. In 1632 King Charles I had granted lands south of Pennsylvania, now called Maryland, to Cecilius Calvert, Lord Baltimore. Boundary disputes resulting from the adjacency of the grants were to trouble Penn and Baltimore for many years, and they would have special impact on the greater York area, since it lay only about 18 miles from the Maryland boundary. When Penn died in 1718, he was still not assured of the safety of his province.

Boundary disputes with Maryland squatters were not the only property problems in store for Penn or for York. One of Penn's first desires in the New

World was to purchase the Susquehanna River and all the lands lying on both sides of it from the Indians. The lands did not, at that time, belong to the Indians living on them, because they had been lost in a brutal war with members of the Five Nations. Penn engaged Colonel Thomas Dongan, once governor of what is now New York State, to travel north to enter into negotiations with the Indians there.

Dongan, "in consideration of one hundred pounds sterling," conveyed the lands to Penn in 1696. Dongan's agreement with the Five Nations included "all that tract of land lying on both sides of the river Susquehanna . . . adjacent, in or near the Province of Pennsylvania . . . beginning at the mountains or head of said river, and running as far as and into the bay of Chesapeak."

Widagh and Addagyjunkquagh, kings (or "sachems") of the Susquehannocks, confirmed Dongan's deed in 1700, but the neighboring Conestogoe Indians —another Iroquois splinter group —were displeased with the transaction, asserting that the Five Nations had no right to make such a sale. They also disputed the portion of the deed which read, "for all the [river] Susquehanna and all the islands therein, and all the lands lying on both sides of the said river, *and next adjoining to same,* to the utmost confines of the lands which are, or formerly were, the right of the people or nation called the *Susquehanna* Indians."

The words "next adjoining to same" left open the question of who owned the lands west of the river, including what would become York. The Five Nations insisted, regardless of the agreement of 1700, on treating the lands and the river as their own territory.

The fact that more than 30 years would pass before the issue of land ownership was settled also did not stop the English from treating the area as their own. In 1722 the heirs of William Penn approved a plan to survey an area west of the Susquehanna River. The area was to be set aside as a "manor" for use by the Penns since they had been authorized to reserve "10,000 acres from every 100,000" over which they would have direct control. The 64,000 acres surveyed extended from the river into what is now York. The land was named Springettsbury Manor for Penn's grandson, who was also his heir. The establishment of its borders formally opened the West to white settlers, who, until the land's purchase from the Indians, had no legal right to settle west of the river. (The word "manor" was then commonly used in England to describe any unit of land for which the owner could expect rents, levy fines, and exact privileges. The Penns, for example, had the privilege of collecting "quitrents"—rents that the settlers paid instead of performing various feudal services—until 1775 on most Pennsylvania lands. They retained their ownership privileges on the manors, however, long after 1775 and last collected quitrents from those areas in 1793.)

Among the first settlers to cross the Susquehanna to take up lands in the newly opened frontier were John and James Hendricks, English by birth. Although no one knows precisely when they made their settlement, it could have been as early as 1728. Even though the lands west of the Susquehanna were not yet fully purchased from the Indians, agents for the Penns had granted certain individuals authority to settle there with the understanding that title to the lands would come later.

The laying out of Springettsbury Manor not only clarified settlement rights in the western lands, it also established boundaries (albeit loosely defined ones) whereby officials could deal with the bothersome "Maryland intruders." Lord Baltimore's followers had, for many years, presented themselves farther and farther north, and their audacity often involved them in "bloody fracases" in the region that Penn's agents strongly claimed as "Penn's

A meeting between William Penn and the Indians, symbolizing "mutual trust," is depicted in this segment of a mural painted by Paul Domville. The mural is now in the collection of the William Penn Museum in Harrisburg. Courtesy, Pennsylvania Historical and Museum Commission.

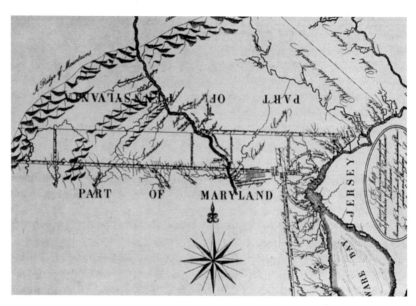

The motto "mercy and justice" appeared on the Penn family coat of arms. The Penns were from the west of England. From *Pennsylvania; Colonial and Federal,* Vol I, 1903.

Above right
The temporary line between Pennsylvania and Maryland is shown on this early map. The provinces were "fixed according to an Order of His Majesty in Council, dated the 25th day of May in the Year 1738, surveyed in the year 1739." (HSYC)

woods." Thomas Cresap, one of the more adventurous Marylanders, seized Pennsylvania lands unabashedly, causing murderous battles, until he himself was seized in 1736 and locked up by the sheriff of Lancaster County.

Although the first settlers west of the Susquehanna were English (and Marylandish), they were soon followed by large numbers of Germans who settled near the site taken up by the Hendrickses on what is now Kreutz Creek. The area originally was called Grist Creek after one of its earliest settlers, John Grist. The Kreutz Creek settlement extended from the Susquehanna southwest to the seven-mile-long area now known as Stony Brook. The Canadochly settlement, probably as old as the Kreutz Creek settlement, encompassed the present-day areas of Yorkana, East Prospect, and Delroy. It had been called the Conojehela Valley by the Indians, who had an established village on the opposite shore in Washington Borough. Corruption of the Indian name, Conojehela, led to different versions of the name, such as "Canajockley," "Jockley," and, finally, "Canadochly."

The English settlers took up land just west of the area now called Spring Grove. The area was surveyed by Penn's surveyor, Joseph Pidgeon, and took the name Pigeon Hills, a name that is still used today.

Most of the settlers moving into these new lands had strong motivation for making a new life. Many had been subject to religious persecution in their native lands, and had watched family members die in the political turmoil of the times. For those Germans who had come from the Palatinate region of Germany, Penn's plan for a free land seemed all the more attractive because of experiences in their homeland that were still fresh in their minds.

The Electoral Palatinate was a beautiful and fertile area in what is now Germany, often referred to as the Middle Rhineland. During the 17th and early 18th centuries, this rich agricultural region, famed now for its wines, was subject to military invasions and the ravaging of its countryside by periodic religious wars and battles for political control. After the Palatinate became involved in the War of the Grand Alliance in 1685, King Louis XIV of France (which bordered the Lower Rhineland in the south) ordered a full-scale invasion and the devastation of the Rhenish Palatinate.

In 1688 Louis XIV sent 50,000 men into the province with orders to level the lush countryside, with its clean, prosperous towns and villages, until the area was, in his words, "a desert." The invasion, which took place in the winter, forced thousands of townsmen and farmers to flee to the fields,

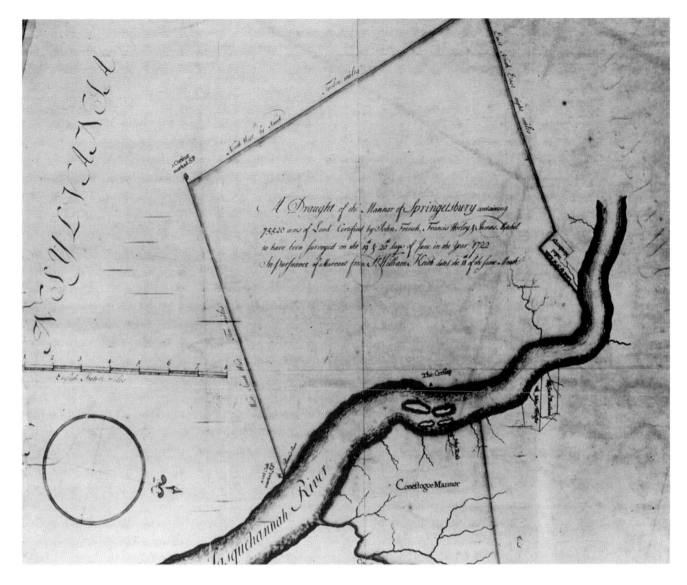

A Draught of the Manor of Springettsbury, includes 75,520 acres of land surveyed on June 19 and 20, 1722. (HSYC)

where many perished from hunger or exposure. The following spring, as the invasion continued, the remaining peasants were forced to plow under their crops.

Other invasions, and religious persecution, ensued in the coming years, so that a steady stream of immigrants found their way to the New World, often by way of sympathetic England. William Penn himself went on recruiting missions to the Palatinate and, as early as 1683, Pennsylvania had its first settlement of Palatine immigrants at Germantown, north of Philadelphia. When Governor Keith informed later arrivals of the already established settlement, many started their journey for that region, coming within 30 miles of the future York settlement. The stream of migration from Germany continued until 1775, and included not only members of the Lutheran and Reformed churches of the Palatinate, but also Mennonites from Germany and Switzerland, and the German Baptists from the Upper Rhine. Even though they could not secure rights to the land until 1733—when Samuel Blunston, the Penns' agent, began issuing licenses for settlements west of the Susquehanna—several hundred Palatines had already settled in York County.

Between 1700 and 1775 approximately 200,000 Scotch-Irish, most of them "rigid" Presbyterians, arrived in America. Comprising the second-largest immigrant group (after the English), many went to Pennsylvania for its available farmland. A large number of them made their home in what they called the York Barrens, a nearly diamond-shaped area whose points are the towns of Craley, Peach Bottom, Delta, and New Freedom. The word "barrens" has been variously defined as "vacant," "not yet bought," "infertile," or "burnt." The last definition referred to the Indians' standard practice of burning vast acreages of forest to force game into a smaller area of woodlands for easier hunting.

Whether the York Barrens was physically "bare" or not, its topography held a fascination for the Scotch-Irish and also the Welsh, who used skills acquired in their homelands to establish slate mines and quarries for the extraction of limestone. They set up family dwellings and later, after the 1736 treaty, settlers moving west from Chester County (the county bordering Lancaster County on the east, as York County later bordered it on the west) moved into the greater York area's Newberry Township. Many were Quakers who founded communities that are now called Newberrytown, Lewisberry, Goldsboro, Etters, Yocumtown, and York Haven. These early settlers called the region "the Red Land" because the soil and rocks were reddish brown. They built crude cabins and occasionally crossed paths with native Indians who taught them how to grow corn and new ways to use the natural resources around them.

Among those first settlers were Thomas Hall, John McFeeson, John Rankin, Ellis Lewis, and Joseph Bennett. A descendant of Lewis later laid out the town of Lewisberry and Bennett's name was given to a small stream. History takes particular note of the arrival of Rankin, Bennett, and Lewis. Their story, which has been questioned by modern historians, recounts how they arrived on the east bank of the Susquehanna, concerned that the river would not allow them to cross on horseback. The terrible threat of having to leave their horses behind hung over them. After an intense discussion, they solved the problem by fastening together two canoes. The horses then crossed the Susquehanna with their front feet in the first canoe and their hind feet in the second.

Just southwest of the Pigeon Hills settlement, during the same period, a group of Marylanders, many of whom were Catholics, were settling on land known as Digges Choice. John Digges, an Irish nobleman who lived in Prince Georges County, Maryland, obtained from the fourth Lord Baltimore, Charles Calvert, a grant of 10,000 acres which was later to encompass the Borough of Hanover. With the assistance of a respected Indian chief named Tom, Digges carved out a 6,822-acre area encompassing lands that were eventually included in York and Adams counties. Lord Baltimore's grant had authorized him to approve settlements in parts of western Maryland before the Penns obtained title to the lands west of the Susquehanna. The questionable nature of the Penn and Baltimore borders, ironically, allowed organized settlements on what was to become Pennsylvania lands by Marylanders.

An initial preoccupation for the settlers throughout the newly opened lands was the building of shelters. Two of the earliest remaining houses in York County were built of stone, although log cabins and "half-timber" houses would dominate the county's architectural scene in a few years. In the town of Hallam (from "Hellam" for the township in which Hallam was located), about six miles east of York's city limits, stands the Martin Shultz House, a Germanic stone cabin that is probably one of the earliest houses in the Kreutz Creek Valley. At about the same time, Johann and Christina Shultz built a two-story stone house south of Stony Brook, and began a new life in lands set aside for a new province.

Life in early York County was hardly easy. The early inhabitants had bitter winters and brutally hot summers to contend with, besides the threat of Indian and Maryland invaders. The streams often flooded and dry periods sometimes

The Johann Shultz house, built by the brother of Martin Shultz in 1734 and located south of Stony Brook, as it looked before restoration. The house had a Germanic central chimney system. Courtesy, The York County Heritage Trust

ruined an entire summer's work in the newly cleared fields. Still the lands in the Kreutz Creek area were fertile, so farmers, including women and children, worked the land and sent up prayers for favorable conditions.

Two of the county's best-known early historians, W.C. Carter and A.J. Glossbrenner, tell us, in their *History of York County, From Its Erection to the Present Time: (1729–1834)*, that the county's early inhabitants lived primitively, even to their clothing. "Their dress was simple," the historians relate, "consisting of a shirt, trousers and a frock," all of tow. In summer they wore only the shirt and trousers; as the weather got colder, they added frocks, "which were bound closely about their loins, usually with a string of the same material as the garments."

"There was neither a shoemaker nor a tanner in any part of what is now York County," according to Carter and Glossbrenner:

> *A supply of shoes for family use was annually obtained from Philadelphia; itinerant cobblers, travelling from one farm house to another, earned a livelihood by mending shoes. . . . The first settled and established shoemaker in the county was Samuel Landys, who had his shop somewhere on the Kreutz creek. The first, and for a long time the only tailor was Valentine Heyer. . . . The first blacksmith was Peter Gardner. The first schoolmaster was known by no other name than that of "Der Dicke Schulmeister."*

The homes of these early settlers were primitive, too. Typical Germanic architecture used a central chimney system; the fireplace cooking area, which also provided light, was often extended through the wall to the adjoining room for heating purposes. Iron-plate stoves were later introduced to house the heating fire opposite the cooking area. Candles and "betty lamps," which burned animal fat, enhanced the light that was given off by the fireplace.

Many of the settlers had brought with them iron-bound chests containing basic cooking implements and other items, such as cloth, small farming tools, candlemaking tools, the family Bible, and sometimes seed with which to start farming in the New World. Furniture was simple, but often incorporated traditional design elements, such as heart shapes and distelfink birds, both of which were thought to bring good luck to the homes of settlers who had also brought, besides basic tools, ideas and customs from their native lands.

People like these farmers and craftsmen were coming to the York area in

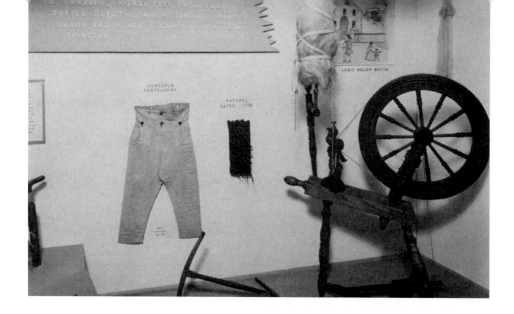

Early York settlers made their simple clothes from flax and wool, using homemade instruments like the ones shown in this former exhibit at the York County Heritage Trust. Courtesy, The York County Heritage Trust

increasing numbers largely because of promotional material, ranging from pamphlets to playing cards, which described Pennsylvania to the inhabitants of Europe. The promise of religious freedom, a better way of life, and "Goodly land, fertile and well-watered" (as the promotional pieces said) drew the Germans from the Palatinate and Scotch-Irish, but also French Huguenots and English (particularly Quakers) to Pennsylvania.

One of York's esteemed modern historians, Joe E. Kindig III, writes that by the time York was laid out in 1741, "it was predominantly a German community....[The settlers] were of the peasant class and numbered among their group farmers, millers, tanners, and tradesmen who had accepted William Penn's promise of new land and religious freedom. They brought with them...not the Baroque culture of the wealthy city merchants, but the peasant culture of medievalism." This culture was transplanted intact. As Kindig points out: "Since few of them [the Germans] did more than pass immediately through Philadelphia, on finding the English language not to their liking, they arrived in York County uninfluenced by English culture and customs." Some historians have noted not every settler in early York was of the peasant class; a few were quite well off.

Ferryboat operators worked at several points up and down the Susquehanna, and the newcomers, usually on horseback and sometimes carrying small children, reached the west side of the river much fatigued but jubilant with the thought of putting down stakes on land they could call home. Some settlers bargained with fellow-countrymen, who had already settled in Chester County, to use their covered wagons in transporting families and their belongings west of the river.

Many Germans, and some Englishmen, followed Indian trails to find homes. Some came to the area where the Monocacy crossed the Codorus and discovered that with its fertile fields, majestic hills, good supply of fish from the Codorus, and woodlands filled with game and plant life—it would make a fine place to settle.

The early record books of the Christ Lutheran Church list the names of "24 heads of family," most of whom had emigrated from Wuerttemberg, Germany. They established a congregation and worshiped together as early as 1733. Among those first congregation members were Christian Groll, Philip Ziegler, Georg Schwaab (later Swope), John Adam Diehl, Jacob Scherer, Georg and Mathias Schmeiser (later Smyser), Martin Bauer, Georg Adam Zimmerman, Georg Ziegler, Christoph Kraut, Joseph Beyer, Jacob Ziegler, and Valentine and Heinrich Schultz.

In spite of the enthusiastic activity involving the establishment of settlements and the founding of congregations, the question of whether these settlements were legal was still in discussion. The ownership of the land had been in dispute since the treaty between Penns' agent, Dongan, and the Five Nations in 1700. Action was finally taken in 1736, when a great council was called to put an end to the quarrels of official ownership between the Penns and the Indians. Gathering in Philadelphia, the sachems and representatives of all the Five Nations renewed old treaties, and, on October 11, wrote a new deed in the name of William Penn's successors: his son Thomas and his two grandsons, John and Richard. In return for the land, the Indians were given:

500 lbs powder, 600 lbs lead, 45 guns, 60 strouds water match coats, 100 blankets, 100 duffle match coats, 200 yds. of half thick, 100 shirts, 40 hats, 40 prs. of shoes and buckles, 40 pairs of stockings, 100 hatchets, 500 knives, 100 houghs [hoes], 60 kettles, 100 tobacco tougs, 100 scissors, 500 awe blades, 120 combs, 2,000 needles, 1,000 flints, 24 looking glasses, 2 lbs. of vermillion, 100 tin pots, 200 lbs of tobacco, 25 gals. rum, 1,000 pipes, 24 dozen of gartering.

The new deed made it clear for the first time that the Susquehanna Valley region of Pennsylvania belonged exclusively to the Penns. It was signed by 23 chiefs of the nations of Seneca, Oneida, Onondaga, and Tuscurora. It granted to the Penns all the land north of the Susquehanna "to the hills or mountains called, in the language of the Five Nations, Taymentesachta [the eastern slopes of the Allegheny Mountains] . . . and "all the river Susquehanna, and all the lands lying on the west side of the said river to the setting of the sun. . . ."

This map of some of the south and east boundaries of early Pennsylvania, date unknown, was intended "to give an account of some of the Province in America, so far as the Relations received from Persons that have been upon the place, could give any light towards it." (HSYC)

John Fisher was a carpenter and one of York's earliest clockmakers and artists. His superb craftsmanship can be seen in this tall case clock, made in 1790. (HSYC)

CHAPTER II

THE FOUNDING OF YORK TOWN

Once the settlements west of the Susquehanna officially belonged to the Penns, the Pennsylvania proprietaries and governors were more open to requests from the area's pioneer residents that an organized town be laid out. In 1739 a petition for the erection of the county of York was presented to the proprietaries. This petition was brought by Ulrich Whisler and Baltzar Spangler, two German immigrants who had built log houses near the Plank Road southeast of what is now downtown York, and was granted in 1741. The Penns then authorized Thomas Cookson, the deputy surveyor for Lancaster County (which York was a part of until 1749), to lay out a town in the "checkerboard" pattern that had been used for Philadelphia a half-century earlier.

With the assistance of Whisler and Spangler, who acted as chainbearers, Cookson laid out the town according to the prescribed plan: lots were to be 230 feet long by 65 feet wide; alleys were to be 20 feet wide; and two streets, which crossed each other to form the central intersection, were to be 80 feet wide. At the corners of the cross streets, 65 square feet were to be cut off to make a "Square," "for any public building or market."

Cookson was from Yorkshire, England, and it was probably his suggestion that led to the name of the proposed town. "York town," as it was then called and written on public documents, also manifested Cookson's English background in the names of its streets. Thus there were streets called King, Queen, Prince (now Princess), and Duke, and, of course, George Street, which had been referred to as Prison Street, or Union Street, before being renamed in honor of King George II.

In addition to being a town, York was considered a "manor," and administered by the Penns in much the same way as Springettsbury and other manors were. Applicants to the town lots had to agree to pay a rental fee of seven shillings a year and to construct "a substantial dwelling of 16 feet square at least, built with lime and sand, within the space of one year." The proprietaries could also collect other quitrents, which in the case of York were often only token in nature, consisting of a peppercorn or barleycorn "paid" each year. York was the second of seven towns established by the proprietaries during their period of governance. The first had been Philadelphia, founded in 1682. After York, in 1741, came Reading in 1749, Carlisle in 1751, Easton in 1752, Bedford in 1766, and Sunbury in 1772.

In payment for their assistance in laying out the town, Spangler and Whisler were granted the lots of their choice, thereby establishing them as the first official residents of the first town west of the Susquehanna. Baltzar Spangler chose a site on the northwest corner of what is now York's Continental Square, where he built a residence and operated the community's first inn and tavern, the Black Horse. The Black Horse was also used, while still in an unfinished state, as the first polling place in York in 1750. Ulrich Whisler, a miller by trade, waited several years before taking up his lot near the Codorus at the intersection of Main Street (now Market Street) and Water Street (now

This early composite map depicts York town as surveyed by Thomas Cookson in 1741. The map shows lots for landowners, the road to Monocacy, and the land outside the town that belonged to Hermanus Bott, Baltzar Spangler, and John and James Wright. (HSYC)

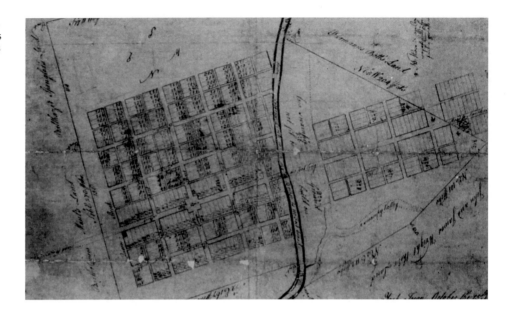

Pershing Avenue). The reconstructed Colonial Court House is now located on property that includes Whisler's original lot.

Others "taking up" lots with Spangler in 1741 were: John Bishop, Jacob Welsch, Michael Schwaab (later Swope), Matthias Onvesant, Andrew Coaler (originally Kohler or Koller), Henry Hendricks, Joseph Hinsman, Christopher Croll, Michael Laub, Zachariah Shugart, Nicholas Stuke, Arnold Stuke, Samuel Hoake (later Hoke), George Swope (who took four lots when no one else took more than two lots and most applied for just one), Jacob Crebill (later Graybill), Michael Eichelberger, and Hermanus Bott. Michael Eichelberger later sold his lot to his brother, Martin, who operated another of York's early public inns and taverns. Now known as the Golden Plough, the tavern was authentically restored in the years 1963–1965. Hermanus Bott obtained a patent for 297 acres of land west of the Codorus and laid out his own town of about 50 lots in subsequent years. Bottstown, with its population of 300, was annexed to the borough of York in 1884.

Shortly after York was laid out, its residents began holding market in Centre Square (now Continental Square) at the intersection of Market and George streets. Although the exact date of authorization is not known, the Penns granted approval to the market through their lieutenant governor, Robert Hunter Morris.

York's first farmers had been Indian squaws, who scratched the land with sticks so that they could plant seed. The Indians passed on their knowledge of the land to some of the earliest immigrants, many of whom knew little about the art of growing things and were forced into farming in order to feed themselves and their families. But Yorkers' farming skills were rudimentary, to say the least, until the arrival of the first waves of German immigrants, who brought with them more advanced agricultural techniques that they had learned in Europe. The German farmers worked exceptionally hard, as did their wives, and many contemporaries remarked that the Germans were the most efficient and industrious farmers to come to the New World.

When the Germans applied their farming skills to Pennsylvania's rich lands, the results were rapid and extraordinary, so much so that Pennsylvania soon became an exporter of food to other colonies. In York their success brought a request for the Penns to allow them to make the farmers' market a twice-weekly event. The Penns granted the request, but designated Wednesday and Saturday as the only market days, thus pleasing both the predominantly German farmers and the citizens from other countries who objected to their

Above
The Golden Plough Tavern, left, built circa 1741, and the General Gates House, built circa 1751, are two surviving reminders of York's Colonial past. The Golden Plough Tavern is the only remaining example of half-timber architecture in York County. (HSYC)

Above right
The kitchen of the Golden Plough Tavern was the center of activity because of the heat and light generated from its central fireplace. Martin Eichelberger ran the tavern for travelers passing through the county. (HSYC)

practice of trading on the sabbath. The farmers' market tradition has survived to this day, making it (along with religious observance and government activity) one of the oldest public institutions in York.

The first markets were held in the open air; as a result, when it rained or snowed, the mud in Centre Square, churned by hundreds of humans and animals, grew ankle deep. Farmers from the outlying areas, who came into York town on market days, peddled their wares from the backs of wagons and from makeshift "stands" on the curbs. During dry spells in the summer, dust flew everywhere, covering the vendors' produce and meat. The building of the market shed, authorized in 1754, alleviated the problems caused by dust and mud, but extremes of heat and cold still made the market activities grueling during several months of the year. The business of market was carried on in prices that often included fractions. Since money was not plentiful, due to the relative isolation of the community and the economic level of most of its residents, bartering was often undertaken in lively sessions.

The market was not the only area of York life that was growing, however. Yorkers were a churchgoing people, and new congregations were springing up throughout the greater York area. Before church buildings and meeting houses were built, worshipers assembled in private homes or, occasionally, in taverns or barns. The churches became important social as well as religious outlets, often serving as focal points in the development of community.

In 1743, too, a group of Germans built "Die Evangelische Luthensche Kanawagische Germeinde" (The German Evangelical Lutheran Church on the Conewago). The first church was in the McSherrystown area, and the Conewago settlement stretched from Hanover to Littlestown. The congregation later built a sanctuary in Hanover Borough and named it for St. Matthew. Its first pastor, the Reverend David Chandler, lived in the middle of a vast Lutheran parish, and among this church's first "subscribers," or financial supporters were Frederick Gelwicks, Michael Carl, Philip Morgernstern, Christoffell Schlegel (later Christopher Slagle), and Nicholaus Beideinger (later Bittinger), some of whose names are still associated with the congregation. The village of Hanover, home to the Conewago Church, developed a thriving economy of its own.

A short time later, perhaps as early as 1744, a Moravian missionary named Jacob Lischy was ministering to the families of the Kreutz Creek Settlement,

including the members of York's German Reformed Congregation, who did not yet have a church building. No one knows exactly when the Congregation was formed, but Lischy writes in his journal of 1744 that "this congregation has been for several years without a pastor." In 1745 church trustees Jacob and Samuel Welsch "took up a lot in the town of York for a meeting house." The lot fronted what is now West Market Street. Later the congregation built a newer church on the lot to the east, known as Trinity United Church of Christ.

After churchmen and businessmen bought up the first 23 lots in 1741, no additional lots were spoken for until the spring of 1746, when 44 were taken up. Between 1748 and 1750, many more applications were made and York town began to take on the appearance of a prosperous community.

In the vicinity of Centre Square were the shops of shoemakers, carpenters, gunsmiths, blacksmiths, clockmakers, harnessmakers, toolmakers, distillers, and weavers. Tanners chose the area along the Codorus, two blocks west of the Square, to establish their shops. The soaking and boiling of hides required a large supply of water, which the Codorus provided, and wood, which was available from the heavily forested nearby land. To expedite travel and development in the area of the Codorus, a bridge was built in 1743. This first bridge was little more than a wooden span crossing the Codorus at High (now Market) Street.

The work of the artisans and shopkeepers who thrived along the Codorus and the Monocacy Road soon earned for York the reputation as a community of fine craftsmen. John Fisher, for example, was a carpenter and also one of York's earliest clockmakers and artists. His shop, which still exists, stood on North George Street about half a block north of the Square. In Fisher's shop, the clockmaker-artist-carpenter built a particularly splendid clock embodying astronomical devices. The Fisher work now stands in an outstanding collection of clocks owned by Yale University. Besides Fisher, York had at least a dozen other fine clockmakers, including Rudolph Spangler (son of Kaspar Spangler, and nephew of Baltzar Spangler), Godfrey Lenhart, Elisha Kirk, and Jonathan Jessop. Clocks bearing the signatures of these men are highly sought after in York County today.

While small craftsmen lived and worked in York's increasingly crowded center, early manufacturers needed more space to work, so they developed their products outside of town. Gristmills and sawmills sprang up all over the area, beginning in the 1730s. Many farmers also grew flax to help supply the inhabitants' need for clothing, rope, and sacks. The fibers of the flax plant were used to make linen or were combined with wool to make "linsey-woolsey," a more elegant fabric much coveted by the women of York.

Alongside the flax fields were wide expanses of rye and Indian corn, which gave rise to York's early spirits industry. Records reveal that there were 16 distillers in Dover Township and 18 in Manchester Township by

1770. John George Charles Barnitz, married to Anna Barbara Spangler, started a brewery and left it to his two sons, Charles and John, when he died in 1796. The elder son, Charles, renounced his share of the business in favor of his brother. John married Catherine Hay, daughter of Colonel John and Julia Maul Hay, during the Revolution.

The Barnitz family, headed by David Grier Barnitz, purchased the manor of Springettsbury in 1841 from William Penn's descendant Granville Penn, who was until then the "lord" of the manor. David Grier Barnitz was obliged to pay two beaver skins per year to Granville Penn "if demanded."

All the businesses being established in the manor had one problem in common: York was still part of Lancaster County, and people had to travel 25 miles to Lancaster, the county seat, crossing the Susquehanna, to do legal business or resolve problems. Complaints from citizens eventually led to the "erection" of York County in 1749 with the county seat located at York town. With the establishment of the county, the citizens also were provided with funds to raise a courthouse and a jail.

While the Court House was being built, sessions of the court were held in the homes of York County's justices. Those first justices included John Day, Thomas Cox, John Wright, Jr., (who had settled at Wrightsville), Matthew Dill (who later founded Dillsburg [1800]), Patrick Watson, George Stevenson (who would later serve as York town's first prothonotary, clerk of the courts, register of wills, and "recorder of deeds"), Georg Swope (one of the fathers of York's first church in 1733), and Hance Hamilton (a Scotch-Irish immigrant who had settled near Wrightsville and who was appointed York's first sheriff). Hamilton was to serve as sheriff until an election for the office was held in 1750.

John Gibson's 1886 history of York County tells of that October 1750 election, the first of any kind in York. Richard McAllister ran against Hamilton, who wanted to remain sheriff after the term of his appointment expired. Hamilton, Gibson says, "was urgently supported by the Scotch-Irish," while McAllister, "although a Scotch-Irishman himself, was the candidate of the Germans. . . . The voting place on this occasion was the unfinished public inn of Baltzar Spangler." Why York's German population supported a Scotch-Irishman in these times when nationality was often foremost in people's minds is not known. The candidate favored by the Germans, as it turned out, had little chance of winning the election, regardless of his national ties.

"By the noon hour," Gibson continues, "hundreds of gallant frontiersmen . . . with great determination and impetuosity began to clamor for their

Below
This carved wooden head of Captain John Carlton, attributed to John Fisher, has human hair, silver, and brass, circa 1786. (HSYC)

Below right
The York County Court House, erected in 1754, was located in York town's Centre Square. The Continental Congress met at the site from September 30, 1777 to June 27, 1778. This authentic reproduction of the Court House stands today at the corner of Pershing Avenue and Market Street. Photo by G.H. Laird. (HSYC)

Below, far right
York artisan John Fisher's painting of the Pennsylvania Coat of Arms is now in the collection of York College of Pennsylvania. It is believed to be the oldest, painted Pennsylvania coat of arms in existence. Courtesy, York College of Pennsylvania.

favorite candidates, and crowded around the voting place." Sheriff Hamilton tried to control the situation by stopping the election, which only made things worse:

> *A general commotion and confusion ensued. A lusty German, insisting on his right to vote, tripped up the heels of one of the Scotch-Irish guards. An affray began. . . . Saplings cut along the Codorus were used as offensive and defensive weapons. Hamilton and his party fled west of the Codorus. During the remainder of the day the Scotch-Irish were not seen east of the creek. There were a few limbs broken and considerable blood was shed, but no lives were lost.*

Gibson ends by noting, "The Quakers, of whom there were a great many present from the northern part of the county . . . took no part in the affray." He explains that because Hamilton could not turn in an election report to the provincial government in Philadelphia, the governor commissioned him sheriff. He served in that post until 1753, when he was succeeded by John Adlum, but Hamilton was reelected in 1755.

York no doubt needed a sheriff during those early years, since land disputes and other legal problems were alarmingly common. Recorder of deeds George Stevenson reported, in April of 1751, that only 50 lots had been used in compliance with the original agreements. Three of those lots were occupied by churches—two by the German Lutheran and one by the German Reformed. Many individuals had taken up lots, but not built on them, as the Penns' dictates required. Some of the lot holders probably did not have the money to fulfill their building obligation; others procrastinated until after the one-year time limit had expired. Houses were sometimes constructed on lots to which the builders had no title. Some Yorkers with ready capital watched carefully until they saw a lot or building that did not meet specifications, then tried to acquire the property through a legal procedure called "forfeiture of rights."

Considering the rising number of legal wrangles that the York community found itself embroiled in, the completion of the new Court House in 1754 was timely. The Court House had been built in Centre Square. William Willis, a Quaker who was one of the first English Friends to settle near York, had been contracted for the brickmaking and bricklaying. Another Quaker, Henry Clark, provided wood "scantlings" for the building. John Meem and Jacob Klein, both Germans, were employed as carpenters; and Robert Jones, a Quaker, had been hired to haul 7,000 shingles from Philadelphia to complete the Court House roof.

To detain those awaiting legal proceedings and punish those convicted of offenses, the new jail was completed two years later. The jail, intended only as a temporary structure, had high stone walls and a wooden roof. It was located at the corner of George and King streets, the present-day site of Sunny's Surplus Store. In 1768 a three-story jail of blue limestone replaced the temporary structure.

But more public and humiliating punishments than imprisonment often awaited York's criminals. In front of the Court House were the pillory, a wooden frame with holes for the head and wrists, and the stocks, which confined the person's ankles. Residents accused of breaking the law were sometimes confined to the pillory and stocks, where they were subject to the scorn of hundreds of people passing through Centre Square. ("Scorn," in those times, often meant dirt picked up from the horse-trod streets.) Offenders were sometimes also lashed, physically mutilated, or hanged.

Records tell of the 15 lashings given to a York woman, Margaret Wilmouth, for stealing a silk handkerchief. Another woman, Elisabeth Irwin, was accused of murder, imprisoned for 20 weeks, then hanged. A crime that was considered nearly as serious as murder was counterfeiting the king's money. James Pitt was convicted of altering a two-shilling bill of credit to a ten-shilling note. For his eight-shilling crime, Pitt had both his ears cut off and nailed to the pillory, where he had to stand for one hour before receiving 39 lashes. He was also fined £100, which he could not pay, so he was sold into servitude for a period of four years.

In York, at this time, individuals were commonly sold to pay for court costs, or as payment to creditors. Imprisoned persons also had the right to sell themselves or their children to obtain their release.

Bondservants, who had sold themselves to pay for transportation to the New World or to satisfy debts, were punished especially hard when accused of trying to escape from their masters. In one case of bondservant punishment, Robert Gamel Hath was sentenced to two additional years of servitude to Baltzar Spangler, Jr., when Hath was apprehended after running away from town. Another servant, Thomas Haughy, was accused of absenting his duties for two months and 11 days, and had to serve an extra seven years.

Despite the quarrelsome and sometimes illegal ways of the York area's early residents, they remained an essentially religious people. The early 1750s saw a new flurry of religious activity and church building that helped give rise to the modern York axiom, "There's a church on every corner."

In 1752 the First Moravian Church was formally organized. The congregation met in a tavern until 1755, when it built a church on Prince and Water streets (now Princess Street and Pershing Avenue). At that location it also operated a school. The church established a burial place in back of the church, which it called "God's Acre." The Moravian dead were buried in seven sections: a section for married men and widowers, one for single men, one for male children, one for married women and widows, one for single women, one for female children, and one for "strangers." The cemetery divisions were made to remind living Moravians that there is no marrying in heaven and that all "the saints" will eventually enjoy a single reunion.

A Presbyterian congregation was formed in late 1753, or early 1754, known as Guinston, 12 miles from York. An Episcopal congregation was established in York, probably in 1755, by a missionary of the Church of England, the Reverend Thomas Barton; three prominent Yorkers—Samuel Johnston, Thomas Minshall, and Joseph Adlum—were appointed trustees.

St. John's Episcopal Church was established in York by the Reverend Thomas Barton, an English missionary, circa 1755. Samuel Johnston, Thomas Minshall, and Joseph Adlum, all prominent Yorkers, were appointed trustees. (HSYC)

Early Catholic records indicate that more than 100 German Catholics and about 70 Irish Catholics lived in York County in the 1750s and probably celebrated mass in private homes. The Amish, the Mennonites, the Dunkards, and Brethren also formed churches throughout York County.

This burst of religious activity faded out when the effects of the French and Indian War (1754-1763) began to reach the York area. Living peacefully with the Indians had not been a major problem for the area's whites. But when the French, aided by Indian allies near Canada, crossed Lake Erie and began to move southeast toward York County, the citizens of the York area were naturally alarmed.

Britain's king, informed of the French and Indian troubles by the Pennsylvania Assembly, sent General Edward Braddock to help the Colonists. Assemblyman Benjamin Franklin, who had urged the furnishing of money to carry on the war, assured Braddock that the Assembly had appropriated £5,000 to support Braddock's army. Unfortunately, as Franklin related in a proclamation to the people of York, Lancaster, and Cumberland counties, "money had not been provided nor any steps taken for that purpose" by either the Assembly or the governor. The Assembly, mostly made up of peace-loving Quakers, was not enthusiastic about supplying war materiel. On learning that Braddock had only 25 wagons in which to transport equipment and supplies over the Alleghenies, Franklin took it upon himself to recruit wagons and pack horses. He came to York and Lancaster, and sent his son William to Carlisle in Cumberland County, with the aforementioned proclamation, which read, in part:

Friends and Countrymen:

Having been at the camp at Frederick a few days since, I found the General and officers of the army extremely exasperated on account of their not being supplied with horses and wagons. . . .

It was proposed to send an armed force immediately into these counties, to seize as many of the best wagons and horses as should be wanted, and compel as many persons into the service as should be necessary to drive and take care of them.

I apprehended that the progress of a body of soldiers through these counties on such an occasion, their resentment against us, would be attended with many and great inconveniences to the inhabitants; and therefore more willingly undertook the trouble of trying first what might be done by fair and equitable means.

The people of these back counties have lately been complaining that a sufficient currency was wanting; you have now an opportunity of receiving and dividing among you a very considerable sum; for if the service of this expedition should continue (as it's more than probable it will) for 120 days, the hire of these wagons and horses will amount to upwards of thirty thousand pounds. . . .

If this method of obtaining the wagons and horses is not likely to succeed, I am obliged to send word to the General in fourteen days, and I suppose Sir John St. Clair, the Hussar, with a body of soldiers, will probably enter the province, of which I shall be sorry to hear, because

> I am very sincerely and truly
> Your friend and well-wisher,

B. FRANKLIN

Within two weeks, 150 wagons and teams and 259 pack horses were on their way to Braddock. They carried 1,200 barrels of flour from Cumberland and York County gristmills.

The war raged on, and in 1756 York area citizens organized a number of military companies to aid the cause. George R. Prowell, perhaps York County's best-known historian, records three companies of 60 men each, three of 100 each, one of 50, and one of 106. In addition to the enlisted men, each company had its own captain, lieutenant, and ensign. Hance Hamilton formed his own company after resigning as sheriff in 1755; in 1756 he marched to Pennsylvania's western frontier to join the fighting. Companies were also formed by the Reverend Thomas Barton of the newly established York, Carlisle and York Springs Episcopal Church; by the Reverend Andrew Bay of the Presbyterian Church at Marsh Creek; by Dr. David Jameson, York's pioneer physician; and by Thomas Armor, a court justice.

As the war edged closer to the York area, some settlers fled eastward across the Susquehanna, while others assembled inside York town itself. The town had been fortified against attack. But the fighting, reaching its peak and then fading out between 1758 and 1760, never did touch York. The Treaty of Paris in 1763 ended French control of America's western frontier, which at that time was York County's western half, and peace returned to Pennsylvania.

Life as usual also returned to York. New businesses were established, new church buildings were erected, and new squabbles over land and lots were heard in the streets and in the courts. Dick's Bloomery, established in 1756, was one of the first iron furnaces in the York area and may have been built to feed the war-born demand for rifle balls, cannonballs, and other metal items.

After the war, the demand for metal goods stayed high. James Smith, York's famed lawyer and signer of the Declaration of Independence, owned the Codorus Furnace, built in 1765 and known then as Bennett's Furnace. In the 19th century it took the name Hallam Furnace and Forge. The expanding availability and use of metals combined with York County's rich cereal crops caused many farmers to erect copper stills. Area farmers became expert in blending various ingredients, and they were soon hauling their whiskey to Baltimore and other communities outside of York. The establishment of iron furnaces made other "exports" possible, such as tools, pots, kettles, spoons,

Benjamin Franklin distributed an impassioned proclamation during the French and Indian War "To the inhabitants of the Counties of Lancaster, York, and Cumberland," calling for wagons, teams, and other supplies for the English forces. Within two weeks, 150 wagons and 259 packhorses were on their way from the area to support the efforts of "His Majesty." (HSYC)

skillets, hoes, and knives, all of which were sold in great numbers. This new idea of exporting products made in York was to have a dramatic impact on the community's economy in coming years.

The iron industry spurred another successful venture in York, the making of fine guns. Early "Pennsylvania rifles" were made in York by Joseph Welshantz, Conrad Welshantz, Ignatius Leightner, Frederick Zorger, and George Eyster. No two Pennsylvania rifles were alike and the work of the early York gunsmiths helped to strengthen York's status as a community of fine craftsmen. After the Revolution, the Pennsylvania rifle was called the Kentucky Rifle, and credit for its origin became clouded.

The York area's iron furnaces also supported another important local industry, wagonmaking. There were at least half a dozen makers of Conestoga wagons working in the county by the time of the American Revolution. The Pennsylvania Germans adopted the wagon as a freight carrier, and it helped many settlers reach the Western lands with the items necessary for beginning a new life. The wagon's partner in transporting newcomers to the greater York area was usually, of course, the horse, but one could also arrive by "shank's mare," a mode of transportation named after a portion of the underside of the human foot.

The Conestoga, a more comfortable way to travel over long distances, had a curved, boat like body sometimes painted blue with red trim. The wagons, with their white canvas tops, were often seen in long caravans, carrying loads of grain, fruit, tobacco, cider, whiskey, oil, poultry, glass, iron wares, and flour. Frederick Lawmaster, John Lever, and Daniel Weaver were among the first Conestoga wagonmakers in York, opening the community's long and rich association with the transportation business.

With the rise of the York area's iron industry, and the expansion of manufacturing that it triggered, Yorkers began talking about holding a special

Below left
Erected in 1765, Bennett's or Codorus Furnace was owned and operated by James Smith, who signed the Declaration of Independence. (HSYC)

Below
Conestoga wagons, such as the one pictured here, were made in York and helped to open Western frontiers to settlement. (HSYC)

Bottom
The rear of the York Friends Meeting House is seen in an 1893 photograph by Gilbert Cope of West Chester, Pennsylvania. The eastern portion of the Meeting House was built in 1766 and the western portion added in 1783. It is the oldest house of worship still used in York and York County. The meeting has been in continuous existence since 1764 and many notable Quakers lie buried in the churchyard. (HSYC)

exposition in which they could show off their products. In 1765 Thomas Penn, then lieutenant governor of Pennsylvania, granted the citizens of York the privilege of holding two fairs a year, in June and November, "for the purpose of buying and selling goods, wares, merchandise and cattle." The community was diversifying and the idea of selling York-made products to the people of other towns was becoming more widespread.

As commerce grew, so did the population and the need for more churches. The first formal Presbyterian services in York probably were held in 1762, when the Presbytery began sending theological students to conduct services and to minister to the needs of the small congregation there. Seventeen sixty-three saw the erection of two new stone churches for congregations that had had only wooden structures before: the German Reformed Congregation and the Christ Lutheran Church, the latter of which built its new church building on the site it still occupies today. In 1766 the York Quakers built a brick structure at what is now 135 West Philadelphia Street, the oldest building in York County still used as a house of worship. In 1783 an addition to the western side of the Meeting House greatly expanded the facility.

Devout though the people may have been, they still fought almost rapaciously over lands. A letter from recorder of deeds George Stevenson—dated June 8, 1764, and addressed to William Peters, secretary to the land office—states:

> Yesterday at 6 P.M. Mr. Homel and myself met the two Doudels [Yorkers Michael and Jacob Doudel] together, with sundry other inhabitants of the place, to try to settle the difference between them about the lots lately granted to Michael. . . . After many things said on both sides, Michael agreed to bind himself by any reasonable instrument of writing, not to build a tan yard on the said lots. . . . But nothing would satisfy Jacob but the lots; and he offered to give Michael the two opposite lots on the other side of High Street, and to plough them and fence them. . . . This offer gave great offence to all the company, What, said they, is no body to have a lot but the two Doudels?

All of this lot-buying, fencing, and building brought with it a greater threat of fire. S.H. Spangler, a 19th-century fireman, compiled a detailed history of York's first firefighting activities. In it Spangler notes that "in 1769 and 70 quite a number of buildings being erected, mostly of logs, which were liable to take fire, the villagers becoming aware of the necessity of making some provision to protect their property, held a meeting at the house of Baltzar Spangler, their 'Bauer Meister,' and discussed the propriety of organizing a fire company, this as in December, 1770."

Spangler tells of another meeting held in January 1771, during which a motion was made to organize a fire brigade and Spangler notes that 24 men "enrolled themselves as members," among them Baltzar Spangler, Jacob Doudel, the Reverend David Chandler, the gunsmith Ignatius Leightner, and the clockmaker Rudolph Spangler. Joseph Updegraff served as clerk at the meeting and Henry Miller was the chairman. (Chairman Miller, born in Lancaster County, had come to York in 1769 to read law with Samuel Johnston. He later participated in 47 battles and skirmishes with the British during the American Revolution, and was captain of the York Riflemen under General Washington. Captain Miller and the Riflemen were, in fact, with Washington during the arduous winter of 1777–1778 at Valley Forge. Among Miller's other positions of note were elected sheriff of York County and the supervisor of revenue for the state of Pennsylvania, appointed by then-President Washington.)

The company was named "The Sun Fire Brigade of York town," and its members agreed to meet every Saturday afternoon to participate in a drill. Those who were absent from a drill paid a two-shilling fine. Members also voted to provide each member with a bucket, basket, and staff, which they kept in the halls or entranceways of their homes. The bucket would be used for carrying water to a fire scene, and the basket (or bag) for carrying valuables out of a burning house. The staff could be used in many firefighting functions.

The company purchased its first fire wagon in 1772 and built its first engine house in 1773. The site chosen for the engine house was a lot on the Square. The red fire engine was decorated on both sides with the picture of a rising sun enclosed in a laurel wreath. The brigade's motto was "*Spectamur Agendo,*" or "Let us be judged by our actions."

The creation of a fire brigade, the fights over lots, the building of churches, the growth of trade —these were all primarily local matters. There were two other events of the time that, while not strictly local in scope, did nonetheless affect York. The first was the disappearance of the Susquehannocks. Though the reason for their population decline is still a mystery, the indications are that disease brought by the white man was a major factor. Droughts came, decimating food supplies and destroying hunting land. Intertribal warfare and decreasing numbers to guard their diminishing frontiers also contributed to their fall, and the strong Susquehannocks slipped out of the annals of history.

Moving stories are told of the last groups of Susquehannocks known to exist. One tale finds a band of Susquehannocks tricked into an army encampment in Maryland where they were blamed for atrocities apparently committed by tribes from the north who had swept through that state. A 19th-century historian, S.F. Streeter, writes: "Here the Susquehannocks, to the number of nearly one hundred, with their old men, women and children, established themselves, and here they were determined to remain."

Six leaders were chosen from among the 100 Susquehannocks and they presented the white leaders with "a paper and a silver medal, with a black and yellow ribbon attached, which they said had been given to them by former governors of Maryland as a pledge of protection and friendship, as long as the sun and moon should endure." Five of the six Susquehannock leaders were killed the next day.

Another story concerning the Susquehannocks' disappearance dates from 1763. Streeter writes that the number of Susquehannocks involved amounted to "only twenty souls." "At that time," he continues, "rioters inflamed by accounts of the Indian war raging along the Pennsylvania frontier, massacred this small band where they had taken shelter in the jail yard in the city of Lancaster."

Hal Conrad, a present-day student of Pennsylvania Indians and a county editor of the *York Dispatch*, notes another story of the final days of the river Indians. "The river . . . was used by many tribes in migration to the north or south," he writes, "and provided sites for intertribal battles, which were the rule rather than the exception. The last Indians living along the Susquehanna were Shawnees, a branch of the Susquehannock tribe, and they resided at Indian Steps where they had hatcheries. Finally, when only 18 remained, they departed westward in 1765. The last glimpse of them was when the chief and his daughter climbed into a canoe and paddled away down the river."

Indian Steps Museum, an institution dedicated to the study of the Susquehannocks and other Indians, today stands in York County's Lower Chanceford Township, about 15 miles from York and along the river where the Indians carved "steps" in the bank to use as footholds while shad fishing. John Edward Vandersloot, owner and builder of Indian Steps "Cabin"

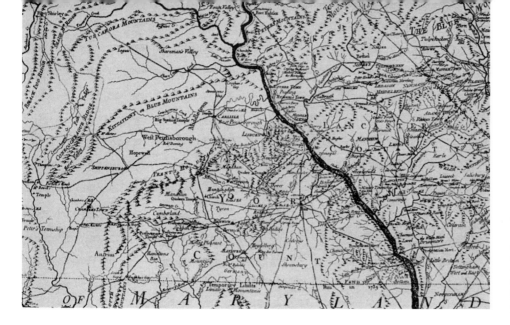

This map of Pennsylvania, including York County, "Laid down from Actual Surveys and chiefly from the map of W. Scull," was published in 1770 and "humbly inscribed to the honourable Thomas Penn and Richard Penn, Esquires." (HSYC)

in 1912, had the following words inscribed over the Museum's main door, facing the Susquehanna: "I entreat all those who pass this way to safely guard and preserve these former possessions of and monuments to an ancient Indian people." Another sharp image which Vandersloot left to York citizens was a photograph of himself, showing a powerful-looking man posed in full Indian chief regalia and standing on the rock steps that reach out into the Susquehanna.

With the disappearance of the Indians another crucial event of the time took the regional focus—the official solution of the old Pennsylvania-Maryland border conflict. In 1760 commissioners representing Lord Baltimore and the Penns agreed to authorize a survey to mark the colonies' mutual border once and for all.

Commissioners from both colonies employed Charles Mason and Jeremiah Dixon to make the survey and the two worked between 1763 and 1767 to establish the now-famous line that bears their names. Mason and Dixon established not only the southern boundary of Pennsylvania but also that of York County. This new line was marked with milestones cut in England and engraved with an "M" on one side for Maryland and a "P" on the opposite side for Pennsylvania. Five special stones were engraved with the coats of arms of Lord Baltimore and of the Penns, and these stones were placed at five-mile intervals. The Mason-Dixon line was resurveyed in 1849 and 1900, but the later surveys found no major error in the boundaries established by Mason and Dixon at the parallel of 39 degrees, 43 minutes, and 26.3 seconds.

Working with the two famous surveyors on the original job was a York County man named Archibald McLean. McLean, a surveyor by profession, served as a chief associator for Mason and Dixon, and later became chairman of the Committee of Observation and Safety for York County. A native of Antrim, Ireland, he also served as prothonotary, register of wills, and recorder of deeds for the county after George Stevenson (1749–1764) and Samuel Johnston (1764–1777).

In the Civil War the line that McLean had helped to survey—dubbed "the Mason-Dixon"—separated the free states from the slave states and took on even greater importance as Americans fought against each other. (Important as this line was, however, it did not give "Dixie" its name, as is commonly believed; the term derives from New Orleans bank notes with the English "Ten" printed on one side and the French "Dix" on the other.)

But in the meantime, Yorkers were planning to fight a different enemy: the British. The American Revolution was coming to York.

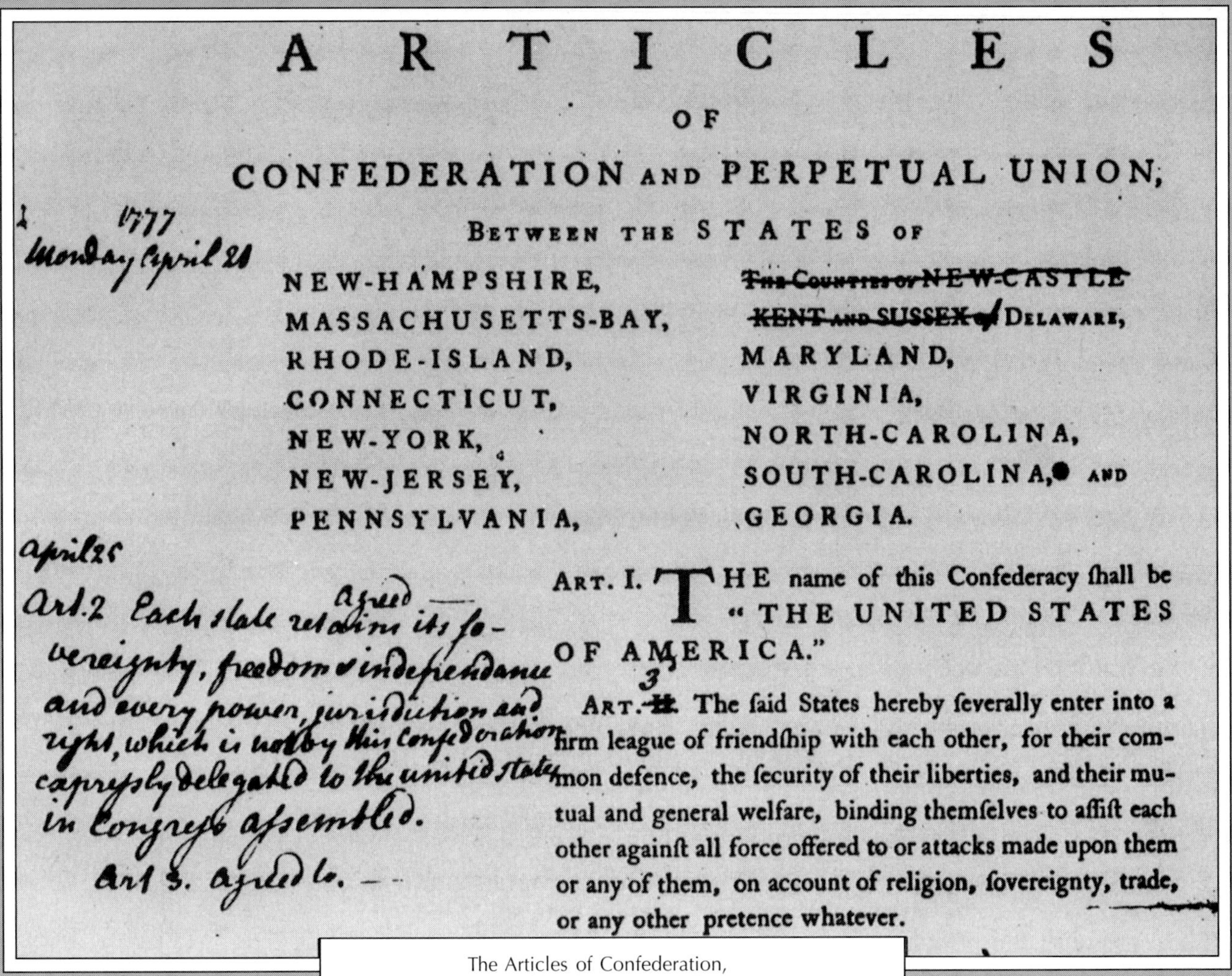

ARTICLES OF CONFEDERATION AND PERPETUAL UNION,

BETWEEN THE STATES OF

NEW-HAMPSHIRE, MASSACHUSETTS-BAY, RHODE-ISLAND, CONNECTICUT, NEW-YORK, NEW-JERSEY, PENNSYLVANIA, ~~THE COUNTIES OF NEW-CASTLE KENT AND SUSSEX of~~ DELAWARE, MARYLAND, VIRGINIA, NORTH-CAROLINA, SOUTH-CAROLINA, AND GEORGIA.

1777
Monday April 21

April 25

Art. 2 Each state retains its sovereignty, freedom & independance and every power, jurisdiction and right, which is not by this Confederation expressly delegated to the united states in Congress assembled. agreed —

Art 3. agreed to. — —

ART. I. THE name of this Confederacy ſhall be "THE UNITED STATES OF AMERICA."

ART. ~~II.~~ 3 The ſaid States hereby ſeverally enter into a firm league of friendſhip with each other, for their common defence, the ſecurity of their liberties, and their mutual and general welfare, binding themſelves to aſſiſt each other againſt all force offered to or attacks made upon them or any of them, on account of religion, ſovereignty, trade, or any other pretence whatever.

The Articles of Confederation, adopted by the Continental Congress during its stay in York, used the name "United States of America" in capital letters. The Declaration of Independence also used the term, but without the same capitalization. Courtesy, The York County Heritage Trust

CHAPTER III

CAPITAL OF REVOLUTIONARY AMERICA

A new spirit was alive in America. It was the spirit of revolutionary patriotism, which struck a responsive chord in York, where the citizens were highly sensitive to the invasion of their lands by outsiders. For many York citizens, horror-filled memories of King Louis XIV's armies destroying their native countryside had already merged with images of Marylanders intruding into York County and the earlier attacks of the French and the Indians. The York patriots, skilled in the use of rifles and Indian methods of warfare, were now ready to use those skills to prevent the incursion of the British "outsiders."

In 1774, after King George III failed to resolve differences between the Colonies and the British monarchy, the first Continental Congress had met in Philadelphia, where its members drew up a declaration of rights to send to the king. The declaration went unanswered and, soon afterward, Massachusetts called a Provincial Congress, which authorized the formation of troops and the collection of supplies with which the tyranny of England could be forcibly resisted.

General Thomas Gage, who had fought under Braddock in the French and Indian War, was the commander of the British regulars at Boston. On April 18, 1775, he sent 800 troops to Concord, a few miles west of Boston, to capture the supply stores there. The next day at dawn, he was met on the Lexington Common by a group of armed patriots, seven of whom died when the group refused orders to disperse and were fired upon by British troops.

When the British arrived in Concord, they were met by an even larger band of armed patriots. A tense battle ensued, the British were turned back, and, on their return to Boston, they were shot at by hundreds of Boston farmers along the way. Three hundred British soldiers died in the skirmishes, and the remaining troops barely escaped capture.

Thus began the Revolutionary War, which would occupy Yorkers, in body and mind, for nearly a decade. When the news of Lexington and Concord reached York, the populace, nearly bursting with enthusiasm for the American cause, readied themselves for action. The second Continental Congress, which had assembled in Philadelphia on May 10, now supported measures for war against Britain. On June 14 the Continental Congress adopted a resolution that eight companies of trained riflemen from Pennsylvania be raised as quickly as possible. They called for two companies each from Maryland and Virginia as well. When organized, the troops were to march to Cambridge and join the army under General George Washington.

There were already three organized military companies in York—some of the members of which were veterans of the French and Indian War—which comprised the York County militia. The required number of officers and the 68 riflemen were selected from the county's militia to head up York's first company.

Recruitment of the other soldiers for the first company took place at sites throughout the region, including the Marsh Creek area (around Gettysburg), the Monoghan settlement (now known as Dillsburg), and in the southern part of the county. In less than a week these "sturdy pioneers" were organized under Michael Doudel as captain, Henry Miller as first lieutenant, John Dill as second lieutenant, and Walter Cruise as corporal. Yorkers such as Thomas Hartley (who would become a colonel under Washington and later York's first Congressman), James Smith, John Kean, Joseph Donaldson, and Michael Hahn led the efforts to prepare the company for action.

Doudel and Miller, who were in charge of recruitment, picked only those men who could hit a small chalk mark with a flintlock from a distance of 150 yards, and it seemed that every man under 50 years of age came to prove himself. Historian George R. Prowell observes that "so many men wanted to enlist that there were more than the soldiers were authorized to accept." Luckily for Doudel and Miller, Horatio Gates—who had recently been appointed adjutant general—happened to be passing through York and he decided that it would be unwise to refuse the enlistment of "such courageous men." He looked them over and declared, "They will make soldiers!"

York's Committee of Correspondence, part of a network of such informal committees that regularly exchanged information on the current state of the fight for independence, wrote to Congress: "The men seemed actuated with the greatest zeal and thought themselves honored in having their names enrolled among the sons of liberty who are to fight for their country and in defense of their dearest rights and privileges. The only uneasiness they feel is that they are not at this moment at the scene of action."

A modern historian, Philip J. Schlegel, has compiled a complete muster roll for the York company. In the publication, "Recruits to Continentals: A History of the York County Rifle Company, June 1775 to January 1777," Schlegel lists more than 100 men as members, including Doudel, Miller, Dill, Cruise, court justice Thomas Armor, Christian Bittinger (son of one of Hanover's founders, Nicholas Bittinger), and tavernkeeper Martin Eichelberger, Jr. Schlegel points out that one of the enlistees, Peter Hammer, was under age, so his mother hired a substitute, a practice occasionally employed by Colonial families. Youths in their early teens were used by the army as drummers and flagbearers, and parents of young teenagers often saw sons just out of puberty march off to join the war.

On July 1, 1775, the men were ready to join Washington. The Reverend John Roth, pastor of the Moravian church at York, recorded in his diary that the men attended a farewell religious service at Zion Reformed Church under the Reverend Daniel Wagner. At one o'clock, after Wagner preached to the men in German and, according to Roth, entreated them to "keep God before your eyes continually and you will be assured of his guidance," the York County Rifle Company started down East Market Street on its long march.

The York company crossed the Susquehanna at Wright's Ferry and arrived at Cambridge on July 25, thereby distinguishing itself as the first military

The Moravian Church and Gemeinhaus were located at South Water (now Pershing Avenue) and West Princess streets in 1830. The Reverend John Roth, pastor of the Moravian Church, wrote extensively of the Revolutionary War days in York. (HSYC)

group to arrive from outside New England. The company's arrival boosted the morale of the local citizens considerably. Because of its superb weapons and superior mobility—the men had marched 414 miles in 25 days, or more than 16 miles a day—the company was assigned to a support function on the perimeter of the Continental Army.

Despite their long march, the Yorkers' desire for action was stronger than ever, as this newspaper article quoted in Frank Moore's *Diary of the American Revolution*, indicates. Dated July 25, 1775, the item from the *Pennsylvania Journal* relates:

> Captain Doudel, with his company of riflemen from York, Pennsylvania, arrived at Cambridge about one o'clock today, and since has made proposals to General George Washington to attack the [British] transport stationed on the Charles River. . . . The General thinks it best to decline at present; but at the same time commends the spirit of Captain Doudel and his brave men who, though just arrived after a very long march, offer to execute the plan immediately.

Though commended by Washington, these aggressive, restless Yorkers soon earned a reputation, according to Schlegel, for "early disciplinary problems . . . manifested in such activities as unauthorized sniping, desertion and mutinous behaviour." Schlegel points out that natural maturation and Washington's ability to provide direction for the Yorker's frustrated zeal made them better soldiers and helped them to earn the generous praise they later received for their service with the Continental Army.

Another newspaper item, which editor Moore included in *Diary of the American Revolution*, describes a maneuver in which General Washington directed the Yorkers. On July 30, Washington ordered two groups to:

> march down to our advanced post at Charlestown Neck, to endeavour to surround the [British] advanced guard and bring off some prisoners. . . . Captain Doudel with thirty-nine men filed off to the right of Bunker Hill, and, creeping on their hands and knees, got into the rear without being discovered.
>
> The other band of forty men, under Lieutenant Miller, were successful

in getting behind the sentinels on the left, and were within a few yards of joining the division on the right, when a party of regulars came down to the hill to relieve their guard, and crossed our riflemen under Captain Doudel as they were lying on the ground. . . . [The British] immediately fired. The riflemen returned the salute, killed several and brought off two prisoners and their arms, with the loss of Corporal Cruise, who is supposed to have been killed as he has not been heard of since the affair.

Cruise was actually very much alive. The British had taken him prisoner and thereby started him on the road to becoming one of York's most unusual heroes. American riflemen such as Cruise were almost legendary in England for the damage they were doing to the finest British troops abroad. Thus the English offered a reward to any person who could bring one of these famous riflemen to England, and Cruise himself, after his capture, was taken to London and put on display.

Cruise fascinated the English. They found his white frock, round hat, durable trousers, and Indian mocasins intriguing. His American manners further charmed them, and his displays of marksmanship brought polite applause from government officials who wondered aloud how British soldiers could successfully counterattack when such remarkable shooting ability was present on the opposite side. After a period of imprisonment, Cruise was taken before the mayor of London, who could find no reason to detain him. He was ordered freed.

Arthur Lee, an American secret agent in London, learned of Cruise's fate and later of his release. He sent for the American immediately. Lee had documents which, he told Cruise, "are of the greatest moment to the liberty of our country." Lee informed the York soldier that the papers had to be delivered safely into the hands of General Washington as quickly as possible. "Can I trust you with this important task?" Lee asked. "You can trust me," answered the man from York.

Cruise delivered the papers to General Washington at the army's headquarters in New York, and the general immediately sent copies to the Continental Congress in Philadelphia. Congress, and the American people for that matter, believed that the king would be sending peace commissioners to hammer out the differences between the crown and the Colonies. But the Cruise papers revealed that the king would be sending not diplomats, but additional troops to augment the English forces in America. Furthermore, King George III planned to hire troops from the German state of Hesse and elsewhere in Germany, to act as mercenaries in the war against the Colonists.

Yorkers and most other Americans were furious at the information contained in Cruise's papers. The papers played a large part in spurring action which, in time, led Congressional delegate Richard Henry Lee to make the motion in Congress on June 7, 1776: "These United Colonies are, and of right ought to be, free and independent states." The motion was carried on July 2 and, in consequence, the Declaration of Independence was passed two days later. Congressional delegate James Smith, from York, was one of those who signed the new document.

While Congress was declaring its independence from English rule, Yorkers were fighting the crown in a more forceful manner. In response to Congressional directives, eight companies— one more than Congress had requested —were formed in other Pennsylvania counties. Two regiments were formed from the York County militia and they became known as the First and Second Pennsylvania Regiments. The First, consisting of eight companies, was commanded by Colonel Michael Swope and Lieutenant Colonel Robert Stevenson. The Second Pennsylvania Regiment was commanded by Colonel Richard McAllister, the unsuccessful candidate in York's first mayoral election and the founder, in 1763, of Hanover. He had served as a member of the Committee of Observation and Safety for York County. He was married to Mary Dill, the daughter of Colonel Matthew Dill who had commanded a regiment in the French and Indian War. Richard and Mary McAllister had 11 children. Two of their sons commanded companies in the Revolution.

The nine Pennsylvania companies, including the York riflemen and a company from Franklin County commanded by two captains, James Ross and Matthew Smith, were formed into what General Washington was to call "Colonel Thompson's Battalion of Riflemen from Pennsylvania."

Born in Ireland, Colonel William Thompson had settled in Carlisle, working as a surveyor there until called to serve in the Revolution. Captain James Ross, co-commander of the Franklin County company, had been born in York County in Peach Bottom Township. He later earned a reputation as a noted orator and statesman, serving for nine years as a United States Senator. He was also a trusted confidante of and counselor to General Washington.

As in most wars, companies of men in the Revolution were massed into

James Smith, the signer of the Declaration of Independence from York, was also an organizer of "sturdy pioneers" recruited from York to fight against England in the Revolutionary War. Smith is buried today in the First Presbyterian churchyard. (HSYC)

larger bodies, then often pulled out and placed in another group for a different campaign. Such was the case with the York soldiers. After the siege of Boston in the summer of 1775, the original company of York troops, under Doudel and Miller, remained with Thompson's Battalion in Boston. Captain Doudel resigned his command and Miller was promoted to succeed him. After further reorganization and command shifts, the York company was soon engaged in a skirmish. Colonel Edward Hand recorded the incident. He writes: "Our battalion formed the picket guard of the two thousand provincial troops who on the evening of the 26th of August took possession of Ploughed Hill . . . and met with its first loss, Private Simpson. . . ."

The young private, who was from the York company captained by Ross and Smith, did not die from his wounds immediately. While near death in a battlefield tent, according to the diary of James Wilkinson: "The young man was visited by General Washington in person and by most of the officers of rank. . . ." Captain Wilkinson, who had joined Thompson's Battalion as a Boston volunteer and who would later become commander-in-chief of the post-Revolutionary army, further relates that Simpson's death "became a common sorrow in an army of twelve or fourteen thousand men." The personal visit to a dying soldier was typical of Washington's concern for his troops, especially in the early days of the Revolution.

Although the war was exacting a high price from Yorkers, including additional lives, the town's citizenry remained united in the cause of liberty. When a copy of the Declaration of Independence was brought to York soon after July 4, 1776, it was read to a cheering crowd at the Centre Square Court House and a bell atop the building rang out the news. The bell, which had been authorized for the Court House by the county commissioners in

1767, was joined by a chorus of church bells throughout the community.

Within days, however, there were few York County people left to celebrate the Declaration. The Reverend John Roth records on July 17 that "York town seems quite deserted on account of the departure for the army of all men under fifty years of age.... All business is prostrated, all shops are closed. How many prayers and tears will now be brought before the Lord, by parents for their children, by children for their parents, by wives for their husbands."

One of the war's oddities was that once local soldiers exited the town, others promptly entered it. During August, Roth writes, "Numerous bands of soldiers from Maryland, Virginia, etc., passed through the town." John Durang, a Yorker who went on to become an actor and America's first native-born professional dancer, was eight years old in 1776. In a later account of his life, *The Memoir of John Durang: American Actor 1785–1816,* he remembers the period:

> *My father was encamped [with Captain George Eichelberger's company] at Lancaster, and a regiment from Virginia was in York....The men [of this regiment were] in poor condition to meet an enemy...some without shoes or stockings, some no coats, some with old muskets and some with fowling pieces. However, when they went on their journey, they were supplied by citizens, who could spare them clothes and provisions.*

Young Durang, without permission, accompanied the Virginia soldiers to Lancaster. Arriving there in a new hunting shirt and trousers ("green with yellow fringe"), the boy was swiftly sent back to York by his father, Jacob Durang. A surgeon, storekeeper, and farmer, Jacob Durang was a typical "country gentleman" of the day.

Captain George Eichelberger, mentioned in Durang's account, was commander of the Fourth company of York County, and had served as a delegate to the provincial convention held in January of 1775. That conference was a forerunner of the one that resulted in the Declaration of Independence. Eichelberger, who kept a tavern in York, was a member of the county's Committee of Safety, a group formed to protect the families and property of those citizens who were away with the army or who were too young or infirm to protect themselves. The committee's duties also included keeping law and order in the town and collecting funds and materiel for the army. Eichelberger was married to Lydia Worley and they had seven children, including Martin, who also became a tavernkeeper. The elder Eichelberger and his brother, Jacob, had established themselves as pro-liberty activists even before Congress called troops in 1775.

Americans were not the only military men in York during 1776. Prisoners of war were boarded in York County and after most hostilities were over, a stockaded enclosure called Camp Security was built about four miles east of York as a kind of prison. The prisoners held here built crude shelters for themselves and their wives and children, many of whom had accompanied them to America. Some of the prisoners had liberal leave policies and, after the war, a few decided to settle in York because of its already large German-speaking population and its similarites to their native land.

Other prisoners were held at the York County Jail at George and King streets, and Durang, in his memoirs, writes that "several of the officers [Hessians] boarded at my father's house." The Durangs lived on East Market Street on the site where a bank now stands, and young Durang says that the Hessians there "had an excellent band of music and occasionally played to my great delight and serenaded the citizens."

The York area, of course, had sources of entertainment other than the enemy's band. Reflecting on calmer days, when the marching of soldiers and the quartering of prisoners were not necessary, Durang describes the semi-annual fairs, or frolics, where Yorkers' many diversions were often brought together in a single celebration:

The country people flock in from all quarters, old and young, of both sexes. . . . The market place is furnished with every description of fineries, with some useful as well as ornamental goods by little merchants from Philadelphia and Baltimore, all kinds of diversions going on during the whole day, the taverns crowded, in every room a fiddle and dancing. Show-folks with their signs out, band and trumpet to invite the people to see the puppet shows, wire dancing, sleight of hand. . . . A great many marriages take place by the young country men and girls at the time of the harvest frolic.

Durang also gives the modern Yorker a peek at one of the area's early vices: "The greatest evil in this town is the collection of gamblers, who infest the country towns at the time of fairs, harvest frolics and the [horse] races. . . . They would draw the unsuspecting into their snare and yet those very same gamesters make the appearance of good moral citizens, when they walk the street."

York town's various entertainments, even in the face of war, drew the community's diverse ethnic strains and religious groups together into a shared cultural appreciation of music, parades, fairs, traveling circuses and performers, and other amusements. In fact, so strong was the community's fervor for music, especially, that if hard work, commerce, and the level-headed observance of religious strictures ruled its body, music could be said to rule its soul.

The Palatines who settled York County had brought with them a long musical heritage, as had the Moravians. Pipe organs were installed in the Lutheran and Reformed churches. Church choirs regularly gave concerts before the Revolutionary War, which brought military bands that added marches to the traditional hymns. Less religious elements were the traveling circuses, which passed through the area in wagon caravans, and York's first "dramatic" offerings, including a performance of the tragedy, *Cato*, as well as a bill offering "Mr. McGrath's Company of Comedians from Virginia and Maryland."

Local taverns also helped York earn a reputation as a town that entertained itself well. One such tavern was the Golden Lamb, located on the south side of East Market Street, which was often the scene of festive entertainments. After the Revolution, the Golden Lamb presented Frederick Durang (John's brother) performing with what was probably America's first touring company of actors.

Although Yorkers before, during, and after the Revolutionary War period gladly took time out for such diversions, they were primarily occupied with their two principal interests—farming and business. York County farmers continued to make advances in agricultural techniques and equipment. They began harvesting their crops with the German scythe, which was manufactured locally by sharpening hot iron on the edge of an anvil. The scythe proved effective on the local crops of spelt, rye, and wheat, but it was eventually replaced by another tool, the grain cradle.

The innovativeness and industry that characterized farmers in York County, and throughout Pennsylvania, had accorded them a high, even slightly romanticized, status by the 1770s. John Durang writes that "The Pennsylvania farmer stands predominant. He enjoys the sweets of his industry in the bosom of his family, his artless simplicity cements their harmony and their barn is the best house." Successful farmers were thought, in the class system of the day, to be the equal of firemen and shopkeepers, but probably a step below county and town officials, ministers, and members of the bar. Adding to their importance in the community was the fact that their barns were often used as religious meeting places for various congregations.

Barn raising, from York's beginnings, had been a cooperative effort. Indians helped some of the first white settlers construct their rather crude log barns, but as the population grew, barn raisings became something of a social event, with family, friends, and neighbors joining in the work. By the 1770s the York landscape was dotted with log barns and "Sweitzer" (Swiss) barns, which were built against a bank with the ground floor opening to one side and the top floor opening to the other. The later "bank barns" were adaptations of the Sweitzer barns built by early Yorkers, whose native lands were only miles from the Swiss barns' country of origin.

Churches, too, continued to be built. In 1776 the local Catholics purchased a property, the present-day site of Saint Patrick's Church, for use as a Mass House.

Seventeen seventy-four also was the year of the formation of another important York religious group. The River Brethren, or Brethren in Christ, originated in Lancaster County with services conducted in the home of Jacob Engel, a Mennonite, who later became the church's first bishop. After much discussion, the "brethren" meeting decided that triune-immersion (baptism by immersion three times) was the only practice acceptable to Scripture. They went to a minister of the German Baptist (Dunkard) faith and asked him to baptize the members of their group. Because the group members would not agree to join the Dunkard's church, he refused their request. The group then cast lots on the banks of the Susquehanna. The one who selected the proper ticket baptized the others and finally one of the newly baptized performed the service for him. One hundred Brethren in Christ settled in York and Lancaster counties during the period around the Revolution and the tradition of requiring women to wear small, net prayer bonnets, because of the Biblical injunction that women should keep their heads covered, is practiced today.

York County, in 1776, already had three German Baptist congregations—one on the little Conewago Creek near Hanover, one at Bermudian in Washington Township, and one in Codorus Township. The first elder of the

From the earliest days of York County history, its churches have contributed immeasurably to the welfare and strength of the community. Many early York County congregations worshipped in homes of members or in crude log meeting houses. This informal sketch depicts the Church of the Brethren, Little Conewago Congregation. (HSYC)

last-named church was Jacob Tanner, a poet, who had once mesmerized a debater with an argument set down in perfect German meter. The German Baptists —or Dunkards, from the German word *tunken*, meaning to baptize or dip —began as a group called the Pietists in North Prussia. They believed in baptism by immersion. The Dunkards, like the Brethren in Christ, the Mennonites, and the Friends, were pacifists upon arriving in York County. Some of them decided to fight during the Revolution but the majority of the members in all these groups stood by their nonviolent principles.

When York men were called away to battle, the activities of the community took on a dramatically different complexion. The women were left behind to tend market stands, farms, shops, taverns, fires, and other matters. They also had to deal with the usual chores involved in taking care of their families—spinning, sewing, weaving, cooking, making candles, and cleaning away the dust and dirt of the street. In fact, cleanliness among early York settlers *was* godliness, and German housewives in front of their homes literally sweeping the street became a common sight. The custom is still practiced by some residents today.

The war often kept the men away for long periods. Some, of course, never returned. On November 16, 1776, during the Battle of Fort Washington on Manhattan Island, nearly 400 York-area soldiers under the command of Henry Miller and Michael Swope were taken prisoner. Some of them were held for three years, suffering from hunger, cold, disease, and other afflictions. Some died and others were wounded, but since records were not always kept during those days, no accurate accounting of casualties is possible.

After the defeat at Fort Washington, commander-in-chief George Washington was forced to order his troops, which included a good many Yorkers, to retreat southward across New Jersey. On December 26 he led his men to victory in the Battle of Trenton, aided by the companies of York captains Henry Miller and Philip Albright.

Captain Albright, who had received his education at the German Lutheran School, owned a flour mill on the Codorus. He married Anna Maria Ursula Duenckle, daughter of a German aristocrat. One of the couple's daughters, Anna Maria Ursula, married George Small, who had a lumber yard. Small's lumber yard was a predecessor of the P.A. and S. Small Company.

Yorkers also distinguished themselves at the bloody Battle of Brandywine on September 11, 1777. Pennsylvania troops there were under the overall command of General Anthony Wayne. Colonel Thomas Hartley of York commanded the First Brigade of this division. Also participating in the Battle of Brandywine were Yorkers Colonel Henry Miller, Colonel David Grier, Major John Clark, Benjamin Stoddard, Evan Edwards, George Ross, Archibald McAllister (son of Richard McAllister, candidate in York's first election), Robert Hoopes, James Kenny, James Dill, Andrew Walker, and Martin Eichelberger. One thousand Americans were killed, wounded or captured at Brandywine and the British also suffered heavy losses. One of the York Countians injured was Ensign William Russel, who lost a leg by a cannonball. Colonel Miller and Major Clark requested that the state award Russel a certificate of meritorious service and a pension to help compensate him for his loss.

Colonel Thomas Hartley, born in Colebrookdale, Pennsylvania, received his early education at a classical school in Reading. When he was 18 he came to York, where he read law with Samuel Johnston, a relative of his mother. He was admitted to the York bar in 1769 and was one of York's earliest patriots. In the fall of 1775, at age 27, he was a member of the expedition to Canada, during which campaign he was promoted to lieutenant colonel under Colonel William Irvine of Carlisle. When Colonel Irvine was captured in Canada, Hartley was put in command. He returned to Carlisle with his men in March 1777.

In the fall of 1777, York County troops went on to the Battle of Paoli, about 60 miles east of York. During the engagement, 300 American soldiers were killed or wounded. General Wayne, who commanded the forces at what was called "the Massacre at Paoli," later wrote to General Washington of the Yorkers' valor, commenting that he "derived every assistance possible from those gentlemen of this occasion."

Shortly after Brandywine, the British general Howe had begun to move eastward into nearby Philadelphia, a move that would have historic consequences for York. Philadelphia, the home of the Congress, could almost hear the Redcoats approaching and delegates adjourned there on September 23, 1777, to meet in Lancaster on September 27. Congress arrived in Lancaster only to find that the Pennsylvania state government, which had also fled from Philadelphia, had already taken over Lancaster's public building. Since the Court House in York was about the same size as the one in Lancaster— 45 feet by 45 feet—and since having the Susquehanna River between themselves and the enemy seemed like a good idea, the delegates voted to adjourn at Lancaster and reconvene in York on September 30. They arrived in a town of about 1,800 people, with some 300 homes, most of them made of logs, and about a dozen "publick houses," as taverns were then called. These taverns, which also served as inns, soon grew busy and crowded, as members, aides, and guards of Congress, the Treasury, and the Board of War all tried to find lodgings and offices as close to the Court House as possible.

John Hancock, president of the Congress, stayed just across Centre Square

from the Court House at the home of Mrs. Eva Swope, the second wife of Michael Swope who had commanded the York troops at Fort Washington and was, at the time, being held as a prisoner of war. A house that later belonged to Archibald McLean at the northeast corner of the Square was chosen to house the Treasury, and James Smith volunteered his law office on South George Street as headquarters for the Board of War and the Committee on Foreign Affairs. (The site of the building used as the Treasury later became the site of Commonwealth Bank and the James Smith property was the site of the Drovers and Mechanics Bank.) At Elizabeth Moore's Inn on the southeast quadrant of the Square, now the site of a Hamilton Bank annex and restored in 1981, Georgia delegate Edward Langworthy took lodgings and became enamored of one of the Moore daughters. He and young Mary Moore were married the next year.

The chaplains of Congress, William White and George Duffield, took advantage of the hospitality of York's ministers. The Reverend White stayed at the Christ Lutheran Church parsonage on North George Street with the Reverend John Kurtz, and the Reverend Duffield stayed on East King Street with the Reverend Daniel Wagner of Zion Reformed Church.

Increased crowding caused discontent among York's visitors. Elias Boudinot, from New Jersey, complained that the town was "full as a tick." Henry Laurens, who would succeed Hancock as the president of Congress, commented that his total accommodations in York were smaller than the hall of his home in South Carolina and that he was forced to dine on nothing but "bread and cheese and a bit of grog." James Lovell, a Massachusetts delegate, wrote that the local "lime water" had done damage to many of his countrymen's bowels and "had forced some delegates home to their native springs." Lovell's complaint stemmed from York's generous geological gift, limestone, which imparted to some early York wells a white, cloudy color and a particu-

Samuel Adams, a representative to Continental Congress, had few good things to say about Yorkers and their political views. (HSYC)

late consistency. Samuel Adams (who tended to villify even America's greatest towns), complained in a letter to his wife:

> *The house where I am is so thronged that I cannot enjoy accommodations as I wish. I cannot have a room . . . The people of this country are chiefly Germans who have schools in their own language, as well as prayers, psalms and sermons, so that multitudes are born, grow up and die here without ever learning English. In politics they are a breed of mongrels or neutrals benumbed with a general torpor.*

Not every visitor shared Adams's low opinion of York and Yorkers. A letter from Board of War member Timothy Pickering to his wife, dated February 14, 1778, gives a particularly favorable picture of the household of a "widow Mihms" (probably the widow of John Meem, who had helped build the Court House). Pickering writes:

> *She is a very neat, clever, obliging old woman, and has agreed to wash and mend my linen and stockings which is a very great thing here. . . . I have not felt so much at home since I left Salem. She lived all alone and now sets from morning till night at her spinning wheel, which, by the way, is a very modest one. And when I am home writing or reading it gives me no more disturbance than the purring of a cat.*
>
> *There is a warm chamber where I lodge. In one corner [his servant] Millet has fixed me a little cabin in which he has put a straw bed. . . . In this manner I have lain every night warm and comfortable. . . .*
>
> *Millet has bought a tolerable veal at a shilling a pound, butter at two thirds of a dollar, eggs at one third of a dollar a dozen, and potatoes at a dollar a bushel. But above all he gets a quart of good milk every night and every morning which with good bread at a third of a dollar a loaf of about six pounds weight makes our breakfast and supper. . . . Thus my diet is perfectly agreeable.*

As delegates and other newcomers to York settled in their lodging places, citizens readied the Court House for the Congressional sessions. The jury benches had to be pushed against the wall to make room for the delegates, and Yorkers brought in their own tables and chairs to accommodate the delegates. A table for each delegate was covered with a long cloth, which in the winter made an effective leg warmer that was augmented by a hot-coal footwarmer. A tall, cased clock—made by York's Godfrey Lenhart—timed the sessions from a corner of the room.

Historian Prowell capsulizes the Congressional sessions with these observations: "There were never more than forty members of Congress present at one time. In all there were sixty-four delegates from the thirteen original states who occupied seats in Congress from the time it came to York until it returned to Philadelphia." At the time of the first Congressional sessions in York, Prowell continues, circumstances were grim: "There was little hope that the army under Washington would eventually defeat the British forces. . . . The patriots who came here, however, continued to legislate for the army and the establishment of the freedom of the United States."

The delegates themselves were under no illusions as to the vast scope of the task ahead of them in York. A few days after they arrived, Samuel Adams wrote: "Our affairs are said to be desperate. . . . The eyes of the people of this country are upon us here." Congress had to unify and strengthen the states, which it did by organizing the country's first government and ratifying its first constitution, the Articles of Confederation. The Articles, the forerunner to the Constitution and often called the first constitutional government of the

New World, had been drafted and presented to Congress on July 12, 1776. In York, on October 2, 1777, the delegates agreed "that the Articles of Confederation be taken into consideration tomorrow morning at 11 o'clock."

Congressional records from October 2 through November 15 contain accounts of extensive and spirited debates, on those and other issues, as the document was hammered into a form acceptable to the Congress as a whole. Little states argued against big states; Southern states argued against Northern states; and some delegates from the same state argued against each other. The frustration and complexity of those sessions are shown in the correspondence and diaries of the times.

Henry Laurens wrote to his son: "The present question is a mode of taxation. Two days have been amused with conning it: some sensible things have been said, and as much nonsense as ever I heard in so short a space."

Richard Henry Lee reminded his colleagues of the vulnerable nature of the new confederation, saying: "I must note that in this great business of forming our first common charter, we must yield a little to each other, and not rigidly insist on having everything correspond to our own partial views. On such basis we would never be able to confederate."

In constructing the Articles, Congress had to empower the government to unify military resources, outline rules for treaties and alliances, build confidence in the government, stabilize currency in a wildly inflationary financial climate, create procedures for taxation and voting, determine the power to fix Western boundaries, and decide the issue of slavery. The delegates debated these issues and revised the Articles for more than six weeks. Then, on November 15, they adopted the Articles officially. Article I of the document read: "The Stile of this confederacy shall be 'United States of America,'" which marked the first time that term was used in an official capacity to signify the Thirteen Colonies as a single force. The Court House on York town's Centre Square had seen within its doors the adoption of America's first constitutional government. Yorkers feel justified in claiming their city as the "First Capital of the U.S.A."

While Congress was taking responsibility for America, York was taking responsibility for Congress. The Sun Fire Brigade had the honor of protecting the Congressmen during their nine months in York. Congress, probably recognizing the added burden that its presence was placing on the brigade, resolved that "an appropriation of $50.00, Continental currency, be granted to the fire company of York town which has a laurel-wreath design painted on its fire wagon." This prompted the fire company to change its name to the Laurel Company, the name under which the organization still exists today.

Congress's printing of resolutions and constitutions soon created the need for a printing facility in York. On October 17, 1777, Congress authorized its Committee of Intelligence to take "the most speedy and effectual measures for getting a printing press erected in this town—York town—for the purpose of conveying to the public the intelligence that Congress may from time to time receive."

Ten days later the Hall and Sellers press from Philadelphia, which had originally belonged to Benjamin Franklin, was brought to York. The press was set up in a building on the southwest corner of High and Beaver streets on the site, familiar to modern Yorkers, of the old Bon Ton department store. Government documents and $5 million of the inflated Continental currency were printed while Congress worked in York. The *Pennsylvania Gazette*, the official organ of Congress at that time, was also printed there.

On October 29, a couple of days after the printing press arrived, John Hancock resigned as president of Congress because of ill health. Henry Laurens of South Carolina was elected to replace Hancock in the president's chair, which was the one closest to the Court House's heating stove. Upon taking the job, Laurens joked that he "might as well be president as anyone else, since a good seat near a warm fire is some compensation for extra

Below
General Horatio Gates, head of the Board of War in 1777, plotted with other critics of General George Washington to have Washington fired from his job and replaced by Gates. The scheme, which included a plan to sway Washington's strongest supporter, the Marquis de Lafayette, is remembered in history as the "Conway Cabal." (HSYC)

Below right
Henry Laurens of South Carolina succeeded John Hancock as president of the Continental Congress and served for eight months while the Congress stayed in York. (HSYC)

labor."

Laurens had been president only two days on October 31, 1777, when Congress received news from the battlefield of an important victory. Major General Horatio Gates, who had passed through York and praised its new recruits in June 1775, had soundly defeated the British under General John Burgoyne at Saratoga, New York, several days earlier.

The members of Congress were elated over the victory, although they chastised James Wilkinson, the young man who had delivered the dispatch from General Gates, for taking two weeks to arrive with the news. Wilkinson, only 20 years old at the time, had been delayed at a raucous party on his way to York. "Perhaps we should strike a medal in his honor," a member of Congress joked.

Wilkinson's drunken reveling nearly had more serious consequences than delays and the barbs of Congressmen, however. At the party he had attended, Wilkinson had been indiscreet about General Gates's efforts to undermine Washington, efforts that would be revealed as the winter of 1777 drew to a close. But, for now, Congress was jubilant about the Saratoga triumph, which later historians would call "the most decisive battle ever fought on American soil." Laurens appointed a "thanksgiving proclamation," and Congress "set apart Thursday, the 18th day of December next, for solemn thanksgiving and praise." Copies of the National Thanksgiving Proclamation were sent to all 13 states. Thus it was in York that the first national thanksgiving was decreed.

A few days later General Washington sent Colonel Thomas Hartley's regiment, composed mostly of Yorkers, to act as special guard for Congress. The delegates directed that "barracks, or sheds be erected with all possible dispatch" to house Hartley's men in York. The regiment earned the title of "Congress's Own" as a result of its service.

As popular as this move no doubt made Washington among native Yorkers, there were many individuals in town actively working to unseat him. Washington's enemies in the military and the government, foremost among whom was Gates himself, Major General Thomas Conway, and General Thomas Mifflin, were even then plotting to have Washington removed and replaced by Gates. Gates's victory at Saratoga fueled the sentiment against Washington, which had been building since the commander-in-chief's disastrous loss at Brandywine. Although the cunning Gates took credit for Saratoga, modern historians point out that he had never even been under fire, and that officers Arnold and Morgan, under Washington's direction, had actually engineered the battle.

But Congressional president Laurens wrote to Gates in October of 1777: "Your name, sir, will be written in the breasts of grateful Americans of the present age and sent down to posterity." The public concurred, and urged Congress to name Gates the head of the Board of War, a position equivalent to the present-day Secretary of Defense. Gates was thereby authorized to dictate military policy for the entire American forces. The letters, conversations, and insinuations that had passed between Gates, Conway, and the other conspirators became known as the "Conway Cabal," and it was the details of this plot that young James Wilkinson had leaked on his way to York.

When this information was passed on to Washington, by Patrick Henry and others, the commander-in-chief had written to Gates telling him that, through Wilkinson's indiscretions, he had learned of the attempts to damage him. Gates raged with anger and shot off several abusive letters to Wilkinson. Wilkinson had become an intimate friend and aide to General Gates at a very young age, and his youth was demonstrated both in his earlier loose talk and in his dramatic response to Gates's last letter, which contained particularly offensive language. In his memoirs, Wilkinson recalls the incident:

Immediately after receiving this letter, I repaired to York, arriving in that town by twilight on the evening of February 23, 1778, to avoid observation. During the night I met my early companion and friend, Captain Stoddert. I recounted my wrongs to him and requested him to bear a message from me to General Gates. He remonstrated against my intention to challenge to fight a duel, and warned me that I was going headlong to destruction. For the first time we parted in displeasure. Soon afterward I met with Lieutenant-Colonel Ball, of the Virginia Line, whose spirit was as independent as his fortune. He delivered Gates the following note: 'Sir—I have discharged my duty to you and my conscience. Meet me tomorrow morning behind the Episcopal Church and I will then stipulate the satisfaction which you have promised to grant. I am your humble servant, JAMES WILKINSON.'

Lieutenant Colonel Ball was met in the doorway of the Gates home by the general. He was surprised at the message from his former aide and friend, but this was the age of dueling. Integrity and honor had to be restored, at least in Wilkinson's mind, so Gates agreed to the terms: "All right, sir," the general said to Colonel Ball, "we will meet tomorrow morning at 8 o'clock."

The next morning at the appointed time, Wilkinson walked down North Beaver Street with Ball, his "second." They saw General Gates and Captain Stoddert standing in the street in front of St. John's Episcopal Church. Gates was not armed. During the night he had decided to attempt a rapprochement with his young friend.

When Wilkinson saw them, he stopped. Captain Stoddert approached and yelled into the crisp air, "General Gates wishes to speak to you."

"I will meet him on the dueling ground in answer to the challenge which he accepted," Wilkinson yelled back.

Stoddert then came closer and pleaded with Wilkinson to walk down to the church and greet his former chief. "General Gates does not wish to fight a duel with a person for whom he entertains the highest regard and affection," Captain Stoddert said. After a tense moment, Gates and Wilkinson ran to each other and clasped hands in a triumphant renewal of their friendship.

"Come, my dear boy," General Gates said, as emotion welled up in his throat, "we must be friends again. There is no cause for ill will between us. Conway has acknowledged that he wrote a letter criticizing Washington and has since made harsher statements." The two men talked over their differences, and it was decided that Wilkinson would assume the duties of secretary to the Board of War the very next day.

When Gates had to come to York to head up the Board of War in November of 1777, three months prior to the aborted duel, he had rented a stone house next to a tavern at the northeast corner of High and Water streets. (Both house and tavern were authentically restored during the years 1961 through 1964.) Gates's wife, reputedly the richest woman in America at the time, comfortably provided for his needs at their new home near the Codorus. Records from Congress indicate that Gates was not shy about presenting extravagant expense vouchers, some of which resulted from lavish entertainments that Gates and his wife held during their stay there. Oftentimes those entertainments were designed, as in the case of a famous banquet in honor of the Marquis de Lafayette, to forward the fortunes of Gates and the Conway Cabal.

Shortly after Gates's arrival in York, to gain Lafayette's favor, the plotters had recommended to Congress that Lafayette lead an expedition to Canada, with Conway as his second-in-command. Congress approved the plan and directed Lafayette, then 22 years old, to come to York to receive his commission. He arrived in February of 1778 and, after stopping at the Court House, found conspirators John Trumbull, Richard Peters, Gates, Mifflin, General Pickering, and probably some sympathetic Congressmen, such as Benjamin Rush and James Lovell, at dinner. Tradition has it that this banquet was held on the second floor of General Gates's lodgings, where a special partition could be lifted and hooked against the ceiling to make a large banquet room.

When Lafayette entered, the diners greeted him with loud, drunken acclamations. They toasted each other and "the men of the day," conspicuously omitting Washington's name. They were ready to adjourn when Lafayette, angry at what he considered treason against Washington, arose and proclaimed, "I propose a toast to our commander-in-chief, George Washington." The conspirators shuffled their feet in awkward silence. Some pretended to drink and some refused to raise their glasses. Lafayette, having turned the tide against the Conway Cabal by effectively opposing it, bowed politely and excused himself.

These events marked the beginning of Washington's rise to a position of greater esteem and popularity than he had ever before enjoyed in America. Lafayette's visit to York and his role in support of General Washington also won him esteem and popularity—particularly in the minds of Yorkers, who adopted Lafayette as a local hero.

About the time of the cabals, York was to host three important visitors, the first of which was Thomas Paine. Paine, whose impassioned writings and tireless propaganda provided the spiritual fire of the American Revolution, is believed to have lived in York from January through May of 1778 while serving Congress as Secretary of the Committee on Foreign Affairs.

Local tradition claims that Paine lived in the "Cookes House," a stone structure built in 1761 by Johannes Guckes (Cookes) and located about a mile southwest of Centre Square. Although no one can tell how he felt about life in the House — or can even prove that he lived there at all—Paine himself documented the historic way that he spent his spare time. A letter addressed to Benjamin Franklin, dated May 16, 1778, reads in part: "After October 23, I returned to Col. Kirkbridge's [Lancaster] where I stayed a fortnight until the latter end of January, 1778. After that I went to York and published [posted] Crisis No. 5 to General Howe. I have begun No. 6 which I intend to address to [British prime minister] North."

While Paine was writing, York was receiving its second important visitor. On February 5, Baron von Steuben, a member of King Frederick the Great of Prussia's military staff, came to town. Congress, after receiving the baron with great praise, gave him the commission of lieutenant general of the American forces. He was sent to Valley Forge, where Washington graciously welcomed him and put him in charge of shaping up the "ragged and motley" American army.

In March the third famous visitor arrived: the Polish count Casimir Pulaski. While in York he worked out of headquarters near the Square at the west side of North George Street. On March 28 Congress made Pulaski a brigadier general and gave him authority to "raise and have the command of an independent corps to consist of sixty-eight horse, and two hundred foot."

Charles Fisher, son of early York clockmaker John Fisher and a friend of Pulaski, made a weathervane in the count's honor, using the silhouette of a Polish dragoon, which has become a familiar symbol to York citizens. The weathervane was installed on the cupola of the Court House and stood watch there until the Court House was torn down in 1841. It was then rescued from the building's rubble by members of the Laurel (*nee* Sun) Fire Company.

Additional help came from Europe on May 2, when Simeon Deane,

One of York's most beloved visitors, the Marquis de Lafayette, quelled General Gates's plan against General Washington by praising Washington: "Gentlemen, here is to one you have forgotten. I propose a toast to our commander in chief, General Washington." (HSYC)

Above
A weather vane depicting Count Casimir Pulaski, made by John Fisher's son Charles, was installed on the cupola of the York County Court House. (HSYC)

Above right
Oral tradition in York claims that Thomas Paine, famous pamphleteer of the Revolution, lived in York from January to May 1778 and published his famous document, *Crisis No. 5*, during his stay. (HSYC)

Above, far right
Philip Livingston, a delegate from New York State, died in York and was buried in the graveyard of the German Reformed Church. His body was later moved to the Prospect Hill Cemetery. Livingston was a signer of the Declaration of Independence. (HSYC)

brother of Silas Deane, one of three commissioners to Versailles, arrived in York from France with a letter for Congress. The letter, written by Benjamin Franklin, also a commissioner, came with copies of the Treaty of Amity and Commerce and the Treaty of Alliance. In those treaties the King of France promised to send an army, a fleet of vessels, and supplies to aid the Americans in the fight for liberty. These documents marked the first time the struggling new government was recognized abroad.

As if in contrast to these encouraging commitments of aid, sad news struck the York community. Philip Livingston, a wealthy landowner and delegate from New York, died after a burdensome illness on June 12, 1778. He was buried that evening in the graveyard of the German Reformed Church. The delegate's body later was removed to Prospect Hill Cemetery, where his burial site was marked with a monument placed there by a Livingston descendant.

After the somber occasion of Livingston's funeral, Congress's attention was drawn again to conditions on the battle front. France was pouring troops and other support into America as it had promised in the letter that Deane had delivered, and its support dealt a crucial blow to English interests.

On June 20 Congress received the news that the British had left Philadelphia. The delegates decided to return to that city, assured of the safety in reconvening the American government there. On June 27, in the little brick Court House in Centre Square, Congress adopted its last resolution in York town: "That Congress adjourn until Tuesday next to meet at the statehouse in Philadelphia."

In the following days Congressmen, government aides, servants, and other visitors left the town of York. The first village west of the Susquehanna had carved a lasting place for itself in the history of a determined new country.

John Elgar's iron steamboat, the *Codorus*, was the first metal-hull vessel built in the United States. This is an artist's rendition of the launch, on November 14, 1825, in the Susquehanna River. (HSYC)

CHAPTER IV

CENTER OF TRADE AND COMMERCE

After Congress had left York and returned to Philadelphia, life in the town resumed an even, progressive pace. Yorkers had enjoyed having important men and women living among them, but they were quite content with the greater privacy and calm occasioned by their isolation from a central role in national controversies. It was certainly not, however, a time marked by stagnation or little excitement. York built its first incorporated school, expanded community services, and offered its men several more times to the cause of liberty.

Assisting in that cause was a noted foreign dignitary who had been commissioned into the U.S. Army. Count Casimir Pulaski had been empowered by Congress to raise an independent regiment, later called Pulaski's Legion, and he came to York to recruit troops. The Polish count had a recruiting station on the west side of North George Street from February to May in 1779. He left York and marched with his troops to the South, where he was mortally wounded when the British attacked Savannah, Georgia.

York did not spend all its time engaged in national and international matters, of course. Except for the occasional foray into the war, it entered a period where it concentrated on making improvements at home.

The first order of business was a school. Reading, writing, and arithmetic were taught to York's children at the Moravian Church and at Christ Lutheran Church's German School, but many Yorkers saw the need for a more advanced program stressing the classics. The Reverend John Andrews, an English missionary, opened a classical school in the 1770s in association with Saint John's Episcopal Church. As rector, Andrews originated studies in the classics to supplement his own income. He left York in 1772, and the school he founded is considered a predecessor of the York County Academy, incorporated in 1787.

The Reverend Andrews continued to distinguish himself in academics throughout his long career. He was made vice-provost of the University of Pennsylvania in 1789 and provost in 1810. He wrote a highly praised textbook and became a close friend of Joseph Priestley, the English-born scientist and theologian who moved to America in 1794. In the 1970s York College of Pennsylvania recognized Andrews's work in York and erected a statue in his likeness on the college campus.

In 1774 the pulpit of the classical school's sponsor, the Episcopal Church, was filled by the appointment of the Reverend Daniel Batwell. The Reverend Batwell, another English missionary, openly espoused the rule of King George III and wrote that he was once ducked three times in the Codorus Creek by local people who thought little of his politics. The Reverend Batwell went back to England, where he was rewarded for his loyalty to the crown. The pulpit of St. John's was left without a minister until 1784 and, during the Revolution, the church was used as a storage place for weapons

and other military equipment.

Perhaps Yorkers took so long to establish a secondary school—after all, more than 30 years had passed since the town's founding—because life had remained simple in York town. Among the many Pennsylvania Dutch residents, there was no great call for an English school. Besides, most York towners were involved with aspects of life more immediately pressing, such as basic sustenance and shelter, than learning or culture. Some in the farming community had not yet built permanent barns or homes and others were still experimenting with the land, which, they soon learned, was not as similar to their homeland as it had at first appeared. The land in Pennsylvania would not grow the grapes the farmers were accustomed to in the mother country—a big disappointment to the settlers—but the farmers eventually found some consolation in the fact that the land could produce bountiful crops of wheat suitable for making fine flour and even finer beer.

While farmers toiled over the land in the countryside, residents of the town tended their own small gardens and the animals that lived behind their homes. The population of the town was slowly growing, though, and since wood houses with "wood and dauble" chimneys were becoming more common, the threat of fire became more worrisome.

By 1781 the number of fire companies in York town had jumped from one to three. Most prominent and long-lived of the three companies was the Sun Fire Brigade, which had renamed itself the Laurel and served York, as it does today, from the northeast corner of King and Duke streets. There were also the Federal company and the Union brigade, (later known as the Vigilant).

Little information remains about the Federal company, although a 1976 history of the York Fire Department states that "the Federal and Union . . . were dissolved" in 1780 or 1781. The Vigilant, which apparently grew out of what was left of the Union, was formed "some time between the years of 1778 and 1781." The founding dates are unclear because the flood of 1817 destroyed the brigades' early records, which were stored in the home of the Quaker clockmaker Jonathan Jessop, a member of the company and later its president.

Carter and Glossbrenner, in their history of York County, give a clear picture of the people and structures that the firemen protected in 1780. York had about 290 houses within its borders at that time and some 1,900 inhabitants, including 335 members of 32 different professions and 43 slaves (who would soon be freed by Pennsylvania's emancipation act that very year). Population of the county, which still included what is now known as Adams County, was about 27,000.

The jobs listed by Carter and Glossbrenner reveal much about the Yorkers of 1780. They must have suffered very little from theft or violent crime, since the town had only four locksmiths and the same number of gunsmiths. Although well-educated—17 teachers, not counting those in classical and theological institutions, served the community—Yorkers were probably not well-read, as they supported only three booksellers, one bookbinder, and no magazine or newspaper publishers. They were, however, well-dressed, having 16 tailors, 13 hatters, eight tanners, four dyers, five weavers, and 40 cordwainers (or leatherworkers), which constituted the town's largest single profession. In a town that had 25 tavernkeepers, 20 butchers, and hundreds of people who prepared their own meals, there was only one cutler, who made, sold, and repaired knives. Homes and farms in those days had their own knife- and ax-sharpening tools, and Pennsylvania Dutch cuisine did not require sophisticated kitchen implements because so many of the dishes were simple.

Most Yorkers were hospitable people, and sharing a meal with a visitor or putting him up for the night was a common occurrence in those days. Although treasuring their privacy, they went out of their way to make visitors feel important and welcome. One of York's distinguished visitors during the early days was the famous General Anthony Wayne. Wayne spent three months in 1781 in York recruiting troops. George Irwin lent Wayne space in his store and residence at the northwest corner of Market and Beaver streets, where the noted soldier worked until time to march off to Yorktown, Virginia. At Yorktown General Wayne participated in the defeat of Lord Cornwallis and the British army.

The following year brought another famous soldier to York with a "legion" of 200 soldiers. France's Marquis de la Rouerie had joined the Revolution under the name Charles Armand. Congress commissioned him a colonel and authorized him to raise a corps of soldiers. Half of Armand's Legion was French and the corps arrived in York after serving with Lafayette in New Jersey and later at Yorktown. Armand had been with Washington's army before his arrival in York and part of his Legion had served with York's Colonel Thomas Hartley in the expedition against the Indians in northern Pennsylvania and southern New York. Some Yorkers, in fact, had served in Armand's Legion, including surgeon John Gottleib Morris. (Morris's son, Charles, was a druggist in York for more than 50 years.) Armand and his command resided in two rows of log houses that met at the northwest corner of Philadelphia and Duke streets. The men were encamped there 11 months before they disbanded and Armand returned to France.

Besides the soldiers' quarters, various taverns, shops, civic buildings, and old churches, Carter and Glossbrenner note, York had by the 1780s added another major religious denomination. The Methodist Episcopal Church had its start as early as 1780 and a few years later Yorker Jacob Sitler erected a building for the congregation. The church soon began to hold meetings "at early candlelight"—the first evening church sessions in York. The evening sessions were controversial enough, at first, to provoke John Joseph Henry, then president of the York County courts, to declare, "there is sufficient time during the day to hold religious services." But the practice soon spread to other York churches. A few years after the congregation moved into its

building in 1807, Francis Asbury, the first bishop of the Methodist Church in America, preached in York to large and appreciative audiences. (Today one of York's most distinguished downtown churches is named in his honor.) The Methodist Episcopal Church was erected on the northwest corner of Philadelphia and Newberry streets, quite a distance in those days from Centre Square.

The principal part of the town in these days of Revolution still lay roughly in a five-block area east of the Codorus between Queen Street and the Codorus Creek. The Codorus—a source of food, recreation, and washing—was a peaceful stream, but had the potential, as Yorkers learned in 1784, to "make an awful display of its terrible destructive power." In March of that year the creek, which was still filled with huge chunks of ice from the winter freeze, rose and spilled over its banks, causing great damage to properties along its bank. After the flood Yorkers rebuilt their ruined buildings. Since public money for flood control was not even thought of in those days, the residents accepted the rampages of the Codorus as another act of God or nature, not unlike death and drought.

In 1784 two wardens of Saint John's Episcopal Church, William Bailey and William Johnston, worked to acquire a minister and, as a result, the Reverend John Campbell came to York. Campbell soon "set about repairing the church, improving the grounds, and raising to build an Academy." He purchased three lots on North Beaver Street, comprising the entire block across from the church, and ordered brick and stone for the construction of the new school. In the *Pennsylvania Gazette* of September 28, 1785, Campbell states his purpose in founding the school: "These counties are inhabited by a great number of Germans, who are daily more anxious for the education of their children in the English language, the knowledge of which may now be obtained at an easy rate; and by this means the roots of those national distinctions and prejudices, which have unhappily too long sustained, will be cut up and destroyed."

Construction soon started in a grove of locust trees. William Bailey lent the church £75 for 6,000 bricks and another sum, four pounds and 10 shillings, to pay for 2,000 shingles. Additional money for the school was raised through a lottery, despite the immoral connotation that many Yorkers connected to any form of chance. Episcopalian clockmaker Godfrey Lenhart was named treasurer of the lottery and eventually Bailey was reimbursed for the money he lent for the school.

Another Christian building, the town's very first Presbyterian church, was also constructed in 1785. Presbyterians applied to John Penn and John

Penn, Jr., for a grant of land. For a transfer fee of five shillings, the Penns conveyed "the piece of ground situated on the corner of High [now Market] and Queen Streets . . . as a site for a house of religious worship and burial ground." The site is probably one of two in the town conveyed directly by the Penns and not through their attorneys. (The other lot was the one on which the Penns' agent, Thomas Cookson, built a house about 1749.)

York, during this period of growth and building, projected the image of a peaceful, productive, almost pious town, but there were occasional controversies. In 1786 an incident which historians now call "The Cow Insurrection" occurred. Jacob Bixler, a resident of nearby Manchester Township, refused to pay a tax that had been levied on farm animals. The tax collector distrained Bixler's cow and drove it to York, where he planned to sell it and take the proceeds in lieu of the tax money.

On the day of the sale, about 100 men from Bixler's neighborhood—armed with clubs, pistols, and rifles—marched into York. At the intersection of Main and Beaver streets, where the taxman was selling the cow, they were met by a large assemblage of Yorkers, also armed. A court justice, "half deprived of his senses," ran out to the crowd, shouting, "I command thee in my name to keep peace," but no one listened to him.

Frederick Hooke, one of the Bixler followers, cut a rope from around the cow's neck. A York official responded by aiming a sword thrust at Hooke, who escaped the blow. A riot ensued and, after it was over, several participants were fined. Moreover, Carter and Glossbrenner say, "Manchester and York were brought together into a fond and loving union."

Whether this "union" was a significant one or not, the complexion of York was changing from a sometimes disorderly frontier town to a well-organized center of local government, culture, and literacy. In 1787 Matthias Bartgis and T. Roberts established a printing office in York for the first time since the Hall and Sellers press had left town, and began publishing York's first newspaper, the *Pennsylvania Chronicle and York Weekly Advertiser*. Bartgis and Roberts moved their office to Harrisburg, however, when James Edie, John Edie, and Henry Wilcocks started a competing newspaper, the *Pennsylvania Herald and York General Advertiser*, two years later.

In 1787, too, the school that succeeded the Reverend Andrews's program of classical studies was formally institutionalized as the York County Academy. Education in the new country was a privilege. Every pair of hands was needed at home. By the age of 12 or 13, most young men were already employed as farmers, or as apprentices to a barber, carpenter, clockmaker, butcher, cordwainer, blacksmith, brewer, or other tradesman. Scholarships were generally only available to the children of teachers, ministers, and widows, or by the recommendation of a member of the faculty.

Headmasters, salaried on the basis of how many students they could recruit, ran the school's day-to-day business. But 21 of York's leading citizens were in charge of overseeing the school's general management, direction, and governance. The 21 included Reformed Church pastor Daniel Wagner, Presbyterian pastor Robert Cathcart, Saint John's Episcopal pastor John Campbell, Colonel Thomas Hartley, Major John Clark, and Colonel James Smith. Of the 21 men, 11 were Revolutionary War heroes.

The Academy, one of the first classical schools established west of the Susquehanna, also served the community as a center for the arts. Theatrical performances and concerts took place periodically throughout the following decades and various societies formed there provided valuable new direction in intellectual development. But the Academy's main function was education and, especially in later years as a college-preparatory school, it would train thousands of young men "who became leaders in city, state and national affairs; in professions of law, medicine, education and the ministry;

An early woodcut shows the York County Academy, which originally served as an educational institution and a center for the arts. Courtesy, York College of Pennsylvania.

and in finance and business."

A 20th-century Academy history points out that, among those who attended the Academy, were at least four judges of the York County courts, 20 others who became members of the bar, 25 who became prominent members of the medical profession, and eight who became educators. Others went on to serve as editors, authors, ministers, high-ranking military officers, and federal or state legislators. The Academy history also records that during the first 140 years of the Academy's existence, no student was graduated. Students, during their regimen of strict discipline and moral instruction, were drilled with the concept that learning never stops.

As the Academy's history suggests, alumni had far-reaching influence after their tenure at the York school. Samuel Klinefelter, for instance, studied at the Academy; at the peak of a full and varied career, he became president of Western Christian University (now Butler University). He also served as Indiana State superintendent of public instruction after pioneering schools in that state. Another alumnus, Levi Clarence Hunt, became the president of Albright College, and still another, Waldo Emerson Gentzler, became assistant provost of Columbia University in his distinguished career as an educator.

Millard E. Glatfelter, an Academy student for two years, began his career as a teacher in York County rural school but left to direct Temple University's High School. He later became the university's registrar, then its vice-president, and finally its provost. John Allen Smith proceeded to Gettysburg College after studying at the Academy and earned his medical degree from the University of Pennsylvania. He accepted a teaching position at the University of Texas, where he became "professor of all subjects taught with the microscope. . . ." Those subjects at that time included histology, embryology, bacteriology, parasitology, and clinical pathology. His work there resulted in the expansion of equipment and curriculum, and his research later with the hookworm led to mass efforts to exterminate the parasite in America's Southern states and in subtropical areas of other countries.

Edgar Fahs Smith, older brother of John Allen Smith, is probably the Academy's most distinguished alumnus. The son of a miller, he was born on the banks of the Codorus and attended the Academy, where he mastered Greek, Latin, and other subjects. During a career marked by substantial contributions to education, Smith held governmental, state, and corporate offices; wrote 13 chemistry textbooks translated into French, German, Italian, Russian and Chinese; and became provost of the University of Pennsylvania. While at the university, he completely revised the courses of study and made its school of science one of the best in the country. He also raised millions of dollars for the university and was inundated with honorary degrees, medals, decorations, and memberships in prestigious intellectual societies. Smith's image was commemorated on the University of Pennsylvania campus by the erection of a bronze statue and, in York, a school overlooking the city was named in his honor.

The success of the Academy's students was probably linked to the seriousness with which classes were approached and to the intellectual stimulation provided by the Academy's superb faculty. A standard of excellence was set at the Academy by such instructors as Thaddeus Stevens, Samuel Bacon, Samuel S. Schmucker, and Daniel Kirkwood.

Samuel Bacon, a native of Sturbridge, Massachusetts, organized a company of Junior Volunteers at the Academy during the period of the War of 1812. The corps included young men such as David Cassatt, son of the president of York's first bank; Samuel Small, who would later establish the firm of P.A. and S. Small with his brother, Philip Albright Small, and who would also erect another important York school, the York Collegiate Institute; and other sons of York pioneers, John Armstrong, Jr., George S. Morris, Henry Miller, Jr., George P. Kurtz, and Baltzar Spangler, Jr. Professor Bacon later studied law, became deputy attorney general, and was ordained an Episcopal priest. In 1817 Bacon started York's first Sunday school, which, within a year, had 300 students. Bacon has also been credited with proposing the first professional magazine for teachers.

Samuel S. Schmucker, after his tenure at the Academy, moved to Gettysburg and founded a classical school that became Gettysburg College. He was the college's first president and also founded the Lutheran Theological Seminary in Gettysburg. Daniel Kirkwood, a Scotch-Irishman born in Harford County, Maryland, taught for three years at the Academy, instructing courses in algebra, geometry, and science. Kirkwood became a leading American pioneer in astronomy, calculating the earth's exact distance in miles from the sun, and became a highly respected authority on comets and meteors. He taught at the University of Indiana, where an observatory, a lecture hall, and a university town street were given his name.

Other faculty members made similar contributions to the worlds of medicine, science, law, and theology, as well as impressing on their students at York the fundamental joy of a keen mind put to challenging work.

The year 1787, which had seen the establishment of the York Academy as well as the town's first newpaper, also marked the date of its incorporation. On September 24, 1787, 46 years of informal organization of the government and town services ended when York was "erected" a borough. Under Pennsylvania law a community of roughly more than 2,000 citizens could incorporate itself as a borough and elect officers to manage its affairs. Upon the borough's erection, Henry Miller was elected chief burgess, David Cantler was chosen burgess, and the assistant burgesses were Baltzar Spangler, Michael Doudel, Christian Lauman, Peter Mundorf, David Grier, and James Smith. The first town clerk was George Lewis Loeffler, and Christian Stoer was the first high constable.

Under the requirements of Pennsylvania law, only the most populous area of the community was included in the boundaries of the borough, and York has been restricted in size by the original incorporation boundaries until modern times. Only through complicated annexations, which have been attempted rarely, has York been able to increase its size. In all other respects besides size, however, the borough would undergo extraordinary changes over the next several decades. Fortunately for historians, the way the borough of York looked shortly after its incorporation, and some of the ways its residents spent their time, have been preserved in the observations of a French traveler. Thomas Cazenove, who visited York in 1788, writes:

> The town is in York valley, on Codorus Creek, a little river always rich in water, permitting several mills of all kinds in the neighborhood; the Common . . . is unusually spacious. The Court-house, placed in the middle of the square, ridiculously shuts off the view of the whole of the 2 main streets.
>
> As in every inland town of Pennsylvania, there is a quantity of taverns and inns, where the people come to talk and drink, morning and evening, as in the cafes of European cities. Also many stores where . . . [y]ou find everything necessary in utensils, clothing, furniture, for the lower class, but nothing dainty of choice.

Cazenove also observed that, "James Smith, Esq. and the families of Mr. Hartley, a lawyer and congressman . . . and General Miller have been most obliging, and are the best society here. Two-thirds of the inhabitants are Germans and mechanics."

These largely uneducated "mechanics"—carpenters, wagonmakers, brick burners, and others—were often victimized by shrewd manipulators who visited York in those days. There was, for example, one Dr. Dady, a German who came to America with the Hessians during the Revolution. His eloquence in both English and German allowed him to move freely between the Englishmen and Germans in York, and his "artful ways" enabled him to dupe the more naive Yorkers. Dady, at various times, passed himself off as a minister, a conjurer of fake ghosts, and a physician who sold a "mineral dulcimer elixir."

In 1788, the year Cazenove made his observations, the capital of the nation was nearly relocated on the banks of the Susquehanna. In fact, York Borough was in consideration for the capital site. Congressman Thomas Hartley made eloquent speeches before Congress supporting the already-proposed site of Wright's Ferry (later Wrightsville), on the York County side of the river. The borough of York and York County's Peach Bottom Township had also been discussed as possible sites for the national headquarters.

William Maclay, a prominent leader in the Revolution and a member of the Supreme Executive Council of the Pennsylvania Assembly, was enthusiastic in his support of York as the national capital. He sent a letter to James Smith at York asking him to prepare a paper in support of the proposal. Smith gathered a group of community leaders, who issued a report revealing that the borough of York now had 12 public buildings (including churches), 412 private homes, 2,884 inhabitants, 46 tradesmen, 23 stores, 18 taverns, and 15 boarding houses.

In lengthy discussions the attention of Congress was again turned to Wright's Ferry. Congressman Hartley told his colleagues that Wright's Ferry, indeed, was the best site available and asserted in his analysis that the

Facing page
These early York structures are from an 1852 lithograph entitled *View of York Pa. from the Harrisburg Road* (counterclockwise): German Reformed Church, Court House, Methodist Church, Railroad Station House, and Catholic Church. (HSYC)

fertility of the soil in York County was "inferior to none in the world." Furthermore Hartley told his fellow Congressmen that, if they enjoyed a sumptuous dish of fish, he could assure them that the Susquehanna held a bountiful supply that would please the most sophisticated palate. The House of Representatives voted 28 to 21 in 1789 to locate the capital "on the banks of the Susquehanna," but complicated arguments ensued and finally the banks of the Potomac were afforded the honor.

Although York was passed over as the site of the new nation's capital, it was not forgotten by its first President. President George Washington paid York a visit in 1791. Few records of his visit exist, but modern scholars do know that Washington came to town to see his friend Thomas Hartley, who had served under the then General Washington during the Revolutionary War.

Historians have also ascertained that Washington attended services with Hartley at the German Reformed Church on West Market Street near the Square on the morning of July 3, 1791. (Washington, an Episcopalian, would have attended the Episcopal church, but its minister was out of town.) The President later wrote in his diary that he was in no danger of being converted during the service since he did not understand a word of German, the language in which the service was conducted. The windows of the Court House were illuminated by candlelight during Washington's visit.

From the time of his nomination to the Presidency, Washington found strong political support from the York community. Many of the newly erected borough's leaders had served under Washington in the Revolutionary War, and had earned deep respect for his courage in the thick of battle. His personal friendships with such Yorkers as Thomas Hartley and John Clark further strengthened the bond of allegiance to the man who would become the nation's first President. Washington, for his part, knew York well from Congress's nine-month stay there. The quashing of the Conway Cabal in York also engendered pleasant associations in Washington. Yorkers' love for Washington was richly displayed in 1799, when the country received news of the former President's death. In his memory a procession walked down the borough's streets, led by Henry Miller, the Reverend Daniel Wagner, the Reverend Robert Cathcart, and the Reverend John Campbell.

As the century drew to an end, York and Yorkers had found themselves more prominent throughout Pennsylvania. In 1796 John Fisher, York's clockmaker-artist, painted Pennsylvania's Coat of Arms for the Court House. A copy of the Fisher painting hangs in Philadelphia's Independence Hall. The original, the oldest painting of the Coat of Arms in existence, is owned today by York College of Pennsylvania.

Yorker Solomon Meyer achieved prominence with *Die York Gazette*, the county's first German newspaper and one of the first in all of southeastern Pennsylvania, which began in 1785. A number of other newspapers followed, springing up throughout the region.

As the new century appeared, it brought with it two reminders of York's past. The 1800 census revealed that the town now had 2,503 people, an increase of more than 20 percent over the 1790 census. Population in the county, which had previously been increasing at a significant rate, received a setback. Through an act of the legislature, Adams County had been carved out of York County's western side, diminishing the area of York County from 1,469 to 921 square miles. The population of the smaller county continued to grow, however, and in 1800 it stood at 25,643. In 1790, when the United States had made its first census count, there had been 37,147 people living in the county including the area that became Adams. Many of the outlying townships, in those days, had supported larger populations than the borough of York because of greater area, shifting boundaries, and further emigration, but York Borough had continued to be the center of all county activities.

In May of 1800 John Adams returned to the Court House where he had served as a Congressional delegate in 1777, but this time he came as President of the United States. Adams congratulated Yorkers on their thrift, industry, progress, and patriotism, then rode off to the newly constructed White House. As Adams left for the banks of the Potomac, a number of Yorkers no doubt had lumps of envy in their throats. A different decision 12 years earlier might have placed the White House on the banks of the Susquehanna near York, or even in York itself.

Although voting statistics for York were not kept until 1812, York had no doubt supported the Federalist Party under Adams in the 1796 election, as it had under Washington for two terms. But with the emergence of the two-party system in 1800, a trend for York County was set that would last more than 100 years. From 1800 to 1916, with few exceptions, Yorkers would cast ballots for Democratic candidates in the Presidential races, as well as electing Democrats to the U.S. Congress, the State Assembly, and the State Senate. This trend was signaled most clearly in 1800 with the election of the first "Jeffersonian Democrat" to a seat left vacant by the death of Thomas Hartley, the last Federalist to be sent to Congress from York.

The shift to the Democratic side was probably precipitated by the Federalist Party's policies that were designed to increase the power of the centralized government. Disaffection with this Federalist tendency had been engendered as early as 1791, with the hated Whiskey excise tax, which directly affected York distillers, but Washington's personal popularity had overridden the suspicion that the new federal government was becoming more like the British crown in assessing unfair taxes. Now that Yorkers had an alternative party, however, they gave it their enthusiastic support.

Besides marking a shift in political loyalties, the turn-of-the-century period also saw the culmination or initiation of a number of transportation developments that were greatly increasing York's importance as a center of trade and commerce. York was fortunate in its location, as it was an important crossroads in the middle of a commercial route going south to Baltimore, north to Harrisburg, east to Philadelphia, and west to the Fort Duquesne [Pittsburgh] area.

In 1792 the state of Pennsylvania had approved a new road linking Philadelphia to Lancaster. The 62-mile road, which was to be paid for by tolls, took two years to build and cost $465,000. The first turnpike within York County's borders was chartered in 1804 by the state legislature and was to link Wrightsville to York. The road was not completed until 1818. The York and Conewago Turnpike was built from York to York Haven in 1818, and extended along the Susquehanna River to Harrisburg in 1835. During the same era, the first bridge was built across the Susquehanna. The wooden structure with its 23 piers was completed in 1814 and greatly facilitated travel between York and Lancaster.

As commerce began to stream through York in unprecedented amounts, a series of strange local incidents brought a sense of uneasiness to the prospering community.

A series of fires threatened York in February and March of 1803. The most shocking fire struck the Academy building. No one knew, at first, how the fires had started, but Yorkers suspected arson.

It was later revealed that the fires had, indeed, been set. A black woman, Margaret Bradley, had been convicted, in February of 1803, of attempting to poison two York sisters, Matilda and Sophia Bentz. She was sentenced to four years' imprisonment, which infuriated some of York's black residents, who were convinced of her innocence. For about three weeks afterward, fires were set in buildings in town every day.

The origin of the fires remained mysterious until one black girl was instructed to set a barn on fire "at 12 o'clock." At high noon, instead of midnight as the instructions implied, she carried a pan of coals into the barn of a certain Mr. Zinn and scattered them on the hay. She was discovered, taken under arrest, and confessed to the crimes with others in her group. The conspirators were soon caught, tried, and punished.

York did not escape the slavery issue. Advertisements in the York papers prior to Pennsylvania's emancipation act of 1780 had publicized an occasional slave for sale, and other advertisements, placed in York papers by Southern plantation owners, offered rewards for escaped slaves who were believed to be passing through the York County area. York, in fact, later became a secret center for the hiding of slaves on their way to freedom. Some black people from the South were brought to York's Public Common, where they lived. The York County census (which included Adams County until 1800) had counted 471 ex-slaves in 1783 and 499 in 1790. In 1810 there were 22 and in 1820 only six were counted. York County's last black citizen who had been a slave died in Hanover in 1841.

The year after the rash of fires in York, 1804, held a sound infinitely more enjoyable to York citizens than the clangor of fire bells. The great organmaker David Tannenberg, a native of Saxony, arrived in town that year to construct a new organ for Christ Lutheran Church. Tannenberg, an accomplished violinist and fine tenor vocalist, had already built organs in Salem, North Carolina; Albany, New York; Baltimore, Reading, Philadelphia, New Holland, and Lancaster. Tragically, though, as Tannenberg was making the last adjustments on the new instrument in York, he was stricken with apoplexy, fell off his bench, and suffered head injuries that would take his life on May 19, 1804. His newly completed organ was played at his funeral service in York and the children of the Lutheran and Moravian congregations sang at his grave. Eventually Tannenberg's last organ became the property of the Historical Society of York County, which still uses it today for special events.

The people of York, during this period, were also becoming social-minded, founding the county's first and only Poor House (or Almshouse) in 1805. The state legislature had authorized the county commissioners to levy a special tax to pay for the building and operation of a house "for the employment and support of the poor in York County." A year later Yorkers Martin Gardner, Samuel Collins, Abraham Grafius, Christian Hetrich, Peter Small,

Peter Stoer, John Henneisen, Henry Grieger, and Daniel Spangler were appointed its organizers. The site that they chose for the home was "a certain plantation, and tract of land, of and from Andrew Robinson, Esq., called Elm-spring farm within one mile of the borough of York." The Almshouse buildings were constructed soon thereafter and "the poor were removed thither from all parts of the county, in April, 1806."

Financing such projects as the Almshouse and encouraging York's surge of rising commerce led in 1810 to the establishment of York's first bank. The York Bank was organized in that year, after Pennsylvania was divided into eight districts and each one was authorized to establish a bank. The York bank's 15 directors, who served until 1824, included members of the venerable Cassatt, Spangler, Hay, Eichelberger, Lenhart, Jessop, King, and Barnitz families. David Cassatt was elected the first president and was followed in that office by Jacob Hay, Charles A. Barnitz, James Lewis, Michael Doudel, Henry Welsh, G. Edward Hersh, and Grier Hersh. Early cashiers were Thomas Woodyear, John Schmidt, Samuel Wagner, George H. Sprigg, and W.H. Griffith. John C. Schmidt, a great-great grandson of cashier Schmidt, later became an officer in that bank.

With social institutions, new churches, a new school, and a new bank, York was taking on urban characteristics. It was changing from a center of informal trade to a center of high finance, and from a center of craftsmanship to a center of fine arts. The famed engraver William Wagner, whose

Services in York's German Reformed Church were depicted by William Wagner in 1830. (HSYC)

watercolors and engravings of York streets give modern Yorkers a sharp and penetrating view of York's past, had been born in 1800 and was learning his trade in the first decades of the 19th century. York's best-known and best-loved artist, Lewis Miller, was also at work at this time. Art critics today, who classify Miller as one of America's most treasured folk or primitive artists, tend to lose sight of the fact that he was a carpenter by trade and made his watercolors for his own enjoyment and for the pleasure of his neighbors.

Born in 1796, "Louie" Miller (as he was called) spent 80 years of his life drawing his *Chronicles*. These sketches depicted, in minute detail, the common, the grotesque, the scandalous, and the eccentric aspects of York life between 1790 and 1870. He was a prolific artist and Yorkers of the 18th and 19th centuries grew accustomed to the sight of Miller drawing in his sketchbook, while attending public events or at other times "just leaning against a lamppost." Miller himself attested to the authenticity of his works with a preface to his *Chronicles*, which reads in part: "I myself being There upon the places and Spot and put down what happened. And was Close by of the Greatest number, Saw the whole Scene enacted before my eyes."

The six volumes of Miller sketches owned by The Historical Society of York County include drawings of elephants bathing in the Codorus, a cow killing a pigeon, a farmer burning his supposedly bewitched hogs, "old Mrs. Schreck laying in the oats," a doctor extracting the skeleton from a corpse for study purposes, a York housewife's attempt to paint a chicken, York's funeral procession for President Washington in 1799, and the surrender of York to the Confederates in 1863. Miller annotated these and many other scenes in both German and English, making his works doubly valuable. In addition to the thousands of sketches, the Historical Society owns a 46-by-64-inch pediment that Miller sculpted in an eerily primitive fashion for hanging over the door of his birthplace home on the east side of South Duke

Street.

Miller's 80 years of work give Yorkers an unparalleled view of life in early America, and the Historical Society's collection is the envy of such museums as the Abby Aldrich Rockefeller Folk Art Center, the New York Historical Society, the Henry Ford Museum, and the Whitney Museum of American Art, all of which own less substantial collections of Miller's work. Donald A. Shelley, executive director of the Ford Museum, writes that York's Lewis Miller "suggests comparison with St. Memin and his profiles of notable Americans, with Audubon and his 'Birds of America' or with George Catlin and his on-the-spot sketches of American Indians."

Miller was 16 years old and already launched on his career in May of 1812, when the call came from President James Madison for 14,000 Pennsylvania men. Pennsylvania Governor Simon Snyder, who had spent his early manhood in York, issued the call and soon had three times more men than he needed. William Reed, a York County native, was Snyder's adjutant general, and his experience as brigade inspector of militia for York County led Snyder to choose him to organize the state militia.

The war, which was for the most part being fought hundreds of miles north of York, came frighteningly close on the night of August 24, 1814. During that evening Yorkers observed a light in the southern sky. The British were burning Washington.

The British troops were coming close—Washington was only 90 miles away—and they were planning to stay. The British sailed to North Point, 14 miles southeast of Baltimore and 60 miles southeast of York. Governor Snyder ordered the Pennsylvania militia to rendezvous at two spots—Marcus Hook on Delaware Bay and York—so that they could prepare to meet the enemy. Six thousand men, including 400 Revolutionary War veterans, gathered on York's Common and were mustered into service for six months

"unless sooner discharged." Among the Yorkers watching them on the Common was Lewis Miller, who stood nearby, executing a watercolor sketch of the men. That drawing has become one of Miller's most famous works. The York Volunteers, under the command of Captain Michael Spangler, marched to Baltimore and offered to help defend the city. They ended up fighting in the Battle of North Point.

On September 13, 1814, the British attacked Fort McHenry, located near Baltimore. It was during this attack that a Washington lawyer named Francis Scott Key, on his way to Baltimore to rescue a friend from imprisonment, wrote the lyrics to "The Star-Spangled Banner." The music, however, was supplied by a Yorker.

When Key arrived in Baltimore, he gave the lyrics to his brother-in-law, Captain Benjamin Eades, who took them to an old tavern that adjoined Baltimore's Holliday Street Theatre. An 18-year-old actor named Ferdinand Durang—second son of the York diarist and dancer-actor, John Durang—was at the tavern, drinking with friends who were fellow players at the theater next door. According to Chief Justice Taney, Eades was discussing the new set of words when an idea seized Ferdinand Durang. Hunting up a volume of old flute music, he jumped up on a chair and impatiently played bits of tunes as they caught his eye. "One called 'Anacreon in Heaven,'" writes Tawney, "struck his fancy and riveted his attention. Note after note fell from his puckered lips until with a leap and a shout, he exclaimed, 'Boys, I've hit it!'" The chief justice later observes: "There rang out for the first time the song of the Star-Spangled Banner."

After the war ended in the fall of 1814, men returned home and the community resumed the business of tending fields and shops. Late in the year, 60 acres of land were added to York town when the heirs of John Hay (a president of York's first bank and the community's market master) laid out lots "after the manner of the rest of the town, extending the streets and alleys north." The lots were sold to the highest bidder and the area became known as "Hay's Addition" or "Haytown."

This welcome acquisition coincided with bad news for most of the community's citizens. Carter and Glossbrenner note that, in January of 1816, the state legislature prohibited the holding of fairs within York, declaring them "common nuisances," after a York citizen was killed in the autumn fair of 1815. Three persons were convicted of manslaughter for the death of the citizen, Robert Dunn.

Also in 1816, the York Water Company was formed, and the York bank's first president, David Cassatt, served as the Water Company's first president. (Cassatt, interestingly, was a cousin of the American painter Mary Cassatt.) The company laid out wooden pipes—logs with holes drilled through their long measure—and brought water from springs.

In addition to an annexation and a water company, the York community got its first church solely for black people during this era. As early as 1800 York had become a crossroads for escaping or manumitted slaves, and, while most of them passed through the town and proceeded to Wrightsville where they crossed the Susquehanna, some settled in York. (Others settled in communities across the river at Columbia and Marietta.) The new York residents met in each other's homes for worship services in the beginning, but by 1819 they were ready for their own house of worship. With the encouragement of other churches in town and some community leaders, they erected a church on North Duke Street. The building also was used as a school for black youths for a period of 60 years. The church's first trustees were John Joice, Richard Butler, John Lindenberger, Edward Young, and Israel Williams.

York's classical school, the York County Academy, also was expanding at this time and Thaddeus Stevens, who would later become one of America's most prominent statesmen, arrived in York to study law in Cassatt's legal offices.

While in town Stevens no doubt lived through the terrible flood of 1817. As an eyewitness reports, "the water rose five feet higher than ever known

Thaddeus Stevens, later noted as a great American statesman and debater, practiced law in York and was a teacher at the York County Academy. (HSYC)

71

before in this town—where two breweries and five tanneries are swept away, and nothing left but a bleak shore—where instead of the hum of industry nothing is now to be heard but the howling of winds and the rustling of water. . . . Our town wears the appearance of having been the scene of military operations. . . . Some are engaged in burying the dead, some in hunting their valuable effects among the ruins while others are dispatched as guards to protect the property floating down the stream."

The flood was only the first in a string of problems that beset York during this period. In 1819 the economic panic that was crippling the nation also came to York, but businesses and banks withstood the disaster. In 1822 the county suffered from a prolonged drought that ended with such heavy rains that they produced another flood. Despite these disasters, the town continued to grow: the 1820 census revealed that York had 3,545 people, more than a 40 percent increase over the 1800 count. The county's population had jumped to 38,759.

A great many members of York's population were on hand a few years later to see the return of an old friend, the Marquis de Lafayette. Accompanied by his son, George Washington Lafayette, the Marquis was touring America. Lafayette arrived in York on January 29, 1825, and was met by Dr. Adam King, Colonel M.H. Spangler, and Jacob Spangler, who took him to Harrisburg. The group returned to York on February 2, and when its members arrived at the turnpike gate, they were met by six military companies and a "vast multitude of people from the town and country." Four gray horses drew a large carriage bearing the general up Market Street, where the ringing of church bells, and Yorkers eager to catch a look at the handsome war hero, greeted him. "Welcome! Thrice welcome, Lafayette," they yelled. After the procession, the Lafayette party was received at the Globe Inn, located on the southwest corner of Centre Square. A reception in the Frenchman's honor was given and a number of Yorkers who had fought under him during the Revolution made speeches praising him.

About 9 p.m., with the town brilliantly lit, Lafayette was feted at a banquet attended by "one hundred gentlemen, citizens of York and invited guests." Flags and evergreens decorated the inn's banquet rooms, and elegant chairs were placed at the tables. Lafayette talked at length to those who attended the banquet. Banker John Schmidt assisted the general as interpreter for the occasion.

The mood of the evening was joyous. As a writer for the *York Gazette* of February 8 put it: "The people of York County poured forth overflowing hearts of gratitude and welcome." Yorkers showered their hero with praise: "We love [Lafayette] as a man," they said, "hail him as a deliverer, revere him as a champion of freedom and welcome him as a guest." Lafayette answered: "The town of York, the seat of our American Union in our most gloomy time. May her citizens enjoy a proportionate share of American prosperity."

Although Lafayette could not have known it, his wish was already coming true. Yorkers would soon take care of a special problem: how to get trade goods in and out of the area more quickly and economically.

In 1793 public attention had been called to the importance "of removing obstructions and improving the navigation of the Susquehanna" for, among

Above right
General Lafayette's arrival in York in an "open Barouch" is depicted in this 1825 drawing by Lewis Miller. Courtesy, The York County Heritage Trust

Below
The seal of the Codorus Navigation Company, chartered in 1825, is shown here. Until the railroads took over, the company shipped lumber, grain, and coal. Courtesy, The York County Heritage Trust

other reasons, the purpose of facilitating trade into and out of York. State and private money was appropriated for the cause but that solution was not good enough. The opening of a navigable area around the Conewago Falls, on the west bank of the Susquehanna at what is now York Haven, was, in George R. Prowell's words: "the initiatory step which inaugurated a great system of artificial navigation and internal improvement." Exhilarated with the progress already being made, a group of Baltimore businessmen formed a company to test the feasibility of running steamboats on the Susquehanna. Some York merchants joined the new company and their plans came to the attention of a master mechanic in York.

The mechanic, a Quaker named John Elgar, had begun working on the development of a steam-powered engine soon after he had joined York's Davis, Gardner and Webb foundry-machine shop. When the Baltimore-York merchant company advertised a need for steamboats, Elgar constructed a sheet-iron vessel in his shop and was ready to launch it on November 8, 1825. Elgar named his five-ton boat *The Codorus*. He loaded it on an eight-wheeled wagon and, on November 14, pulled it from the foundry as a multitude of Yorkers gathered to watch the welcoming parade. The boat was lowered into the Susquehanna and sailed upstream to Harrisburg.

Thousands gathered on the river banks to watch the vessel with its party of 100 Yorkers depart. When the boat reached Harrisburg, the party, headed by "Captain Elgar," was royally welcomed, then escorted to Buehler's Hotel for a hearty banquet. The Baltimore Company's York-born steamship had proven the Susquehanna navigable from York to the rest of the state. Yorkers, seeing the success of the growing waterways, realized that they could use their own Codorus Creek with similar success. In late 1825 a charter was granted for the construction of a slack-water navigation system from York along the creek to the Susquehanna. Incorporators included Jacob Spangler, George Small, George Loucks, Jacob Eichelberger, Michael Doudel, and Jonathan Jessop. For many years the Codorus Navigation Company oversaw the transportation of large shipments of lumber, coal, grain, and other products, before bowing later to the coming of the railroad.

While most of the Navigation Company's founders were preoccupied with the development of other businesses, Jonathan Jessop was experimenting with a new apple. Jessop had a number of fruit trees in his nursery just south of York. A friend, John Kline, told Jessop about a tree on his farm near Hallam that produced apples that had been covered with snow all winter but remained firm and tasty. Jessop grafted stems from Kline's tree onto seedlings at his farm, producing an apple that became known as the York Imperial. Jessop sold his new strain of apple trees in York, Baltimore, and Virginia, mostly to fellow Quakers. Eventually more than 60 percent of Virginia's rich apple country was growing the York Imperial.

Other agricultural advancements, including the use of burnt limestone as a fertilizer, coincided with Jessop's development of the York Imperial. The county's farmlands, thus, were keeping up with the "hum of industry" and transportation developments that were transforming the York Borough. By 1825 the York Borough had been formally incorporated; its new municipal services were firmly in place; its churches and industries had long since settled in; it had survived natural and manmade disasters and bred artistic triumphs; and it had clear connections to the outside world. York was ready for the future, a future that would turn out to be far stranger than any Yorker of the day could have imagined.

Below
This German version of *The Nonpartisan York Gazette* is dated May 20, 1796, but local historians assume the first issue was printed in late 1795. Solomon Meyer, an educated, German-born printer, saw the need for his German friends and neighbors to have a native-language newspaper and printed a four-page weekly, *Die York Gazette*. The newspaper today is recognized as the 13th oldest in the nation and is now called the *York Daily Record*. (HSYC)

Phineas Davis invented and developed the first American anthracite-burning locomotive engine and called it the "York." Davis was awarded first prize for his invention in a competition sponsored by the Baltimore & Ohio Steam Railway Company. (HSYC)

CHAPTER V

RAILROADS ABOVE AND BELOW THE GROUND

From the 1830s to the beginning of the Civil War, York experienced a period of almost unparalleled prosperity and growth. The antebellum era saw the completion or expansion of many of the transportation developments initiated at the turn of the century, the establishment of a public school system, increasing sophistication in city services and utilities, and an industrial and agricultural boom that proved resistant to financial panics and natural disasters. York was beginning to "Anglicize" and "Americanize"—though it would never completely outgrow its German village roots.

The 1830 census revealed the previous decade's expansion. While York Borough itself showed only a 10 percent increase over 1820 to 4,216 residents, the county was still expanding at a remarkable rate. Its population in 1830 stood at 42,859, up from the 1820 figure of 38,759. The fertile agricultural communities of the Susquehanna Valley, and the growing number of businesses and industries, were attracting still larger numbers of people to the area. Some of the new Yorkers came from Eastern regions of the United States, while others arrived in the continuing waves of immigration from Europe.

The era of transportation advances began, ironically, with a minor setback. An ice flood in 1832 swept away the wooden bridge spanning the Susquehanna, reminding Yorkers for the two years it took to build a replacement bridge just south of the original structure, what York had been like before easy transportation across the river was available.

The loss of the wooden bridge in 1832 was offset somewhat by the completion of the slack-water navigation system, which was first used when Gottlieb Ziegle, James Schall, and Daniel Ford launched the *Pioneer*, a 40-foot boat. Also in 1832 James Chalfont sent a 70-foot boat that could carry 150 passengers sailing down the Susquehanna toward York. On November 18 Chalfont's large, flat-bottomed riverboat, the first "ark," arrived in York carrying 40,000 feet of lumber. It was greeted by about 100 people, who celebrated its arrival with wild cheers and singing.

Canal and river traffic was a much cheaper method of transporting freight than the slow wagon trains from places like Philadelphia to the Western territories, but it was doomed to be short-lived. Canal building had been initiated in 1816, when New York announced plans to build the Erie Canal. That canal, completed in 1825, had secured for New York its preeminence as a river capital. State and local concerns began their own canal projects, however. Locally, the Susquehanna and TideWater Canal was chartered in 1835, with 24 men from Philadelphia, Baltimore, Harrisburg, and other areas serving as commissioners. Yorker Charles A. Barnitz was among the chartering group of businessmen.

A large crowd celebrated the opening of the Susquehanna and TideWater Canal. Nicholas Biddle, the noted Philadelphia financier, made a dramatic speech on the internal improvements that were leading the country toward greater wealth. The canals of Pennsylvania were coming into their own and the next 30 years showed a continual increase in traffic. The capacity of the boats increased, too, so that they were soon descending the canal with cargoes of up to 150 tons instead of the 60 tons they originally carried.

The railroad system would eventually replace the canals in their premiere position of moving freight across the land, however. The doom of the canals had been foretold as early as 1826, the year after the Erie Canal was opened, when the first U.S. railway was constructed outside Quincy, Massachusetts. The little horse-drawn railway was soon itself to be outstripped by the chartering of the Baltimore & Ohio Steam Railway Company. The Baltimore & Ohio Company would establish an intimate connection with York, and the future of American rail transport was promoted in the process. That connection was to be established by young Phineas Davis, who had come to York from New Hampshire.

Davis was an orphan boy, "in search of a situation," when he wandered into the shop of York clockmaker Jonathan Jessop. Jessop employed the young man immediately and he soon showed his inventive genius by designing a gold watch that became the talk of clockmakers in York and other towns.

During his leisure hours while working at Jessop's shop, Davis studied natural philosophy and became fascinated with an idea that he had recently heard discussed: "steam as a motor." He tinkered with many of Jessop's tools and learned from the Quaker shopkeeper's friends all he could about the production of steam energy. He soon joined York's Gardner foundry and machine shop and, while making tools and implements there, he found that many of the clockmaker's tools were just miniatures of the ones he was now operating. After experimenting for some time, his attention was turned to creating a steam-powered locomotive engine. The only locomotives being produced at that time had English-made, wood-burning engines that needed many improvements for easy use in America.

On January 4, 1831, Davis heard of an offer by the Baltimore & Ohio Steam Railway Company. The company promised a $3,500 prize to whomever would invent and manufacture a new American locomotive engine. The competition's rules stated that the engine must burn coke or coal and "consume its own smoke." Davis, now half-owner of the shop on the Codorus (the same one in which John Elgar had built York's first steamship six years earlier), set to work. On June 1, 1832, the day of the competition, he delivered his steam engine, named "the York," to Baltimore.

The *Baltimore Gazette* of July 31 describes the locomotive's trial run: "It started from the Pratt Street depot . . . with a train of fourteen loaded cars, carrying together with the engineer, a gross weight of fifty tons. The whole went off in fine style and was out of sight of the depot in six minutes. The rapid gliding of the immense train was one of the most imposing and beautiful spectacles we have ever seen."

Five other inventors entered locomotives in the competition, but on August 4, 1832, "the York," sporting steel springs invented by Davis, was awarded first prize. Davis and Gardner later built several other locomotives for the B & O. Along with Ross Winans and John Elgar, who invented not only the steamboat but also railroad-drill bearings, switch turnstiles, and plate wheels, Davis solved many of the problems connected with railroad travel and inland transportation.

Since York now had its own railroad manufacturer, the coming of the railroad line to York seemed only natural. Selling trains to the Baltimore & Ohio could prove profitable for a few York merchants and manufacturers, but the benefits of a local train line that many Yorkers could use became a priority. The desire for such a line was enhanced further on April 16, 1834, when several York shopkeepers and merchants went to Columbia, a town on the shore of the Susquehanna opposite Wrightsville, to join Governor Wolf on the first train over the just-completed Columbia, Lancaster & Philadelphia Railroad. The pleasure of train travel and the possibility of moving vast amounts of freight quickly intrigued Yorkers and they joined their neighbors in Maryland to petition the Maryland legislature to build a track to the Pennsylvania state line at York County's southern border. The track could go no further than the state line without a charter from the Pennsylvania legislature, so York County citizens began petitioning that body. Four years later Governor Wolf recommended extending the railroad into Pennsylvania and the legislature passed a bill to that effect on March 14, 1838. When the news reached York, people fired cannons, rang bells, danced in the street, formed a parade, and celebrated into the night.

Building the railroad that would prove immensely profitable for York businesses was a backbreaking task. Workers had to drill a 217-foot tunnel through solid rock and build 82 bridges over the rugged, stream-cut terrain between Baltimore and York. Further delays were caused by a strike in which workers demanded more money for their arduous and dangerous work as well as a supply of whiskey. Eventually, though, the workers finished laying the track and on August 23, 1838, the first train from Baltimore arrived in York.

That trip, and the thousands that would follow it, took only four hours. The train's daily arrival in towns soon became a public event, as passengers going to Columbia, Harrisburg, and Pittsburgh disembarked in York and continued their journey by stagecoach. York was already established as a commercial crossroads for wagon trains.

The railroad would revolutionize York in other ways, including an immediate boom in population. And, as the capacity to accommodate trade through York increased, so did the capital accrued from it. Many local businesses and industries flourished during this period, changing the look of the town as a result. One of the first indications of the new-found affluence was the appearance of more modern and expensive clothes. Carter and Glossbrenner describe York women "in silks and crepes, and jewels and gold, in lieu of [the old] tow frocks and linsey woolsey finery." York's residential neighborhoods, too, underwent a metamorphosis, as greater prosperity allowed York's leading merchants and manufacturers to build elegant homes in the town and the surrounding countryside. One such home was a beautiful Georgian-style townhouse on the corner of Duke and Market streets, a block from Centre Square.

Living in the Georgian townhouse were Philip Albright Small and his wife, the former Sarah Latimer. Sarah's father was Philadelphian Hugh Latimer, a descendant of Bishop Latimer of Worcester, England. George Small, Philip's father, had run a wholesale and retail business in York. George Small was also president of the York Water Company for two terms, during the time when it began an extensive improvement program. The 16,000 feet of bored logs that served the town as water pipes were connected to iron and lead pipes installed in York's new public buildings.

George Small owned a home on North George Street, where Philip and his younger brother Samuel had been born. Philip had attended the York County Academy and was apprenticed as a teenager to a prominent Baltimore merchant, Penrose Robinson. When he returned to York, at the age of 22, Philip was taken into his father's retail and wholesale business, which was renamed George Small and Son. In 1833, after a well-planned expansion, Samuel joined the firm, Philip was named president, and it became the P.A. and S. Small Company. Its diverse interests included purchasing grain, manufacturing flour, retailing groceries and hardware goods, and eventually iron. The firm served dozens of counties in Pennsylvania and Maryland, all without the assistance of salesmen, and at one point, P.A. and S. Small business represented one-sixth of all the freight moved over the Northern Central Railroad between York and Baltimore.

The firm's flour mills were remarkable in their own right. The Smalls built a mill on the Codorus northeast of York, another mill farther downstream north of York, and a larger concern at Goldsboro. The Smalls also operated the old Loucks mill for awhile. The P.A. and S. Small Company mills purchased, for many years, one-third of the grain grown in York County. They developed customers as far away as London and, at the peak of the flour-mill operation, shipped some 90,000 barrels of flour a year to Brazil. The Smalls went on to become partners in various Maryland iron companies, and their philanthropy would be felt throughout the York community.

A second company, established in the 1830s, proved important to York's industrial expansion. Frederick Baugher and E.I. Wolf owned a tannery on the north side of West Market Street that later became known as Eyster, Weiser and Company. The firm employed 100 men initially in tanning activities, and later expanded into foundry and machine-shop work. Dozens of other shops and industrial plants sprang up throughout York County during this period.

This depiction of the beautiful Codorus Creek was done by William Wagner in 1830, when a covered bridge crossed the Creek at Main Street (now Market Street). (HSYC)

The rest of the country, however, was suffering the widespread inflation and failure of financial institutions that would culminate in the Panic of 1837–1839. Many state financial institutions, including the Bank of the United States, went under, but York's one bank fared well during the crisis. The diversification of York businesses and the ability of many in the York community to handle finances in an efficient, conservative, and profitable manner helped York to weather hard times, as they would in the future.

The 1830s saw, as nearly every decade before it had, the visits of national leaders. For the last time, however, they would arrive by the older forms of transportation rather than the newly constructed railroad or later transportation innovations. General William Henry Harrison arrived in York in a "handsome barouche" on October 8, 1836, while campaigning for President. But as the Whig Party candidate, Harrison had little chance of winning over the strongly Democratic Yorkers. Yorkers voted against Harrison in 1836, and again in 1840 when Harrison won, only to die from pneumonia a month after his inaugural. Harrison's predecessor, Martin Van Buren, had arrived in York by horse and carriage on June 21, 1839. President Van Buren's popularity was at a low ebb during his visit to York, probably because of the unresolved difficulties of the recent financial panics. His visit coincided with the announcement of the York Bank that it had suspended specie payment. The President stayed in his hotel room at the White Hall on the corner of Market and Beaver streets, and the next morning took the York Haven turnpike on his way to New York.

More impressive to the York community, probably, than the decade's visits of national leaders was a visitation from the heavens in 1833. A spectacular meteor shower in that year is described by modern historian George Prowell as "the most remarkable known to the whole history of astronomy and the display was more brilliant in central and southern Pennsylvania than in any other part of America or Europe." Yorkers saw luminous meteors shooting from what seemed to be one point directly overhead. Within an hour's time, the entire sky was filled with shooting lights. Some Yorkers thought the world was coming to an end, but hours later, after the sky had cleared leaving no visible damage to the community, the event became only an entertaining topic of conversation.

An increasingly high percentage of that conversation, in the era's most significant social change, was in English. The English-German debate had been with York from its very beginnings. While the vast majority of York's citizens were of Germanic origin, the new province where they immigrated was originally owned and operated by British subjects. As the Pennsylvania government began to form, many Germans were dismayed because the legal language of the day was English. For 25 years, too, after the formation of York County in 1749, the presiding officers of the court had been English-speaking. Martin Eichelberger and Michael Swope were the first Germans who earned prominence in the York County courts and few German names were found among county offices for years afterward.

But in the churches, in homes and businesses, German was widely spoken until the 1830s, when the English language was used more often in church services. The Reverend Lewis Mayer had introduced English into his services in 1821 and the church's next four ministers gave sermons in both languages. The Presbyterian Church was growing, increasing the English-speaking population through larger families and new residents.

Two German newspapers, *Der Republicanische Herald* and *Die Evangelical Zeitung*, had faded from the York picture by the opening of the decade, a further sign that the English language was gaining power over the traditional German. The *People's Advocate* was one of several English newspapers

printed in York during the 1830s.

The public schools were also instrumental in the spread of English usage. An optional public school system had been established in Pennsylvania in 1834. Governor Wolf, Thomas H. Burroughs, a prominent state educator, and Thaddeus Stevens, a leading state legislator formerly from York, joined forces to win approval for the tax-supported educational system. The adoption of public schools had to be approved on the township and borough levels, and much controversy arose out of the voting process used locally. The county commissioners—Jacob Dietz, Samuel Harnish, John Schultz, Christian Inners, and Joseph Small—met with delegates from each township and borough at three separate conventions. Heated discussions, often centering around the public schools' English requirements, greeted the issue whenever it was discussed. Only Joseph Small voted for passage of the act at all three conventions.

But, after the third convention, York and Hanover boroughs, and the townships of Fairview, Chanceford, Lower Chanceford, and Peach Bottom accepted the plan. Newberry and Fawn townships voted in favor the next year, and the year after that Warrington, Hallam, Shrewsbury, Monaghan, Hopewell, Carroll, and Springfield townships accepted. West Manheim, 44 years later, was the last township to approve public schools.

The public school act established the office of county superintendent of public schools, but when the salary was set at $500, three of the four leading candidates for the job dropped out. The job went to the remaining nominee, Jacob Kirk, a Quaker from Fairview Township. By 1854 there were 247 schools in the York County system. The average salary for the 233 male teachers was $19 a month; the 33 female teachers were paid less, averaging only $13 a month. Kirk left his position after a year and was succeeded by Christopher Stair, later editor of the *People's Advocate*.

The already-established schools, especially the York Academy, also became strong influences in the community. The Academy's trustees had added a Young Ladies' Department in 1829, which taught Latin, Greek, English, and "moral, mathematical, and physical science." Besides the classroom work, the Academy's students of both sexes could participate in literary societies, perform in plays, and enter spelling bees. Spelling bees enjoyed enormous popularity and the winners of these elaborately produced events went on to state contests that afforded them a kind of celebrity status in York.

But life at the Academy was not all moral instruction and spelling bees. There are records that tell of students putting rubber in the Academy's pot-bellied stove and of stealing the master's coal to pack into snowballs. Sleighing parties and coasting sessions made central Pennsylvania's winters seem like fun to the Academy students and, on fairer days, they could attend outdoor circuses that often played on a lot nearby. Sometimes they attended such functions on school time. But one of the students' favorite pastimes were the periodic balloon ascensions.

Balloon ascensions appealed to the general public as well. One historian writes that the first balloon ascension in York occurred in 1798. By the 1830s the "sport" was well-established and York's inhabitants turned out by the thousands to see the big, colorful balloons lift off the Public Common or the Square. In 1842 York had two ascensions and the August *Gazette* of that year reports that 6,000 to 10,000 people witnessed the event, which took place despite the blustery weather. The dangerous but thrilling climb was made by John Wise, described at that time as "the celebrated American aeronaut." The second ascension took place in weather that was questionable, too, but the *Gazette* (the forerunner of the *York Daily Record* published

today) reports that Wise was so afraid of disappointing the crowd and "being mobbed that he made the ascension anyway.

Another balloonist who entertained York was the community's own James A. Dale. Dale owned a drugstore near the Square and his hobby was "the exploration of the atmosphere." Dale made numerous ascensions from the York Square, and one of them is described in another *Gazette* article: "We never saw a more gratified multitude than were assembled on this occasion. All seemed delighted, and to be at a loss for words to express their admiration of the sight presented by the daring aeronaut. . . ." The *Gazette* describes the parting gesture of the York pharmacist as "a graceful wave of his hat to the cheers that continued to greet him as long as his features could be distinguished."

And thus balloon ascensions were added to the list of entertainments—with parades, music, and drama—that most appealed to Yorkers in this period. The last two of these entertainments were presented at the Academy by the same students who spent their spare pennies for sugar-plums, mint sticks, horehound, licorice, and rose almonds. But making music and drama were not the only means of entertainment there. Professor Daniel Kirkwood, the noted astronomer, wrote of school outings that included a stop in a hotel in Columbia for dinner, and he told of Academy students going to corn-huskings and "quiltings."

But many York Countians, especially in the rural Pennsylvania Dutch country, were little impressed by balloon ascensions and not overly worried about the spread of English. These things only affected them during occasional forays into town. The Pennsylvania Germans (also called the Pennsylvania Dutch) had developed a dialect that was a lively mixture of English and German long before the rest of York "went English." (The influence of this dialect can still be heard today in communities throughout eastern Pennsylvania. Certain words and inflections originating in the dialect are used by some York countians and adopted by some newcomers who find them both colorful and useful for clear expression.)

The Pennsylvania Dutch, during the antebellum period, still represented the majority of the population, and they had developed a distinctive and colorful way of life. Their culture contained within it considerable diversity. Predominantly, there were "the church people" and "the plain people," but even within these groups there were many subgroups. To understand the complexity the student today must explore the beliefs, practices and experiences of "the church people" like the Lutherans and the Reformed, (and remember that some members of the early Reformed congregations later affiliated with the United Church of Christ) and "the plain people," taking in the Mennonites, the Brethren and the Amish, among others. Fredric Klees, a scholar of the early migrations to Pennsylvania provided a general guideline when he wrote, "I think of the Pennsylvania Dutch as the descendants of the Germans and Swiss who came to Pennsylvania before the Revolution. To the Germans, most of whom came from the Rhineland, I would add the handful of Moravians, whether from Bohemia or Silesia or Moravia itself and the French Huguenots who had fled to the Rhineland and who came to Pennsylvania with the Palatines and Wurtembergers..." (From the book, *Pennsylvania Dutch* by Fredric Klees, The Macmillan Company, New York, 1961, p. 7)

Much of the confusion surrounding the Pennsylvania Dutch to this very day stems from the identification of the "quaint" dress and customs of the "plain people" with all denominations. But for most Pennsylvania Dutch, life was far from "plain."

Many of the denominations present in York at this time soon became embroiled in the antebellum period's most controversial political issue: slavery. The oppression experienced by the forefathers of the Pennsylvania Dutch had made them keenly sympathetic to any kind of human or spiritual bondage. H.G. Wells points out, in *The Outline of History*, that "almost the first outspoken utterances against Negro slavery came from German settlers in Pennsylvania."

But opinions in the community varied, as they did everywhere in the country, and many Yorkers felt that the slavery issue was splitting the nation. They were afraid that further exacerbation would damage their good trade relations with the South. On the whole, though, Yorkers were a law-abiding people and they worked toward compromise solutions. The York County Colonization Society worked for many years on a program established by then-President James Monroe to set up in Africa a "colony for any free person of color who may choose to go there." The republic was called Liberia and its capital named Monrovia in honor of the President. Led by such York figures as Jacob and George Barnitz, Jacob Eichelberger, Charles A. Morris, John Gardner, and John Schmidt, the local group was organized a full eight years before the Pennsylvania Colonization Society.

With their sympathetic but no-nonsense views, Yorkers greeted "outside" abolitionist leaders with suspicion and sometimes scorn. When famous antislavery speakers such as Lucretia Mott came to York, they were likely to be greeted with jeers—and an occasional tomato.

But many York-area residents were so moved by the plight of the slaves that they became active in speeding "freight" along the underground railroad. Many believe, in fact, that the term "underground railroad" first came into use in the York area. Slave owners who followed their fleeing "property" northward were perplexed to find that slaves would often seem to disappear, as if the ground had swallowed them up. They are said to have exclaimed, "There must be an underground railroad somewhere!" The expression soon became a part of the American language.

Various people and places in York figured prominently in the underground railroad's operation. William Willis's house, built in 1767 southwest of Prospect Hill Cemetery (and restored in the early 1980s), became an underground-railroad "station," as did the home of Ezekiel Baptiste in the "Bald Hills" of Newberry Township. Amos Griest and his wife Margaret Garrettson were also among the railroad's operators. Edward J. Chalfont, whose maternal grandfather was Jonathan Jessop, helped the abolitionist cause in York by distributing antislavery literature. Among the other workers on the railroad was York Academy's Thaddeus Stevens, who may have found in York the antislavery sentiments that he would carry with him into his political career.

One of the most important persons to figure in York's underground railroad was also one of the most remarkable people in York's entire history: William C. Goodridge. Goodridge lived two blocks from the Court House, at 123 East Philadelphia Street, and slaves knew him as a man with whom they could hide, which was hardly surprising since he, too, was an ex-slave. Goodridge had been born in 1805 to a slave who belonged to a Baltimore doctor. His grandmother had belonged to Charles Carroll, of Carrollton, Maryland, the namesake for Maryland's Carroll County. In 1811, when William was just six, the doctor sent

The Willis House and barn in North York was a York County stop on the Underground Railroad. Hundreds of slaves passed through York County on their way to freedom in the North. Courtesy, The York County Heritage Trust

him to apprentice with the Reverend William Dunn in his York tanning yard. Goodridge was to be apprenticed until the age of 21, at which time he was to receive "an extra suit and a Bible" and go off to seek his fortune.

But Goodridge was ready to leave at 16 and, with the Reverend Dunn's permission, he traveled to an Eastern town and learned the trade of barbering. He later returned to York and developed many lines of business, such as newspaper distribution (he is believed to have introduced the sale of daily papers in York) and the ordinary "above-ground" railroad. At one time he had 13 railroad cars making regular trips to Philadelphia which carried many escaped slaves out of York. Goodridge also erected the tallest building of the day in York, a four-story structure devoted to his various lines of business. His success inspired considerable envy among York's other businessmen, and one merchant began construction on a larger building that he hoped would literally "overshadow" Goodridge's business complex.

It was Goodridge's courageous efforts on behalf of the "underground railroad" that would eventually spell his downfall in York, however. He frequently spirited slaves to freedom in Northern states and Canada, through his own railroad cars and by other means. Among those he helped to freedom were three fugitives who had participated in the Christiana Riots of 1857, and Osborn Perry Anderson, who had fought alongside John Brown at Harpers Ferry. While in York, Anderson hid out in Goodridge's "skyscraper" on the southeast corner of Centre Square. According to Stuart D. Gross in *Saginaw: A History of the Land and the City*, Goodridge "was so well known for his activities against slavery that a price was put on his head by irate Southern slave owners. Many old York histories claimed William C. Goodridge and his family fled York in June 1863 as the Confederates approached the city, but three of the Goodridge daughters had gone west earlier. One of the Goodridge sons, Glenalvin, had been sent to prison in February 1863 after a jury found him guilty of a rape charge many believed to be trumped up by a woman believing she could exhort money from him. The eldest Goodridge and his son, William O. Goodridge, remained in York through 1864, and according to historian John V. Jezierski, "the elder Goodridge continued his barbering trade and father and son undertook a Herculean effort to obtain a pardon for Glenalvin." (see *Enterprising Images: The Goodridge Brothers, African American Photographers, 1847-1922*, by John Vincent Jezierski, Wayne State University Press, Detroit, 2000.) In late December, 1864, Gov. Andrew G. Curtin signed the pardon with the condition that Glenalvin leave the state. The next spring or summer William C. Goodridge, traveled west with Glenalvin and his family to East Saginaw, Michigan. Later, the older William Goodridge returned to his York barbershop, Jezierski writes, "but by the end of 1865 he had settled in Minneapolis with Emily and her family." He died in early 1873." Wallace and William O. Goodridge established a business in East Saginaw specializing in the most modern photographic images, including panoramic, flash, and motion pictures.

The history of York is filled with other dramatic tales of Yorkers who worked on the underground railroad. William Wright, descendant of Wrightsville namesake John Wright, was credited with helping more than 1,000 slaves to freedom. One of those he helped was James W.C. Pennington.

When Pennington fled his master on his twenty-first birthday, he made his

This photo of the southeast corner of Centre Square shows the six-story building erected by John Hartmann in 1846, and the spire of Christ Lutheran Church. (HSYC)

way north to the home of Wright, whose name was well known among slaves in the South. The young man was apprehended near Reistertown, about 35 miles from Wright's home, and put under the care of a woman tavern owner. He negotiated with the woman for a moment of fresh air outside, gaining her confidence by taking off his hat, coat, and shoes before leaving the barroom. A boy sent to watch Pennington found him doubled over in apparent pain, crying out for water. When the boy ran to fetch the water, Pennington took off running through the cornfields. He arrived at the Wrights' home after a harrowing journey, but Wright and his wife, Phebe, immediately made Pennington feel at home. He stayed with them for several months, helping them with household chores while Wright taught him to read, write, and do arithmetic.

When Pennington left, he went to New Haven, Connecticut, where he acquired a position as janitor at Yale College. The brilliant young ex-slave also completed studies in the college curriculum, eventually moving to Germany, where a doctor of divinity degree was conferred on him. Friends of the Wrights later told them of a curious painting they had seen at an antislavery fair in London. Among the pictures for sale there was one called, "William and Phebe Wright Receiving James W.C. Pennington."

During the 1840s, while the underground railroad was striking blows for freedom, workers were laying down the lines above ground of the new York-Wrightsville Railroad. The railroad company was headed by Thaddeus Stevens, former York Academy professor. The company combined its operations with those of the Wrightsville & Gettysburg Railroad Company, so that the tracks could be extended westward from York through Abbottstown and New Oxford to Gettysburg. A state grant of $200,000 was applied to the $800,000 cost of the project.

York's growing railroad system would, at last, be used by a distinguished visitor arriving in York. The 1842 visit of the famous English writer, Charles Dickens, would be remembered by Yorkers for years to come. Dickens was only 30 years old when he arrived in York, but had achieved widespread fame and extraordinary popularity in England and its former colony. On a tour of America that he would preserve in his book, *American Notes*, Dickens

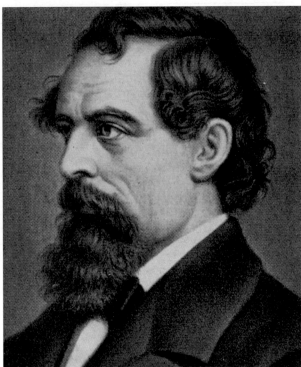

Above
English novelist Charles Dickens visited York in the spring of 1842. Local legend claims that Dickens was served "the best beefsteak he ever ate" in York. (HSYC)

Above left
Peter Wiest, after opening a "foreign and domestic dry goods store" in the York County community of Dover, set up a retail business on West Market Street. Wiest's Department Store would become a popular shopping spot in downtown York for over a hundred years. (HSYC)

stopped in York to dine at the White Hall Hotel. He later wrote that he had entered the area "by railroad; and got to a place called York, [at] about twelve. There we dined, and took a stage-coach for Harrisburgh [*sic*]."

Dickens liked York's stagecoaches, which he described as "like nothing so much as the body of one of the swings you see at a fair set upon four wheels and roofed and covered at the sides with painted canvas." But he seems not to have liked Yorkers; he was disappointed, generally, in the Americans he encountered. Local tradition, however, states that Dickens considered the beefsteak that he ate at the White Hall the best that he had ever eaten in America, and historian Prowell, who has retold the story, agrees. Unfortunately modern historians have been unable to find any such statement in Dickens works and the story has become another legend handed down unverified from generation to generation.

When Dickens traveled through York he undoubtedly noticed a tremendous amount of building and expansion of the area's shops and homes. Because of improved agricultural methods, a large population, and especially the better transportation provided by the railroads, the community was growing rapidly.

The year 1840 had seen the establishment of the Small and Smyser iron works, which had small shops along North Beaver Street adjoining the railroad. The company eventually became the Variety Iron Works, manufacturers of wrought-iron ornamentation. The company sent tons of wrought-iron decorations to New Orleans, where its architectural uses can still be seen in parts of the French Quarter.

At the corner of Market Street and Pershing Avenue, Jacob Hantz, once sheriff of York County, opened a hardware store which supplied tools for the town's new construction. This store later became the York Paint and Hardware Company and developed a large interstate wholesale division. Supplying lumber for the new construction going on in York County was the firm of A. and E. Wolf in New Holland (now Saginaw), about six miles north of York. The Wolfs packed lumber onto rafts traveling upstream to a landing on the west bank of the Susquehanna and thereupon unloaded the wagons and transported the wood to York. That firm eventually became the Wolf Supply Company—another business still in operation today.

Through the stories of other businesses, we discover bits of how Yorkers lived and what products they used. In the town of Dover, six miles northeast of York, Peter Wiest opened a "foreign and domestic dry goods store." Soon after, he moved to York, which had more people and thus more potential customers. He set up business at 218 West Market Street and sold "everything from buttons to butter, from rakes to cinnamon, from calico to herring." Many of Wiest's farmer customers traded him nails, which they made in their blacksmith shops, for goods in his store. Because molasses and mush was a popular dish of the day, Wiest also did a lot of his trading in molasses. He sold eggs for 10 cents a dozen, 14 pounds of flour for about 37 cents, and a customer could walk away, if he wanted to, with "five cents of whiskey." (After numerous expansions Wiest's firm became the Wiest's Department Store—a flagship store in the still booming downtown area of later years.)

A "wholesale retail dry good store" stood on the southwest corner of Centre Square in 1852. (HSYC)

Nathan Lehmayer, who became one of York's most prominent haberdashers, opened his first store in York in 1847, selling beaver hats, tailcoats, checked pantaloons, and other clothes for men and boys. (Almost a century later, in 1945, Lehmayer's, as the business was called, would move to a site next door to the Strand Theatre.)

The storekeepers, in this period, often used an informal system of bartering to provide consumers with needed supplies and food. This awkward system may have created a demand for a more organized and workable form of capital exchange, since in 1845 York saw the opening of its second bank, the York County Bank, which had 153 subscribers dividing the bank's 5,000 shares. At a meeting on May 29, the shareholders elected 13 directors, including Michael Doudel, the nephew and namesake of the Revolutionary War hero, and other community leaders such as Daniel Hartman, Christian Lanius, Charles Weiser, and Adam Smyser. They opened the bank on the north side of East Market Street nearly opposite the Court House and "four doors" from Centre Square. In five months the bank had total resources of $71,000.

Commerce was not the only area of city life undergoing expansion in the 1840s. This period saw innovations and growth in almost every aspect of Yorkers' experience. The town's first telegraph line was completed in the year 1845. Yorkers now had an alternative in long-distance communication to the use of horse and rider. A few years later when President Zachary Taylor came to town, either the York City Band or the Spring Garden Silver Coronet Band (soon to change its name to the Spring Garden Band) could have greeted him with a fanfare, for both bands were born in that year. While in town in 1849, he may have been warmed not only by York hospitality but also by the York County Gas Company, which got its start that same year.

The gas company also was incorporated in 1849 when 14 York men (including two of those who had been involved in establishment of the York County National Bank a few years before, Daniel Hartman and Charles Weiser) established the company. Dr. Alexander Small was elected the firm's first president. Gas at that time was manufactured from rosin and the incorporators sold shares of stock to partially cover the $35,000 cost of building the gas works. The era of flickering lights in homes and schools had come to York.

The next year would be just as busy. A railroad was built to haul freight from York to nearby York Haven and Harrisburg. The census revealed that York now housed about 7,000 people, a rise of nearly 70 percent over the

last census for the borough. The county population had climbed to 57,450. Such growth was partly attributable to the railroads, which made it easier for large numbers of people to get in and out of York. Another new development was the building of the Odd Fellows Hall on the southwest corner of King and George streets, and the Washington Hall on its second floor soon became home to many popular dramatic events. These included an appearance of Joseph Jefferson, noted actor of the day, who played Rip Van Winkle, and, later, Tom Thumb and the original Siamese Twins. (The building at one time housed the Hub Store).

The 1850s saw a continuation of York's commercial advancement. While the California Gold Rush was drawing a few of York's younger sons (some of whom did not have inheritances of farms or shops to look forward to), a group of prominent citizens met in the Court House and organized the York County Agricultural Society to convince the state legislature to permit fairs again in York.

The first fair under the auspices of the Agricultural Society was held on the Public Common (now Penn Common) on October 5–7, 1853. The Society in 1856 held the annual fair on a new site on the south side of East King Street just east of Queen Street. That plot, later expanded by seven acres, was used for 31 years, after which the Agricultural Society—formed to operate such an exhibition of York County's agricultural products—moved to a 73-acre farm owned by Samuel Smyser in West Manchester Township. With additional purchases of land, the 120-acre property became known as the York Interstate Fair Ground. The fair was originated to display and encourage the county's agricultural production, and fair days became official festivals with county schools giving students a holiday to attend the educational exhibitions.

Today the York Inter-State Fair, still held under the auspices of the Agricultural Society but also offering "wide variety of commercial attractions," is recognized as the oldest continually operating fair in America. "School Day" at the Fair was ended in the 1960s as educators argued that the annual fete had become too commercial.

In the 1850s, too, a young man named A.B. Farquhar, a Quaker from Sandy Springs, Maryland, was starting to build an empire. His autobiography, published in 1922, tells that he came to York on April 4, 1856, and acquired an apprenticeship in the shop of W.W. Dingee and Company, which manufactured farm equipment and heavy machinery.

Farquhar's grandmother was the sister of the inventor John Elgar, who met the young Farquhar when he arrived in town. Elgar arranged to have Farquhar put up at the home of Edward Jessop, son of Jonathan Jessop and a friend of Farquhar's father. At the Jessop house on his first night in York, Farquhar met his future wife, Elizabeth, daughter of Edward Jessop, whom he would marry in 1860.

In 1860, when Farquhar was just beginning to amass his millions, the number of people in York Borough had reached about 8,600. The county population had risen to 68,200. These people were, by and large, conservative politically and regularly voted Democratic, including in the 1860 election, when they favored Stephen Douglas over Abraham Lincoln in the Presidential race. Although many Yorkers appreciated Lincoln's stand against slavery, even more felt that his policies were widening the split between North and South, thus endangering York's strong trade relationship with the South. York was well-established as a central trade route between the North and South, but its particularly close ties with neighboring Maryland (especially to the city of Baltimore) and its lucrative trade with other Southern states probably led to the development of what some thought of as a quasi-Southern climate in York that strained some business and social interactions.

Even though Yorkers had voted against Lincoln (and would do so again in 1864), they were still firm believers in the maintenance of the Union. It is not surprising then that when the Battle of Fort Sumter began the Civil War and forced them to choose sides, they favored the North. After Sumter, on April 12, 1861, the newly elected President Lincoln called for 75,000 volunteers to fight in the Civil War. Yorkers quickly gathered and, as in 1775 and 1812, exceeded enlistment quotas. By the close of the war, 3,780 men from the greater York area had served, including all members but one of the Spring Garden Band. The band, with its president William Frey (a descendant of Tobias Frey, founder of Freystown, now a part of York), became the 87th Regimental Band of the Pennsylvania Volunteers.

Meanwhile the Worth Infantry under the command of Captain Thomas A. Ziegle and the York Rifles under Captain George Hay were sent immediately to Maryland, where they were to guard railroad bridges. Eventually York County soldiers would participate in important engagements, such as the battles of Mechanicsville, Antietam, Frederick, Charleston, Petersburg, Richmond, Monocacy River, and Gettysburg. Some Yorkers rode with General Philip Henry Sheridan and others with Ulysses S. Grant.

As the days and battles passed, the war's focus shifted from town to town,

Below left
"The York Depot, September 28, 1861, and the Departure of Passenger Trains to Baltimore and one Regiment" at North Duke Street was done by Lewis Miller. (HSYC)

Below
A Civil War proclamation issued in York on September 8, 1862, required citizens "to assemble at suitable places within their limits, and organize military companies under the Act of 1858, to aid each other in repelling invasion of the county." (HSYC)

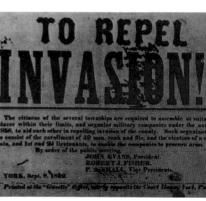

and from conflict to conflict, but in June of 1863, the war was brought frighteningly close to home.

The Confederates' main army began an invasion of Pennsylvania, planning to take Harrisburg and Philadelphia and thereby break the stronghold of Union power. General Robert E. Lee had advanced his troops over the Mason-Dixon line by June 15 and arrived in Chambersburg, about 57 miles west of York, on June 26. He ordered General R.S. Ewell to take Harrisburg and General Jubal Early to take York and move across the Susquehanna toward Philadelphia.

The next several days would be dramatic and terrifying ones for York. Streams of merchants and farmers with wagonloads of goods crowded the Gettysburg Pike (today's U.S. Route 30). They passed through the borough, crossed the river, and entered Lancaster and Chester counties. Some families buried valuables, such as silver, or hid them in wells. Some residents sent goods and valuables to Philadelphia for reclaiming later on. This escape route was soon to be cut off, however, as Confederate troops entered Wrightsville Borough to burn the bridge across the Susquehanna.

Earlier, while the Confederates were only a day from York, Farquhar relates, "the leading citizens went into session in the counting room of P.A. and S. Small's hardware store. The Smalls . . . were the big men of town and David Small, one of the proprietors of the *York Gazette*, was Chief Burgess. Among others in the meeting were W. Latimer Small, General George Hay, Samuel and Philip Small, Thomas E. Cochran [an attorney], Thomas White, and other leading citizens who had formed a Committee of Safety."

The meeting of that group of community officials and captains of local industry embodied a long-practiced custom to meet community needs, whether urgent or less demanding.

Farquhar entered the meeting and suggested that "it would be well to meet the Confederates before they entered the town—that we could make a good deal better bargain with them then than we could after they saw how little of our property we had been able to remove." Although the committeemen did not give his plan serious consideration, Farquhar told them that he would try to dicker with the Confederates anyway. He hitched up his buggy and started off.

Just beyond Abbottstown, which lay on the Pike about 14 miles southwest of York, Farquhar struck the Confederate line and by coincidence met an old classmate, Lieutenant Redik from Georgia. Farquhar asked him who was in charge and Redik informed him that the troops were under the command of General John B. Gordon. They thereupon went to see the general.

The York man later wrote that "the General was exceedingly courteous. . . . Having stated exactly the object of my mission, I said: 'General Gordon, unless you have entirely changed from the character you used to have, you are neither a horse thief nor a bank robber, and fighting is more your line than sacking a city.'" Gordon agreed, and the two made an agreement that would save York from destruction. The Civil War, after all, was a war between gentlemen, and leaders on both sides made agreements such as the one made between Farquhar and the Southern general.

When Farquhar returned to the Small's store, the Committee of Safety was still in session. He told the members of his accomplishment, but attorney Cochran argued that since Farquhar "was not authorized by the Committee to make the agreement, the Confederates would not feel bound to carry out their promises. . . . The Smalls joined me in insisting that a committee be appointed with full authority to arrange the terms, and that evening, David Small, General George Hay, Latimer Small, Thomas White, and myself, as this committee, went out to the Gettysburg Pike bearing a flag of truce."

The burning of the Wrightsville-Columbia Bridge on June 28, 1863, was depicted by artist A. Berghous. This view is from the Columbia side looking across the Susquehanna River toward Wrightsville. (HSYC)

The Confederates entered the town the next day, June 28. Cassandra Morris Small, a York girl and daughter of W. Latimer Small, described the invasion in a letter to her friend and cousin, Lissie Latimer. "Sunday morning," she writes, "Mother, Mary and I dressed for church; all the rest expected to stay home. Just as the church bells rang, the cry was heard, 'They are coming!' Oh, Lissie, what did we feel like? Humiliated! Disgraced! Men who don't often weep, wept then. They [the Confederates] came with loud music, flags flying. First we saw a picket in front of our door. Where he came from or how he got there, no one knew, he came so suddenly and quietly. [Other pickets were all along the street.] When we spoke to him, he said they were only to keep the [York] men in line."

These first soldiers carried shovels, spades, and pickaxes. The troops who arrived later had guns, but all of the soldiers, no matter where they came from, were ragged, dirty, and unshaven. Among this disheveled band some York girls recognized boyfriends from Baltimore. Thirty thousand troops in all entered the town.

General Gordon later writes of this scene in his book, *Reminiscences of the Civil War,* that " . . . the grotesque aspect of my troops was accentuated here and there, too, by barefooted men mounted double upon huge horses with shaggy manes and long fetlocks. Confederate pride, to say nothing of Southern gallantry, was subjected to the sorest trial by the consternation produced among the ladies of York. In my eagerness to relieve the citizens from all apprehension, I lost sight of the fact that this turnpike powder was no respecter of persons, but that it enveloped all alike—officers as well as privates."

Cassandra Small related to a relative that General Gordon's division came after the first group of men: "They halted in the Square and took down our flag. Mr. Farquhar [A.B. Farquhar] persuaded them to make our hospital buildings a camping place [they were so near residences they couldn't be burnt]." The Confederates took Farquhar's advice but nevertheless many houses were ransacked throughout the county and the Confederates appropriated horses, mules, cattle, and other items. "Our beautiful hospital!" the Small girl writes, "I would be ashamed to tell you all they did there, and to think Lissie, there are some who call themselves ladies, who went there to see them and entertained them."

These "ladies" were not the only Yorkers to welcome the Confederates. Because of York's proximity to the Mason-Dixon line, some townspeople were openly sympathetic to the Southerners and even waved red streamers as Gordon rode through the streets. Even Small, describing Gordon during his ride through town, paints a picture not of a rapacious monster but of a more

or less humane soldier: " 'I want to say to you,' " she recalls him announcing, " 'We have not come among you to pursue the same warfare your men did in our country. You need not have any fear of us. You are just as safe as though we were a thousand miles away. That is all I have to say.' He bowed and, turning his horse, rode away."

In General Gordon's book, another remarkable event during the Confederates' invasion is recounted. Upon entering the Square, a girl not more than 12 years old walked toward Gordon's horse with a bouquet of roses. The general accepted the gift, but before riding off noticed a note inside the flowers. The note told of a secret gorge at the entry to Wrightsville that would take the general's forces unseen to a spot where they could force the Union soldiers stationed there to retreat or to surrender.

General Gordon reached Wrightsville the same evening and found that the information he had received in the bouquet of roses was indeed correct. The 1,200 Union troops immediately retreated across the bridge and burned the span behind them. Gordon noted that, as the bridge burned, no fire buckets could be found, but when the town later caught fire the buckets seemed to appear from everywhere.

Meanwhile, at about two o'clock on the first day of the Confederate invasion, General Early and his staff set up a meeting in the Court House. He demanded from York "165 barrels of flour or 28,000 pounds of baked bread, 3,500 pounds of sugar, 1,650 pounds of coffee, 300 gallons of molasses, 1,200 pounds of salt, 32,000 pounds of fresh beef or 21,000 pounds of bacon or pork . . . to be delivered at the market place on Main [now Market] Street." The general also demanded "2,000 pairs of shoes or boots, 1,000 pairs of socks, 1,000 felt hats, and $100,000 in United States money."

About $28,610 and its equivalent in merchandise were collected and given to the general, along with a "due bill" for the balance. The general appeared satisfied, although the take never reached the proportions that he had demanded and the Committee of Safety gave receipts for the contributions to the contributors. (Later the Borough reimbursed them through a special tax.)

The soldiers, who had camped not only in the hospital but also on Penn Common, the Fair Grounds, and around Louck's mill, butchered cattle and roasted them over huge fires. They set up a bakery near the United States Hospital on the Common and took flour from the mill to make bread. They also tore down wooden fences to fuel their outdoor fires. General Early asked the Committee of Safety for access to the county's deeds and records so that he could burn them. He was persuaded not to burn the records but then threatened to burn the railroad shops north of the Square.

A United States Army Hospital for the wounded was located on Penn Common at York during the Civil War. The soldiers' chapel is shown here, circa 1863. (HSYC)

At about that time a foaming horse galloped into York carrying a soldier from General Lee's camp. The soldier had a dispatch from Lee that ordered Early to proceed with his men to Gettysburg. While collecting horses along the route, he marched off to Gettysburg and the decisive battle that took the town's name.

Before the Confederates vanished into the distance, they left York one more thing by which to remember them. Small relates, "as they were leaving the town on Tuesday morning, going through the main street, they tore [the Union flag they had taken down during the invasion] into strips, then others took the strips and tore them into little pieces, all singing, 'We'll Plant Our Colors on a Northern Hill.' "

Farquhar says in his autobiography that he followed the Confederates to Gettysburg as a member of the Hospital Service, and when he returned he was shocked to find Yorkers pointing and jeering at him. They accused him of being a Rebel, deciding that, as Farquhar put it, "I, as the man who had opened the negotiations, was something near to being a traitor."

Farquhar, a proud and pious man, was so hurt by this accusation that he went to Washington to seek President Lincoln's view of the situation. There he met John Hay, the President's secretary, whom he knew. Hay, who would later become Secretary of State under Presidents William McKinley and Theodore Roosevelt, tried to convince Farquhar that Lincoln was very busy and that Farquhar did not really need his help since he had acted honorably. But the York man insisted on waiting.

When President Lincoln came out of his office to go to a meeting at the War Department building, Farquhar waylaid him. He blurted out his story to the President, adding, "I am going with you; I want your advice, and to know what you think of our action." Lincoln acquiesced, and as they walked together, the President asked the 25-year-old Farquhar about his life: " 'Was I married?' Lincoln asked. 'Did I have any children? Had I a business in York? What kind was it? Was it prosperous?' "

They arrived at the War Department building and entered a room where Secretary of War Edwin M. Stanton and a number of distinguished-looking generals were gathered. The President, leading Farquhar to the front of the room and giving his hand a squeeze, took him before the Secretary of War and addressed him with these good-humored words: "Stanton, I have captured that young chap who sold York, Pennsylvania, to the rebels. What are we going to do with him?"

Afterwards Farquhar returned to York and resumed his manufacturing duties, somewhat relieved by the President's blessing on his controversial action. He suffered occasional jeers from townspeople for years after the Civil War, but he was confident that he had done right.

As Farquhar's business grew, sending materials around the globe, so did many other York firms. The community already had achieved great prosperity, but it was slight compared to that which the postwar era would bring.

Centre Square in York was decorated during the September 1899 Sesqui-Centennial of the erection of York County. The four triumphal arches, built in the Classical style, were 40 feet wide, 30 feet high, and 12 feet deep. Flags and bunting adorned the Colonial Hotel and other buildings in the city. (HSYC)

CHAPTER VI

POST-CIVIL WAR PROSPERITY

When the Civil War ended, Yorkers put aside national politics and military matters. Instead they concentrated on developments at home and ushered in an era of tremendous growth and industrial expansion. The town's small shops, mills, foundries, and other businesses adapted to changing times and many new businesses began, further stimulating the building of the city. Construction continued to improve with larger factories and grander homes, such as those established in the 700 block of South George Street.

The designer of most of those homes, as well as many of the other buildings that would rise in York's cityscape over the next five decades, was J.A. Dempwolf. Born in Brunswick, Germany, Dempwolf came to York in 1867 at the age of 19 to work for the P.A. and S. Small Company. Seeing construction all around him, Dempwolf became interested in the building trade. He was apprenticed in 1869 to Jacob Gotwalt, a York carpenter, then went to work for Nathanial Weigel, a York building contractor. While with Weigel, Dempwolf made full-size architectural details for St. Paul's Lutheran Church then under construction at King and Beaver streets. The church building's design, by the noted Philadelphia architect Stephen D. Button, intrigued Dempwolf.

Realizing that he needed professional training, Dempwolf went to New York, where he studied architectural drawing and design in night courses at the Cooper Union Institute. He worked full time during the day. Upon graduation, Dempwolf went to Boston, where he supervised the construction of Holy Cross Cathedral. He returned to York to design St. John's German Lutheran Church on West King Street.

After completion of the church, Dempwolf went to Philadelphia to assist Stephen Button in designing some of the buildings for the Centennial Exposition to be held there the next year. In 1876 Dempwolf returned to York and, with the help of Samuel Small and other friends, opened an office in the Cassatt Building for the practice of architecture. From his office on Continental Square, Dempwolf completed designs for the York Trust Company, the York National Bank, the City Market, the Fluhrer Building, and many other landmark structures. Dempwolf, his brother Reinhart, and J.A.'s son Frederick (who also became architects), are credited with creating many of the stately and beautiful buildings that still dominate the York scene. The elder Dempwolf was active with the American Institute of Architects. He was appointed to the Pennsylvania State Arts Council, and elected that body's chairman in 1926.

Factories providing jobs for hundreds of employees sprang up in the 1860s and the community continued spreading in all directions. As the borough's population grew, so did the populations of the townships and boroughs surrounding it. One of the developments reinforcing this growth was the increasing specialization of businesses.

Richard Watt, a Scotsman, came to York in 1865 after serving as an apprentice in the painting and decorating trade. After working in one of York's first photography shops with Fitz James Evans, Watt opened his own

painting shop. In 1866 his brother Andrew joined him and they moved to 108 East Market Street to specialize in sign painting. When Richard died, their shop was continued by Andrew under the name Watt and Brother. Andrew Watt acted as president and James Webster as secretary and general manager.

Upon Andrew Watt's death, Webster became president and his son Richard Watt Webster became secretary. Realizing the need for skilled craftsmen in the trade, the two Websters opened a school for apprentices. This school's first two students, Frank P. Connolly and Ray Reisinger, both won top prizes at the Pennsylvania Master Painters' and Decorators' Association convention, held in York. Richard W. Webster opened a branch of the business in Harrisburg, and churches as far away as Brooklyn soon were employing the master craftsmen to do work for them. Watt Brothers also provided the street decoration for the town's 150th birthday celebration in 1899. Connolly later became president of his own shop.

Specialization also brought success to Christian Charles Kottcamp, a tinsmith who opened a small shop on the 100 block of North George Street, where he made cooking utensils, spouting, and roofing. Many years later, in 1895, Kottcamp realized that plumbing and heating services were coming into demand, and he sent his son Harry to pursue a course at the New York School of Plumbing and Sanitation. When Harry returned to York in 1901, he joined his father's business and, with his newly acquired knowledge in plumbing, helped expand it.

The Kottcamps moved into the plumbing and heating fields at the right time. York's new buildings were becoming more modern, and now that York's water and gas companies were well established, the community needed the

This stenciled and turned settee exemplifies the craftsmanship of York County artisans during the 19th century. (HSYC)

specialized service. Outdoor toilet facilities would linger in York's backyard environment, though, for many more years. At the time of the establishment of York's first plumbing service, the small structures behind York homes were as common a sight as the family cow or chickens.

Local farmers, after the Civil War, were enjoying their own prosperity. They were doing so well, in fact, that the Farmer's Market, which still operates on its original site at Market and Penn streets, was built in 1866 to serve the population growing in the open lands west of the Codorus. The market, incorporated by John H. Baer, Jacob Baer, John Winter, C.F. Winter, and Israel Laucks, was an instant success and was enlarged twice.

The Farmer's Market stands offered sumptuous displays of fat chickens, polished apples, fresh eggs, tender asparagus, home-cured meats, home-baked breads, pastries, and such Pennsylvania Dutch items as egg noodles, scrapple, snitz und knepp, soft pretzels, chowchow, red beet eggs, pot pie, and hog maws. Visitors found a cascade of fresh-cut flowers and just-picked produce, as well as stands showing off home-made bonnets, aprons, and household decorations. Yorkers began to consider the visit to market as important a social occasion as going to church on Sunday morning. After all, one met the same friends and neighbors there as at church, and strong and healthy bodies were needed to carry on God's work here on earth. Some families in York markets have passed their market stands down through five generations. Market in York was—and still is—a festival to be enjoyed several times a week.

Yorkers were increasingly concerned about the welfare of their children and young adults, and the late 1860s and early 1870s witnessed an unprecedented boom in institutions for community youths. Yorkers built a new Children's Home in 1865, formed the town's YMCA in 1869, opened on Duke Street one of the town's first high schools, and in 1872 opened a second one.

Despite Yorkers' initial reluctance to welcome the public school system to the county, the inhabitants soon learned the value of mass education for its citizens. Several new public schools were opened and the parochial schools continued their work. The York County Academy still offered concentrated courses of study for the community's "gifted" students and educated generations of community leaders. York's first high school was established on South Duke Street in 1862, and in 1868 another building was erected on its back lot.

With York's continuing growth a bigger high school was needed by 1872

and York taxpayers contributed $35,500 for a building on Philadelphia Street opposite the Friends Meeting House. Among the school's four faculty members was historian George R. Prowell.

In 1873 Samuel Small and his wife, Isabel Cassatt Small, envisioning another privately run institution of liberal education, built still another school on the northeast corner of Duke Street and College Avenue, known as York Collegiate Institute. The Smalls appointed their own board of directors and opened with five faculty members and 50 students.

As York entered the 1870s, it housed 11,003 people, almost 30 percent more than 10 years before. The county population had zoomed to 76,134. The population rise created a demand for products that only new businesses could supply. These businesses gave York even more diversity and led to the formation of new institutions to serve them.

In 1870 Addison Shaffer started a chain shop on South Pershing Avenue. About nine years later, John C. Schmidt established a new chain company on East Walnut Street and hired Shaffer as foreman. Later Schmidt built a larger factory on State Street and used electric welders and mechanical formers that greatly improved his manufacturing process. The chain manufacturer then acquired plants in other Pennsylvania cities, as well as in Ohio, and formed the Standard Chain Company. That company eventually was sold to the American Chain Company, which used York as its headquarters and later became known as Acco Industries. That company employed 800 people as it neared its 100th anniversary and then disappeared from the York scene.

In 1871 David F. Stauffer took over a cake and cracker business that Jacob Weiser had begun in 1858. A good rate for the company was five barrels a day, some of which Stauffer delivered himself. The company later specialized in pretzels and helped make York the "Pretzel Capital of America."

The York Manufacturing Company was formed in 1874 and became the world's largest manufacturer of refrigerators, ice-makers, and air conditioners. That company became the York Division of the Borg Warner Corporation and still later York International. In 1875 Hermann Noss' Sons, Inc., began producing paneling for buildings, such as Atlantic City's Marlborough Blenheim Hotel. Soon afterward Stephen Morgan Smith opened what would become the largest plant in the world devoted exclusively to hydraulic turbines and allied equipment. His products were also sent around the globe. The company was eventually sold to the Allis Chalmers Corporation and once employed 1,900 people. It also disappeared from the York industrial scene.

The rise of all this new business may have helped to perpetuate York's

unbroken support of Democratic candidates in Presidential elections. They favored Democrat Horace Greeley over Ulysses S. Grant in 1872, probably because Greeley supported a high tariff to protect American businessmen against foreign competition and Grant opposed it.

American inventiveness was entering an extremely active period and the new technologies and inventions found an eager public in York. In 1876 Hiram Young, owner of the local weekly newspaper, the *True Democrat* (later the *York Dispatch*), visited the Centennial Exposition in Philadelphia and brought back an incandescent lamp. He hooked it up to a battery and displayed it in the window of the newspaper office to the great interest of Yorkers.

Another man who went to the Centennial Exposition, the York dentist Dr. Charles A. Eisenhart, became intrigued with a demonstration there of transmitting a voice over the air. After returning to York, Eisenhart installed a telephone line from his office to his stable so he could call for his horse. About the same time another Yorker, W. Latimer Small, strung a telephone line from his home to Codorus Mills two miles away.

A few years later John K. Gross, who was a passenger and freight agent with the Northern Central Railway, unveiled a system of 27 telephones connected to stores and offices in York and to a central office that handled calls. Albert Galbreath started a similar exchange in Columbia and connected his lines to the community of Wrightsville. Frank A. Ziegler gave Hanover its first system the same year Gross introduced the new-fangled instrument to York. Gross sold his business in 1883 to the Southern Pennsylvania Telephone Company, which was consolidated with the Pennsylvania Telephone Company, a subsidiary of the Bell Telephone System started in 1877.

Perhaps the experience of seeing a local company swallowed up by a large system induced a group of York businessmen to establish another telephone company in 1895. Headed by Dr. Eisenhart and George B. Rudy, the group organized under the name, the York Telephone Company. Within a decade, the company had 2,600 telephones and 300 miles of pole line connecting towns and villages across York County. That company later became a part of the General Telephone Company, which established headquarters in Erie, Pennsylvania, but later became part of a larger corporation.

As York was developing its intricate telephone system, new businesses were being added to the commercial community. In 1877 Edward C. Reineberg opened a shoe shop on South George Street. In 1880, when York housed 13,940 people and 87,841 people lived in the county, George W. Hoover and his three sons started manufacturing horse-drawn buggies in the iron-front

York's Telephone and Telegraph Company was organized in 1895 by Dr. Charles Eisenhart, a York dentist who was interested in telecommunication. These women were photographed at the telephone-company switchboard. (HSYC)

building, located on East Philadelphia Street's north side, which later became the home of the *York Dispatch*. A well-known York musician, J.O. Weaver, formed the Weaver Piano Company in 1882 and the company turned out to be the primary developer and supplier of lightweight portable pianos to army camps, hospitals, hospital ships, and USO canteens all over the world. Israel Forry Laucks established (also in 1882) the York Safe and Lock Company, which made products that were installed in the Bank of France in Paris, the Bank of China in Shanghai, Tokyo's Bank of Japan, and other financial institutions around the world.

In the late 1870s and early 1880s, two more significant businesses were begun. The first was the establishment of the City Market at 211 South Duke Street in 1878, brought about by a population increase in the town's southern parts. J.A. Dempwolf designed the 225-by-80-foot building, which, like its predecessor, the Farmer's Market, was enlarged twice. The City Market, razed after generations had used it, is said to have been one of the most architecturally pleasing buildings ever put up in York.

A few years after the City Market was established, the Arnaux Electric Light Company came to York. The company connected four arc lights to the flagstaff on the Square and they burned "with a light rivaling the daylight itself," in the words of a reporter from the *York Dispatch*. The newspaper also reports: "A large number of people gathered in the Square and neighborhood to witness the exhibition, and many were the expressions of approval and delight over the new light. . . . We ought soon to have plenty of electric light and bright streets at night, instead of the dark, dingy ones through which we have heretofore had to find our way." The time of the lamplighter igniting gas lamps in front of York taverns and stores was coming to a close.

In the late 1870s, the York community diversified in other ways as well. By 1877 increasing numbers of Jews were immigrating to York and a group of them organized under the name Beth Israel. Within two years they were holding congregational devotions in the home of Solomon Kahn of West Market Street; the officiating rabbi was Joseph Lebach. Soon afterwards the group rented a room for use as a synagogue and Hebrew school, and the congregation was established with Lebach, the Reverend Doctor Nathan Rosenau, Isador Walker, and Abram Simmons leading the services and supervising the Hebrew school. The congregation, in 1907, erected a temple on South Beaver Street in the "Little Moscow" area of York. (Hanover Jews had held services in homes as early as 1826, but the Civil War dispersed the community and a synagogue did not open there until 1953.)

Although Temple Beth Israel was the first Jewish house of worship, York's Jewish citizens had enjoyed prominence almost from the community's earliest days. Before and during the Revolution, a Jewish merchant, Elijah Etting, had operated his shop in York. Jews who left the Palatinate to escape persecution often gravitated to Pennsylvania. Finding the Pennsylvania Dutch dialect in York similar to their own language, many set down roots.

The first son of York merchant Elijah Etting and his wife, Shinah, followed his parents to Baltimore after the Revolution and became an early proponent of the "Jewish Bill," which sought to abolish discrimination against Jews desiring to hold public office. At that time holding such offices required a vow of adherence to the Christian religion and naturally excluded members of other faiths. President Thomas Jefferson appointed the Ettings' York-born son, Reuben, as United States Marshal of Maryland in 1801. The "Jewish Bill," with the young Etting's unflagging support, was adopted in 1825.

In 1879, just two years after Beth Israel was formed, another group of Jewish immigrants arrived in York, principally from Austria and Hungary. The new Jewish group, strictly Orthodox in their beliefs, established its own congregation. Anshe Hadas (People of the Faith) Congregation was chartered in 1883 and Jacob Sirovich, father of a well-known Congressman from New York, became its first rabbi.

Charles Beck, a member of Anshe Hadas Congregation, organized the Adas Israel (Congregation of Israel) for the purpose of following the Nussach Sephard of the Chasidic tradition. In 1904 the congregation erected a synagogue on South Pershing Avenue. Among its leaders were Jacob Feder, Samuel Williams, Benjamin Feldman, Jonas Piperberg, and Michael Leibowitz.

Two years earlier the followers of the Ashkenazic ritual of the Anshe Hadas had gathered at the home of Max Tewel, deciding to change their congregation's name to Ohev Sholom (Lovers of Peace) and to build a new synagogue. The synagogue was dedicated in 1904 with Abe Trattner as president. J.T. Ziegler and David Katz comprised the building committee.

In addition to Jews from various countries, York was benefiting from an influx of many other nationalities at this time. From the end of the 19th century to World War I, Poles, Hungarians, Czechs, Russians, and Greeks gravitated to Pennsylvania Dutch country. York became home to many of the new immigrants, especially the Italians and Greeks.

York's steady population growth made its lack of formal medical facilities increasingly burdensome, and community leaders established the building of a hospital as a high priority. York's early physicians had received their training in European medical schools; it was not until 1827 that the first American medical school was developed in Baltimore. Philadelphia had educated physicians as early as the 1760s, but few of them took up practice in York town.

In the early days of York, as in other parts of the country, medical care was usually relegated to the barber's chair. Inflammatory illnesses, such as pleurisy, bronchitis, pneumonia, and rheumatism, were common, and sometimes fatal. York town was plagued with periodic epidemics of cholera, whooping cough, and scarlet fever, and even such relatively mild afflictions as measles, dysentery, and diarrhea could have tragic results in the absence of proper medical attention.

Immigrants, who had brought old customs and beliefs from their homelands, were likely to rely on herbs or other forms of folk medicine. Such herbs as rosemary, rue, wormwood, sage, thyme, blue mint, woolly nut, fever few, and horehound were often grown in home gardens and used for medicinal purposes. From the woods, people gathered tansy, camomile, yarrow, sassafras root, penny royal, mandrake, and witch hazel, from which they concocted tonics and "cures." The practice of "powwowing," a form of faith healing that sometimes used herbs and natural concoctions, was practiced throughout the Pennsylvania Dutch regions, including York County.

The coming of scientifically based medicine then was greatly welcomed in the York area and Yorkers banded together to see this needed modernization become a reality. On a blustery day in January 1880, 10 years after Lister had discovered antiseptic surgery and while Pasteur was studying bacteria and its relation to disease, Samuel Small gathered a small group of Yorkers in his office to create the York Hospital and Dispensary Association."In attendance were a relative of Small, David E. Small, Jere S. Carl, Dr. Thomas Cathcart, Frank Geise, Dr. William S. Roland and Dr. John Wiest. Samuel Small contributed a three-story building on West College Avenue and the group agreed to raise $70,000 to convert the house into a hospital. The hospital's new board of managers purchased 12 wrought-iron beds for $98 each and hired one nurse. There was no full-time physician. In 1881 Dr. A.R. Blair became the hospital's first consulting physician and Dr. James W. Kerr became the first consulting surgeon. The board of directors was made up of

Cathcart, Roland, Wiest, Blair, and E.W. Meisenhelder. A Board of Lady Managers, formed at the same time to serve in auxiliary functions, numbered Mrs. D. Pentz, Mrs. Israel Laucks, Mrs. Chauncey Black, and Mrs. A.B. Farquhar.

Physicians connected to the growing facility sought new ideas and techniques to help better serve the people of the community. Some doctors traveled to Baltimore to hear or give lectures and to sit in on seminars, and others conducted their own research in York. The most notable researcher was Dr. George E. Holtzapple, who discovered that oxygen could be used in the treatment of pneumonia. While tending to a critically ill 16-year-old boy in a Loganville farmhouse in 1885, Dr. Holtzapple, relying on his own ingenuity, rigged up an apparatus of rubber tubing, test tubes, and a spirit lamp. The lamp was used to heat a mixture of chlorate of potash and black oxide of manganese, generating oxygen which traveled through the tubing and bubbled to the surface of the water in a bucket at the patient's bedside. The oxygen saved the boy's life. Afterwards Dr. Holtzapple worked at perfecting the technique, then introduced his discovery to the medical world. Not long after that Dr. Meisenhelder began using nitrous oxide (laughing gas), but because he was worried that it might harm patients if used without extreme care, he brought a skilled anesthetist to the hospital at his own expense. Soon the hospital hired its own professional anesthetist and added a nursing school. One of the school's early graduates, Florence Gipe, left York to found the School of Nursing at the University of Maryland. York's hospital prospered from the beginning and the community supported it financially as well as with volunteer service.

In 1885 the York Hospital and Dispensary facilities were pressed into emergency service. When the York Collegiate Institute, also founded by Samuel Small and located on the same street as the hospital, caught fire, the

hospital volunteered shelter. Although no one was hurt in the fire, this experience inspired the Institute to lend space for the holding of classes.

Two years later the Institute was rebuilt by Small's nephew, W. Latimer Small, and George Small. (The senior Small had died just a few months before fire razed the first Institute Building.) The new building was completed using a J.A. Dempwolf design and was described by a newspaper reporter of the day as "larger, more convenient and more elaborate than the first."

If the windows in the new Collegiate Institute were any measure of its elaborateness, the building deserved the reporter's generous evaluation. Stained-glass panels were installed throughout the building by artisans and craftsmen from the J. Horace Rudy Company. The company's owner had attended the Pennsylvania Academy of Fine Arts and then worked for a Philadelphia firm as a woodcarver and engraver. His firm eventually made windows for more than 500 churches, as well as for hospitals, schools, colleges, and private homes in the Midwestern and Southeastern areas of the United States.

J. Horace Rudy's son, Charles, born in York in 1904, received his early training in his father's shop, graduated from his father's alma mater, and won major scholarly awards including a Guggenheim Fellowship. He later received awards for his sculpture and was praised by magazines such as *Life*.

York was a thriving center of activity in the 1880s. In 1884 Fluhrer's Jewelry Store opened, a Presidential election was held (Yorkers supported Democrat Grover Cleveland over Benjamin Harrison), and the 17-acre Fairmount area on the Codorus's north side was annexed to the city. But the event of the year that had the greatest local impact occurred on June 15, when heavy rains and a wind of hurricane force killed several Yorkers. The storm swept away all the structures along the Codorus, including the Pennsylvania Railroad Bridge, and caused more than $700,000 worth of property damage. In 1885 York Borough was enlarged again when the areas of Freystown, Bottstown, and Smysertown were annexed to it. The Edison Electric Light Company was formed that year, and the Eastern Market was added in the 400 block of East Market Street.

In hectic 1886 the People's Electric Light Company was formed and for the first time institutions such as the York Hospital had electric light. "Electric Light Can't Blow Out," an advertisement in the *York Dispatch* told Yorkers, and as more and more inhabitants became familiar with the non-flickering radiant new light, they had electrical lines installed in their houses and schools. The age of light had come to York and residents were quick to put its new inventions to work.

During the same year that York's second electric company came into being, Milton D. Martin, who would become a leading auto manufacturer, founded the York Spring Wagon Works on the site where the Strand Theatre would be built almost 40 years later. Money left by Martin helped in establishing another important public institution—the Martin Memorial Library.

But the biggest event of 1886 was the incorporation of the York Street Railway Company, which aided the people immensely in getting around their expanding town. The company immediately put eight closed horsecars, six open ones, 15 horses, and eight mules into service. Each driver was given a set of rules, which included a provision for ejecting stubborn tobacco smokers, "using only so much force as is necessary."

Eighteen eighty-six was also the year of the controversial market shed affair. In that year the City Council authorized George Heiges, Luther Small, and Dr. Jacob Hay to investigate the removing of the Centre Square market sheds, which many people considered eyesores. The three men advocated tearing down the sheds, which "brought forth violent opposition"

The second York Collegiate Institute building, dedicated on March 15, 1887, featured magnificent stained-glass windows made in York by the J. Horace Rudy Company. Courtesy, York College of Pennsylvania.

from people who leased stands in the sheds. But on June 26 the council labeled the sheds a "public nuisance" and voted to remove them.

On June 30, at 2:00 a.m., 20 city workers brought several ropes, three horses, and seven mules to the Square to begin work. They tied one end of each rope to a shed support and the other to a horse or mule. Just as the animals were about to pull the sheds down, someone turned in a fire alarm and pandemonium broke loose. Firemen rushed to the scene, bringing with them crowds of Yorkers who thought there was a fire in Centre Square. They arrived just in time to see the shed roofs come crashing down. Great clouds of dust rose into the sky, which, seen from a distance in the moonlight, looked like smoke, alarming the latecomers even more. By 3 a.m. the sheds had all been flattened and the excitement had died down. The debris was removed the next day. Markets were held on the perimeter of the Square until the 1930s. People were then forced to go to the Farmers, City, Central, or Eastern markets.

The destruction of the market sheds prefigured the events of 1887. The

destruction was a municipal action, and so were the major events of the new year. For one thing, York was incorporated as a city almost exactly 100 years after its incorporation as a borough, but not before many years of debate on the subject. Heated discussions on the issue ensued and many people were quite vociferous in their objections.

The Central Market, another J.A. Dempwolf building, was built in 1887. Six investors invested sums ranging from $1,500 to $9,100 to build the market facing on both Beaver Street and Philadelphia Street. The building was opened in 1888 and many of the same families that leased space at the time of its opening are still operating "stands" there. By this time York was well known as a center of agricultural abundance. Tons of fresh produce, fruit, meats, and chickens were shipped out of York every year.

Outstanding local favorites developed at the markets, especially snow peas, with their tender, thin skins, and lush, red strawberries. But almost as popular among Yorkers were such seasonal favorites as the famous Pennsylvania Dutch pumpkin pie at Thanksgiving; plump, red, home-cured hams at Easter; and turkeys at Christmas. Elaborate holiday meals are still very much a part of Pennsylvania Dutch heritage. Two or three kinds of meat, and numerous vegetables, salads, breads, condiments, and desserts make up the average holiday meal, and the Pennsylvania Dutch hallmark for gracious dining is "quantity as well as quality."

York's official government had begun in 1787 when the York Borough was erected; it was really a town, but the use of the strange-sounding Pennsylvania governmental unit of borough persisted. Soon after York's erection as a borough, its burgesses asked for additional powers, including the right to issue ordinances. A supplement was passed by the General Assembly of Pennsylvania granting the new "Board of Burgesses" much greater jurisdiction than they had previously enjoyed. The board, in effect, became a town council. Until the enactment of this statute, the state legislature had been able to arbitrarily pass rules that changed the borough's laws. The sophistication which the new form of government brought with it would signal a new direction for York.

In 1859 another supplement was passed, establishing a town council and abolishing the old Board of Burgesses. The borough was then divided into five wards with two councilmen each. The councilmen served two-year terms and each ward staggered the elections, so that they voted for only one representative a year. At this time the job of second burgess was abolished

Below left
A Saturday Market Day in Centre Square in the 1890s is shown here. York's longstanding farmers' market tradition began in Colonial times and continued to play an important role in the city. Courtesy, Sunday News.

Below
Daniel K. Noel was elected the first mayor of York when it was incorporated as a city in 1887. After his two three-year terms as mayor, he devoted many more years to public service. (HSYC)

and the former chief burgess presided over the council. York was protected by a guard of watchmen headed by a night constable who passed through the streets during the night yelling the time and the weather conditions. (The job of night constable had been provided for in the original borough charter. One indication of the amount of activity in the city offices in those years was the fact that the rules for selecting the night constable changed five times while the borough form of government existed.) In 1865 the town council passed legislation that would create a police force.

By 1882 the borough had outgrown its town council form of government and in April of that year the "General Borough Law" was passed, making York subject to general Pennsylvania law. Although adopted, opponents of the law argued that York would soon outgrow even this larger form of government. The pro-city advocates campaigned for their cause enthusiastically and were able to get the issue on the November 1882 ballot. During that election the majority of York voters cast ballots for a city government. Their opponents organized a hearing before the governor, however, which resulted in his refusal to give York a city charter because it had neglected to fulfill certain technicalities in filing for the license.

Four years would pass before the issue again appeared on a public ballot. The city advocates won the election, and further objection by incorporation opponents were disallowed by the governor. Thus, almost a century after its incorporation into a borough, on January 11, 1887, York became a city in the eyes of state government.

The first mayor of the new city—Daniel Noel—was a typical York Countian. His father, Jacob Noel, had come to America from the Rhine area of Germany and had served as a private in Captain Spangler's company of York soldiers in the War of 1812, during which he was wounded at the Battle of North Point. Jacob Noel's son, Daniel, was born in York on July 7, 1820. He studied diligently and became a teacher. He taught for 12 years, then became superintendent of schools for Cumberland County. He also served Cumberland County as prothonotary for three years. He moved back to York in 1871 and was to serve two three-year terms as York's first mayor, after which Noel devoted many more years to public service before his death in 1898.

On September 24 and 25 of 1887, York held its Borough Centennial. More than 30,000 people celebrated and the borough was bedecked with flags, evergreens, and bunting for the occasion. Cannon fire and bell ringing ushered in the special 100th anniversary day, which also saw two parades. On September 24, in late morning, 3,000 schoolchildren—boys in uniform caps and girls in white—proceeded down the street. In the afternoon a parade of the military, the firemen, the secret orders, and 30 bands and drum corps marched proudly along the same route. After the parades, Governor James A. Beaver, in town for the occasion, held a reception at the Opera House. In the evening, for all of York to see, a spectacular fireworks display took place on the Public Common. The next day, the Honorable Chauncey F. Black, Pennsylvania lieutenant governor and a Yorker, concluded the celebration when he presented an oration at the Opera House.

Chauncey Forward Black was the son of Jeremiah S. Black of York. Jeremiah Black had been born in Somerset County of Scotch-Irish parents and had a distinguished career as lawyer and statesman. In 1857, while Chief Justice of the Supreme Court of Pennsylvania, he was appointed by President James Buchanan as Attorney General of the United States. Black succeeded Lewis Cass as Secretary of State in 1860.

Black's lasting claim to fame as a jurist was his brilliant defense of Lambdin P. Milligan in 1866. Milligan, with two other defendants, had been sentenced to death by a military commission in Indianapolis, where the civil

Above
Although York artist Horace Bonham passed the York County Bar, he never practiced law. Instead he went on to study art in Munich and Paris, eventually receiving recognition for both his paintings and poetry. (HSYC)

Top left
The cast of *Nittaunis, the Fairy of the Codorus* presented the play for Yorkers in a benefit at the York Opera House. (HSYC)

Top right
The York Opera House provided a variety of entertainment for Yorkers at the turn of the century. It was located on South Beaver Street near the present-day General Telephone Company. Courtesy, Sunday News.

courts were open. The case hinged not on their guilt or innocence, but on their right to be tried by a civil court rather than a military tribunal. Black, assisted by the future U.S. President James A. Garfield, won the decision of the Supreme Court, which literally marked the end of military rule by restoring the Constitution. This decision has been recognized as "a bulwark of liberty, a landmark of jurisprudence." Study of the "Ex-Parte Milligan" case is, to this day, a basic requirement for students of Constitutional law.

After Jeremiah Black's retirement from the Cabinet, he moved to York. He lived in town while "Brockie," a large mansion he commissioned, was being built two miles southwest of York. In 1873 he moved into Brockie and lived there until his death on August 19, 1883.

Chauncey Forward Black was born before his family moved to York. He attended private academies, than enrolled at Hiram College, where one of his instructors was future President James A. Garfield. The younger Black then enrolled at Jefferson College in western Pennsylvania. At age 17, when his father was appointed to Buchanan's cabinet, Chauncey followed his family to Washington. Afterwards, he returned with his family to York and opened a law office with his father. Chauncey also worked at journalism before being elected lieutenant governor. After his term was completed, he returned to his estate, Willow Bridges, southwest of York in Spring Garden Township. Black and his wife, Mary Dawson Black, lived at Willow Bridges until the death of his mother in 1897, when they moved into Brockie. Both generations of the Blacks entertained distinguished leaders of the country at Brockie, including President Garfield who was a frequent visitor.

Another prominent York family of the day was the Bonhams, who lived on East Market Street. Horace Bonham, the best known member of the family, received his early education at the York County Academy and then entered Lafayette College at Easton, Pennsylvania. Three years after his graduation in 1856, Bonham was admitted to the York County Bar. He never practiced law, but when the internal-revenue assessor's office was opened in York, he was appointed to that post by President Lincoln.

"Being a man of excellent literary training and possessed of an aesthetic nature," Bonham became interested in art and was encouraged by his first painting attempts. He went to Europe, where he studied art in Munich and in Paris. He had widely praised exhibitions in Boston and Philadelphia, and also received recognition for his poetry. Bonham's painting, *Nearing the Issue at the Cockpit*, is one of the prized pieces in the collection of the Corcoran Gallery of Art. Bonham died in York in 1892.

Elizabeth Bonham, Horace's daughter, lived in the East Market Street residence among paintings and porcelains acquired on the family's many travels, until she died in the 1960s. She left the house and its furnishings to The Historical Society of York County.

Affluence and recognition came to many other York families during this period. Henry Wasbers, Sr., a former state senator, opened a laundry and the Buckingham family started a wastepaper and rag business at 129 West Philadelphia Street. In 1888 John Mayer built a cigar factory on 63 acres on the east side of North George Street, one of the first of the many cigar factories that would soon constitute a major local industry. (A settlement called "Mayersville" soon sprang up around the factory, and in 1899 the settlement was incorporated as North York Borough.) In 1890 John T. McFall was operating one of the oddest businesses in York history, a combination hat and bicycle shop.

The year 1890 saw the city's population reach 20,793, a rise of almost one-third over the 1880 number. The county's population had grown to almost 100,000 (99,489 to be exact). The decade just beginning brought more technological advances and increased industrialization. New businesses and transportation systems sprang up as always, but not the stagecoaches or retail clothiers of earlier years. These new enterprises were machine-oriented manufacturers, who expanded the range of York's businesses and, in doing so, helped cushion the impact of the nationwide Panic of 1893. York's businesses, as in earlier panics, suffered a slowdown but the local economy remained sound.

Among the most important of the new developments of this era were the formation of the York Wagon Gear Company (founded in 1892), and the introduction of the electric trolley to city streets by the York Street Railway Company. The York Street Railway Company, in order to encourage people to use the trolleys, also gave the town parks.

Robert Cathcart Latimer, a distinguished Yorker, reminisced about the York Street Railway shortly before his death in 1974. "During the heyday of street railway prosperity," he recalls, "the local company established and maintained a recreation area southwest of town called Highland Park. It was a wooded hillside and hilltop on the north bank of the Codorus. . . . The

This was one of the York Railways Company's electric streetcars. (HSYC)

Park was reached by a car line that made a complete loop around it."

Latimer's memoirs tell us that the park's chief attraction was a summer theater with a stock company that performed the works of Gilbert and Sullivan and other light operas: "At least to the young people, inexperienced theater-goers that we were, the performances were a delight. The car fare each way was five cents. Admission to the theater, I think, was not more than ten cents."

Latimer also offers some rare and gentle glimpses of summertime plea-sures in another railway park: "Springwood too was a wooded hillside, but the stream at the foot of the hill was a shallow brook of clear water, fine wading for the youngsters. For some of an older group it was an annual custom to walk to a small store that I think must have been at the edge of Dallastown. The fact that the walk was on the railroad track almost all the way gave it a special zest; pop and sarsaparilla bought and drunk at the store were its sufficient purpose." Brookside and Cold Springs were other parks the railway company established.

Terrible autumns and winters followed these bucolic summers. On October 6, 1893, fire destroyed several buildings on the York Fair Grounds and killed two horses. On November 19, 1895, fire destroyed the York Wall Paper Company. On September 29, 1896, a powerful cyclone destroyed the main building, the grandstand, the carriage house, and the stove buildings at the Fair Grounds.

These scattered disasters, though damaging and inconvenient, did not severely impede the actions of most people, especially those with leisure time to fill. Upper-class Yorkers began to organize some of York's first social and historical organizations. The Out Door Country Club opened in 1892, and The Historical Society of York County was established in 1895. One of the most prestigious of the new groups, however, was the local chapter of the Daughters of the American Revolution, organized on October 10, 1894, at the East Market Street home of Mrs. Henry D. Schmidt. Its members, including women of the venerable Small, Croll, Miller, Lanius, Latimer, Doudel, Spangler, Cassatt, Barnitz, Smyser, and Schmidt families, elected Mrs. Schmidt vice-president and Louise Black regent (the equivalent of president). Louise Black was the wife of Chauncey Forward Black.

The York Town Chapter of the DAR began an ambitious educational program designed to point out York's rich contributions to the Revolution and to the founding of America in general. DAR members presented papers on

Below
Highland Park was a popular stop on the trolley line. This 1899 photograph shows a group of boys posed on a long flight of steps called "Fat Man's Misery." (HSYC)

Below right
This summertime group photograph shows the York Collegiate Institute class of 1895-1896. Courtesy, York College of Pennsylvania.

historical topics and sponsored the placement of historic plaques in honor of various York Revolutionary heroes. The DAR is still among the important social organizations today, and its members count among their ancestors those people who settled York, participated in its development, and fought in the war that won America its independence.

One of the early families represented in the founding of York and later the local chapter of the DAR were the Smysers. The Smyser family was noted for its contributions to local and state matters throughout York's developing years. Michael, Henry, and Philip all served in the state senate during the crucial years of 1790 to 1833. Adam was on the first board of directors of the Central Market in 1887; and Edward sold John Mayer the 63 acres that would become Mayersville or North York.

Mathias Smyser was one of York County's first settlers. In 1745 he made his home in West Manchester Township. His great-grandson, Samuel, owned a section of land west of Penn Street and south of Princess Street. The area became known as Smysertown and was eventually annexed.

Although conventional businesses, such as Schmidt and Ault Paper Company (founded in 1897), and Max Grumbacher's dry-goods store (opened the next year), continued to spring up, the last years of the century generally featured establishments of a kind that had never been seen before in York.

Above
This view looking west shows Market Street Bridge during the flood of June 1889. (HSYC)

Above right
The Bon Ton Department Store opened in York in 1898 at 22 West Market Street. The store's slogan was "Walk In and Look Around." The owner, Max Grumbacher, is shown wearing a hat, circa 1899. Oil cloth at the Bon Ton was eight cents a yard and gingham was four cents a yard. (HSYC)

Below right
This 1893 view of East Market Street was taken from the Square. The P.A. and S. Small Company building is at the left. (HSYC)

A group of merchants gathered in 1897 to draw up the constitution and bylaws for the Merchant's Association of York. The organization's first slate of officers included W.H. McClellan, Isaac Bennett, C.A. Geesy, and D.H. Lafean. The association grew and a program of community involvement was adopted, creating a natural tie between York's commercial and industrial segments. As a result the group's name was changed to the York Chamber of Commerce. York was the eighth locality to acquire a charter from the national Chamber of Commerce. Alexander McLean was elected first president of the York Chamber in 1909. He was followed in office by H. Wasbers, A.B. Farquhar, J. Calvin Strayer, D. Scott Bruce, Max Grumbacher, and Walter McBlain.

The year 1891 saw the formation of an exclusive club for some of York's businessmen. Named to honor the Marquis de Lafayette, the Lafayette Club eventually took over the Philip Albright Small house on the corner of Duke and Market streets. The club now welcomes women and still serves as an important sounding board, where community leaders can review the events of the day and stimulate action on community or business projects. Exclusivity came to York County in another form that year when John Luther Long, a Hanover resident, saw the publication of his short story, *Madame Butterfly*, in *Century Magazine*. The story was later staged by David Belasco, then turned into an opera by Puccini. The now-famous opera had its American premiere at the Metropolitan Opera House in New York City in 1906.

The next year, 1899, brought to York another prestigious social organization. The York Country Club was formed by Grier Hersh, Francis Farquhar (son of A.B.), Smyser Williams, W.H. Lanius, Horace Keesey, S. Fahs Smith, and several other leading York businessmen. Hersh had laid out his

own golf course in 1894 on his estate called "Springdale." That property covered the present 800 and 900 blocks of the east side of South George Street and the estate's carriage house can be seen today at 950 South Duke Street. The Hersh home had separate wine and mushroom cellars, a large octagonal ballroom, a natural outdoor amphitheater, croquet grounds, and a conservatory crowded with exotic plants. Hersh was so enthusiastic about a country club that he erected a clubhouse (designed by J.A. Dempwolf) on land on the north side of the present-day Country Club Road, which he had bought with Francis Farquhar. He leased it, along with the grounds, to the new country club board. Those grounds, many years later, became the York College of Pennsylvania campus.

The club's nine-hole golf course was opened on July 1, 1900, and in 1915 Francis Farquhar bought Hersh's interest in the estate, which was still being leased to the club. Farquhar lived on the hill at the south side of Country Club Road and he had promised his wife that as long as they lived at their residence, called "Edgecomb," their property would front on a golf course.

In 1925 the club, outgrowing its first home, acquired land to the southwest in the Crow's Nest area, built a new 18-hole golf course, and a new clubhouse that is still used today.

The year after the local Chamber of Commerce was organized, B.M. Root founded the B.M. Root Company to manufacture woodworking machinery, becoming the first company of its kind in York. In 1899 the Dentists' Supply Company was founded.

This period ended with the grandest celebration in York's history—the Sesqui-Centennial of the erection of York County, held September 3–6, 1899. On the morning of September 4, M.B. Gibson, chairman of the committee that organized the celebration, gave an address of welcome at the Opera House. Then the Honorable John W. Bittinger gave a speech on the Germans, Robert C. Bair discussed the Scotch-Irish, and historian-teacher George R. Prowell talked about the Quakers. These three speeches highlighted "the three classes of people who composed the original settlers of York County." Though the makeup of York's population had changed considerably, there was still strong evidence of those three original groups in York's bloodline.

There were many other activities connected with the Sesqui-Centennial celebration, but the most remarkable was the September 5 industrial parade. One hundred thousand people crowded the streets to watch the parade of 168 floats. Many of the parade decorations had been created by Watt Brothers and Company. (York's industrial parades were popular community events in those days and combined the community's love of parades with its pride in the ever-growing number of highly praised industrial products.) For this parade, according to George Prowell, "Centre Square was decorated with four triumphal arches . . . forty feet wide, and twelve feet deep, so that they could be seen at a great distance. Between the arches in each angle of the square were two heroic columns, supporting Corinthian capitals and globes, stuck full of flags. These arches and columns were . . . provided with electric light. The scene at night, when the several thousand lights were lit, was very impressive and delighted the people."

It is likely that some of the music used in the Sesqui-Centennial Parade had been composed in York. Roland F. Seitz, born in Shrewsbury Township, wrote dozens of marches and other compositions, and his works were performed and recorded by some of the country's leading music groups. Seitz had been educated at Dana's Musical Institute (now a part of Youngstown State University in Ohio) and his music was often compared to John

Above
The elegance of the Colonial Hotel on York's Centre Square reflected the city's era of growth and maturity at the turn of the century. The H.S. Schmidt and Company building is shown at right. Courtesy, Sunday News.

Above right
The use of electricity added to the festive air of many of York's celebrations, including the "Moneybak" display at P. Wiest's Sons store. The arch in front of the store proclaims "Welcome Knights." (HSYC)

Right
At night, thousands of electric lights decorated the 1899 Sesqui-Centennial arches. (HSYC)

Philip Sousa's.

A little more than a year after the celebration of the Sesqui-Centennial, the community engaged itself in another joyful festivity. On New Year's Eve, 1900, hundreds of people gathered in Centre Square to await midnight. When the hands of the town clock in the steeple of Christ Lutheran Church indicated the arrival of the new century, a cannon at the soldiers' monument of Penn Common fired a salute and bells rang from churches, factories, and fire-engine houses. The city band struck up a patriotic march and Company A of the Pennsylvania National Guard fired a series of salutes. Then came fireworks, and York had welcomed itself into the 20th century.

In 1901 the Maryland & Pennsylvania Railroad, which Yorkers affectionately called the "Mom and Pop," was formed by consolidating several smaller lines. In 1902 the Carlisle Market was established at Carlisle Avenue near the York Fair Grounds.

The manufacture of cigars in York County involved 80 separate factories by 1907. The town also had become an important carriage manufacturer. As H. Dietz Keller, a great-grandson of one of the founders of York Wagon Gear and a great-nephew of another, has written: "York, in the heart of an area with natural resources of fine timber, with fine craftsmen, and with a great deal of agriculture, was a natural spot for the manufacturing of a large number of vehicles. From among its number of small carriage builders emerged several companies which later became nationally known."

The area also became known for its production of many other varied commodities, including chemicals, candies, roofing paper, silk clothing, furniture, wallpaper, machine parts, and wire products. All of this diversity and growth prompted local businessmen to form the Manufacturers' Association in 1906. A year later, Prowell describes the one-year old Manufacturer's Association as "an active and energetic body, composed of the leading manufacturers of York, who have aided in developing the material interests of the city." John C. Schmidt was elected the group's first president. Serving under him as vice-presidents were Thomas Shipley, S. Forry Laucks, and Francis Farquhar, successively.

The new century saw Yorkers voting Republican for the first time in decades, favoring Theodore Roosevelt over Democrat Alton B. Parker in 1904. At about that time the Woman's Club, which still flourishes today, started out at the home of Mrs. Grier Hersh on South George Street and Rathton Road. (The 47 founding members, incidentally, included women from the Eichelberger, Farquhar, Jessop, Smyser, and Small families.) In 1906 the York Art Club, a predecessor of the York Art Association active today, held its first meetings. Two years later the Visiting Nurse Association acquired its charter.

On April 6, 1904, York had one of its worst fires in history. A blaze swept through the York Carriage Company, claiming the lives of three city firemen. The Vigilant Company's John Henry Saltzgiver, Lewis M. Strubinger, and Horace Frank Strine all died in the blaze, which leveled the plant on North George Street. In 1928 York's Rescue Fire Company voted to take its name off a large statue that it had erected on Penn Common in 1900, rededicating it to the three men who lost their lives in the 1904 disaster and to seven other firefighters who had died in the line of duty subsequently.

After the Carriage Company fire, York's carriage industry experienced a decline. Some manufacturers saw this trend developing in the nation and, as in other times, they retooled and adapted their businesses for new products—in this case a new form of transportation, the automobile. In the next two decades, York would become one of the nation's leading auto centers.

The first stirrings of automotive interest in York arose in 1900, when, as Keller relates, "the first horseless carriage in York came down Main Street and then past the largest livery stable—chugging along, scaring the stable operator and a nearby coachman with his passengers and horses. The several large carriage and wagon builders in York realized what was happening."

Lowell W. Williams, Dietz's coauthor, takes up the story to tell about the most important car company to arise in York, the Pullman Company. "Nineteen ten and 1911 brought national fame to York's Pullman automobiles," he writes. "A [Pullman] Model 'K' was the winner in an 1,100-mile endurance race between Atlanta and New York, June 6–11, 1910. . . . On October 8, a Pullman Model 'O' won the Fairmount Park Road Race in Philadelphia." Pullman, Williams reports, began shipping automobiles to places as near as Philadelphia and as far away as Australia.

In 1914, when the town held 45,000 people and the county had more than 130,000, a healthy 10,851 worked in 247 plants to turn out almost $23 million worth of products. While York industrialists were forging state and national reputations in the automobile and other businesses, reports of the conflicts in Europe reached York. York leaders, in their board rooms and over lunch at the Lafayette Club, discussed the day's disheartening headlines. Some of them increased inventories in anticipation of future supply shortages and others reinforced manufacturing policies preparing for the worst.

The *York Dispatch*, anticipating war, took a survey of the community's resources and found that there were many factories in York that could be

A fire broke out at the York Art Store at 239 North George Street on April 21, 1912. The sign on the building across the alley advertises Coca-Cola for five cents. (HSYC)

pressed quickly into action for war production. "The plant of the W.H. Ottemiller Company has automatic machinery which could in a moment be turned to the manufacture of hand grenades," the *Dispatch* relates. "The A.B. Farquhar plant could turn out huge armored tractors and artillery carriages, and wagon bodies could be manufactured by the Pullman Company, the Bell Motor Car Company and the Martin Carriage Company. . . ." Even canteens could be made in York, it was reported.

But while war was presenting a sobering influence on community life, the city and county were still on the upswing. The Ancient Order Knights of the Mystic Chain, the Knights of Malta, the Fraternal Order of Eagles, the Brotherly Protective Order of Elks, the Order of Red Men, the Order of Odd Fellows, and the Tall Cedars of Lebanon all had York representatives in the new century. Their members made the community a center of fraternal activity. Yorkers' personal wealth had never looked better. The tax rate for that year was four mills on the dollar.

But the general prosperity could not save the once-mighty Pullman Company. As Lowell Williams tells it, "sales were down, working capital was at a low ebb, and the sterling reputation of Pullman [a reputation born of the Yorkers' devotion to fine craftsmanship] had been tarnished by some 'lemons' that had been allowed to reach the marketplace. . . . [In addition], a few crucial bad management decisions were made by 'big city experts' brought to York. However, this damage could probably have been overcome had not World War I occurred at this time. Export business 'dried up,' financing became tight and competition from well capitalized mass-production manufacturers usurped the market from the limited production, modestly funded York auto producers."

The Pullman company's death was the major industrial calamity that York suffered during the World War I period. For the most part, the five decades after the war had been amazingly good ones. York had developed most of the characteristics that remain with it today, from the architectural flavor of its streets, to the diversity of its industries and the number of its people. York, after 300 years, had achieved the mark of a mature city: stability. Despite the failure of the Pullman company, York was enjoying prosperity in generous proportions and the population was generally content.

World War I would soon change that, however.

This 1908 Pullman automobile was built in York. It is parked in front of St. John's Episcopal Church on North Beaver Street. (HSYC)

Lorie Satz, a member of the York Collegiate Institute class of 1920-1921, dressed in the style typical of fashionable young ladies in York when "the Roaring Twenties" began. Courtesy, York College of Pennsylvania.

CHAPTER VII

WORLD WAR I AND THE "ROARING TWENTIES"

The evening edition of the *York Dispatch* on April 6, 1917, used a two-column, front-page headline to declare the news: "President Proclaims War Between U.S. and Germany." Despite his election promise to keep America free from the burgeoning conflict in Europe, President Wilson decided to enter the United States in "the war to end all wars." He had requested authorization from Congress four days earlier, and on April 6, Congress voted 373 to 50 to declare war. York's Congressman, A.R. Broadbeck, was among those in favor of the act.

Another headline in the same edition of the *Dispatch* commanded Yorkers to "Enlist at Once or Be Drafted." Predictably, the command was not necessary for York. The community already had prepared for the probability of war and for sending its men again to the battlefield. Even though 4 million of the eventual 4½ million Americans who fought in World War I were draftees, most of the 6,000 men and women who served from York County were enlisted participants.

Commodore C.M. Fahs, who was in charge of the Harrisburg district of mobilization, noted that the district, of which York County was a part, had 62 applicants per day even though its daily quota was only five. "There is no lack of patriotism here," he said. Pennsylvania, in fact, led the New York State district by 700 percent in number of men signed up for the armed services. York County's draftees totaled 2,592—less than half the number of county citizens who served.

While so many of York-area men and women were engaged directly in the war efforts, county residents were aiding the cause on the home front. President Wilson called for higher food production on the nation's farms and Yorkers were prompt to act on his suggestion. Farm production was accelerated with the help of city people who volunteered to work the land, but, nevertheless, shortages soon occurred. Sugar had to be rationed at four pounds per person each month, and since many farmers sold their herds of milk cows, butter and related products were also in short supply. Most citizens, even in the city, kept their own gardens so that the shortages were little more than inconveniences.

Sadly for most Yorkers, the city's two breweries, the Keystone Brewing Company and the York Brewing Company, were forced to close their doors as a grain-conservation measure in November 1918. A *Dispatch* article, however, pointed out that there were enough alcoholic beverages to last the county until May, making Yorkers better off, in this respect, than most other communities. Theodore R. Helb, owner of the Keystone Brewing Company, announced that he would not lay off the firm's employees, but would put them to work in painting and repair jobs. In the northern part of the county, the York Haven Paper Company announced that its 300 employees would receive a five percent salary bonus to offset the increased cost of living, and other companies followed suit.

The York community supported the war effort in other ways. York bakers created a "Victory Loaf," which substituted other cereals for wheat in order to save that valuable grain for the men at the front. Campaigns were held to collect worn clothing for Belgian and French refugees and to gather linen for French hospitals. In order to ensure that the military had enough carbon, which was used in gas masks to absorb the poisonous mustard gas, Yorkers gathered peach stones, apricot pits, plum pits, olive pits, date seeds, walnut shells, hickory nut shells, butternut shells, and cherry pits for use in the manufacture of this important commodity. Yorkers adopted "heatless Mondays" and other conservation methods, and collection drives were headed up by community residents, such as Clinton W. Schultz, Charles E. Moul, C.F. Bauserman, J.V. Kleffel, M.W. Naill, Charles E. Sprenkle, and H.W. Miller.

The Woman's Club of York initiated a War Relief Committee to do sewing for French hospitals that were caring for American soldiers. Members of the Woman's Club also made garments for refugees and collected gold to sell in fund-raising drives for the hospitals. The club "adopted" four French orphans and after war's end organized the establishment of a veteran's memorial—a living row of trees lining the highway from Wrightsville to Abbottstown.

Yorkers subscribed $30.5 million to five "Liberty Loans," and leaders of the bond promotions proudly pointed out that the sum represented an average of $200 per person for the entire county. A total of $2.18 million in "War Stamps" was sold in the York Square, from a replica of the Colonial Court House (quickly renamed the "Victory House"). A War Chest was subscribed at $425,000 during the same period.

Several Yorkers achieved national prominence for their efforts on behalf of the war. Grier Hersh, president of the York National Bank and the York Gas Company, was appointed chairman of the National Defense Committee and the Liberty Loan Committee. Hersh also served as the Federal Food Administrator for York County in charge of distributing food to the hundreds of Yorkers who were without basic sustenance. Working with Hersh was John C. Schmidt, chain manufacturer and the president of the Schmidt and Ault Paper Company. Schmidt called a meeting of influential York citizens to form the local chapter of the American Red Cross. He devoted his energies full-time to the organization of the York County chapter until the spring of 1918, when he was called to Washington to head up the Chain Section of the War Industries Board.

But before the war was over, 196 Yorkers would die either on the battlefield or in hospitals. As a tribute to them, the community erected a large white replica of the "winged Victory of Samothrace" in front of the Court House. Four bronze plaques bearing the names of those who had died were installed on the Court House's pillars, and memorial services were held in churches across York County.

Several of the York volunteers had been women. Jeannette Zinn, a resident of West College Avenue and an honor graduate of York High School, had been valedictorian and class poet, and before volunteering for the service was captain of the winning team in the War Thrift Stamp contest. She died, like so many other Americans during the war, a victim of pneumonia in the United States Hospital in Liverpool, England. Her former employers at the C.H. Bear & Company furnished a room in her memory in the Girl's Club of York.

Facing page

Left
A sign displaying the slogan "Lest We Forget" on the York County Court House reminded Yorkers of their sons and daughters who fought in World War I. The *Winged Victory* statue was erected in front of the Court House in memory of York Countians who fought in the war. (HSYC)

Right
C.H. Bear, dry-goods and notions store, became Bear's Department Store, one of the most popular retail businesses in York. (HSYC)

Facing page

Left
Yorkers celebrated the end of World War I with a parade on November 16, 1918, five days after the Armistice. Courtesy, Sunday News.

Right
An emergency open-air hospital was set up on the York Fair Grounds when a flu epidemic hit the city in 1918. From the first of October 1918 to mid-January 1919, more than 6,500 cases of influenza were reported in York. (HSYC)

One of the first Yorkers who had entered the war—and one of the youngest to die—was Corporal Raymond F. Knighton. Knighton, who had lived on Walnut Street, had enlisted on July 6, 1916, at the age of 15. He was killed in France, in the Meuse-Argonne offensive, on October 4, 1918, a little more than a month before the Armistice ended the fighting on November 11.

The Yorker who most distinguished himself for heroics, however, was Captain Rodney W. Polack. A resident of the McClellan Heights section of York, Polack led his company in capturing 205 prisoners, including several German officers, before he was killed at Cunel, France, on October 14, 1918.

Toward the end of World War I, news of American victories reached York and the community began planning its Armistice celebrations. Ironically, inaccurate information triggered a false Armistice celebration in York several days before the Tuesday, November 11 signing. When reliable news came that day, however, the city and county joined the nation in exclamations of victory, including bell ringing, singing in the streets, and the banging of pot lids.

There was only one appropriate way for the community to celebrate an event as important as the Armistice: a grand parade was planned for the

following Saturday. Lining the streets to view the proceedings were 100,000 jubilant Yorkers, who applauded the 20,000 participants, including 50 bands and 13 drum and bugle corps, in the 7½-mile parade.

Undercutting the mood of celebration that the end of World War I inspired was a terrible flu epidemic that swept York between October and December of 1918. From the first of October to mid-January, when the epidemic was finally controlled, more than 6,500 cases of influenza were reported. On a single day, 2,012 children were reported home sick from York County schools. Three members of one family died within days of each other and makeshift hospitals were set up in a Beaver Street hall and also at the York Fair Grounds. Many of the community's women were active in treating the sick, including Helen V. Delaplane, who wrote a column about her experiences for the Lutheran Social Services' newsletter. "In many families," Miss Delaplane recalls, "all members were ill, so that no one was left to care for them. People were warned not to gather in crowds. All places where crowds were accustomed to assembling—movies, schools, churches, etc.—were closed. Everyone was urged to stay at home. Doctors and nurses were working at top speed. . . . Neighbors and relatives were helping each other. Under all of it was fear. Flu was a killer—what could be done? An open-air hospital seemed to be the answer. The York Fairgrounds was chosen as the site. . . . Volunteers became nurses' aides . . . the greatest number being teachers. . . . The nurse who had been appointed as [our] supervisor came down with the flu the third day." (The nurse later recovered.)

Even while York County was experiencing a terrifying flu epidemic, it was gaining in population. The 1920 census showed that 47,499 people lived in the city and 144,521 people lived in the county. And some of those people were making an impact that reached far beyond York's borders, especially in politics.

In 1919 York's state representative, Henry Lanius, who was himself blind, introduced Pennsylvania's first legislation to provide the handicapped with special education. In 1921 Samuel S. Lewis, a past president of the Vigilant Fire Company, became Pennsylvania's state auditor, initiating a 33-year political career that would see him elected or appointed state treasurer, secretary of highways, secretary of forest and waters, and lieutenant governor. A county park was named in his honor. Yorkers, in this era, were undergoing a political change that had been, perhaps, presaged in 1904, when residents broke their long Democratic trend by voting for Theodore Roosevelt rather than the Democratic candidate Alton B. Parker. Yorkers' preferences for practicality over dogma, and moderation over excess, pointed them to a different party in this election and those characteristics rule county politics to this day. Roosevelt, too, was a friendly grandfather type with sparkling eyes—in contrast to the dull Parker.

In the 1920s Yorkers supported all three Republican candidates for President, helping to elect Warren G. Harding in 1920, Calvin Coolidge in 1924, and Herbert Hoover in 1928. They were all given warm welcomes when they visited York during the decade. Harding and Hoover made campaign stops on September 27, 1920, and July 14, 1928, respectively; Coolidge visited York as President on November 19, 1926. Future President Franklin D. Roosevelt also campaigned in York in 1920. Then assistant secretary of the navy, Roosevelt had been selected as the running mate of Democratic nominee Governor James M. Cox of Ohio.

The Yorker shift to Republican loyalties had been effected, in part, by the feeling that President Wilson had gone too far in his expansion of federal power and that his zeal for reform had derailed traditional Democratic, laissez-faire business policies. But the abandonment of the Democratic

Party extended into state and local politics as well. Yorkers supported Republican gubernatorial candidates Gifford Pinchot, elected in 1922, and John S. Fisher, who was sent to the Governor's Mansion in 1926. Republican Congressmen also received York's backing, except in 1922, when Democrat Samuel Glatfelter was favored over shoe-merchant Mahlon Haines, the Republican nominee.

Haines, though a well-known York philanthropist, was probably too much of a local character for Yorkers to entrust with high office. He owned a chain of shoe stores in Pennsylvania and Maryland and called himself the "Shoe Wizard." He promised young people money if they would give up smoking immediately and forever, and he kept a small herd of buffalo on his farm for the amusement of Yorkers. Haines often sponsored essay contests, offering a $190 first prize to the student who wrote the best essay on the "Shoe Wizard's" accomplishments. Haines also waged an unsuccessful campaign to rename York's Royalist street names, including George, Princess, King, and others. But Mahlon Haines was as magnanimous as he was eccentric; he devoted himself to many community-service organizations, especially the Boy Scouts, and when he dissolved his business, he divided its assets among his 50 employees. Haines left an ersatz monument to his personality and accomplishments: a shoe-shaped house that now houses an ice cream shop and is still a tourist curiosity.

The postwar period was one of continuing prosperity for York, even though the number of industrial corporations had actually dropped to 218. But this was due to mergers and consolidations, not to a decline in growth. Those 218 factories produced finished products valued at $62,610,816, compared with a yield of $22,943,328 by the community's 247 plants in 1914.

During the late 1920s, York gained a reputation as the "Gateway to the East," because of its attractive location between Eastern and Western trade regions and because of its good transportation facilities and varied industry. The town also boasted 10 of the largest industrial plants in the United States. Those plants, according to a *Dispatch* article of 1928, led "all others in volume of production in icemaking and refrigeration machinery, bank safes and vaults, water turbines, artificial teeth, wallpaper, roofing paper, pretzels, baker's machinery, auto tire chains and commercial auto bodies."

York's prosperous automobile industry earned the community another nickname—the "Detroit of the East." During the peak of York's remarkable auto-manufacturing era, which spanned the years 1903 to 1930, there were some 30 factories in the county producing thousands of cars and trucks every year. During 1904 the Martin Parry Corporation alone turned out 20,000 vehicles. In the 1920s Martin Parry produced 65 body styles, including the Model T, which came off the factory lines at 500 a day.

This was the era, too, when York acquired a brand new hotel. Businessmen in the community had long felt the need for a high-quality modern hotel; in 1924 the Chamber of Commerce appointed a committee to study the acquisition of such a structure. A temporary board of directors was created that spearheaded a campaign to sell $1,175,000 worth of stock to cover the building costs of the new hotel. On that board were John L. Gerber, Charles H. Bear, W.S. Bond, Dr. C.P. Rice, Max Grumbacher, C. Elmer Smith, and Thomas Shipley. Land was purchased on the southwest corner of Market and Duke streets and the 198-room Yorktowne Hotel was opened on October 5, 1925. The community now could boast of an elegant downtown hotel that served both Yorkers and visitors from many miles away.

York's economic and political stability was challenged, however, by sweeping social changes—mostly affecting the town's youth—that had

Above, top left
Mahlon N. Haines, the "Shoe Wizard," was known for his philanthropy and was a noted figure in York for many years. The house he built in the shape of a shoe east of York is located today along busy Route 30 and remains a curiosity for passing travelers. (HSYC)

Above left
The first Pullman automobile, shown here, was built in York in 1903. York's automobile industry expanded to such an extent that the city earned the nickname "Detroit of the East." (HSYC)

Above
Members of the 1918-1919 York Collegiate Institute basketball team pose on the front steps of the school. Dr. Bruce Grove, later a well known York physician, is shown holding the ball. Courtesy, York College of Pennsylvania.

begun to trouble the more conservative members of the older generation. The first issue to divide the York community was Prohibition, which had been enacted as a temporary city ordinance on July 1, 1919. Prohibition became law on January 16, 1920, when the federal Volstead Act went into effect.

But Yorkers had a family tradition of drinking that went back to Colonial days (and even further back through the families of European immigrants, especially Germans and Scotch-Irish), so Prohibition was often ignored or circumvented. Yorkers frequented speakeasies, bought bootleg liquor, or experimented with various "home brews" (which they drank themselves or sold to others). They found that "properly fermented, dandelions made a fairly decent wine with an equally decent kick." They also tried, with varying degrees of success, to make alcoholic beverages from raisins, cornmeal, vinegar, cider, and berries. Some resorted to drinking items with high alcoholic content, such as vanilla extract, cough syrups, bay rum hair tonic, and even wood alcohol. The more creative Yorkers discovered that pouring two quarts of boiling water into an old whiskey barrel, and letting it stand for awhile, produced a drink "with sufficient kick to paralyze a healthy elephant." As a result, the demand for old whiskey barrels reached unprecedented proportions.

According to a 1928 *York Dispatch*, bootlegging became so profitable that farmers spent much of their time engaged in this activity, leaving their wives sometimes to harvest the fields. Mayor E.S. Hugentugler said that bootlegging was so prevalent and accepted that he could do little to stop it, admitting that even members of the York Police Department were involved. Prohibition, at least in York, proved to be a disastrous experiment in which a majority of its citizenry simply ignored the law. An even more significant development in the "Roaring Twenties," however, was the growing schism between the generations. More and more young Yorkers became "flappers" and "sheiks," and their parents, for the most part, were not pleased.

According to authors Carl E. Hatch, Joseph B. Hicks, and Richard E. Kohler, in their Martin Library booklet, "York, Pa., in the Roaring 20s" (1973): "Older women were appalled to see younger women in short skirts, low-cut blouses, rolled-down stockings and peek-a-boo waists."

Citizens registered complaints with Mayor Hugentugler, asking him to revive an old borough ordinance that made it unlawful for women "to expose their calves or shoulders or to appear on the street or in public in any dress such as attracts undue attention to the body or is in any way immodest." But the mayor refused, saying that he believed in personal liberty and thought that "people, both minors and adults, should have freedom to dress according to their individual tastes."

Another community leader who received complaints regularly was the Superintendent of York City Schools, Atreus Wanner. Wanner told the complaining citizens that he, too, was a believer in personal liberty and would, under no circumstances, institute a dress code for city schools.

The youths of York, of course, were merely responding to the "Jazz Age" ethos that F. Scott Fizgerald had chronicled in *This Side of Paradise* (1920), and which his own example helped to popularize. Movies, popular songs, novels, endless magazine articles, and especially advertising all served to reinforce the carefree, sophisticated, distinctly urban image of "Flaming Youth" that was having an effect on even America's smaller communities. Radios and automobiles also helped York out of isolation felt by many county teenagers. Although York did not yet have its own radio station, thousands owned the new entertainment box and listened to stations in Harrisburg, Washington, D.C., and other places. More people were moving into the city, too, and finding life there much more exciting than the routine of the farm.

But the changes in dress and manner, especially among women, were not well received by many York citizens. In addition to the short skirts and immodest blouses, citizens lodged complaints about the use of cosmetics. The Reverend Silas C. Swallow, a Methodist minister, sadly rebuked the "face-painting" women of the community. "In my boyhood days, about 80 years ago," the Reverend preached, "paint, powder, and rouge on a lady's lips and cheeks was so dim as to justify her denial of its presence. . . . Now . . . it is no uncommon thing to see a lass 'a la Paree,' walking the streets with her lover, peering into a mirror held in one hand, while with the other she smears her angel face with a bag of powder, paint and rouge— meanwhile, with the escort blowing his fetid breath surcharged with tobacco smoke into the same angel's face."

In 1922 one of the town's oldest druggists told a *York Dispatch* reporter that cosmetics sales had increased 200 percent over the last few years. He went on to add that not all his customers were young women and "the way some of the old girls doll up, you can't tell them from their daughters."

In 1924, when bobbed hair became the rage, Superintendent Wanner was again besieged with demands to institute appearance codes, this time covering hair as well as dress. Didn't the Bible itself, some of the complainants urged, say that it is an abomination for a woman to cut her hair? Wanner's response once more dismayed York's conservative older generation. "The school controllers of York," he declared, "have one regulation in regard to hair . . . and that is that the hair of the heads of pupils be free of pediculosis. That means, in plain words, 'cooties' are not allowed in pupils' hair."

The intensity of reaction that these changes in fashion and mores evoked was not entirely unwarranted. More than any previous generation, the young people of York—indeed of the whole country—considered themselves a distinct group. They had just been through the disrupting, emotionally devas-

Farquhar Park was the site of a large Easter egg hunt in the 1920s. Courtesy, Harry J. McLaughlin.

tating experience of World War I, and in the subsequent peacetime prosperity, they went on something of a rampage. Jazz music, speakeasies, fancy cars, and flamboyant dress were not insignificant; they were symbols of a virtual revolution in the social structure, and represented, at least to the young people, a break from the past. As authors Hatch, Hicks, and Kohler put it: "Whereas Yorkers were offended at bobbed hair, cosmetics and short skirts, they were shocked at the younger generation's smoking, vulgar dancing and petting. . . . They were horrified at rumors that the young were frequenting speakeasies and brothels. Bobbed hair, cosmetics and short skirts entailed a revolution in manners. But smoking, vulgar dancing, petting, and the spread of venereal disease involved something far more serious. This was a revolution in morals."

As in every revolution, there were counter-revolutionaries. York's first policewoman, Mabel Rozelle, was foremost among them. On a Saturday night, April 1, 1922, Officer Rozelle raided a favorite York dance hall, pulling apart dance partners and announcing that henceforth "there are certain dances that will not be tolerated by the York police department, two of which are 'The Toddle' and 'The Cheek to Cheek.' " She also set up special classes for York men, where she warned them of "flappers who looked for pickups in dance halls and who give you venereal disease."

York's movie houses and theaters were often mentioned in complaints to authorities during this era, and they, too, no doubt contributed to the "revolution in morals." To take a typical year, in 1925 the newly opened Strand Theater was offering Colleen Moore in *The Desert Flower*, with musical accompaniment provided by "Herbert Seiler at the Wurlitzer." The Orpheum featured a live show—"McIntyre and Heath, in Trumping the Ace"—and reminded patrons that Monday was "Burlesque Day" at the theater. Reginald Denny starred in the film, *California Straight Ahead*, at the Jackson Theater; and the Coliseum was hosting a Charleston Queen contest and a Fox trot-waltz competition. Yorkers could see *A Girl of the Limberlost* at the Hippodrome; Evelyn Brent was appearing on the screen at the Wizard in *Midnight Molly*; and the Scenic featured *The Hidden Menace* with Charles Hutchison.

While the majority of Yorkers, young and old, enjoyed these new diversions, and soon made visits to dance halls, and movie and vaudeville houses a part of their weekly routine, one segment of the community demonstrated strong opposition—the Ku Klux Klan. York, because of its many theaters, was being called a "banner burlesque town," and its entertainments were attracting large numbers of out-of-town visitors. Spurred on by the "old stand-pat conservatives," the Klan began waging war against the

Facing page
The Hippodrome theater at 121 West Market Street screened the film *The Serpent's Fang* in 1913. (HSYC)

Below left
A York Collegiate Institute party was held in 1920 in Mary Gotwald's barn at the rear of 153 East Market Street. Mary Gotwald is the first on the left in the back row. Courtesy, York College of Pennsylvania.

Below
The annual Halloween parade is a tradition in York. One department of the York Manufacturing Company marched in a Halloween parade in the mid-1920s dressed as clocks, with Father Time leading the group holding a sign, "Don't be Alarmed—Time Is Passing." The group assembled in front of the plant on North Hartley Street. The parade is still one of York's most popular yearly events. (HSYC)

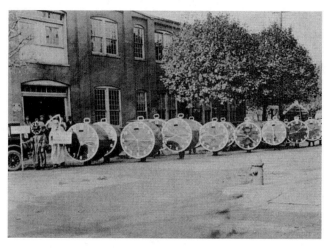

new turpitude and the changing morals that preceded it.

A June 10, 1924, article in the *York Dispatch* tells the story of one of the KKK's many raids: "Forty hooded and gowned members of the KKK, said to be from Shrewsbury and Jacobus, attended a picnic in a woods near the Susquehanna Trail, 12 miles south of York, Saturday night, and put a stop to numerous petting parties that were in progress. . . . It is said the Klansmen rounded up a number of women who were deserted by their male escorts when the Klansmen approached. One of the ardent male wooers, however, was identified. He is a married man with several children and resides in a town in the southern part of York County. The women were taken into custody and promised the Klansmen to reform and never again return to the picnic woods."

While the Klan, in other parts of the country, were known for their violent vigilantism against blacks, Catholics, Jews, and other minorities, in York they appear to have tried to assume the role of "moral caretaker." With the exception of an occasional cross burning on a Catholic family's lawn, the group's activities in York did not have a racial tone or a strong impact. As late as the 1970s and the 1980s, though, the Klan in York County made itself visible by planning rallies and parades, many of which never came off. Perhaps the no-nonsense, law-abiding attitude of Yorkers has all along dampened the spirit of the KKK in its York mission.

But the Klan received early and vehement opposition from Mayor Hugentugler, who proclaimed: "I do not intend to tolerate in this city such an un-American organization as the KKK." The mayor may not have been as upset at the challenge to his authority that the Klan represented as he was at

This view looking west shows Market Street in 1924. The Bon Ton Department Store is in the left-hand corner. (HSYC)

their principles, since he soon began a moral crusade of his own. On October 20, 1928, he launched a campaign to break up the "canned heat" parties, which a tailor on South Hartley Street had been hosting. The daily newspapers reported arrests of several people, who were drunk on a dozen or more different alcoholic concoctions.

Other events toward the end of the decade, especially the York Sesqui-Centennial in 1927, the "Hex Murder" trial in 1928, and the stock market crash of 1929, took Yorkers' minds off the changing moral climate. But the "Roaring Twenties" had altered the social structure of the town forever, and the order and piety of its early years were significantly changed.

York's Sesqui-Centennial, marking the 150th anniversary of the time when it had been the nation's capital, gave the community an opportunity for self-congratulation. It responded by producing a lavish gala, including parades, music, decorations, and grand pageantry. But the Sesqui-Centennial was a strictly local concern. The next year a bizarre murder would bring reporters from newspapers and magazines across the country flocking to York.

On November 28, 1928, three men robbed and brutally murdered Nelson Rehmeyer, at his rural York County farmhouse. A robbery-murder, while hardly an everyday occurrence in York, was not by itself enough to send shock waves around the world. What attracted the attention of reporters was the motive for the crime: the murderers wanted to obtain a lock of Rehmeyer's hair, thereby enabling them to break a spell they believed him to have cast.

Nelson Rehmeyer was a large, powerfully built man. He stood over six feet tall and weighed close to 200 pounds. His wife had left him, taking their two daughters with her, but they made frequent visits and there was no bitterness. When the young girls were sick, they were taken to their father to be "tried for." Rehmeyer, like many of the rural folk in York County, was a practitioner of faith healing and "powwowing."

Powwowing was based on John George Hohman's book of recipes, incantations, and talismans, *The Long Lost Friend: A Collection of Mysterious and Invaluable Remedies Good for Man and Beast.* The book had been published in German in 1820, in Reading, Pennsylvania, and was widely read throughout Pennsylvania Dutch country for generations afterwards. The

Below left
This view, looking north from Centre Square, shows George Street in 1927. Paintings depicting heroes of the American Revolution were part of the city's Sesqui-Centennial celebration marking the time Congress was in York. Courtesy, Sunday News.

Below
The house of Nelson Rehmeyer in Rehmeyer's Hollow in southern York County was the site of the famous York County "Hex Murder" on November 27, 1928. Courtesy, Harry J. McLaughlin.

strongholds of powwowism (also referred to as witchcraft and "brauching") were communities, or areas of communities, where the people were largely uneducated and subject to superstitions passed down from the old country.

The three men charged with Rehmeyer's death were believers in, and sometime practitioners of, powwowism. John Blymire, 32, was a fourth-generation, self-proclaimed witch, who worked in a York cigar factory on East Princess Street. He had recently moved into town to take a room in a boarding house on Prospect Street after a series of failures. His wife had divorced him; his crops had failed; his chickens laid no eggs. He was forced to support himself at the cigar factory, and with the small amount of money he received from powwowing. But his "patients" often complained that his "trying" for them did not help, and eventually Blymire could not even perform the lowliest of witch duties: "the stopping of blood." Trying for a patient, in powwow lore, involved the recitation of chants by a witch and the offering of strange prescriptions to overcome hexes cast by another pow-wower, or to cure ailments or achieve ends.

Blymire had befriended John Curry, who looked several years older than his age of 14, at the cigar factory where Curry was also employed. The third man in the Rehmeyer case was Wilbert Hess, 18, whose father had a farm outside the city where he and his sons tended their plentiful crops. Mrs. Hess had a stand at the Central Market three days a week, which brought her "pin money" for the niceties of Pennsylvania Dutch life. But the Hess family, like Blymire, had been visited recently by disaster. Mr. Hess's crops had failed, his hogs had become ill, and he had suffered nervousness and loss of appetite. He visited many powwowers, convinced that someone had put a hex on him. When he consulted Blymire, he was told that a hex had, indeed, been put on his farm and Blymire assured him that for $40 he would find out who had cast the spell. Hess only had $10 and Blymire accepted the money with no complaint.

Blymire attempted to determine who had bewitched the Hess farm, but eventually visited another witch in desperation. Mrs. Nellie Noll, a resident of Lancaster County's riverside community, Marietta, was 90 years old and the most famous practitioner of powwowism in the area. For the same $10 Hess had given Blymire, she divined that the witch who had cast the spell was Nelson D. Rehmeyer of Rehmeyer's Hollow in York County's North Hopewell Township. For good measure, she added John Curry's name to the list of people Rehmeyer had hexed. She then gave Blymire instructions on how to break the spell. "Get the old witch's Bible and a lock of his hair," the River Witch said, "and bury the hair under eight feet of ground."

Blymire, accompanied by Curry, made a trip to Rehmeyer's Hollow. They sat around Rehmeyer's home chatting as old friends, and at Rehmeyer's invitation spent the night. Blymire "tried" for hours to beat down the supposed power of the man asleep above him, but to no avail. The following morning they returned to York, determined to return with help.

The next night, under a full Thanksgiving moon, the two men returned with Wilbert Hess, and what had begun as the breaking of a spell ended up in brutal murder. The three men struggled with Rehmeyer in an attempt to obtain a lock of his hair. Blymire, Curry, and Hess all struck Rehmeyer with various heavy objects; he was tied down and his shirt was set on fire. After the men left, the braying of Rehmeyer's unfed mule led a neighbor to discover the murdered man's blood-soaked and charred body.

Wilbert Hess, apparently plagued with guilt, made a full confession the next day to District Attorney Amos W. Herrman. On November 30, the *York Dispatch* carried the headline: "Murder Farmer to Get Lock of Hair to Break Spell, Three Confess."

The resulting trial, involving weeks of testimony by 34 witnesses, caused a national sensation. The city of York sat in resentful shock as the murder story, and the press reaction to it, unfolded. The *Philadelphia Record* called the Rehmeyer case "the weirdest and most curiously fascinating trial in the history of modern jurisprudence." The *New York World*, believing apparently that everyone in York was a powwower, called Yorkers "stupid clods" and "twentieth century anachronisms bound by fifteenth century superstitions." It was hinted in the national press that there were more than a thousand witches, "powwowers," hexers, or "brauchers" in York County practicing their art, using the witch's handbook, and distributing protective cloths called "himmelsbriefs."

There is no doubt that the reporters' hunger for a dramatic story blew the "Hex Murder," as it was called, out of all proportion. Most Yorkers were embarrassed that their town was suddenly being viewed as a hotbed of superstition and black magic. They knew that powwowing existed; many had been "tried for" without incident; and believers in witchcraft had largely been viewed as an eccentric, but harmless element in the community. The trial, and the unwanted attention it garnered, would change that, however. The three men who had caused the uproar were convicted of first-degree murder. Blymire and Hess were sentenced to life imprisonment, and the minor, John Curry, was given 10 to 20 years.

A wide educational campaign against the practice of witchcraft was launched, led by prominent physicians, business leaders, local reporters, and others. The York County Medical Society conducted a study of powwowing and the state departments of health and education offered help in eradicating the various superstitions and practices from Pennsylvania Dutch lore. York County Coroner L.U. Zech, in later investigations, reported seven known powwowers who practiced witchcraft as a business, and four deaths that were believed to have been caused because individuals had relied on witchcraft instead of seeking proper medical attention. Those who participated in the educational campaign asserted that "York County is not any worse or so bad as some other places in the incidence of powwowing practice," and "no witches ever were hanged in Pennsylvania for their beliefs."

With the coming of radio, television, and increased travel and educational opportunities, powwowing has all but disappeared in subsequent generations. The murderers eventually were released. Blymire, after serving 23 years, had his life sentence commuted by Governor John S. Fine, and he moved to Philadelphia where he worked as a janitor. Hess and Curry were each paroled after serving 10 years.

Forty years after the "Hex Murder" made front-page news across the nation, interest in the case was revived by a book about it by Arthur H. Lewis. Tourists and reporters trudged down the roads of southern York County looking for "Rehmeyer's Hollow." In 1969 advance men for a movie producer began gathering material and scouting locations, but the proposed film was never made, and the incident once again faded into welcomed obscurity.

While the attention of some Yorkers in the late 1920s was on powwowing, others in the community were preoccupied with more positive developments. The York Hospital board of directors announced it would begin construction, in January 1929, of a new facility on top of a hill in the Springdale section of Spring Garden Township. Coinciding with the start of construction was the annexation of the Springdale area into the city; a section of West Manchester Township became the city's 14th ward when it was also annexed.

During the same period Lee Reineberg, president of the York Chamber of Commerce, joined Mayor Jacob E. Weaver to lead efforts to acquire new

Christmas decorations for the city, and the York Gas Company, which had been purchased five years before by the Pennsylvania Gas and Electric Company, announced plans for a $140,000 improvement project. Conditions seemed just as favorable for the York Water Company, where president C.M. Kerr announced that water company capital stock would double from $3 million to $6 million. This was also the era of great expansion for the York Water Company, with the construction of Lake Williams. The company's reforestation program benefited the community and brought widespread notice from faraway places. In the area of transportation, the Pennsylvania Railroad was adding extra trains to its routes and handling the highest number of shipments since the war.

As a further indication of the era's prosperity, Lancaster and York counties were planning a new one and one-quarter mile long bridge over the Susquehanna at a cost of $2 million. The possibility of an airport for the York area also was being discussed. The city had $1,691,193 worth of building projects near completion and the evening newspaper reported that new shopping records had been set in the Christmas season of 1928 for downtown stores. The milling crowds that year had to dodge construction on the Square, too: the city was in the midst of building its underground comfort facilities. Above the ground, volunteers were collecting for the welfare drive to benefit York's poor people.

At the same time, 800 volunteers from 50 York churches were taking a census of the community's religious population as part of the celebration attending "the 19th Centenary of the Ministry of Jesus Christ." Heading that effort was the Reverend Doctor W.H. Feldmann of the Union Lutheran

Church who was, no doubt, pleased with the final census, which showed that more than half of York's churchgoing population was Lutheran. Helping the Lutheran minister and his large band of volunteers were numerous York companies—including the A.B. Farquhar Company, the Home Furniture Company, and the York Body Corporation—which blew their factory whistles when York churches marked the Centenary with other Christians around the world.

The jubilation, however, was in sharp contrast to events of the coming months, as America faced the impending failure of its economic system. But York, because of its healthy economy, its many locally owned and operated industries and businesses, and its fiscally conservative outlook and continued expansion, was cushioned from many of the disastrous effects that other American communities suffered from after the stock market crash of 1929. The York community maintained its hopeful spirit, drawing on the pioneer strength that had been handed down to most of the community's leaders. York was a stable center of diverse power and, while the world seemed to be falling apart around them, Yorkers worked on, convinced that this adversity, too, would pass.

Facing page
Streetcars traverse York's Centre Square in the 1920s. The speed limit is posted at 10 mph and parking is allowed for 15 minutes. Bear's Department Store is at the right. (HSYC)

Below
Smiling York residents find pleasure in the water at Eim Beach in the late 1920s, unaware of the hard times to come. Courtesy, Sunday News.

The last streetcars on Market Street, looking east from the Square, were seen in 1939. The kiosk in the background was restored and returned to the Square in the spring of 1981. Courtesy, Sunday News.

CHAPTER VIII

THE DEPRESSION YEARS

While the stock market hovered on the precipice of disaster in October 1929, York was enjoying almost unbelievable prosperity. The previous month had been a banner period for the county's cigar industry, which employed some 10,000. York Mayor Jacob E. Weaver announced that no tax increase would be necessary for the next fiscal year, and York stores and shops were still experiencing their best pre-Christmas sales ever. Banks in York were issuing record numbers of savings checks—13,072 in all—and total clearings for the year would also set new records.

Construction in the county was in high gear. A new $30-million dam project was approved for the Susquehanna River, with construction slated for spring. A new junior high school—named for York inventor Phineas Davis—was being erected in the city. Still another construction project was in the works: the new bridge, spanning the Susquehanna between Wrightsville and Columbia, less than 10 miles east of York. The concrete multiple-arch structure, which at one and a quarter miles long was said to be the longest bridge of its type in the world, joined U.S. Route 30 running from York to Lancaster. During opening day ceremonies, on October 1, 1930, crowds stood cheering on the banks of the river.

Two Yorkers were among the first to cross the newly opened bridge. A.B. Meisky, who lived on Court Avenue, drove his motorcycle across; and Guy Leber, who resided at 1206 West King Street, battled sand left over from construction to rollerskate back and forth across the length of the bridge.

Another event related to York's expanding transportation network would later close out the decade: the dedication of the York Airport, 10 miles west of York, on October 25, 1939. Thirty thousand people were on hand for the official opening of the new airfield. The field accommodated small planes traveling to and from York and was eventually heavily used by many executives of York industry and business who invested in their own planes. One York man who watched airplane traffic of the day with special interest was W.H. "Jack" Hespenheide, who had much earlier become fascinated by the science of aeronautics.

Hespenheide had first become interested in flying as a young man in the 1920s, when barnstormers had flown into York to perform their antics. He left town in 1929 to train as a pilot in Texas. When he returned, he joined four other York men—Lester Sipe, Roman Smyser, Raymond Ruth, and Addison Millard—to form the York Flying Service in 1931. Their first airfield, located east of the city on a farm owned by York historian Joseph Kindig II, became known as Fayfield. Hespenheide and his group later moved to the York Airport at Thomasville, where they operated until World War II. At that time some of the partners were wooed into service as pilot trainers.

The year 1930, however, saw about 2,500 Yorkers out of work due to the beleaguered national economy. On the brighter side, 500 people were employed on the new Safe Harbor Dam; 250 were at work on the Phineas Davis School; and still other workers were employed by the local utilities and the city, which had enacted special work programs for the jobless.

York's 62 churches, with 28,285 members, also initiated help programs, and even the Ku Klux Klan was distributing food to the unemployed.

By 1931 there were nearly 5,100 people out of work in York County. Hundreds of garments were distributed to the community's poor at a distribution center set up to aid the jobless and penniless. Even that year had its good news, though. Construction of a new sewer on the city's west end would put many people to work; 20 acres of city land was set aside for the poor to farm; hosiery mills in the county were operating on 24-hour schedules; and a United States industry study revealed that York trade had topped the $36 million mark for the previous year. The York Telephone Company, the York Oil Burner Company, the York Water Company, and the A.B. Farquhar Company all had expansion programs under way and a government loan was granted York that created 500 new jobs.

Railroad transportation was further expanded in 1932, when the Pennsylvania Railroad Company added two passenger lines to its schedule of more than 50 trains passing through York every day. Communications were also expanded, well beyond York's surrounding lands, with the city's first radio station, WORK, which went on the air in 1932. Located at 13 South Beaver Street, WORK's middle-of-the-road programming soon made it an informational and entertainment mainstay of the York community. Its news coverage won numerous state awards. The station changed hands several times, and its call letters changed with new owners and new formats.

The year 1932 saw a decline in York's jobless number as 3,000 were counted among those with relief cards. At the same time several York industries were receiving government contracts and a new paper factory was being built in York Haven.

Nineteen thirty-two was also the year of another visit by a well-known personage — even though when he came he was not yet well-known, and had he been, York would not have been pleased to receive him. Bruno Richard Hauptmann, later connected to the kidnapping and murder of the baby of American flyer Charles Lindbergh, came to York County in the late summer, several months after the Lindbergh kidnapping. He was looking for a farm property. Spring Grove realtor Clayton E. Moul showed the German emigrant several farms, but the potential buyer said that none was quite what he was looking for. Local residents later speculated that Hauptmann had probably been searching for a hideout, and that he came to York County because he knew that many of its inhabitants spoke Pennsylvania Dutch, a dialect close to his own language. The Spring Grove realtor noticed the man's picture in a national newspaper some time after his York County visit, and only then realized that he might have been an unwilling accomplice in a bizarre and sad murder.

It was the uncertainty of the times—even though the community fared better than most—that caused York once again to shift political loyalties. In 1932, Yorkers voted for a Democratic President, Franklin D. Roosevelt, for the first time in more than three decades. In 1972, a booklet by Dr. G.A. Mellander and Dr. Carl E. Hatch, both of York College, stated that, after the late 1920s, Yorkers "perceived that Republican 'laissez-faireism' if carried too far . . . could be as undesirable as dogmatic, Democratic-Wilsonian 'interventionism.'"

One of the "practical and moderate" local candidates that Yorkers favored, regardless of political affiliation, was Herbert B. Cohen, counsel for John Blymire in the hex murder trial. Like Samuel S. Lewis before him, Cohen went from membership in the Vigilant fire brigade to political success. In 1933 Yorkers elected Cohen to the State House of Representatives.

He later became State Attorney General, and a member of the Pennsylvania Supreme Court until his retirement in 1970. Cohen was active in many community activities and, among other public-service projects, he helped a group of deaf Yorkers form the York Association of the Deaf in 1934. York eventually became a center for deaf activities, led by such people as Samuel Shultz and Henry Senft, who also held offices in state and national organizations serving the deaf. The Pennsylvania Society for the Advancement of the Deaf has had state conventions in York, and York deaf people are known across the country for their enthusiastic work in improving the standard of life for the hearing-impaired.

Probably because of York's relatively sound economic state, citizens were able to devote a good deal of time in the Depression years to entertaining themselves. They did so in grand style. The York Association of the Deaf initiated a wide social program that included captioned movies and shuffleboard tournaments. The York Little Theater was begun in the winter of 1932–1933. After informal meetings at various homes of theater-minded Yorkers, the theater had its first production (of Oscar Wilde's *Lady Windemere's Fan*) on December 14, 1933, directed by two of the founding members, Ida Frances Moody and her future husband, S. Barnitz Williams. On January 24, 1934, the York Little Theater hired J.F. Foster as its first full-time director. The Little Theater was sponsored by the York Recreation Commission, and used two rooms on the second floor of the York County Academy Building for rehearsals and other dramatic activities. Early York Little Theater presidents included George Hay Kain, Jr., Gilbert A. Dietz, Lucy Smith, Cassandra S. Brown, Samuel A. Gotwalt, William C. Wanbaugh, and Alverta Herbst Keller. (In May 1956, the community group moved into the former Elmwood Theater, which after several remodeling programs still serves YLT today.)

After a night at the theater, Yorkers could go to the corner bar and have a beer, since Prohibition had been repealed on April 6, 1933. Owners of 200 restaurants, hotels, cigar stores, and drugstores flooded the Internal Revenue Service after that date for federal permits "to relieve the extreme thirst of those who obeyed the restrictions imposed by the Prohibition laws."

For those who preferred music, the York Symphony Orchestra gave its first concert on April 18, 1933, under conductor George K. Raudenbush. Seven months later, the York Symphony Orchestra announced the next year's full season, under resident conductor, Sylvan Levin. Levin was succeeded by Louis Vyner and the symphony baton was later passed on to George Hurst, Robert Mandell, Francois Jaroschy, and James C. Pfohl.

As York was finding new sources of entertainment in 1933, it also battled with economic conditions at home. Theaters cut admission prices to lure moviegoers who could no longer afford normal prices, and the York Fair also cut its entrance fees in an attempt to assist fairgoers in hard times. Twenty-four thousand Yorkers that year were given aid of some kind, ranging from foodstuffs to clothes and shoes.

York's Louis J. Appell was appointed to lead the community's National Recovery Act efforts and NRA funds brought 1,436 jobs to the York area. Twenty-six WPA projects were employing 6,112 people and, in contrast to the discouraging conditions, York was being hailed as a leader in United States production of pretzels and artificial teeth.

In early March of 1933 a banking holiday was declared by the federal government; York quietly accepted the order, although business would not be interrupted. By March 11, York banks had asked for permission to reopen and a few days later the city would share the honors with Lewistown

as the only two cities in Pennsylvania with all banks open and operating under near-normal conditions. York, in fact, was called a "bright spot" in Pennsylvania as far as banking was concerned, and a *Dispatch* article announcing the reopening of York banks on March 14 was even more generous with its analysis of the York economy.

"Happy days are here again," the *Dispatch*'s lead article told Yorkers, "for York banks and their thousands of depositors. With a clean bill of health from the federal government, every bank in the city opened at 9 o'clock this morning with power to resume normal banking functions . . . hoarding has become decidedly unfashionable. . . ." On the same day J.W. Gitt, chairman of the local emergency relief committee, was speaking in Harrisburg on York's successful dealings with bad times. The program, for relief board members of surrounding counties, also featured Governor Gifford Pinchot.

The 1930s were also a great time for moviegoers. Emory Myers, who was a Strand Theater projectionist from 1929 to 1970, recalls the local premiere of *Gone with the Wind* in the 1930s: "No movie ever hit York like *Gone with the Wind.* People used to line up from the front of the Strand to Bear's Department Store on the Square. Scarlett and Rhett took the city by storm."

Live performances were sometimes offered at the Strand, the Orpheum, and the York Opera House. "I remember when Abbott and Costello, the famous comedians, were there," Myers says. "They were so poor at the time that we had to give them something to eat. And then there was Sally Rand, the famous fan dancer. She was a big hit in York." The Strand discontinued its live shows in the World War II years, because Yorkers could no longer afford the increasingly high ticket prices.

M. Valerie Groff, who worked for 15 years at the Strand and Capitol theaters, recalls that York had many other entertainment opportunities, including popular concerts at Valley View Park, which "used to get such names as Gene Autry . . . and other shows were performed by the renowned Kinley Players [now at Warren, Ohio] at the York Theater. The York County Academy combined with the York Collegiate Institute in the 1930s to produce dramatic offerings at both school sites. The York Music League sponsored concerts by the Cleveland Symphony Orchestra, among others, which were held at William Penn Senior High School. Big-name groups and "homegrown" entertainment were featured at such places as the Penn Hotel, the York Country Club, the Dutch Club, the Yorktowne Hotel, and private functions sponsored by various York industries.

These entertainments were temporarily halted in 1933, however, when York was the victim of another natural disaster. On August 20 of that year, a tropical hurricane entered the Delaware coast heading west. According to Helen V. Delaplane, the hurricane "brought torrents of rain—nonstop day and night rain," which continued for four days. The Codorus Creek overflowed, bridges were under water, and all exits to York flooded. "King's Dam had broken," Miss Delaplane recalls, "causing the water to rise suddenly. . . . Upstream from College Avenue the Codorus makes a sharp bend to the west. In that angle the flood waters advanced from two directions. This area was the worst flooded part of York, also the most densely populated."

Two people were drowned, thousands left homeless, and there was hundreds of thousands of dollars in immediate property damage. The main plant of the Edison Electric Company was flooded, stalling the generators, and all electrical activity in the city ceased. Streetcars stopped in their tracks, lights went out, and the power outage caused further damage. The rain finally stopped at 3:15 Thursday morning, August 24, and York heaved a collective sigh of relief. According to Miss Delaplane, the flooding had "reached a peak of 13 feet 9 inches near Doll's Pontiac Garage," and stretching from there was "a great lake covering central York and far beyond on the south side." Flood damage was ultimately estimated at $4,261,000.

The *York Dispatch* termed it "the most disastrous flood in the history of the city." J.W. Gitt, the editor of the rival paper, the *York Gazette*, was determined to help the town get back on its feet after the flood. Gitt, a Hanover-educated lawyer, had bought the paper in 1915 out of receivership, and had originally intended only to revive it and profit from a resale. But in 1918 he bought another paper, the *York Daily*, merged the two morning editions, and became so involved in journalism that he never returned to law. Through his reasoned, reform-minded editorials and his civic activism, Gitt soon became an important community spokesman.

Governor Gifford Pinchot (who was a close friend of Gitt) appointed him to head up relief operations in York County. Gitt saw the flood as an opportunity to put many of the more than 10,000 people who were on relief at the time to work in a useful community project. Gitt, in a book about him, *Sweet Land of Liberty* (1975), recalls the period: "I was having a real fight with the politicians over the W.P.A. in York. Most of the politicians in the country . . . used it for political purposes. I conceived the idea that we would use it for something . . . worthwhile . . . so we put our money into digging out and widening the Codorus Creek. The people on relief were so . . . anxious to get jobs that they went down to work in the icy creek in the winter, bookkeepers and all kinds of people, with shovels and things. I'm telling you, it was terrible for awhile."

Gitt also set up a commissary to feed thousands of York citizens during the Depression. Afterward he continued to serve as the community's conscience, writing forcefully against self-aggrandizing politicians and inspiring the wrath of grocers, milk dealers, coal-company owners, and anyone else who did not meet his high standards of "faith, hope, and charity."

As York began to return to normal after the flood, it resumed its nightlife. The Valencia Ballroom entertained Saturday-night crowds of up to 2,000, who came to dance to the big-band music of Duke Ellington, Benny Goodman, Glenn Miller, Cab Calloway, Tommy Dorsey, and many others. The Clooney sisters and Ozzie Nelson and Harriet Hilliard (later the well-known television team, Ozzie and Harriet) also played the Valencia, which featured a ballroom with an overhead revolving light and a bar downstairs called the Rainbow Grill. Located in the 200 block of North George Street, the Valencia entertained patrons for more than 30 years, and people came from as far as 200 miles away to take in the Valencia during its heyday.

The Valencia was owned and operated by eight members of the Tassia family, who earlier had established a fresh produce and fruit business in York. The family members formed a partnership and, in 1928, bought a huge building in the 200 block of North George Street. The building, erected in 1911, was called the Coliseum. The Tassias transformed the building into a splendid entertainment palace. The ballroom was furnished with over 700 bentwood chairs. Fourteen floor-to-ceiling murals were commissioned to decorate the ballroom and they exquisitely mirrored the Valencia's Spanish theme. On October 8, 1934, they were ready for their grand opening. Sadie Tassia was manager and her brother, Steve, was her assistant. About 40 waiters and waitresses were on hand and a half-dozen girls were on duty in the cloak room. Warming up on the newly installed stage that evening in 1934 was Mal Hallett and his orchestra, and Miss Teddie Grace, affectionately nicknamed the "sweetheart of the Dixie circuit."

Joel Michael, writing in the *York Daily Record* on the occasion of the Valencia's closing in 1973, reminded Yorkers of some of its finer moments: "The dance band could have been . . . Sammy Kaye and his Swing 'n' Sway Orchestra or Kay Kyser and his College of Musical Knowledge, or two dozen other big-name possibilities. Vaughan Monroe did York's first coast-to-coast radio commercial for Lucky Strike 23 years ago from the tiered stage of the Valencia Ballroom." In addition to the great names in American music of the time, the Valencia had its own band, the Blue Moon Orchestra. The Blue Moon was popular with York's young people, who attended the Valencia's Friday night hops. The Blue Moon Orchestra played 788 "sets" in the Ballroom.

Another York band, "The Black Diamonds," also played to "swinging

and swaying" members of the community during those days when "Dance and Music" ruled the York spirit. Because it was common for young people to come to the Valencia as "stags," many romances budded at the Valencia and some of them moved into marriage. One of the young men likely to be in attendance during the Valencia's most popular evenings was a friend of the Tassias who was a reporter for the *York High Weekly*. The young journalist turned his early interest in reporting to a full-time profession and was still reporting the news and interviewing celebrities in the 1980s.

The reporter, Harry McLaughlin, generally had the company of a fellow photographer on the *York High Weekly*, William Thomas. Together they interviewed the celebrities at the Valencia, or at the Yorktowne Hotel, where many of them stayed. The more "uncooperative" stars who stayed at the Yorktowne were interviewed by the two young reporters as they made their way, often rapidly, west on East Market Street then north on North George Street to the Valencia.

The 1930s, mixed with crowd-pleasing entertainment and jolting economic news, was a study in contrasts for York. Though it had not escaped completely the impact of the Depression, York was responding well to treatment afforded by many community plans and a few national ones. By the end of 1934, things were looking bright again. The commissary, where the poor had obtained food, was closed and York County was listed 49th in the state in the number of unemployed workers. Nineteen thirty-four saw a new wire plant for York, another hosiery trade boom, and 81,818 of York County's citizens enrolled in a Sunday School program. That year also saw the visit of another President to York. President Franklin D. Roosevelt passed through the city by train after speaking at a Memorial Day program in Gettysburg. His special train slowed down as it entered the borough of West York in the late afternoon, and a crowd of cheering Yorkers greeted him as he waved from the rear platform of the train. Children placed pennies on the railroad tracks and valued them as unmatched souvenirs.

Yorkers also achieved prominence in sports during the 1930s. Dick Bachtell, and brothers Bill Good and Walter Good, were York barbell standouts and on August 3, 1936, "Little Tony" Terlazzo won the gold medal at the Olympics for weightlifting. As a featherweight, he lifted a total of 687.5 pounds, including one lift of more than twice his weight. Two other York weightlifters, John Terpak and Robert Mitchell, also competed in the Olympics, and Terpak took fifth place in his division with a total lift of 709½ pounds. Another Yorker John Grimek was named Mr. America in 1941.

In 1940 York weightlifters made a clean sweep of the National A.A.U. titles in the annual tournament in New York City. Joining Olympic competitors Terpak and Terlazzo were Steve Stanko, Joe Fiorito, and John Davis. So impressive was the Yorker weightlifting sweep that the Associated Press declared: "The city of York, Pennsylvania, can rightfully claim to be the weightlifting center of the nation today . . . ."

York's domination of weightlifting competitions came principally through efforts of Yorker Bob Hoffman. Hoffman was named a world-class athlete in 1925. He also was a world canoeing champion and later served as the U.S. Olympic weightlifting coach for 20 years. He ran the York Oil Burner Company with Yorker Ed Kraber, but his interest in weightlifting led him to begin reproducing cast-iron weights in 1932. This resulted in the formation of the York Bar Bell Company, which is still one of the largest such firms in the country.

·Another Yorker who distinguished himself in sports during the 1930s was Tom Keesey, who set a national junior-college basketball scoring record of 501 points in a single season. Keesey had graduated from York High School

Below
York's young reporter, Harry J. McLaughlin, used the Valencia Ballroom as his turf to search for interviews with the famous and infamous entertainers who came to York to perform, including Ozzie Nelson and Harriet Hilliard (later Ozzie and Harriet), Kay Kyser and Ginny Simms, and Glenn Miller. Miller is shown here with reporter McLaughlin. McLaughlin would later become well-known in York for his reportage for the *Sunday Patriot News*. Courtesy, Harry J. McLaughlin.

Bottom
Tony Terlazzo from York was the first American to win an Olympic weightlifting championship when he captured the featherweight title in 1936. (HSYC)

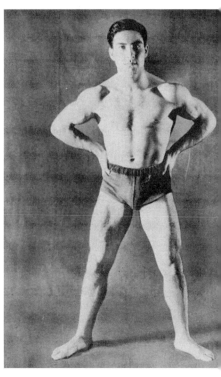

in 1937. His teammates that year included Joe "Nardie" Stock, "Hunk" Stover, Bill Hunter, and Charlie Falkler, and they were considered one of the best high-school teams in history.

While York athletes were achieving fame in sports, a York woman who had moved to Baltimore was gaining attention more akin to notoriety. The death of Pearl Snow, who had run a "high-toned" brothel in the Maryland seaport city for 35 years, was mourned by no less a personage than H.L. Mencken, American author, journalist, and linguist. He wrote about her passing in a letter to his friend Edgar Lee Masters, the writer of the *Spoon River Anthology*. "She was buried from St. John's Evangelical Church," writes Mencken, "and a large congregation was in attendance, including many public men." Snow's establishment had catered to "members of Congress, many of whom dropped over from Washington to discuss public matters with her. Her staff of interns was mainly recruited from York County, Pennsylvania, where she was born herself." Mencken immortalized another Yorker in his saucy "A Girl from Red Lion, Pennsylvania," published in 1914. That story was about a Dunkard girl who fled to Baltimore when she found herself "with child." Mencken befriended the girl and told of how she was persuaded to return home and marry her boyfriend.

As rumors of war were being sounded again in Europe, another York woman, Katherine Haviland Taylor, was bringing fame of a more respectable sort to York. She wrote more than 20 books of light fiction, including two set in her home town, *Yellow Soap* and *Nine Hundred Block*. One of her many short stories, "One Man's Journey," was made into a movie starring Lionel Barrymore and May Robson, and retitled *A Man to Remember*. York named a road after her in the Shiloh area of the county. After her death in 1941, her ashes were returned to York (from St. Cloud, Florida, where she had been living), and interred in St. John's Episcopal Churchyard. Her father, the Reverend Dr. Arthur Russell Taylor, had served St. John's as rector.

By the end of the decade, York had undergone many changes, not the least of which was a further rise in the population. The number of inhabitants in the city stood at 56,712 in 1940, a 2.6 percent increase over 1930. The county's population rose to 178,022. Local transportation in this era had been greatly improved by the building of the Pennsylvania Turnpike, which came within 20 miles of York. Buses had replaced the town's electric trolleys by 1939, and the York Street Railway became the York Bus Company. The company's employees were retrained to drive Twin Coach motor buses and the original "barns" at 520 North Hartley Street were adapted to house the buses.

Several new buildings had been added or improved during the decade. The Post Office on South George Street, built in 1912 as a memorial to the Continental Congress, underwent an enlargement program in 1940. So did the York Court House. The Crispus Attucks Association Center was dedicated, at 125 East Maple Street, to serve as a community center primarily for York's black citizens. Dr. Edward Meisenhelder, Jr., sold the West Side Sanatarium, which he had established in 1913, and it became the West Side Osteopathic Hospital in 1945 with facilities on West Market Street near the York Fair Grounds. (The hospital was renamed the Memorial Osteopathic Hospital and moved to South Belmont Street in 1961.)

All these improvements and accomplishments—in transportation, community services, public buildings, private businesses, sports, literature, and other fields—were gradually raising York to an even higher plane of prosperity. War, however, was soon to thrust York into yet another worldwide conflict. Yorkers would demonstrate the patriotism and adaptability that, by this time, were hallmarks of the community.

The residence built by the Emerton family in 1918 and 1919 for $1.6 million became the Hahn Home for Women in 1958. The mansion, at the corner of East Springettsbury Avenue and South George Street, remains one of York County's most elegant and magnificent buildings. Courtesy, The York County Heritage Trust

York celebrated the 1976
Bicentennial in its favorite
fashion—with a parade down
Market Street. Courtesy, Harry J.
McLaughlin.

CHAPTER IX

THE RISE OF THE GREATER YORK AREA

The Japanese attacked Pearl Harbor on Sunday, December 7, 1941. The next day the *York Dispatch*, in a three-column headline, told Yorkers: "United States Suffers Heavy Losses As Japan Risks Empire In Audacious Attack on Far-flung Pacific Bases." Inside the *Dispatch* Yorkers read these editorial lines: "Now that the United States has become—without choice and as the result of treacherous and unprovoked attack—the major power in a world war the magnitude of which at the moment strains the imagination of any man to comprehend, there is a goal toward which all Americans have set their eyes undeviatingly—Victory."

Immediately, York officials conferred and named Colonel William H. Beckner Director of Energy Defense. Beckner told the community in the next day's *Dispatch*: "York is a target to the new type of warfare. For the present we do not expect long, sustained, repeated attacks. This is a war not so much of armies and navies as of production. We can get out of this mess only if we can produce." He concluded with this challenge: "York is a vital defense area, so proclaimed by the government of the United States, and industry must continue to produce defense material regardless of hardship or inconvenience to all of us."

The war effort soon reshaped daily life in York County. Individuals, groups, and industries contributed to the cause of freedom, and a plan developed in York to maximize war production was adopted nationally. The "York Plan," as it came to be known, was a new set of guidelines containing 15 points that would organize workers and machinery to greatest possible efficiency. The plan was developed by four local industrialists—William S. Shipley, W.J. Fisher, Robert P. Turner, and Warren C. Bulette—and was endorsed by the local Manufacturers Association.

S. Forry Laucks, another York industrialist, had laid the groundwork for the York Plan years earlier. In 1938 he went to Washington, D.C., and obtained the first ordnance contract for the coming war. Remembering his experiences in World War I, he did not attempt to reequip his factory for the new job, but surveyed the community to determine the extent of idle machinery. As a result, more than 45 percent of the machining operations on the gun mounts ordered from him by the government were subcontracted.

The York Plan gained considerable national publicity and York Ice Company president William W. Shipley toured the country, giving details of the plan to leaders in other communities. Many adopted the system for greater defense production.

While Americans were reading about the York Plan in the *Saturday Evening Post*, *Business Week*, and other publications, they also were reading about a native son who was earning recognition for himself and his community. Jacob Loucks Devers, born in York of Irish and Pennsylvania German ancestry, served in the army as commanding general of the armored forces from

August 1941 until May 1943. He was made a four-star general and was decorated with numerous military honors, during and after the war, for his extraordinary record of service. General Devers coordinated armor, infantry, air power, and supply services for the enormously important Normandy Invasions. In four and a half months after the invasion, the Sixth Army, under General Devers, liberated more than half of France, captured more than 170,000 prisoners, penetrated the Maginot Line, and boldly entered Germany.

After the war, General Devers served in many important private and governmental arenas, returning to York occasionally to visit family and friends. In 1949 York honored him by naming an elementary school and a road after him. He died on October 16, 1979, at the age of 92, after giving his personal papers to the Historical Society of York County.

Although war-related activity dominated the local scene, York was not just a manufacturing and fighting machine during the World War II years. People lived as normal lives as possible and the town continued to grow. Citizens formed a Young Woman's Club in 1941, and on May 30, 1942, a new City Hall was dedicated at the corner of King and Beaver streets on the site of the old St. Paul's Lutheran Church, which had been destroyed by fire. York's new city hall was built to commemorate the 200th anniversary of York's founding. It was of Colonial brick design, using white Georgian marble trim and a slate roof. The building's architects, Yorkers Robert Stair and Frederick Dempwolf, designed the lobby as a replica of the one in Philadelphia's Independence Hall, and its total cost was $225,000.

Many new community-service organizations were founded during this period. Foremost among them was the York County War and Welfare Fund, formed by the York Welfare Federation in 1943, which was responsible for raising both local welfare and national war-relief funds. During that year the federation collected $239,577; offices were provided at no charge by the

Below
Actress Hedy Lamarr came to York during World War II selling war bonds to the citizens. She is shown here outside the Yorktowne Hotel. Courtesy Harry J. McLaughlin.

Below right
Jacob Loucks Devers, a native of York, was Commander General of the European Theater of Operation and Deputy Supreme Allied Commander in the Mediterranean Theater during World War II. General Devers was largely responsible for the planning of the Normandy-area landings and was one of the country's few four-star generals. Courtesy, York College of Pennsylvania.

York Area Chamber of Commerce. The organization later became the United Way of York County.

Out where the shooting was going on, another Yorker performed an even greater—and considerably more heroic and famous—act of charity. Alexander D. Goode, rabbi of York's Temple Beth Israel from 1937 to 1942 and contributor to the York County Chapter of the American Red Cross, the Rotary Club of York, and the York YMCA, enlisted in the Navy and served as one of four chaplains on the S.S. *Dorchester*. On February 3, 1943, when the *Dorchester* was lying off the coast of Greenland, most of the crew was below deck, some because of illness, others simply because of the danger from submarine fire. Chaplain Goode was with them, busily caring for the sick crewmen, when a torpedo hit.

Orders were given to abandon ship. The men panicked and stampeded to the lifeboats. Meanwhile Chaplain Goode calmly gave his gloves to a Coast Guard officer, Lieutenant John J. Mahoney. As the *Dorchester* was sinking, Goode and the other three chaplains gave their life belts to crew members. The four chaplains, with arms joined and voices lifted in prayer, died as the *Dorchester* went down.

Later Mahoney told the story of the four chaplains, saying that the gloves Chaplain Goode had given him prevented his hands from freezing and allowed him to cling to a lifeboat for eight hours before being rescued. The story of Rabbi Goode and the other three chaplains soon circled the globe and their actions became famous as one of the war's noblest gestures.

In 1951 a 200-seat interfaith chapel was dedicated to the memory of the four *Dorchester* chaplains in Philadelphia. In 1958 the U.S. Senate posthumously awarded special Medals of Honor to the men, and in 1959 Yorkers were chosen to unveil a new tableau featuring them at the National Wax Museum in Washington. Other recognition included the naming of an elementary school for Chaplain Goode in York in 1955 and the establishment

Below left
First Lieutenant Alexander Goode, rabbi of York's Temple Beth Israel from 1937 to 1942, was one of four chaplains who drowned when the S.S. *Dorchester* sank on February 3, 1943. Goode and the other three chaplains were awarded posthumous Medals of Honor in 1958 for having given their life jackets to crew members. (HSYC)

Below
The York County town of Red Lion honored its ex-military men and women with a homecoming parade in October 1946. Courtesy, Gazette and Daily File Collection. (HSYC)

of a national humanitarian award, the Chapel of the Four Chaplains Gold Medallion.

Before World War II ended, 10 percent of the county's population had served in the armed forces. By May 8, 1945—the day that the Allied nations proclaimed an end to the war in Europe—1,238 countians had been killed or wounded, 155 were reported missing, and 95 were being held as prisoners of war.

Because of the heavy losses, York's mayor appealed for a "simple and dignified celebration of Victory," and asked that merchants close for the afternoon to allow employees to join citywide church services. In autumn of the same year, war in the Far East ended.

After the war York, along with so many American cities, experienced a surge of industrial expansion and development. As a result the downtown area, where much of this growth was centered, began suffering from traffic congestion. A new York planning commission placed a high priority on the problem and in 1950 instituted one-way traffic on the city's main through streets: Market, King, and Philadelphia (east and west); and George, Duke, and Beaver (north and south).

While all this growth was being discussed, however, the town itself received some discouraging news. The 1950 census showed only a slight population increase of 2.6 percent over the 1940 figure, giving York 59,704 people. This proved the apex of York's population, and in succeeding decades, Yorkers would bemoan the lack of further growth. Manufacturing firms continued to move into the area, but large outside companies were purchasing many of York's already-established industries. In order to accommodate what Yorkers still hoped would be the increasingly large numbers of people and companies, the community built a new $5 million sewage-disposal plant and York school authorities began a $4.5 million expansion program.

York was not allowed to settle comfortably into its new plan of community improvements. The Korean War soon pressed York Countians into battle and called upon the talents and expertise of York leaders. The York Plan was reinstituted on a national level. A five-man group of York industrialists was named to pilot the new York Plan. William J. Fisher, president of the A.B. Farquhar Company, was named chairman and Robert P. Turner, vice-president of the New York Wire Cloth Company, was named to assist him. Both men had served on the World War II committee. Also named to the 1950 group were Stewart E. Lauer, president of the York Corporation; John H. Padden, executive secretary of the Manufacturers Association; and Beauchamp E. Smith, president of the S. Morgan Smith Company.

Thousands of Yorkers entered the service during this war. Among them was Marc Green, who introduced the games of softball and baseball to a group of youngsters in a Catholic orphanage on the island of Paengnyŏng, off the coast of western South Korea. Green had played for Little League, American Legion, and high-school teams in York before pitching on semi-professional teams and winning tryouts with the New York Yankees and the St. Louis Cardinals when he was only 16 years old.

While Green and his fellow Yorkers were gone, the town continued developing along the same lines as before. Yorkers back home were as conservative as ever: in 1952, when the issues were "Corruption, Communism and Korea," York County voted, with the nation, for Eisenhower over Stevenson.

There were, as before, new schools and further additions to old ones. In 1952 Yorker A.I. Watts acquired a license for the York Academy of Arts which, after several moves, found a home in the former Ridge Avenue School at 625 East Philadelphia Street. Pennsylvania State University opened a York branch, in 1953, in the Shiloh Elementary School Building. The York campus offered the first two years of college training to York students as well as a variety of noncredit and master's-level courses. York College of Pennsylvania received approval to award its first master's degree in 1977.

Radio station WSBA, which had gone on the air in 1942, added a television station, WSBA-TV, in 1952. That station was the first UHF station to go on the air in the East. WSBA's FM-radio counterpart was a pioneer in FM operation in the United States. WSBA merged with the Pfaltzgraff Pottery Company in 1954 and purchased the first of a number of affiliate stations, WARM of Scranton, in 1958. In 1981 WSBA Radio, under the leadership of Louis J. Appell, Jr., served as the "flagship" for 11 other stations.

By the end of the Korean War at least 29 York Countians had been killed. Total casualties, including those missing, prisoners of war, and men killed or injured in front line accidents, reached 125. About 7,000 countians were eligible after the war for Korean War bonus payments.

Those who returned to York saw a town that was beginning to take on the characteristics of a sprawling metropolis. The city, locked in on all sides by growing townships and boroughs, was experiencing a time of great strength as the county's population turned to its urbanized center city for shopping, banking, government, and entertainment facilities. A trend was developing, however, that gradually would take away a lot of the city's middle-class citizens and sap the center city of many of its most popular department stores and shops.

The move toward the suburbs by middle-class families and shopping-complex developers began in 1953 when the York County Shopping Center was planned east of the city near Haines Acres, where many city residents relocated and newcomers chose to settle. Soon after the York County Shopping Center was opened, a group of consultants studied the York area and told

Below
Softball has traditionally been one of York County's favorite sports and the city has played host to numerous national softball competitions. Ed Glacken of the York City Softball League is shown here in 1946. Courtesy, Harry J. McLaughlin.

Bottom
York in the 1950s was known for its beautiful Christmas decorations, including a huge Christmas tree in front of the York County Court House and a brilliant star hung in the middle of Continental Square. Courtesy, Gazette and Daily File Collection. (HSYC)

the York Area Chamber of Commerce that officials should "modernize the downtown shopping center rather than develop neighborhood centers."

In 1954 a shopping center south of York was approved, and in the same year one for the southeast was planned; a shopping center for the Fireside Terrace area was begun in September; and a fifth was approved for the 900 block of South George Street in December of that year. The town saw the planning of 11 more centers within as many years.

York became the first American city to be linked with a foreign sister city in 1954. The pioneer program with Arles, France, was established after Dr. Victoria Lyles, superintendent of the French program in elementary schools, accepted an invitation from LeMonde Bilingue in Paris to set up a people-to-people program with the 2,000-year-old city in the south of France. The program grew, and in 1957 a York exchange teacher, Margaret Boltz, married the Mayor of Arles, Charles Privat. By 1981 the birth of eight Franco-American babies and the marriages of eight Franco-American couples would be credited—at least in part—to the program.

Yorkers were also forging ties between their town and the city in England for which it was named. Because of the natural interest in the British city, America's Yorkers had adopted its nickname, the White Rose City. In the 1930s the Women's Bureau of the York Area Chamber of Commerce called for an official recognition of the designation. In ensuing years government officials and residents of America's York hosted English visitors on a regular basis.

York voted for President Eisenhower's reelection in 1956. That Eisenhower's farm was just minutes from York County's western border, and that he periodically visited York to play golf at the Country Club, only strengthened his political support locally.

Yorkers forged still another tie with the nation as a whole in the 1950s, although some Yorkers who participated in the venture—such as York Little Theater's Bert Smith—would, as Smith said, "just as soon forget it." In 1958 several Yorkers were called to do small roles in a movie that later became a classic horror picture. Smith was one of the Yorkers to appear in the science-fiction film, *The Blob*, in which Steve McQueen (in the role that launched his film career) struggles to rid humanity of an "insatiable formless creature from outer space."

But during that era, York's most famous former resident was perhaps Cameron Mitchell. Mitchell, the son of the Reverend and Mrs. Charles M. Mitzell of Shrewsbury, told a *York Dispatch* reporter in 1956 that a role in the York American Legion's production of *Maryland, My Maryland* and a subsequent *Dispatch* review of the show made him decide that show business would be his life's work.

Mitchell received two Oscar nominations, for his supporting roles in *Tall*

Men and *Love Me or Leave Me*, and was nominated for an Emmy Award in television's "Oxbow Incident" and "Man on the Ledge." He made dozens of other films and television shows, including the long-running series, "High Chaparral." Mitchell visited his home town in 1958 to see his father perform in the York Little Theatre production of *Inherit the Wind*. When his father became ill during rehearsals, Mitchell took over the role, playing to packed houses and delighted audiences.

York's connections with the outside world increased dramatically with the construction of Interstate Highway 83. The highway, carrying traffic around York between Harrisburg and Baltimore, was opened in sections from 1958 to 1961; its Route 30 bypass followed in 1970 through 1973.

In 1960 the U.S. Census Bureau reported that York, perhaps because of the traffic that I-83 was bringing to the area, now lay for the first time along the western boundary of the "supermetropolitan area" stretching from New Hampshire to Washington, D.C. The report said that the "ever-growing area" had 31.5 million inhabitants. The report also had shocking news for York city officials: for the first time ever in a census, the city itself had lost residents. Although population in the county as a whole continued to rise, the population in the city proper fell from 59,704 in 1950 to 54,504 in 1960.

The year of the 1960 census was also the year of the 1960 Presidential campaign, during which Senator John F. Kennedy stopped in York to greet throngs of townspeople at the York Interstate Fair. With Governor David L. Lawrence, County Democratic chairman Luther Yohe, and former governor (and native Yorker) George M. Leader at his side, Kennedy toured the Fair Grounds, stopping to pat the head of a donkey and to shake hands with members of the excited crowds.

Despite his campaigning Kennedy lost York County, polling 38,710 votes to Richard Nixon's 55,109. Nixon's connection with York probably served as a factor in his countywide support: his parents had resided in York County between 1946 and 1953. They bought a farm at Menges Mills so that they could be near their son, who had been elected to the House of Representatives. Nixon's younger brother Edward had graduated from West York High School.

As the 1960s began, Yorkers made plans to restore two of their prime historic properties: the Golden Plough Tavern and the General Horatio Gates house at the corner of West Market Street and North Pershing Avenue. As the preservation work on the run-down buildings started, many people in the community discovered York's historic importance. Historic York County, Inc., which later merged with The Historical Society of York County, worked with the latter organization, the Junior League, and many other organizations to bring about an awareness of history in the

Below left
John F. Kennedy visited the York Interstate Fair on a campaign tour in 1960. Courtesy, Harry J. McLaughlin.

Below
The Golden Plough Tavern and the General Horatio Gates House appear here as they looked before restoration by The Historical Society of York County. Restoration of the properties began in July 1960, and the buildings were opened to the public in June 1963. (HSYC)

community.

The area was not only preserving its past. it was also building for the present and future. Shopping centers rose on all sides of the city's borders and more people exchanged residences in the city for suburban homes. The Queensgate Shopping Center was opened and J.W. Fields Department Store opened in the North Mall.

The town had other attractions in the early 1960s, especially for young people. The drive-in restaurant at Avalong was a popular meeting place for teenagers, and the White Swan Drive-In west of York (later Clair's Restaurant) offered yet another social outlet. Their older brothers and sisters spent their time studying at York Junior College, which had an enrollment of 326, a new campus along Country Club Road south of York, and a new president, Dr. Ray A. Miller. Dr. Miller, who ran the school from 1958 to 1976, initiated a Town and Gown Concert and Lecture Series. The Town and Gown concerts attracted capacity crowds to hear, among others, flamenco guitarist Carlos Montoya, flutist Jean-Pierre Rampal, violinist Eugene Fodor, the Norman Luboff Choir, the U.S. Marine Band, pianists Ferrante and Teicher, and a group that became a widely hailed York favorite, the Preservation Hall Jazz Band. At about the same time, Dr. Frank Mussano took over the college's student-activities office and launched a program of extremely popular contemporary music concerts.

The 1960s was also the decade when women emerged to take an even more active role in York's community life. At the forefront of this move was Mary (Mrs. Charles) F. Stephenson who, as editor of the *Sunday News* women's section, reported on the burgeoning of hundreds of women's organizations in York County. She became an honorary member of many of these groups, including farm women's clubs, musical societies, hospital organizations, processional committees, church coteries, historical societies, and educational associations.

Mary Stephenson had moved to York in the 1940s to attend Thompson Business College, which had been founded in 1921. Besides her energetic work on behalf of women's groups, she became an almost legendary figure in York community life. Her collection of costumes, drawn from her everyday use as well as for special occasions, earned her such titles as "Queen of the Beaux Arts Ball" and "first woman to wear a pantsuit." She won other, somewhat dubious, titles as well. Her home-pond frog was twice the winner in York's Codorus Frog-jumping Contest. Mary Stephenson, during the 1960s, not only received recognition for her community work and professional achievements, but was a part of every major social event in York, including one of the grandest celebrations in recent history.

During the summer of 1966, the entire community threw a party for itself. The 225th Anniversary Observance of the town's founding included the participation of hundreds of Yorkers and climaxed with a grand pageant, "The York Story," presented at the York Fair Grounds. The celebration culminated on July 4, a day jammed full of celebration activities, including a spectacular fireworks show.

The summer of 1966 brought York one of its worst droughts on record. By July 15 a rainless summer had caused the York Water Company's impounding basin surface to fall 48 inches below normal. Strict water restrictions were issued to the community, and outdoor hoses, water-cooled air conditioners, and the washing of cars were banned. Despite conservation measures, however, the water company's impounding basin, by August 24, was decreasing by eight million gallons over a 24-hour period.

On September 3, 1966, President Lyndon Johnson visited the nearby York County community of Dallastown. Otis B. Morse IV, one of the press coor-

Below
President Lyndon B. Johnson made a visit to York County's Dallastown on September 3, 1966, to celebrate the community's 100th anniversary. Courtesy, Harry J. McLaughlin.

Bottom
Construction of the Peach Bottom atomic plant in southern York County is shown in 1962, five years before its opening. Courtesy, Gazette and Daily File Collection. (HSYC)

dinators for the event, estimated that more than 30,000 people, most of whom had probably come from York, turned out to greet the President.

York County saw the opening of its first large-scale nuclear power plant in 1967, under way for six years. The Peach Bottom I plant was installed on York County's southern border in the Lower Susquehanna Valley and two additional plants were planned for operation in 1972 and 1973.

In the same year that Peach Bottom I opened, cable television came to York. It was a part of the Susquehanna Broadcasting Company, which owned WSBA and its affiliate stations, along with the Pfaltzgraff Pottery Company. The cable added a half-dozen stations to Yorkers' television reception.

Yorkers' increased exposure to television programming, along with improved highways and other means of transportation, brought them ever closer, at least psychologically, to the other large metropolitan areas in their part of the country. Yorkers, who had visited surrounding cities in small numbers since the 1700s, now made frequent trips to neighboring communities. The theaters, sports facilities, restaurants, and the other attractions of Philadelphia, Baltimore, and Washington now lay within an evening's drive of York, and major recreation areas—Atlantic City, Ocean City, and Wildwood in New Jersey, and Ocean City, in Maryland—were just as conveniently situated. Soon Yorkers were agreeing with executives of large firms that had relocated in York that one of the town's biggest advantages was its location.

Three years after man's footprint was placed on the moon for the first time, the Codorus again showed men and women in York how powerless they really were. Seven to eight inches of rain drenched the city formerly known as York town. As in Colonial days, the river spilled its banks, killing several York County residents and causing hundreds of thousands of dollars worth of damage. Mayor Eli Eichelberger declared a city emergency.

Rains, occurring over the night and morning hours of June 21 and 22, covered whole blocks of York housing and forced hundreds of citizens to flee their homes. A Red Cross emergency care center was set up at the Edgar Fahs Smith Junior High School.

Metropolitan-Edison workmen, responding to innumerable trouble calls, found the body of an elderly woman in the Elmwood section of York and authorities guessed that it was the body of a woman whose Camp Betty Washington Road house had been smashed and washed away by flood waters. City police, meanwhile, were scuba diving for the body of a man believed to have drowned in the city's Poorhouse Run flood-control project, and Pennsylvania Department of Transportation crewmen had run out of road barriers with which they had been closing off flooded streets.

Flood waters from the Codorus licked the brick sidewalks in front of the restored Golden Plough Tavern and General Gates House, threatening the invaluable properties with their rooms full of costly antiques. A few blocks away, in the Newberry Street neighborhood, flood waters invaded the home of an elderly York minister and destroyed a lifetime collection of papers, sermons, and books.

Rains from Hurricane Agnes created a devastating flood in downtown York on June 21 and 22, 1972. The Codorus Creek was forced over its banks and into the city streets. Courtesy, William J. Schintz.

Flood damage was set at more than $34 million, including $1.5 million worth of damage to utilities alone. As waters slowly receded clean-up operations began over the weekend of June 23.

Congressman N. Neiman Craley, who had snatched the seat of former Congressman George A. Goodling, made a petition to the Army Corps of Engineers for federal help in alleviating the problem and in expanding York's water sources for the future. Goodling regained his seat in 1966.

Fortunately the month of September brought rich rainfalls, and by October 4, bans were lifted. Water Company president George S. Schmidt thanked industries and housewives for helping to conserve water during the drought and promised that water supplies for the future were being carefully studied. The Army Corps of Engineers assisted the York community in expanding fresh-water resources.

The war in Vietnam was on everyone's mind in the late 1960s and a massive anti war rally in Washington involved the arrest of two Yorkers. On the York College campus students held a peaceful demonstration that drew a small crowd. In the Presidential election of that year, in which Vietnam was, of course, a major issue, Yorkers again favored Richard Nixon, despite a mild familiarity with Hubert Humphrey. Humphrey had visited York in 1952 and 1959, and again after the election in 1969 and 1972.

As the 1960s drew to a close, some Yorkers took a breather from politics and glowed with pride as York Countian Trudy Pedersen was named Miss Pennsylvania at the Miss Pennsylvania pageant in nearby Hershey. Her former schoolmate Margaret Louise Walker won the same title the very next year.

The breather was short-lived. Racial violence erupted in York in the summer of 1969, leaving behind thousands of dollars in property damage, 37 injured Yorkers, and two deaths. The two people killed were 27-year-old Mrs. Lillie B. Allen of Aiken, South Carolina, and York policeman Henry C. Schaad. The death of Officer Schaad was the first known killing of a city police officer in the line of duty in the history of the city. Mayor John L. Snyder imposed a curfew from 9 p.m. to 7 a.m. during the period of unrest, and members of the National Guard patrolled the streets. The national news media carried the developments of York's racial disturbances across the land.

Out of the disturbances of that summer, Yorkers established a community charrette, which led to the founding of York's community-improvement agency, the Community Progress Council, whose goal it was to halt what was seen as York's "decline." The cause for the worry was that, although the 1970 census revealed that the county had gained 32,119 people since 1960 (setting a record high of 272,455), the city's population was set at 50,355, representing a decline of more than 4,000 people. Yet another loss surprised and saddened people almost as much: the sale, in October 1970, of J.W. Gitt's nationally reputed *York Gazette and Daily*.

Journalists across the country mourned its departure from the newsstands and mailboxes of America, demonstrating that while the paper's views were not always compatible with those of Yorkers, they found a good reception in many other places. The *New York Times* said: "The *Gazette* was one of a kind . . . fifty-five years of colorful, outspoken, personal journalism have ended." The *Times* described J.W. Gitt as "an editor who crusaded unequivocally against the war, racism, and infringement of human liberties." But the *Gazette* did not disappear without a trace. After its purchase the name was changed to the *York Daily Record*, and in some respects the new paper's antecedent is quite visible in its pages.

In 1974, a few years after the sale of the *Gazette and Daily*, George

Goodling handed down his well-warmed Congressional seat to his son, William F. Goodling. The younger Goodling served in Washington until 2001, carrying on duties such as serving as chairman of the Foreign Affairs Committee and working as a tireless advocate of improving the public school system.

Congressman Goodling is best remembered in his home town of Loganville, however, not for surviving the Washington chicken-dinner circuit, but for his own chicken dinner of sorts. While still a youngster, Goodling earned a reputation as one of the area's best makers of a favorite Pennsylvania Dutch "dish," chicken corn soup. Congressman Goodling recalls preparing his chicken corn soup for various community fundraisers, and was always amazed to learn that the quantity of soup he made for sale would often be expanded by enthusiastic volunteers, who added water before delivering orders from door to door.

The migration of people and businesses out of the city continued in the late 1960s. Many people preferred the suburbs because of their attractive living conditions, such as parks and recreation areas for children. As a result of the exodus, stores in downtown York began closing or moving. In 1970 Grant's left the downtown area, followed in 1972 by Wiest's and the Golden Glow Cafeteria. In 1974 People's Drug Store, in the Colonial Hotel building, closed, as did Lehmayer's located next door to the Strand Theater, and the Thom McAn Shoe Store, located on West Market Street. In 1975 Bear's Store was sold to the Zollinger's Company. In 1976 the Strand closed, along with Les's Cafeteria, and they were followed, in 1978, by Zollinger's and the Penn Hotel.

To many Yorkers it seemed that the city itself was dying. They called on community leaders to take steps to prevent the city's further decline. The plan to save York that emerged could be summed up in one word: revitalization.

The first step that the city fathers took in revitalizing York was to give the city a new look, or rather revive its old one. In 1976 York's Office of City Planning presented its "Historic Buildings and Preservation Plan," and outlined York's architectural development. Under the direction of Planning Director Charles H. Maneval, planner Thomas M. Foust prepared an extensive report which gave new direction to city leaders. Foust stated that "most of the promotion done by [local agencies] emphasizes York's Colonial Period and its role during the American Revolution. However, in terms of the architectural character of York, little remains from the Colonial period. . . . In fact, probably only five or six . . . buildings [still standing] were here during the Revolution, namely the Gates House and Plough Tavern at 157 and 161 West Market Street, the Cookes (Thomas Paine) House on South Penn Street at the Codorus Creek, probably the (John) Fisher house at 19 North George Street, possibly the small houses at 322 West Market Street and 22 South Beaver Street."

The report went on to say that York, in terms of surviving structures was actually an industrial town, the architecture of which was predominantly Victorian in style. In order to authentically restore York, the plan recommended: "All of the ugly siding and windows added to many downtown stores in the 1940s and 1950s would be replaced by authentic looking brick facades. Public improvements, such as trees, brick sidewalks, and appropriate street furniture, would be installed to add to the restored atmosphere."

One of the first buildings to be revived was not from the Victorian era, however. It was the Yorktowne Hotel, built in the 1920s by a group of local businessmen, who had wanted York to have a gracious building in which the town could show proper hospitality to visitors. In the mid-1970s the hotel, standing just east of the Court House, underwent extensive renovations in order to bring about what the local media and publicity people called a "return to elegance."

The nation's Bicentennial added momentum to the renaissance effort. A replica of the York County Court House, in which Congress had convened during nine months of 1777-1778, was built on the corner of Pershing Avenue and West Market Street at the Codorus Creek. William C. Doze, the York architect who designed the New York Federal Savings and Loan building, drew up the plans for the replica. York's participation in America's 200th birthday was led by the York County Bicentennial Commission. Attorney John F. Rauhauser, Jr., served as the commission's president and was the leading spirit behind York's observances.

The Bicentennial left York with much more than a replica of its first county Court House. A new pride in York's historical heritage had grown in and around the city, and Yorkers felt a new surge of honor at having played a role in national developments throughout the city's 232 years of existence. The issuance of two U.S. Postal Service stamps from York— one commemorating the 200th anniversary of the adoption of the Articles of Confederation, issued on September 30, 1977, and the other commemorating the signing of the French Alliance in York and issued on May 4, 1978—added to York's developing sense of its importance to the nation as a whole.

Yet another facet of York life was on the upswing. When Dr. Robert V. Iosue took over the presidency of York College of Pennsylvania in the fall of 1976, he emphasized the college's academic growth. Moreover, enrollment was climbing and for the first time the college faced the question of limiting it. In 1981 Dr. Iosue oversaw the construction of three new "mini-dormitories" (as the facilities were called) to alleviate the unprecedented crowding.

Even industry has expanded in recent years. In 1970 the York Labor Market area (all of Adams and York counties) had 146,700 workers; in 1978, 18,500 had been added, for a total of 165,200. Moreover, the York Area Chamber of Commerce reported in that year that retail sales for the county in 1977 had topped one billion dollars, and that almost one-third of the nation's population lived within 250 miles of York. The figures implied that the York area, or at least the county, had become a true business and population center.

In only one area did the town remain unchanged: York Countians were politically as conservative as ever. In 1976 they voted for Gerald Ford over Jimmy Carter, and in 1980 they voiced resounding support for Ronald Reagan.

One thing interrupted York's smoothly running revitalization, and most Yorkers weren't even aware of it at first. Yorkers who picked up the morning newspaper on March 28, 1979, probably had no idea that the "worst commercial nuclear power station accident in history" was taking place. Many

of them, even after reading the front-page story of the emergency, went about their business with little real concern of happenings at Three Mile Island, located only 10 miles north of the center of the city.

The next day, however, the *Dispatch* said in a two-column headline, "3-Mile Island Still Leaking Radiation," and Yorkers began to worry. On the same day reports of the emergency received national attention. Telephone lines into the area were jammed, and some Yorkers vacationing outside of the city phoned for hours before reaching family members at home. Even people as far away as Arles were calling in, worried about what was going on.

On Friday, March 30, officials told preschool children and pregnant women from the four counties surrounding TMI to leave. Some Yorkers had already left the area.

A few days after the accident at Three Mile Island, experts told the American public that the effects of the TMI disaster might not be known for 40 years. Yorkers already had a hint of the accident's long-range effects. Musicians booked at area colleges refused to come into the "Three Mile Island" zone, tourism dropped sharply, and a *Dispatch* article on April 2, 1979, called the accident a "realization of a Twentieth Century Horror."

It was Wednesday, April 4, when Yorkers were told that the threat of an "immediate catastrophe" was over, but for many residents the near disaster would never be "over." Two years later, the mental-health impact of the accident was still being studied and Yorkers were hearing further reports of radioactivity from local power plants.

In the aftermath of the Three Mile Island accident, an eery shadow was cast over York County when the Philadelphia Electric Company announced it was installing dozens of sirens within a 10-mile radius of the TMI site. Other sirens were being planned for the area around the Peach Bottom Nuclear Station.

As "the country's worst nuclear-energy plant accident" faded from mem-

ory, Yorkers turned to the business of the day. They had other problems to deal with and, regardless of the shock of the nightmare in their backyard, Yorkers showed the resiliency that is part of their heritage.

The business of nurturing the renaissance of the downtown area received top-priority attention after the Three Mile Island accident. Despite the Yorkers' revitalization efforts in the 1970s, the 1980 census showed 44,464 people in York proper compared to 50,335 in 1970—an 11 percent drop.

But York's leaders were not discouraged. The approval of downtown's new multimillion-dollar Market Way project—a plan in 1979 to turn Bear's Department Store into an $11 million shopping and entertainment complex, and the opening (on April 12, 1980) of the Strand Capitol Performing Arts Center all gave the city evidence of the hoped-for renaissance.

Like so many other structures in the downtown area, the Strand and Capitol theaters had been closed and vacated. Mayor John D. Krout stepped in when the theater buildings were threatened by the wrecking ball, and a group of community leaders assembled to transform the theaters and the Lehmayer's building south of them into a performing-arts complex. In ensuing months Yorkers gave a million dollars and hundreds of hours of volunteer work to make the restoration possible.

In 1981 the York area was a model of slow but steady growth. York's three market houses—Central, Farmers, and the New Eastern—were flourishing. The York Area Chamber of Commerce reported in 1981 that there were two York-area industries (Caterpillar Tractor Company and York Division of Borg-Warner Corporation) that employed more than 3,000 people, and that eight others employed well over 1,000. In terms of land area the county had, in 1981, 914 square miles, according to the York Area Chamber of Commerce, and the city had 5.81 square miles. The "Greater York" area had 17 square miles. The designation "Greater York" came about when the city, small in size, became completely surrounded by heavily populated townships and boroughs. In 1981 the term "York" generally meant "the Greater York Area" and the nonspecific use caused the city some awkward moments when crimes or other unpleasant incidents were tagged to "York," when actually they had occurred outside the city boundaries.

Some Yorkers complained that the city's population figures were misleading to people unfamiliar with the Greater York Area who used the city population count to appraise the area's importance and possible offerings. The situation is frequently made more complicated when "York" is used to denote "York County." Evidence of Yorkers' sensitivity to the problem can be found in the great number of businesses and other groups using the term "York Area" in their names in 1981.

One of the newest York-area groups is the Hispanic community. Father Bernard Pistone, pastor of Cristo Salvador Hispanic Catholic Church at 235 East South Street, has said that there were between 4,000 and 5,000 Hispanics in York when the church was founded in October of 1980, making up some 10 percent of the city's population. He said that most of York's

Hispanic citizens came from Puerto Rico, specifically from the towns of Adjunta, Vega, Baja, Vega Alta, Ponce, and Ajuja.

"I see the Hispanic population here growing even more in coming years," Father Pistone said. "York's industrialization has provided many opportunities for jobs and many times one member of the family will come, get a job, and then send for the rest of the family." The transition from Puerto Rico to York, Father Pistone said, is "very painful because of the language barrier and because the weather is so severe." (The county's average winter temperature is only 40.8 degrees Fahrenheit.)

Father Pistone points out that the transition is even more difficult for Puerto Ricans than for other immigrants. "The Greeks, the Vietnamese, the [other] Asians—they have come to make America their new home. They are quickly assimilated. The Puerto Ricans who come here already are Americans and they tend to hold on to ties to their native island. They can travel back and forth." He predicted that the transition would become easier and in 10 or 15 years there would be no need for a Hispanic Catholic Church, however the population has continued to grow steadily.

York is, indeed, from all indications, revitalizing itself. In February 1981, Jack Kay, Director of Community Development for York, said in a speech before the Cosmopolitan Club of York that York had "turned the corner and is coming back."

Mayor Elizabeth N. Marshall, in an address downtown on March 28, 1981, confirmed Kay's remarks: "Downtown will never be the retail center it was in the 1940s and 1950s. The Downtown area is and will be, however, a center of banking, law, cultural arts, and unique shops. York City will always be the heart of the county and the county seat and York will always hold the rich architectural beauty that makes it truly outstanding."

In commenting on the city's "rich architectural beauty," Mayor Marshall reconfirmed the city's new dedication to the promotion of York's physical uniqueness. A visiting art historian from New York City had told Yorkers that the downtown area was "like a marvelous living museum." He said the juxtaposition of Colonial, Victorian and modern buildings held a charm that was "probably more diverse and interesting than anywhere else in America." The art expert, owner of a 200-year old gallery in London with a branch in New York, visited York's Currier and Ives Gallery, housed in a "spectacular"

Below left, top and bottom
The Greater York Area is home to more than 450 houses of worship representing 45 denominations, including St. Patrick's Catholic Church on 231 South Beaver Street and Ohev Sholom Synagogue on 2251 Eastern Boulevard. Courtesy, Sunday News and HSYC.

Victorian building across from City Hall, and made a stop at the Victoria home left to The Historical Society of York County by the heirs of Yor attorney and artist Horace Bonham. He said he was "astounded" that Yor "held such beauty."

With York's heightened awareness of its architectural heritage, commu nity leaders took positive steps to earn maximum benefits from the increase interest in the city's appearance. The York Area Chamber of Commerc launched an annual two-day Victorian Heritage Festival and the city reape considerable publicity, especially from out-of-town news media.

Yorkers are not only adjusting to taking pride in their town again, they ar also working together to rebuild their center city, to strengthen the area economy, and to promote York throughout the country. Henry R. Merge editor of the *York Dispatch*, summed up feelings about the York communit in an editorial printed on January 14, 1981. It read:

> *York County is a good place to live. One of the reasons why, pe haps the most important reason, is the jobs available to support familie churches, schools and other social institutions serving the community. Yo County is blessed, too, because of the diversification of its industry, supple mented by commerce and agriculture. All of these facts came to mind wi the announcement that York County's unemployment rate of 6 percent below national and state levels. It is vital that we continue to work to crea conditions which will not only encourage the business we already have, b attract others as well. We must give a just day's work for a just day's pa We must have good schools, good recreational facilities, cultural opportu nities, safe streets and pride in our achievements.*

Pride in past achievements has been a guiding beacon to Yorkers in forgin the community's future. Yorkers have survived everything from living amon occasionally hostile Indians and the encroachment of Marylanders in th 1730s to the coming of the Klansmen in the 1920s. They have survive financial difficulties by establishing diverse businesses and industries tha have shielded them from the effects of every economic problem from th panics of the 19th century to the recessions and Great Depression of the 20t century. They have survived massive takeovers from Congress's occupatio in 1778 to the Confederate invasion of 1863. Yorkers have survived, as wel everything from overflowing rivers and destructive fires to a nuclear plar disaster, and it is probable that they will survive calamities as yet not seer In recent years, the York community has survived by attracting people whether by building new freeways, by restoring or rebuilding old landmark or by producing quality goods demanded around the globe.

York's experience today confirms the unwitting suggestion of the India deed of 1736, which stated that York County's influence would extend inf nitely, ". . . to the setting of the sun." With the export of products an ideas, and the moving about of its people, that influence, indeed, seems t have no limits. This, perhaps, is the greatest achievement of all, and on which will set the stage for making York's future as magical as its past.

Below
Mitch Gibbs, a young artist from York, is shown with one of his watercolors depicting the bandstand at Farquhar Park, seen in the background. York artists, such as Virgil Sova, William A. Falkler, and Othmar Carli, have reached national and international prominence. Courtesy, Sunday News.

Below right
The Codorus Creek bike path provides a relaxing and pleasant diversion for health-conscious York citizens. Courtesy, William J. Schintz.

Looking east through Center
Square at the old colonial Market
Shed just west of the County
Court House, this William
Wagner painting typifies life in
1830s York. On the right is the
sign of the Globe Inn where
Lafayette was honored in 1825.
Courtesy, The York County
Heritage Trust

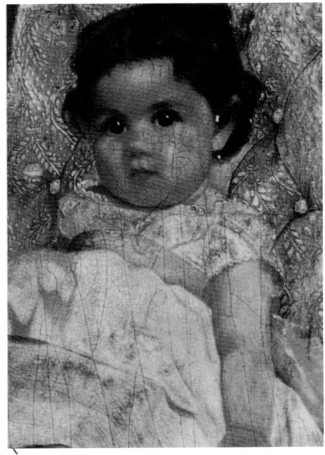

Facing page

Top
The Community Swimming Pool, east of Farquhar Park, boasted a 125-foot by 275-foot pool with depth varying from eight inches to eight feet. This early recreational center offered 1,000 steel lockers, private dressing rooms, and showers with springboards, high dives, rafting equipment, and fountains of bright clear water. Postcard published by the York News Agency. Courtesy The Schintz Studio

Bottom left
This painted window, seen in a bank building on York's Continental Square, depicts members of the Second Continental Congress gathering in the original York County Courthouse. Congressional delegates met in the 1756 structure, located in the middle of the square, from September 1777 to June 1778 and the York community witnessed some of the greatest moments in American history. Scenes such as this one are recreated during many patriotic events remembering York's role as "crucible of a new nation." Photo by Gerald Reimold. CourtesyThe Schintz Studio

Bottom right
York artist Horace Bonham painted this portrait of Mary Lewis Bonham in 1871 or 1892. Bonham's works have been cited as excellent examples of 19th century American genre art. Courtesy, The York County Heritage Trust

This page

Top
WIth its wood-block printed borders, which have been hand-colored and stippled, this 1806 birth and baptismal record of Johannes Willem is truly a work of art. Courtesy, The York County Heritage Trust

Bottom
The handwritten, illuminated watercolor birth record of Jacob N., Elizabeth B., and Joel N. Myers (1846, 1845, and 1871) is pictured here. Courtesy, The York County Heritage Trust

This page
Top
The so-called "Quakers" migrating to northern York County in the early days built this meetinghouse in 1769 and doubled its size just 12 years later. The Warrington Friends Meeting House, located near Rossville, is still used today and its burial ground, partially visible in the foreground, contains both old and new style markers. Photo by Cindy Roach. Courtesy, The Schintz Studio

Bottom
The dining room of the General Horatio Gates House is seen here with its wall partition that lifts from the floor to create a larger banquet room. During a banquet held in this house, the French diplomat, the Marquis de Lafayette, squashed a plot to replace General George Washington with General Gates, who was residing here as Congress met in the nearby courthouse. Courtesy, The Schintz Studio

Facing page
Top
Continental Square in downtown York on a snowy eve is illuminated by holiday lights and old-fashioned lamps recalling the city's heritage in both colonial and Victorian times. Courtesy, The Schintz Studio

Bottom left
The Civil War Monument standing in the Hanover Square was given to the town by the Commonwealth of Pennsylvania to commemorate the Battle of Hanover. The clash between Confederate and Union brigades began at 8 o'clock in the morning of June 30, 1863 and continued until 2 o'clock in the afternoon with many casualties on both sides. Courtesy, The Schintz Studio

Bottom right
The long-familiar animal barns at the York Fairgrounds became history at the close of the 2002 annual fair. These structures were demolished to make room for a new arena that would attract year-round patrons. The fairgrounds, once locked up except for a few weeks each fall, now hosts large and small events all year round. Courtesy, The Schintz Studio

The area around the Farquhar Park bandstand/gazebo, seen above, brings autumn country splendor to a site minutes from Continental Square in downtown York. The old bandstand, in a park donated by industrialist Arthur Briggs Farquhar, is a favorite place for weddings and the subject of many paintings. Courtesy, The Schintz Studio

Above
From Farm to Market is the title of the mural seen on the brick building at right and some of the people depicted in the lower portion of the painting still "tend market" in Central Market House seen at left. Note how the arches and turrets of the 1888 farmers market building are reflected in this mural by Marion Stephenson. Courtesy, The Schintz Studio

Right
The updated, classical columns of the York Water Company building seem to form the ideal frame for this American flag. The people seen in the lower portion of the photo are gathering for the parade that celebrated the county's 250th anniversary in 1999. The facade of the water company building gives little hint of the elaborate murals that decorate the structure's interior. Courtesy, The Schintz Studio

Above
Artist Virgil Sova created this pastel for reproduction as a bookplate for Martin Memorial Library. In this painting, *The Gift of Knowledge*, the artist weaves a group of symbols which the viewer is free to interpret as he or she sees fit. The Library has served as a community center, a platform for the exchange of ideas and a forum for free speech since its founding in 1935. Courtesy, Martin Memorial Library

RIght
This fanciful drawing by Martha Hendrix shows members of *The Breakfast Club*, at one of its meetings in the Yorktowne Hotel coffee shop. In this drawing, newsman Harry J. McLaughlin is depicted at top left with notepad and former Chamber of Commerce president Carl F. Neu is pictured at lower right with a pipe and coffee cup. The informal group is joined occasionally by celebrities lodging at the downtown inn and it is said that no subject is closed to discussion. Reproduction courtesy, The Schintz Studio

Dover native Jeff Koons, seen in this photo with his work entitled *Puppy Vase*. During his many visits to his father's interior design store in York as a small child, he became fascinated with the enchantment that art objects, mirrors and furnishings brought over the human spirit. Born in 1955, he studied at the Maryland Institute College of Art and the School of the Art Institute of Chicago. It was his success as a commodities dealer in New York City, however, that earned him the freedom to create art that has inspired—and shocked—art consumers and critics around the world. Photo by Clifford Norton. Courtesy, Art of this Century, Inc.

BREAKFAST CLUB

Right
These young people enjoy a game on the Small Athletic Field, one of the sites considered for a new baseball stadium. The city of York is visible in the background with the dome of the County Courthouse peaking into the skyline at left. Courtesy, The Schintz Studio

Below
Carnival barkers, thrilling rides and crowds of hungry people are some of the features of the York Fair held each September. The building in the background houses vendors who rent stalls on the ground floor while the upper portion contains thousands of seats for those attending harness racing and concert events. Courtesy, The Schintz Studio

Left
Cherry Lane Park, seen on a summer day, greets visitors before or after they return to one of the nearby farmers' markets. This park offers lunch-time concerts with beautiful art and architecture as a backdrop. Courtesy, The Schintz Studio

Below
The Strand-Capitol Performing Arts Center is seen here as the marquee beckons fans of country music, Broadway and art films. Courtesy, The Schintz Studio

Top
This old mill near Wrightsville recalls York County's past when structures like it dotted every creek. A few mills, including the one above, are still in service after many decades of use. Courtesy, The Schintz Studio

Right
The oldest house in York County was built by Johann Shultz soon after he arrived here in 1734. The home, south of Stony Brook, was used as a public inn and tradition claims members of the Continental Congress stopped here on their way from Philadelphia to York during the fall of 1777. Photo by Gerald Reimold. Courtesy, The Schintz Studio

Left
These two pigs captured during a restful moment at the York Fair reflect the farm tradition that still pervades the York County conscience and landscape. Courtesy, The Schintz Studio

Below
The daily chores of rural farm life are pictured here in a recent photograph in Hallam Township. Scenes like this one unfold everyday just minutes away from the cities, towns and villages that dot York County. Courtesy, The Schintz Studio

Top
Samuel S. Lewis State Park is a favorite spot for picnickers and naturelovers. The two individuals seen here are looking across the Susquehanna River to the western boundaries of Lancaster County. Courtesy, The Schintz Studio

Bottom
A fresh layer of snow brings beauty and a sense of tranquility to downtown York. This photograph was taken on Market Street just east of the square. Courtesy, The Schintz Studio

Above
This York County farm scene shows the diversity of agriculture at a time when farmland is being lost to development. In the forefront are rows of fruit trees, a mainstay in York's agricultural production. Rows of dried cornstalks and grains are interspersed in this landscape with woodland, but a well-built red barn dominates the scene. Note the architectural features of the buildings pictured here. Courtesy, The Schintz Studio

Right
This flock of geese is captured by the camera as it flies above a farm near Bair Station. York's rolling hills contain some of the most fertile farmland in America. Courtesy, The Schintz Studio

New Year's Eve brings crowds of celebrants to the York Square for a night of entertainment that combines music, magic and theater. The finale pictured above draws participants as a giant White Rose drops into an oversized vase at the moment the New Year begins. Courtesy, The Schintz Studio

CHAPTER X

INTO A NEW MILLENNIUM

Gains and losses, celebrations and disappointments. These four themes played out in dramatic fashion as the people of York, grounded in history, faced the challenges of the 1980s and 1990s and entered the new millennium. While the population of the county increased from 313,000 to 382,000 during this 20-year period, the population of the city of York declined from 44,600 to about 41,000. Areas around the city were growing, some at astonishing rates. It was becoming clearer that the 72 autonomous municipalities in York County were dependent on each other for the well being of the entire community.

This remarkable growth affected individuals and businesses in all of York County's governmental bodies. From the Susquehanna River in the east, to the Adams County line in the west, and from the Mason-Dixon line in the south to the scenic towns of the north like Wellsville and Dillsburg, growth around the city helped to revitalize this landlocked county seat. The city grew more important as a center of commerce and government even while the number of residents declined. In the city and in the areas around it, private and public sectors invested hundreds of millions of dollars in new building projects and in the rehabilitation of old structures.

Reflecting its heritage as a good place to settle, York's location and natural resources continued to serve as the key to its development and the door to opportunity. These elements were underscored by the work ethic of the men and women living here, offering "a good day's work for a good day's pay." At the same time developers using "the next available farm" approach to building shopping facilities, industrial plazas and housing tracts, threatened the pastoral qualities that allowed agriculture to thrive for generations on some of the most fertile land in existence. Topography limited the size of farms but the growing of fruits, grains and certain livestock, especially chickens, gave York County a leading edge in state agricultural production.

Natural resources like lumber, limestone and dolomite still played roles in the economic structure while wildlife like deer, fish, and fowl still played roles in the social structure as well. One indicator of the continuing importance of wildlife to the region today is found in the number of York countians holding hunting licenses issued by the state. According to state officials 38,051 individuals purchased a general hunting or fur taker license in York County during the 2000 license year. Clearly, though, York was turning more and more from a culture steeped in farming and hunting to an urban-suburban economy based on industry and service.

As fewer people were working the land to produce crops and meat products, more people were finding jobs in related industries like food

processing, candy making, wine production and the manufacture of snack foods. Food processing made up one of the four most important components of the York County economy. Distribution made up a second important component and the papermaking, pre-press and printing industries accounted for a third important segment.

The fourth component to economic stability remained in manufacturing. As in the past, the economy remained highly diversified; but in some cases, the focus narrowed. In the area of manufacturing, for instance, precision assembly and precision machining work became more important while other manufacturing specialties declined or disappeared.

Health and government-related companies increased their workforces; the construction industry grew and other businesses, like retail stores, restaurants and motels and hotels brought jobs.

Mergers, such as those occurring in health and banking-related institutions, often shifted workers from one job or one location to another and changed attitudes that had been passed on from mother to daughter and father to son over decades of experience. The ideal shared by past generations, that a worker would stay with one company all of his or her life, became increasingly rare.

One perspective, false in many ways, that York remained isolated from the rest of the world, seemed ludicrous as York County faced one of its most perplexing problems, outmoded highways and traffic congestion. Growth in the surrounding regions punctuated the importance of accessibility. The 2000 census showed that there were 1.7 million people living within an eight county area defined by economists as "the midstate." This area included Adams, Cumberland, Dauphin, Franklin, Lancaster, Lebanon, Perry and York counties. More than $8 billion in new residential construction had been added to this geographic base in the period spanning 1990 to 2000 and despite many failures to merge and form coalitions the so-called midstate was becoming a vast metropolis relying on neighbors in many areas but fiercely independent in others.

Economists looking at the southern tier of York County, affected both by Maryland farmlands and the Baltimore suburbs, saw another view of York County. Depending on the point of view there was further potential or

U. S. Representative Bill Goodling, a Republican from Seven Valleys, is shown at right, welcoming the Dale Petroskey family to his home district. In the 1980s Petroskey served on Goodling's staff. He later became president of the National Baseball Hall of Fame and Museum in Cooperstown, New York. Courtesy, Harry J. McLaughlin.

additional danger lying here and many of the rules defied present-day political boundaries and underlying colonial sensibilities.

Even when the representatives of the 13 original colonies chose the York County Courthouse as the headquarters for their meetings to form a national government in the late 18th Century, York was a crossroads of migration, especially west and south. The highways crisscrossing the county today, notably U.S. Route 30 and Interstate Route 83, provide easy accessibility to vast markets. The Pennsylvania Turnpike with exit and entrance ramps just north of the city, and easy connections to the major north-south artery, Interstate 81, help to ease the flow of goods and speed travelers on their way.

Airports like Harrisburg International and Capitol City were complemented by numerous smaller facilities within easy reach, along with the airports of the Baltimore-Washington region. Facilities in the Philadelphia area also competed for the dollars originating in, or passing through York County and associated with distribution of goods and travel for business and pleasure.

U.S. Route 30, still known as the Lincoln Highway to locals, now carried hundreds of thousands of tourists through York County to first-choice destinations nearby like Gettysburg and Lancaster. These towns, also located on the famous road that spanned the nation, had been tremendously successful in marketing their historic and cultural alliances as the era of the automobile took hold. The road, even with its shortcomings, allowed Americans to discover the treasures that made those two towns unique.

Though York held significant national history and communities of devout religious people, like Gettysburg and Lancaster did, its attractiveness as a tourist stop on its own merits, did not fully emerge until the 1980s and 1990s. Major progress was achieved in this important arena and Yorkers discovered that the "clean" money produced by tourism could pump millions of dollars into the local economy and improve the county's image at the same time.

The connection to the past became more important to those with long-time ties here, at the same time it intrigued newcomers thirsty for an anchor in America's vast heritage and a sense of place crucial to a meaningful lifestyle. While sense of place was especially important to families with longtime ties to the region, a startling development troubled the waters for some of these proud and devoted natives. For the first time in history, people who moved here from other regions were outnumbering residents born and reared in York County.

Building on nostalgic memories of railroading, Yorkers worked in private and public sectors to create the "Rail Trail," using the beds of old

Artistry in iron, like the example seen here on Market Street in downtown York, ornaments many of the region's most beautiful buildings. Decorative ironwork became one of York's most significant exports early in its history, along with artificial teeth, wallcoverings, equipment for the hydropower industry, and air conditioning and refrigeration units, to mention a few. Ornamental ironwork made in York can be seen throughout the South, including the picturesque neighborhoods of New Orleans. Courtesy, Schintz Studio

railroad lines to bring visitors from the Maryland line into downtown York.

York County solidified its attractiveness as a gathering place for toy train collectors, antique dealers, Native Americans, street rod owners, motorcycle riders, and racing car enthusiasts, among others. Polishing a gem discovered in earlier days, leaders began to market York County as a place for factory tours. Factory tours, farm tours, garden tours, house tours and even ghost tours spotlighted the fact that York County had a vast heritage and was pleased to share its treasures, some long-hidden from view.

Cultural institutions like York Little Theater, the York Symphony Association, the York Art Association, Yorkarts, the Eichelberger Performing Arts Center and the Strand-Capitol Performing Arts Center, not only entertained and enlightened, but served as the training ground for young actors, artists and musicians who reached for the stars, and in notable instances, were successful in their pursuits. Among many York County natives making international news were the actor Craig Sheffer, the artist Jeff Koons and the rock band, LIVE.

And if local institutions did not offer the kind of culture desired by natives and newcomers, residents of York County were not far from the larger centers of culture and recreation like Baltimore and Philadelphia and even New York City. Most importantly, for thousands of Yorkers, they could reach the beaches of the Atlantic Ocean within a morning's drive.

From its vantage in the middle of the eastern corridor, within a population center extending from Boston to Norfolk, York County continued to foster economic stability and growth.

Many communities located in "the Rust Belt," as York was, broke down under the burden of deteriorating infrastructures and the "brain drain" resulting in flight from the home community. And while York County fared much better than some other communities, these issues troubled educators, politicians and developers here, as they did in places that were not infused with new blood and increased development. With support from the York County Chamber and other groups, an internship program with Howard University brought bright young people to York businesses. Local colleges, technical schools and academies instituted programs to attract people from diverse backgrounds. Similarly, programs to keep York County's best students working in their hometowns were instituted, directed by focus groups; surveys and polls that helped leaders understand the need for proactive efforts in meeting the competition.

Replacing leadership that grew out of patriarchal beginnings and modernizing infrastructures became major challenges for York County as it entered the new millennium. Industries, bank operations and medical facilities, in particular, underwent changes unimaginable in earlier days. Many businesses originating in York County and reared here for generations were sold to outside firms. Control of these operations moved to faraway places, in some instances, and the shift resulted in the loss of decision-making power that affected various elements of the economy from political persuasiveness to philanthropic generosity.

In some notable cases, control of firms that moved out of the county were brought back to York County as employees or other local interests returned operations after brief forays into a larger environment.

On the other hand, firms like the one that made York Peppermint Patties and one that made shoes with the Hanover name seemed to be lost forever to outside control. The sewing industry, once a staple of the York economy, almost disappeared because of competition from cheaper labor and the trend towards mega-mergers. Other industries, once common here, suffered the same fate.

With all the concern for manufacturing developments, interest in York County land, once its chief resource, seemed to wane during the 1980s and 1990s, except for a few small groups that kept the issue of land management alive. Long-term strategic plans helped to designate growth along the highway corridors and attempted to put in place programs for the preservation of the most desirable farmland. Industrial plazas, many located along these corridors with access to major highways, attracted new industry through tax abatement programs and other governmental incentives such as the Keystone Opportunity Zone (KOZ) program. The York County Economic Development Agency, the York County Planning Commission, Better York Inc., Main Street York, and a myriad of other agencies worked together to nurture growth where it was deemed desirable.

The damage growth and activity brought to the Susquehanna River and the Chesapeake Bay were addressed in public and private sessions. To resolve the age-old challenge of restoring the Codorus Creek Watershed an Endowment was created with a $2 million gift from Glatfelter of Spring

The Elmwood Mansion on Belmont Street in East York is a sterling example of building restoration and reuse. In the early 1900s this building was moved from its original site on logs pulled by mules. It was purchased by Memorial Hospital from the last of many families residing here and is used as a meeting and conference center. Former residents tell of at least three harmless ghosts still residing here, but the light of scientific evidence has not yet proven that the legends have validity. Courtesy, The Schintz Studio

Barbara Bush is seen in this photo during a visit to York's Crispus Attucks Community Center. Bobby Simpson, longtime executive director of the center, is seen at left of Mrs. Bush as she salutes the staff for its educational, recreational and child development programs. Courtesy, Harry J. McLaughlin

Grove, as part of a consent decree settling litigation. The gift was placed within the York Foundation and a committee of environmental, business and civic leaders was appointed to direct the Endowment's work. A Foundation spokesman explained, "The committee will lead and support development of promising initiatives to protect and improve the watershed over time, and will award annual grants for projects of local not-for-profit and/or governmental organizations, in response to competitive proposals."

In this development and others, the increasing importance of the York Foundation was evident as this charitable endowment emerged as a major force in helping York County face its challenges. In 2001, the York Foundation made grants to more than 160 charitable organizations. The York Foundation was one of many agencies that contributed to the welfare of the county and its people. Lutheran Social Services of South Central Pennsylvania, the Adams-Hanover Counseling Services and Family Service of York and York County provided funds and expertise that touched almost every resident of York County during his or her lifetime. The United Way of York County alone raised more than $7 million in 2000 for community agencies.

Efforts to preserve the community's cultural resources were also formalized in this era as the York Cultural Alliance was formed to raise money for nine member agencies. In its first three years, the Alliance raised nearly $3 million to benefit such agencies as the Strand-Capitol Performing Arts Center, the York County Heritage Trust, York Little Theater, the York Art Association, Yorkarts, the Colonial Courthouse, the York Symphony Orchestra, the York Junior Symphony Orchestra, and the York Youth Symphony Orchestra. Faster communication with focused appeals aided the efforts to make York County a better place in which to live, work and play.

The revolution in communications affected almost every citizen in this 20-year period. York County was wired for the cable television industry and the worldwide web was introduced. Soon everyone had some access to a larger vision of the world, the global picture, as close as his or her local library.

An official at Martin Library recalled with a sense of wonder, her introduction to what became known as the world wide web: "It was sometime in 1988. I was asked to be part of a group, a cross-section of citizens," she reported, "that would discuss the future of communications and how it might affect York. Someone asked us, 'if you could get anything you wanted over your television set, what would you want?'"

"We were told to let our imaginations run wild," she explained. "As a result, we explored all kinds of possibilities. Someone suggested it would be good to be able to look at a restaurant menu without going to the restaurant. It would be good to be able to register to vote without leaving our office, look at a bus schedule, find out what movies are playing, and acquire forms we needed. We decided we should be able to find out more about current issues and research topics as if we had our own reference library nearby."

"Little did we realize," this observer noted, "that we were the citizens group letting the cable company know what we would want on this new thing called the Internet."

Looking back to the months and years before the Internet swept through thousands of York County businesses and homes and changed the lives of nearly everyone, the daily lives of people and the events of the seasons seem to foreshadow the decades that followed. The twists and turns of recent history might have caught many by surprise but as usual, the past provides road signs that can help prepare for the future. When the eighties began, the United States census verified many of the trends that planners expected. Population of the county was set at 312,963 and population of York City was set at 44,619.

In the preceding ten years, the county had grown by 40,000 people. The U.S. Census Bureau reported that York formed an economic triangle, with Harrisburg and Lancaster that was the fastest growing population center in Pennsylvania. The number of homes, apartments and housing developments in this area had jumped 30 percent since the last federal count ten years before.

The city lost residents but the numbers of Black non-Hispanic people residing in the city was rising along with the numbers of Hispanic people identified "of any race." The number of people in the workforce was growing, but the number of people working in farm-related occupations fell sharply. Still, York County's 2,260 farms comprising 300,000 acres of land were producing almost $84 million worth of goods.

The year 1981 was filled with news making events, from the approval of York Bancorp, the bank holding company that would own the York Bank and Trust Co., to the closing of the city's last department store. When the Bon Ton vacated its landmark department store at Market and Beaver streets it seemed to many the city had suffered a final, terrifying blow. Nevertheless, York City Council members authorized a $7.2 million 30-year bond issue to pay for two new parking garages. Though "business as usual" would never be the same, signs of growth and perennial optimism seemed to overwhelm the signs of gloom and despair.

Parking of automobiles in the downtown area remained a primary push and pull issue. City Council approved parking rate hikes up to 50 percent and the city police bureau enforced parking restrictions at the same time retail choices were dwindling. Some residents left their homes and apartments on this issue alone while others philosophized that parking fines were necessary for the smooth conduct of business. And the city used funds gained from parking fines to supplement its annual budget, which now exceeded $9 million.

This photo shows the interior of the old Borg Warner complex after renovation was completed in 1995. The old crane that was used to carry gigantic air conditioning and refrigeration parts from one place in the factory to another, was saved to add visual interest and serve as historic reference. Courtesy, Buchart-Horn Inc./BASCO Associates

Outside the city, there were more opportunities for shopping and less chance of incurring fines for leaving an automobile unattended. A new 700,000-square-foot climate-controlled mall opened in West Manchester Township, minutes away from downtown congestion. Strip malls, convenience stores, and farm stores outside of city boundaries seemed to pop up at every intersection and these businesses captured the dollars of even those who dubbed themselves back-to-the-city activists.

People who lived in the rural areas of York County had problems of their own. A severe drought and the invasion of gypsy moths cut into farm production as well as farm income. Meanwhile, industrial, governmental and private development in the county took fertile farmland out of production while in many cases it created jobs and steadily changed the face of the region once based primarily on agrarian principles.

Groundbreaking for the Margaret E. Moul Home for the Handicapped occurred on a rainy day in February, 1981 and speakers on hand for that event noted this facility, built for mentally-alert but physically-handicapped adults, was perhaps the only one of its kind in the nation.

The year was full of news making events: the Harley-Davidson Company severed its relationship with AMF, a long-time York employer; York's stand-out athlete, Loretta Claiborne, ran the Boston Marathon breaking barriers and turning a national spotlight on her old hometown as political activists saw history in the making, too. For the first time in 50 years, more people registered as Republicans. Republicans numbered 58,563 and there were 58,024 Democrats on the books.

This development helped Republican William Althaus sweep into the city's mayoral office the following year with a victory over Mayor Elizabeth N. Marshall, the first woman elected to that office. Mayor Marshall played a key role in the revitalization of the city. Among other accomplishments, Market Street, the east-west corridor through the downtown area was narrowed to discourage heavy trucks damaging architecture and to create a more inviting atmosphere for pedestrians. Dozens of Bradford Pear Trees were planted along refurbished sidewalks. Eventually the trees became an unofficial tourist attraction when they began showering the streets with white petals each year in early April. (Althaus was elected again in 1986 and 1990, serving the city for three terms.)

Based just outside the city, the Allis-Chalmers Corp.'s Hydro-Turbine Division won a $30 million contract with Egypt to provide four additional turbines for the Aswan Dam. In contrast to this triumph in York's industrial

The Junior League of York hosted General Colin Powell during his visit to York in April, 1996, and provided a rare opportunity for local officials to chat with an American figure known throughout the world. General Powell is flanked by police chief Michael Hill, pictured at left, and Sargeant Gene Fells at right. Courtesy, The Schintz Studio

Facing page
These before and after pictures show what can happen when an old factory complex is renovated and adapted for reuse. The former Borg Warner complex, comprising 6.7 acres and bounded by West Philadelphia Street and Roosevelt Avenue, was renovated in the mid-1990s. In 1995 Buchart-Horn Inc./Basco Associates, designers and engineers for the project, became the first of several tenants to share the new facilities. At left is an aerial view of the complex before renovation began. At right is an aerial view of the complex today, featuring plenty of free parking and bright, airy spaces for hundreds of workers and visitors. Running from left to right across the top of both photographs is Roosevelt Avenue. At the bottom or each photo West Philadelphia Street can be seen just before it intersects with Roosevelt. Courtesy, Buchart-Horn Inc./ BASCO Associates

outlook, another bedrock employer, the York Division of Borg-Warner Corp., saw most of its workers walk out on strike. A majority, who were members of Local 1872 of the United Auto Workers, voted to strike when talks about a new three-year contract reached a stalemate. Soon after this strike was history, the York Area Labor-Management Council was founded to help resolve differences between workers and their supervisors. York County now had 65,000 workers in manufacturing production alone, and the total labor force in the York-Adams district reached 175,700. Holding to tradition, York ranked among the most highly diversified manufacturing communities of its size in the world.

A major player in creation of jobs and economic development, the York County Industrial Development Authority, was active on many fronts during this era. The Authority approved the purchase of a 69-acre tract just east of Hanover for an industrial park and became an indefatigable advocate for industrial and economic health. A factory and business place tour supported by the Authority and promoted by tourism workers offered an insider's look at numerous York businesses and helped to build a tradition continuing today. This tour included visits to the Borg Warner Corp., the Caterpillar Tractor Co., Dentsply International, the *York Daily Record*, the Dispatch Publishing Co, the General Telephone Company, Green's Dairy, the P.H. Glatfelter Co., Rutter Bros. Dairy, the St. Regis Paper Co., the York Container Company, the Yorktown Paper Mill, the York Bank and Trust Co. and the Rodney C. Gott Motorcycle Museum at the Harley-Davidson assembly plant.

Near the end of 1981, York's newest climate-controlled shopping center, the West Manchester Mall, opened and shoppers praised the 700,000-square-foot facility for its comfort, variety, and acres of free parking. In the city of York, meanwhile, authorities stepped up enforcement of the two-hour free-parking limit designed to encourage people to shop downtown. York County attempted to add shopping outlets to tourism offerings.

In 1982 many of the trends occurring in the previous years gathered force and shaped a community that stayed the same in many ways, but changed forever in other respects, some unimaginable even today. The number of acres in food production fell to about 300,000 acres during this era but York County held its number two position in the state in terms of farm acreage, just behind Lancaster.

Historic structures in downtown York provide a backdrop for Harley-Davidson motorcycles converging here during a pilgrimage of important places In Harley lore. The Harley-Davidson assembly plant in East York attracts thousands of visitors each year, some riding their own Harleys from places faraway. York Bike Nite is one of the highlights of the conven-tion and tourism year with a parade that vrooms east on Market Street as thousands of owners and wannabe owners gather to celebrate the only motorcycle made in the U.S.A. Courtesy, The Schintz Studio

As a national recession begun in 1982 lingered, York County moved ahead, defying state and federal trends as it had in many instances throughout history. From 1983 to 1987, the county planning commission approved building on 30,343 acres. In counterpoint, during the same period, York lost an additional 21,640 acres of farmland, four times the rate of the preceding five years.

As part of its role in nurturing business and creating jobs, the York County Industrial Development Corp. established a CYBER Center in a city industrial park. The word CYBER is an acronym for the County of York Business and Entrepreneurial Resource Center, described as a business incubator where tenants shared critical amenities such as telephones, fax machines, conference rooms and receptionist services. At the same time the YCIDC and other agencies were nurturing expansion in other areas, the New Cumberland Army Depot, one of the area's largest employers, broke ground for a $200 million distribution center, covering 850 acres. York industries such as York Wallcoverings, Hanover Brands, York Graphic Services, the Glatfelter Insurance Agency, the Stauffer/Meiji Biscuit Company, Stewart Connectors, the American Hydro Corp., Gichner Mobile, the Kling Corp. and Trenwyth Industries launched expansions.

In 1986, U.S. President Ronald Reagan visited the Harley-Davidson motorcycle assembly plant and saluted managers who bought the company with new financing and protective tariffs. The president fostered an All-American pride as he pointed out that Harley was the only U.S. based motorcycle maker and recalled that Harley had converted the manufacturing plant used by AMF, which made bomb casings and bowling balls. Harley Davidson was listed on the New York Stock Exchange and experienced steady growth that continues today.

York's old air conditioning company returned to York hands in 1986, and renamed, York International, the company earned a yearly profit of $8.2 million. Amidst the industrial and business expansion, Yorkers kept an eye on social issues. York County Commissioners formed the York 2000 Commission and York's Habitat for Humanity celebrated completion of its first house in the city. In 1987 voters elected the county's first female judge, Sheryl Ann Dorney, age 37, and representatives of the reconstructed York County Colonial Courthouse hosted John Sununu, Chief of Staff to President George Bush. In 1988, the Young Family, publishers of the *York Dis-*

patch for 112 years, sold the paper to an out-of-town firm. This move by the region's only evening, or afternoon, newspaper stunned and dismayed many readers. It also foreshadowed future changes that would end an era in which York was signaled out for its unique blend of competing evening, morning, and Sunday newspapers.

The *Dispatch* and its competitors were quick to cover the news of a local business, the Pfaltzgraff Company, as officials at Pfaltzgraff announced the firm was entering the bone china market. This meant intense national and global competition and came at a time when the pottery's parent company, Susquehanna-Pfaltzgraff, was fortifying its position as a leader in downtown improvements. Engaged in radio broadcasting, cable, and Internet services, real estate and other businesses, Susquehanna Pfaltzgraff was one of York County's largest employers.

The York Chamber of Commerce summarized the economic climate of the times when it reported that within three blocks of the town square, $26 million in private funds and $500,000 in public funds were at work. The Susquehanna Pfaltzgraff Company was building a six-story office building near the Square on South George Street and downtown York was being "transformed as the county's business and commerce center..."

David B. Carver, a long-time cheerleader for York development with astonishing accomplishments to his credit, echoed the Chamber's optimism: "York's continued economic growth is assured by its geographical location, the strong work ethic of its population, and the management and productivity of its companies." Carver was executive director of the York County Industrial Development Corporation and later would be credited with bringing more than 11,000 jobs to York County before he left the organization that came to be called the York County Economic Development Corporation. As the Chamber and the Industrial Development authorities were tallying the advances of the era, they could point to specific areas where expansion was taking place. The Engel USA Co., Continental Insurance Co., the American Hydro Corp., the AC Valve Corp. and Crown Cork and Seal were undergoing multi-million dollar expansions and the local economic climate seemed bright compared to similar regions in the state and the nation.

Not all the news from the industrial sector was palatable. One of the major candy companies that carried the York name to the far reaches of the country, was acquired by an out-of-town firm and manufacturing operations here were closed bringing a loss of jobs and a blow to the "Made in York" sensibility that had developed over two and a half centuries. About the time the Hershey Foods Corporation was taking over production of the York Peppermint Pattie, another surprising development occurred bringing a sense that things would never be the same. York's morning, evening, and Sunday newspapers agreed to a Joint Operating Agreement, an idea that would have been scoffed at just a decade before. Under the agreement, later approved by the attorney general, business activities would be merged but the newspapers would maintain editorial independence.

In the heat of that memorable summer, a former president made a visit to York full of symbolic and nostalgic significance. President Nixon visited the Richard M. Nixon County Park in southern York County and recalled some of the events that brought his family to York County from California in the early days of his congressional tenure. The business pages of the local newspapers, touted another local achievement. Buchart-Horn Inc., the largest engineering firm in York, had been awarded a $3 million contract to design an addition to Baltimore's Back River Wastewater Treatment Plant, one of many prestigious assignments the York company undertook in this country and abroad.

Former President George W. Bush chats with Representative Bill Goodling, Democrat from Seven Valleys, during a lecture stop at the Yorktowne Hotel in May, 1999. Courtesy, Harry J. McLaughlin

John Sununu, at right, chief of staff to President George W. Bush, is photographed here as he walks from the reconstructed York County Courthouse in 1987. His host, seen at left is the late Judge John F. Rauhauser Jr. Judge Rauhauser was a tireless crusader in promoting York County history. The two men are seen in front of The Golden Plough Tavern, built in 1741. Courtesy, Harry J. McLaughlin

York also saw the opening of another major shopping center, the Galleria Mall, in 1988, and dedicated a multi-million dollar Jewish Community Center that became a popular facility for residents of many faiths. A few years into the future, this community center would become the cynosure of the Jewish community, while it attracted non-Jewish patrons to its recreational and educational programs. The declining membership at Congregation Ohev Sholom (Conservative affiliation) lead the membership to place its building on the market and move ahead with plans to move up to the "Jewish Campus" formed by Temple Beth Israel (Reformed) and the Jewish Community Center. Facilities would be shared and members of Ohev Sholom considered building a smaller sanctuary for its use on the site.

As the eighties drew to a close, change was in the air, but one constant, York's role in defense of the country, remained strong. During this period, 16 York companies shared in annual defense contracts of about $183 million and another 120 York County firms divided contracts of about $25 million awarded by the U.S. Department of Defense.

Defense work continued to be a strong factor in economic stability during the following years, even while the decade of the 1990s took twists and turns unimaginable to many, even those who had become accustomed to change and welcomed growth. The 1990 census identified many trends that would continue steadily into the following decade, especially in the areas of population, education and economic developments.

York County's population rose to more than 340,000 and the city, once again, experienced a drop in population and a dramatic change in racial makeup. Census workers, in 1990, counted 42,192 living in the city with the Black non-Hispanic population rising 17.8 percent from 8,968 in 1980 to 10,558 in 1990. The numbers for Hispanics (of any race) rose from

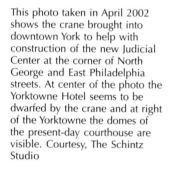

This photo taken in April 2002 shows the crane brought into downtown York to help with construction of the new Judicial Center at the corner of North George and East Philadelphia streets. At center of the photo the Yorktowne Hotel seems to be dwarfed by the crane and at right of the Yorktowne the domes of the present-day courthouse are visible. Courtesy, The Schintz Studio

2,700 in 1980 to 5,165 in 1990—up 91.3 percent in official counts. Accuracy of the figures was called into question, but it was clear that the Spanish-speaking community in the city was growing by leaps and bounds.

The number of people employed in managerial, sales and support, and service also rose, and as might be expected, the number of York countians employed in farming, craft, and repair, and those classified in labor dropped. Tony Dobrosky, a former Penn State Agricultural Extension agent, still in touch with the pulse of York's agricultural heartbeat, noted that two out of every 100 York County residents were involved in agriculture during this era and one farmer could feed 78 people. Prior to 1940, he explained, one farmer was producing enough for only three to five people. Dobrosky reminded Yorkers of a reality replete with a responsibility for land stewardship: York County still had 2,700 acres of the deepest, most tillable farmland in the world.

According to the 1990 census records, the number of families in poverty dropped slightly and York County's population was better educated than ten years before, too, with 13.9 percent holding college degrees (up from 11.2 percent) and 72.8 percent owning high school graduation diplomas (up from 61.7 percent ten years before.)

While jobs in farm-related occupations declined, jobs in the hospitality industry increased. Tourism was bringing $135 million into York County and 2,900 people were employed in the industry. Prospects for growth in this field seemed brighter than ever. In response to ever-increasing numbers of travelers in and out of York County, officials formed the Air Transportation Authority of York County to study needs for the present and the future. These officials, and others of like mind, also considered the role railroads might play and lobbied legislators for improvements in highways. The Route 30 Bypass, infamous for its stop and go character, and its bottlenecks around populous intersections became a target of activism. Millions of dollars in improvements were made but, even before large sections of the roadway were expanded, they seemed inadequate for the volume of traffic. Funding and engineering plans that would provide long-term relief seemed light years away, if attainable at all.

Despite frustrations and overwhelming odds in some aspects of planning, the following years brought hope and optimism in many forms. In 1991 the first fish ladders allowed migrating shad to overcome longtime barriers placed by humans and return to traditional breeding grounds. Members of the local band, LIVE, all graduates of York's William Penn High School, realized the dream of countless young people when a major record company offered them a contract and helped turn them into rock stars. Millions of fans bought the group's compact disks and they were featured in sold-out concerts in the United States and around the world. LIVE accomplished a feat reserved for the elite of the rock world when *Rolling Stone Magazine* carried a picture of the band on its cover and discussed the group's success in a feature article.

Another dream, this one built on the hopes of local business and social leaders, came to fruition in 1991 as the Agricultural and Industrial Museum of York County opened its doors in the former Eastern Market Building under the direction of C. Warren Smith. The Museum's board of directors later acquired a complex of buildings once used as an industrial plant.

While the new agricultural and industrial museums were greeting visitors in downtown York, racial tensions were heating up in downtown Hanover, even while that major York County community, officially a borough, but a town in size and appearance, was celebrating its own accomplishments in agriculture and industrial production. Home to important food processing plants, horse farms and shoe manufacturing facilities, Hanover had always

A monument honoring 9,300 veterans from York serving in World War II was dedicated in August, 2002 on Continental Square. The larger than life eagle mounting the top was sculpted by Lorann Jacobs, a resident of Dallastown. York County men and women have served their country in conflicts ranging from the long-ago French and Indian War to the recent conflicts in Vietnam, the Persian Gulf, Bosnia and other hotspots throughout the world. Courtesy, Harry J. McLaughlin

Everyone in York County loves an outdoor festival and this scene shows hundreds enjoying the fresh air and a contemporary music group performing on the steps of the York County Courthouse. Events like the Olde York Street Fair, the Golden Plough Oyster Festival, Yorkfest, York Bike Nite, and First Night York bring crowds to the city on a year-round basis. Note the banners hanging from lamp posts showing the city's official symbol, the White Rose. Courtesy, The Schintz Studio

seemed distant to some citizens from the hustle and bustle of York City, the county seat. But historical, political, economic and genealogical ties to York City kept "the Black Rose City" and "the White Rose City" close to each other in a spirit of interdependence, despite their many differences.

In response to incidents that showed a possible lack of tolerance for minority groups in the borough of Hanover, common ground was found when citizens formed an organization called Hanover United. This group helped to promote communication among all the citizens of the borough and launched programs that widened understanding and restored peace.

Hanover's bigger "sister," the city of York, was thrust into the national spotlight once again when presidential hopeful Bill Clinton opened his campaign with a drama-filled stop in 1992. Hilary Rodham-Clinton, the candidate's wife, accompanied him on this stopover, as did Clinton's running mate, Albert Gore Jr. and his wife Tipper. The future president and his entourage seemed quite knowledgeable about York and its culture, and undoubtedly won many voters with their *savoir-faire*. Hilary Clinton made friends with vendors at Central Market and her husband went jogging along Market Street near the Yorktowne Hotel where the party spent the night. Al and Tipper Gore posed with locals who wanted photographs and the press corps which followed the candidates reflected the "feel-good" spirit of this visit to the city that once served as the home of Congress.

Media from around the world covered a development in 1993 as the York County Commissioners signed a deal with the U.S. Immigration Service to detain more than 150 Chinese after their ship, *The Golden Venture*, wrecked on a New York beach. Once settled in the York County facility, the stories of the detainees' pilgrimage to freedom became subjects of media broadcasts and political debate here, in Washington, D.C. and around the world. By this time, the city of York had inaugurated a new mayor, Charlie Robertson, a retired city policeman who championed the return of baseball to York, promoted race car events and tried unsuccessfully to annex surrounding municipalities. Robertson was reelected in 1998.

The good news that a West Coast coffee company, Starbucks, had chosen an Emigsville industrial park for a new bean roasting plant in 1994 was welcomed by York planners but even this bright note could not cheer the 1,100 employees of the Caterpillar Company which closed its York facility in 1996. In the years following it seemed each positive economic sign was followed by bad tidings. While bright, welcoming outdoor murals appeared throughout downtown York another major employer, AMP, Inc. closed its Loganville plant. As The Historical Society of York County and the Agricultural and Industrial Museum merged to form The York County Heritage Trust, the city continued to lose population while most of the municipalities around it flourished with new housing, new shopping and new industry. Goodyear Tire & Rubber Company built a $22 million distribution center and "super stores" like Wal-Mart, Target and Kohl's extended the growth rings outward leaving older facilities in jeopardy.

In 1999, as hundreds of residents helped to stage a 250th Birthday Anniversary Party for the County, the 30th anniversary of the so-called 1969 Race Riots opened wounds and promoted political bickering. A cry for justice in the two unsolved murders of 1969 opened new investigations and the arrest of individuals allegedly involved, including Mayor Charlie Robertson who had been serving as a city policeman when the troubles erupted. A trial held in October 2002 led to two convictions, but the former mayor was acquitted.

As the investigation into the 1969 killings continued, white suprema

Top
On a chilly day in April, 1993, Democrat Charlie Robertson was inaugurated mayor on the steps of City Hall. Judge Michael J. Brillhart, at left, is seen here swearing in the new mayor. Behind him stands Helen Rohrbaugh, a former city councilwoman who became aide to mayor Robertson. Robertson was reelected for a second term, succeeded by John S. Brenner, also a Democrat. Courtesy, The Schintz Studio

Bottom
Future First Lady Hilary Rodham-Clinton is captured in this photograph making friends at York's Central Market. She accompanied her husband and Al and Tipper Gore to York in 1992 to launch his presidential campaign. In this photo she jokes with long-time market vendors about restoring broccoli to the White House kitchen after a former president banned the vegetable from the executive mansion. Courtesy, The Schintz Studio

A giant postcard made of donuts dominates this scene as weatherman Willard Scott greets Yorkers celebrating the 250th anniversary of the laying out of the town. Townspeople, seen in the foreground, enjoyed greeting each other in colonial garb as the nationally-televised event spread the word across the nation of York's birthday party, occurring in 1991. A York company, Maple Donuts, supplied the rich in calories backdrop. Courtesy, Harry J. McLaughlin

cist groups from out of town targeted York as a recruiting ground for their causes. A rally in early 2001 attracted more people concerned with racial tolerance and cooperation than individuals seeking to divide, but the cost of security and the cost of free speech suffered in the process.

The city of York, scarred by old wounds and suffering from new ones, dipped in population again in the 2000 census, even as a new mayor, John Brenner, offered hope with programs to increase home ownership and clean-up of deteriorating structures like the old York County prison on Chestnut Street. York County's population increased to 381,751 and to help meet the need for more office space and increasing growth, the Commissioners approved the construction of a $22 million Judicial Center. They chose a site in downtown York opposite the Strand-Capitol Perform-

These members of the York City Police force were photographed patrolling East Market Street while white supremacists attempted to recruit members at a rally occurring in York in April, 2002. This rally "fizzled out" according to some local media reports and tranquility returned to the streets.   Courtesy, Fran Keller

ing Arts Center, another success story which helped to balance the scales of stability for the battered city.

Meanwhile, a multi-million dollar business center was rising on a site known as the Old Smokestack Property, and millions of dollars were being invested in properties downtown. Martin Library, the Strand-Capitol Performing Arts Center, the York County Heritage Trust, were all planning expansion programs within blocks of Continental Square. Expansion, construction, and renovation projects throughout the city and the county were reflecting growth, prosperity and optimism at the same time major challenges were being confronted in face-to-face diplomacy.

In 2002, York countians were uniting again, this time to celebrate the nine-month period in 1777 and 1778 that Congress made York County its home. One of the international figures meeting with congressional delegates during that period was the French nobleman, the Marquis de Lafayette. Recalling that era during a later visit, the Frenchman, now an aging diplomat, toasted York in words that seem as fitting today as they did when he first said them: "The town of York, seat of our American Union in her most gloomy time. May her citizens enjoy a proportionate share of American prosperity."

Crowds of celebrants, fireworks, holiday lights and the extraordinary architecture of downtown York were all part of the First Night York extravaganza starting on the last night of 2001 and ending on the first morning of 2002. This scene shows the finale in Continental Square. At right the familiar Temple of Justice pillars of the York County Courthouse can be seen. Courtesy, The Schintz Studio

York's newest downtown office center, erected by the Susquehanna-Pfaltzgraff Co., is seen nearing completion in this photograph taken in fall 2002. Note the umbrella tables around the patio of the Codorus Creek restaurant in the foreground. Courtesy, The Schintz Studio

CHRONICLES OF LEADERSHIP

The town of York, the seat of the American Union in our most gloomy times. May its citizens enjoy in the same proportion their share of American prosperity.

The Marquis de Lafayette, on his return visit to York in February 1825, proposed this inspiring toast wishing Yorkers a promising future.

Prosperity for York Countians had been abundant since the days of the earliest European settlement. The land was virgin and clearing the forest laborious, but the York County soil proved fertile, yielding bountiful crops and a good life for the pioneers. The settlers of German, English, Quaker, and Scotch-Irish heritage shared a common goal: to work hard and make their little town on the frontier of America a thriving community.

York grew, and soon merchants, craftsmen, and artisans flourished, all striving to create and sell superior products. The town became a borough, and with the advent of the Industrial Revolution, an innovative group of men and women set new goals for York. They were people willing to accept the changing times, and used their unique skills and ideas to establish their own businesses and industries.

Plants and firms started by one man soon employed five people, then 25, then over 100. As York became a city, more new businesses were born and some old firms died. Other industries that were becoming obsolete regrouped their interests and formed new industries based on their equipment, material, and skills.

The spirit of the early craftsmen survived into the age of machines. Business leaders and York workers still believed in manufacturing quality products, and took pride in their work. From the clocks of the early colonial days to the complex technology of today, this standard of excellence has remained solid in York businesses.

The efficiency of York industry in the 20th century became a model for the nation and the world. The "York Plan," devised by area business leaders to pool skills and machine tools to increase productivity would be adopted quickly across the United States. Huge multinational corporations in later years would be impressed by the competence and success of York businesses and acquire them in their corporate families.

No longer was York a community on the edge of the wilderness. Products manufactured in the area were shipped and used around the world. Air conditioners, equipment for weight lifters, costumes for dancers, bricks, printing presses, boxes and containers, swimming pools, paper, labels, stoneware and dinnerware for the tables of the world—the list of products and services headquartered in York is extensive.

The variety of business and industry in York has proved a key to the steady economic growth of the area. No single industry has ever dominated York, but rather the city has become a diversified manufacturing, distributing, and agricultural center in the heart of the heavily populated East Coast region.

Floods, depressions, and the vagaries of time have pressed often upon York businesses, but through imagination, hard work, and determination, many have survived to provide jobs for Yorkers, helping them experience the prosperity Lafayette wished for them in 1825.

JNO. Z. BARTON, INC.

In January 1914, 19-year-old John Z. Barton of York signed an electrical apprenticeship agreement to work for the John E. Graybill Company. Mr. Barton worked the first 1,524 hours for three cents per hour, served in World War I, and then returned to complete the apprenticeship for wages gradually increasing to 11 cents per hour. He was given $100 when he successfully completed the required 12,000 hours. Mr. Graybill (best known for Graybill's Supply on North Broad Street) signed his first name using the Irish abbreviation "Jno.," which influenced the young John Barton to later use that abbreviation as his own. While with the Graybill Co., Barton assisted in the installation of an underground power line at the Carlisle Indian School. In 1965, the line was replaced by Jno. Z. Barton, Inc., under the supervision of John Barton. The school was renamed Army War College during the interim.

Barton and an associate, Luther Doll, started a small electrical business in 1920. They opened their storefront company at 537 West Market Street and concentrated on

John Z. Barton (1894–1977), founder of Jno. Z. Barton, Inc., circa 1960s.

house wiring. Contractors sold, installed, serviced, and wired for new appliances. Barton founded his own business in 1922, performing repair work on consumer products such as refrigerators and oil burners. Two employees who joined the firm in those early years, Chester Stump and William Strickler, would stay with the company until their eventual retirement. Robert McCarthy, who joined the company in later years, also was to spend his entire working career with the company.

Barton's electrical business weathered the Great Depression, but not without his constant perseverance. He would often follow trucks delivering refrigerators, then being sold by the old Edison Light & Power Company, offering to install the machines for the new owners. He moved his business in the early '30s to 261 South George Street, later to the first block of West King Street, and eventually to College and Stone avenues in the mid-1930s. The 1932 flood instigated the search for higher ground. The first floor office of John Z. Barton was flooded to the extent that his desk, papers, etc., on top and intact, was found floating near the ceiling. In 1950, the company moved to 317 West Market Street, where it remained until 1970. The store front idea was abandoned with this move. The Barton Company purchased the old Campbell Chain complex at the corner of Norway and Elm streets in 1970 and remains in a portion of that property today, at 413 Norway Street.

In addition to his electrical business, for many years John Z. Barton was also the owner of Paradise Orchards in East Berlin, which was sold upon his death in 1977 and Barton Fruit Farms (formerly Anderson) in Stewartstown. The latter was operated by Mr. Barton's son, John S. and is now owned and operated by his grandson, Richard.

Barton's company served many local industries in its formative years. During World War II, the electrician and his workers had industrial clients in York that included A. B. Farquhar Co., B. M. Root and Company, York Corporation, Blue Bird Silk Co., Century Ribbon Mills, and York Hoover Body. The business was incorporated under its current name, Jno. Z. Barton, Inc., in 1953. Barton's sons, Frank L. and George H. Barton, became officers in the organization and new markets were found for the firm's electrical contracting services. Major projects were completed in Newark, Ohio; Charleston, South Carolina;

Don "Bear" Sechrist and Greg Neff, members of the line department pose with bucket and auger—pole trucks.

Jno. Z. Barton Inc.'s office employees shown on the company's front steps, left to right: Drew Barton, Michael Myers, Derek Barton, and Doug Barton. Back row, left to right: Carl Hays, Lace Ziegler, Tom Zellers, Robert Schmuck, Gary Miller, and Kevin Sowers.

Atlanta, Georgia; Poughkeepsie, New York; Ithaca, New York; Lynnhaven, Virginia; Middleburg, Vermont; Baltimore, Maryland; Raleigh, North Carolina; Hilton Head Island, South Carolina; and others.

Frank and George both obtained electrical engineering degrees, Frank from Drexel and George from Cornell, following service in World War II. Frank served with the Navy aboard the *Essex* in the Pacific. George served with the Army Air Corps as a navigator.

Douglas A. Barton, George's son, became an officer in 1984 and owner of the business in 1998.

Electrical engineering services grew steadily, and in 1968, George and Frank Barton founded the majority interest of Barton Associates, Inc., a mechanical/electrical consulting firm. It was sold to one of its employees in 1988 and is still active today.

Since the early 1950s, the corporation has expanded its electrical construction to include almost every conceivable type of project: industrial, commercial, institutional, underground, pole lines, high-voltage substations, sewage plants, shopping malls, large retail stores, hospitals, housing developments, distribution centers, warehouses, paper mills, defense plants, and auto manufacturing facilities. Jno. Z. Bar-ton, Inc., is also engaged in the design, fabrication, assembly, and wiring of instrumentation and control panels and related work.

In 1957 the company replaced its manual assembly system for electrical estimating with a mechanical/electrical system for takeoff, pricing, scheduling, and purchasing. It was the 24th such system manufactured by Estimatic Corporation in the United States and served the company well for 30 years until replaced with the modern day computers that are now used for all departments of the business.

The firm offers Construction Management Services-Electrical (CMS-E) for each project. By mutual agreement, design, pre-purchase and construction services will be included in one contract. The contract can include a Guaranteed Maximum Price (GMP). The design services consist of pre-design services such as studies, approvals and licenses, preliminary drawings and specifications, budgets, and coordination with other trades. Final design services will include drawings and specifications suitable for bidding, installation by the Barton firm or another contractor, and quotations by suppliers for subsequent pre-purchase services by the CMS-E.

The firm maintains a full-service philosophy and assumes complete responsibility for its electrical work. Qualified and experienced personnel in accordance with the latest design codes and standards execute the electrical design.

More than 60 people are employed by Barton and the firm's market stretches from Vermont to Georgia. The officers of the company are Doug Barton, chairman/CEO; Gary Miller, president; and Kevin Sowers and Michael Myers, vice presidents. The firm is entering its fourth generation of operation. Derek and Drew Barton, great-grandsons of the founder, are active today in the family business.

The firm has a bright and rewarding future made possible by its continuing desire to serve its clients with experienced and qualified employees and management—to continue to build on the principles established by John Z. Barton in 1922.

Barton's 1922 Model T Ford and modern-era service van are shown by George Glatfelter, service electrician.

THE BON-TON STORES, INC.

One autumn day in 1897, a New Jersey shopkeeper named Samuel Grumbacher received a letter from his son, who had recently arrived in York, Pennsylvania. "I think we will do good business here," wrote Max Grumbacher.

The young merchant was right. York held great promise. It was to the city's burgeoning middle class that Max Grumbacher aimed to bring the fashions current in the larger East Coast cities. So Max and his father, Samuel—incorporated as S. Grumbacher & Son—signed a yearlong lease for a one-room storefront at 22 West Market Street. Max opened his store in York on March 10, 1898, aptly named The Bon-Ton, a French idiom for "good taste" or "stylishness." The store would emphasize a combination of fashion and value. With his own brand of service, he distinguished the store from other retailers in town, so successfully, in fact, that in little more than a decade, The Bon-Ton would outgrow its store-

Patrons never had to carry home their own parcels. The horse-and-carriage was the common vehicle. Edwin H. Tauser (below) joined Bon-Ton in 1903 as its delivery man—and was the first employee to achieve the distinction of serving 50 years with the company.

front setting. Max was preparing for a big move, although the distance was just half a block away: His one-room millinery and dry goods store was about to become a department store.

From its modest beginning, The Bon-Ton has grown to 73 department stores operating in nine states, employing approximately 9,000 associates in its stores, distribution

At the turn of the century, self service was all but unheard of, as attested to by the battalion of sales clerks pictured in front of the original Bon-Ton in York, Pennsylvania in 1899. Max Grumbacher, the store's founder, wearing a hat, stands in back.

facilities and corporate offices. Since its inception in 1898, the company has been building upon the legacy and beliefs established by its founding family: emphasize a combination of fashion and value, customer service redefined with the times, convenience of location, a family feeling that pervades the corporate culture and a company that gives back to the communities in which it operates.

In 1912, The Bon-Ton reopened as a grand new emporium at the southwest corner of West Market and Beaver Streets. In that transformation, The Bon-Ton reflected a retail evolution that was taking place across the country, as merchants expanded their shops into department stores to meet the diverse needs of their blossoming markets. The store sold a wide variety of merchandise, including the recently introduced ready-to-wear apparel, as well as dry goods and home furnishings. The new building rose three stories above a granite

198

base, with an ivory-glazed, terra-cotta façade; copper trimmings and 200 running feet of store windows. The Grumbacher family name was carved into the parapet, with "The Bon-Ton" emblazoned above the entrances. Advertisements trumpeted the opening of the new Bon-Ton flagship, the hallmark department store of York. Over the course of the next five decades, the store continued to grow by expanding into adjoining properties. The grand building is still in use today, having been acquired by York County in 1989 for use as the York County Government Center.

The next generation of the Grumbacher family joined the company in 1931 amidst troubled times: the Great Depression had created a difficult economic climate, and Max's health was rapidly deteriorating. Tom, Max's eldest son, quickly learned the retail trade and soon realized that if The Bon-Ton were to survive, management had to slash expenses. To his sharp business instincts, the Depression added an aversion to risk, a dislike of debt and a mistrust of banks, all of which

Tim Grumbacher, chairman of the board of directors and chief executive officer. Tim is the third generation of the Grumbacher family directing the course of the company. The company strategy is to remain an independent retail department store, true to its roots.

influenced the way he guided the company over the years.

While he was understandably cautious, Tom Grumbacher was willing to experiment and eager to further develop the store. Keenly observant of the retail industry and the marketplace as they evolved, Tom developed a then-uncommon approach that became the company's signature growth strategy: expansion into similar markets, spreading risk geographically. He was among the first merchants to identify the importance of smaller markets, and his decision to develop new stores there contrasted sharply with other retailers' business plans at that time, as growth for the typical family-owned department store was limited to expansion of their downtown location.

As The Bon-Ton began to grow, it demonstrated the determination and flexibility to position itself as the premier retailer in smaller markets—expanding its department stores by both acquisition and new development, as well as tapping new retail concepts and exploring new real estate configurations as

---

Bon-Ton continues to refine and reposition its merchandise mix to better reflect its customers' buying patterns—and to emphasize a combination of fashion and value. Bon-Ton customizes the mix by store to best reflect lifestyle and fashion preferences.

they arose. The company planned to expand to other small, underserved towns and follow Max Grumbacher's formula: Bon-Ton stores would supply service, fashion and value to customers who otherwise would have had to travel far to satisfy their needs.

At the same time that Tom Grumbacher was growing the company, he began to cultivate his son's interest in the business. Tim Grumbacher started working for The Bon-Ton in 1964, bringing to the company a keen, analytical mind and the ability to take charge. Like his father, Tim kept raising the bar to make Bon-Ton stores better places to shop, better places to work and better neighbors in the community.

By 1987 The Bon-Ton was operating 19 department stores in

To distinguish Bon-Ton from the competition, it supplements branded offerings with its own distinctive, exclusive merchandise brands, which offer exceptional value and create customer loyalty.

Pennsylvania, Maryland, West Virginia and New York. Its stores were geographically dispersed in small towns, with decentralized management. Tim Grumbacher made several bold moves in an effort to enhance the company's operations and management: He built the first distribution center, started investing in automated systems and upgraded the management talent. He felt the company was going to have to grow significantly to survive and compete.

An opportunity for rapid expansion presented itself that year when the 13-unit Pomeroy's chain, based in Harrisburg, Pennsylvania, became available. The acquisition was a perfect geographic and strategic fit. With the rampant consolidation of the retail industry, the acquisition was critical to the company's long-term survival.

Change was taking place at every level of the organization, as The Bon-Ton worked to both absorb Pomeroy's and better position itself for future acquisitions. Banking on continued rapid expansion, the company began investing heavily to develop an infrastructure comparable to that of retail organizations several times its size. Due to the Pomeroy's acquisition and the subsequent investment in the company, it was time to address the financial drain of debt service and the need to raise capital for expansion.

The solution was to take the company public. After more than nine decades in the family, the company made an initial public offering in October 1991. Tim became chairman of the board, and the family retained voting control. Four million shares of the stock were sold on the NASDAQ exchange; the infusion of equity improved the company's balance sheet by significantly reducing debt.

With proceeds from its initial public offering, The Bon-Ton began acquiring single or two-unit department stores. But none of that prepared the company for the flurry of activity that occurred in 1994—when The Bon-Ton doubled its number of stores with three acquisitions involving 35 stores, including 19 stores from Hess's in Allentown, Pennsylvania; the ten stores of Adam, Meldrum and Anderson Co., based in Buffalo, New York; and the six stores of Chappell's, in Syracuse, New York. In 1995 and 1996, The Bon-Ton entered the Rochester and Elmira, New York markets with four acquired stores and the opening of one additional store. The company has since opened 10 additional stores and continues to explore future opportunities for new stores in new markets. The Bon-Ton is dedicated to bringing to an ever-expanding customer base the same high-quality merchandise and tremendous value that characterized its founder's business over one century ago.

Since the days of old metal charge plates, the Bon-Ton credit card operation has been an integral component of the company's strategic plan and a meaningful contributor to profit. To sustain this growth, the company continues to invest in its Best of The Bon-Ton customer loyalty program.

The Bon-Ton has learned that today's customers define service by ease of shopping: how quickly they can find what they're looking for, make the purchase and get on their way. The Bon-Ton put in place a variety of initiatives to make its customers' shopping experience more efficient, such as conveniently located, highly visible service centers.

generation of Grumbachers. Today, The Bon-Ton Stores Foundation carries on this philanthropic tradition. Established in 1988, the foundation allocates monies from company profits to underwrite nonprofit organizations' programs in community health, youth education and for the economically disadvantaged. The Bon-Ton also maintains a strong partnership with the United Way in all its communities. Good citizenship is part of The Bon-Ton's mission, and one of the many ways the company supports volunteerism and charitable activities in the communities it serves is through its Bon-Ton Retail Associate Volunteer Outreach program (BRAVO!). Bon-Ton associates are encouraged to partner with organizations and individuals in local markets, volunteering their time, energy and talents to improve the quality of life in those communities.

One hundred four years after Max Grumbacher opened his one-room dry goods store, the Grumbacher family continues to direct the course of the company with Max's grandson, Tim, as chairman of the board and chief executive officer. The Bon-Ton's competitive strengths continue to be its commitment to customer satisfaction, hands-on management, tight control of operating expenses and a carefully executed real estate strategy: It thrives by serving targeted secondary markets that larger retailers typically overlook. The company's strategy is to remain an independent retail department store based in Pennsylvania, offering a distinctive mix of quality, nationally recognized vendors and private brands—with special emphasis on apparel, accessories, cosmetics and home furnishings at price points targeted to the moderate and better shopper. Four years into its second century of business, The Bon-Ton retains a strong presence in its hometown and proudly reflects on its rich heritage and history.

Like the store, the Grumbacher family became an important thread in the fabric of York. While working diligently to establish his business, Max had made time to be active in the community. He was one of the founders of the York Merchants Association in 1898, which became the York Chamber of Commerce in 1909. Max and his wife, Daisy, prized community activity—a trait they passed to each succeeding

BRADLEY LIFTING CORP.

Harvey and Win Bradley did not start out to become world-class weightlifters. Yet they have successfully pumped up a business that crafts the Herculean equipment necessary to lift heavy components that drive the production of many of the world's leading industries. As founders of Bradley Lifting Corp., the Bradleys have chiseled a specialized niche in the global manufacturing marketplace, applying strategic entrepreneurial vision to a well-muscled engineering foundation.

The Bradley's journey to York began in 1957 when Harvey, a design and development engineer for a British pharmaceutical company, and his wife, Win, left their native Yorkshire, England to accept Bradley's new professional opportunity as a crane engineer for the Steel Company of Canada in Hamilton, Ontario, Canada. There, Bradley gained recognition as a leading expert on below-the-hook lifting devices, designing the specialized equipment that was required to efficiently move heavy components in the manufacturing industry. In 1961, the couple crossed the border

The Bradley family in 1979. Back row, left to right: Colin, Heather, and Lorraine. In front are Harvey and Win.

into the United States upon Bradley's appointment to chief engineer for Mansaver Industries in New Haven, Connecticut. When American Chain and Cable Company acquired Mansaver and moved the company to York, Pennsylvania, Bradley also moved and became sales manager in 1964. But in 1972, when the company decided to move Bradley's division to the Midwest, Harvey and Win made

another life-altering decision to remain in York with their three young children and start their own company.

In the basement of the Bradley's home Bradley Lifting Corp. was born. Harvey took charge of all sales and engineering; Win was charged with everything else necessary to operate the business, from typing and accounting to telephone answering. A nearby fabricating company was located, and with a project assignment from its first customer, York Container Corp., the fledgling company started its climb to success. (York Container Corp. remains a Bradley Lifting customer to this day.)

In the beginning, the Bradleys did it all. In fact, Harvey Bradley recalls one particular client in Connecticut that challenged him to wear a multitude of hats. After designing the ordered piece of equipment and supervising its fabrication, Bradley himself loaded the lifting device in his truck and hit the road to the northeast state. Pulling up to his customer's unloading dock, he helped empty his cargo and watched closely as it was successfully tested. Then to complete the delivery, Bradley hand-delivered his invoice to the customer's purchasing department, climbed back in his truck, and steered towards home.

Shortly after its start, the new company outgrew its basement headquarters, and Bradley rented an office next to the company's fabricating shop. The first outside employee, Charles Meads, formerly with Mansaver, was hired and remains with the company today as vice president of engineering and production. Additional experienced employees were brought on board as the company grew, necessitating a move to larger facilities—an 8,000-square-foot building at their present location. Today the company's 50 employees occupy 40,000-square-feet of manufacturing space) two plants along with an office addition) on Elm Street.

Some of the shop personnel with a large plate lifter for a customer.

At a Christmas party, from left to right: Harvey Bradley, Win Bradley, and Charlie Meads.

At the company-owned manufacturing facilities, the Bradley Lifting Corp. team designs, engineers, sells, produces, and technically supports specialty below-the-hook lifting devices that meet the demanding specifications of numerous manufacturing industries, including aluminum, automotive, crane, paper, rail, and steel. In their product portfolio can be found coil grabs, sheet lifters, slab tongs, vacuum lifters, and specialized material handling equipment for use with overhead cranes. Special assignments to solve a complex manufacturing problem is the norm at Bradley Lifting. Aluminum producer Alcoa, for example, needed a strategy to lift and transport 25-ton crucibles of molten aluminum to an area of the plant not serviced by overhead cranes. Bradley engineers, working with Alcoa engineers, crafted an innovative piece of lifting equipment that combined with Mobile Transportation to produce a single solution that performs safely and efficiently.

The engineers under Bradley's command are a very special breed of industry veterans. Many of the highly skilled staff averages 25 years of experience and actively participate in industry trade organizations to maintain proficiency in the latest technological advance-ments. When it is time for a new hire to the seasoned team, Bradley often considers the older, more experienced workers, many of whom are in the process of leaving large corporations with an eye on returning to the York area. With a current workforce of approximately 50 employees, Bradley believes that his company is in the ideal position to secure a successful and profitable future. To Bradley, allowing too much employ-ee growth would take the company to a new and complex level of increased government regulation, ultimately resulting in loss of the control that has brought the company to the high standard it enjoys today.

Currently generating over $6 million in annual sales in the United States, Mexico, Australia, South America, Europe, Africa, and the Far East, Bradley Lifting Corp. holds six engineering patents. Because increasing sales throughout the world have strengthened the company's position as a global leader in below-the-hook lifting devices, Bradley Lifting has established licensing agreements with colleagues in both England and Australia for the manufacture of proprietary Bradley products. The company is a member of numerous industry organizations including the American Society of Mechanical Engineers (ASME), the National Society of Professional Engineers (NSPE), the American Welding Society (AWS), and the Association of Iron and Steel Engineers (AISE). They also actively participate in several codes and standards organizations that provide safety information to users of below-the-hook lifting devices.

As well known as the company is in the global manufacturing arena for exceptional products, Harvey and Win Bradley are themselves personally known for their extraordinary contributions to the region's community service organizations. Benefiting from the Bradley's leadership and financial support are organizations that include the Rehabilitation and Industrial Training Center of York, Inc., the Margaret E. Moul Home for individuals with cerebral palsy; Access York, an organization for abused women; Planned Parenthood; the York Literacy Council; York Little Theatre; the Children's Home of York; the Strand-Capitol Theatre; and Historic York. Also reaping great rewards is Penn State York where Mr. Bradley

Building a 'Fitz' Water Wheel, 16 feet in diameter, for the Grist Mill in the Agricultural Museum in York. One of many Bradley donations.

Harvey Bradley as a keynote speaker at the Pennsylvania Free Enterprise Week, 2000.

is a leading member of its Advisory Board. In the heart of the campus can be found the direct result of Bradley philanthropy—the Bradley Building that houses the continuing education offices. A former president of the Manufacturers' Association of South Central Pennsylvania, Mr. Bradley was named York Area Chamber of Commerce Small Businessman of the Year in 1992.

In recognition of their numerous contributions, both Harvey and Win Bradley were also honored by the York Area Chamber of Commerce as joint recipients of a community service award for their extensive involvement in community activities. Mr. Bradley was the first recipient of a tribute dinner organized by the Rehabilitation and Industrial Training Center of York where he served as a tireless board member who helped raise money for a training program for the center's disabled clients. Win Bradley also has taken a leadership role in the organization that provides vocational training to York county citizens with mental and physical disabilities, along with the operation of an elderly day care program under contract from the York County Area Agency on Aging.

Another notable contribution combines Bradley's generosity with his love of old mills. At the York Agricultural and Industrial Museum, once a six-building industrial complex, is the reconstruction of an 1830s grist mill. Under Bradley's supervision, the three-story maze of gears and belts was constructed, complete with an operating water wheel. He likewise has donated his time and talent to the preservation of the 1826 Wallace-Cross Mill, a rare example of an operating water-powered grain mill—one of the few still standing. He also delighted the preservation society of the historic Muddy Creek Forks Roller Mills by taking time to explain the operation of many parts of the mill that were previously unknown, developing a better understanding of the importance of the preservation and ensuring the proper interpretation of the mill's operation to visitors.

One of Bradley's fondest memories is his participation in the Pennsylvania Free Enterprise Week, a program where students, teachers, and business leaders from across the state come together at Lycoming College in Williamsport to experience a week of the American free enterprise system and learn what it takes to be successful in an increasingly competitive global marketplace. As keynote speaker in the July 2000 program, Bradley addressed the high-school age scholarship students with details of his true life story of building Bradley Lifting Corp. from his home's basement to its current international presence. The rapt attention paid by the budding entrepreneurs, their obvious appreciation, and their youthful enthusiasm combined to produce a most rewarding experience for the veteran businessman. And so, in addition to designing the specialized equipment to lift integral components in the world of industry, Harvey Bradley has managed to lift something of even greater virtue. He has selflessly lifted the aspirations of a whole future generation of Pennsylvania's brightest minds, those that will become the leaders of the business world of tomorrow.

At an industrial trade show in Chicago.

YORK COUNTY CHAMBER OF COMMERCE

Mayor John Brenner, (first row second from left) and Chamber staff gathered at the Market St. Bridge overlooking the Codorus Creek. Chamber staff signed the Codorus Creed pledging to help make York a clean, healthful and vibrant community.

Since 1898, the York County Chamber and its predecessors have been the business link for a better community. In 1898, York's downtown storeowners met and formed the York Merchants Association, the area's first business organization.

On January 28, the same group met again and unanimously adopted a constitution and bylaws of the Merchants Association of York, electing J. Frank Gable president. The Association gradually developed a program of civic improvement which resulted in a merging of interests of commerce and industry in York to form the Chamber of Commerce in 1909.

From the beginning, every day, every year, and every decade the Chamber has been leading the way for business and the community, focusing on jobs, growth, individual initiative, quality of life, and limited government and community leadership. The Chamber is proud of its many accomplishments, which include: playing a key role in forming the York County Industrial Development Corporation (1958); supporting I-83 (1960); helping to found York VoTech (1969); adopting a formal policy to support affirmative action (1971); holding the first Member Mixer—now called Business After Hours (1975); earning the title of "Accredited by the U.S. Chamber of Commerce," one of only 319 chambers out of 5,000 nationwide to receive accreditation status (1976) (accreditation is a process consisting of a complete re-examination every five years, and in 2002 the

To commemorate a century of dynamic leadership, past and present (1898–1998), Chamber leaders form "100" for an historic aerial photograph.

Chamber is in its 25th year of reaccreditation); working to form SCORE (Service Corps of Retired Executives) (1979); sponsoring the first Business Expo at York College (1980); sponsoring *To the Setting of The Sun: The Story of York* (1981 and 2002); awarding the first Small Business of the Year award to Carl's News Stand (1982); becoming affiliated with the Tourism Bureau, which is renamed York County Convention and Visitors Bureau (1984); launching First Capital Compact (York County Alliance for Learning), York's first business and education partnership (1989); building a political network in response to high business taxes (1990); forming York County International Network to promote international business opportunities (1991); establishing an internet task force to create www.YorkChamber.com (1996); holding a drive for Route 30 improvements, beginning a new era of increased transportation funding for York County (1997); celebrating its 100th birthday with a Centennial Celebration (1998); creating Acts 67 & 68 incentives for municipalities to do regional planning and tax revenue sharing (2000); unveiling a new logo and brand, Business Leading the Way (2001); President Tom Donley receiving the Keystone Award for outstanding service and contributions to the profession of cham-

ber management (2001); and the *Chamber News* wins PCCE Newsletter Award of Excellence and goes online (2001).

A major part of the Chamber's success is constantly asking members what they need and value, and what they can do together to grow a better community. In 2001, the Chamber surveyed members extensively and developed and updated their strategic plan through a series of leadership, board, and staff meetings. The plan and priorities will guide the Chamber through 2005 with a more focused vision: "Your Business Link for a Better Community."

Its priorities are to:
• Become a customer-driven organization.
• Develop a stronger alliance with other business-affiliated organizations to create a positive and unified network of organizations.
• Position the Chamber as the leading pro-business advocate and voice of business driven by its core customers.
• Support an economic and workforce plan for the community.

In its third century of business and community leadership, the Chamber is leading York County's business effort to grow better and provide the foundation for a winning, livable community, the model for the Mid-Atlantic region.

DROVERS BANK, A DIVISION OF FULTON BANK

A meeting of citizens interested in the proposed Drovers and Mechanics National Bank of York was held at the Motter House in the borough of York, Saturday, April 28, 1883. A temporary organization was effected by appointing Mr. Israel Gross as chairman and Mr. William H. Bond as secretary.

The bank opened for business on June 12 of that year in the 200 block of West Market Street and later moved to 25 South George Street.

In those days, York was strictly an agricultural region. Many cattle on their way to market were driven through the area. The word "drovers" represented those drivers and the word "mechanics" represented the old-time blacksmiths who shod the horses and re-rimmed the wheels of the wagons.

A short time later, the bank moved to 30 South George Street in a building constructed specifically for banking.

On this site, Mr. James Smith,

The first president of The Drovers & Mechanic Bank, Mr. Nathan F. Burnham, 1883.

one of the signers of the Declaration of Independence, maintained both a residence and a separate office for his law practice during the time the Continental Congress met in York. His home was a place of meeting for many distinguished statesmen who were then serving as delegates and on important committees. His law office was used as a meeting place for the Board of War when it was presided over by John Adams of Massachusetts in 1777.

In 1958 the old Ritz Theater building at 28 South George Street was purchased. The theater was demolished and the building of the bank followed.

A new structure arose and now houses the bank's current main office facilities. A mural by York artist Herb Leopold was commissioned for the facility and represented the many different professions served by the institution.

In the years that followed, expansion became a key for the bank, with new branches being added in Windsor and the

York County Shopping Center (1955), Roosevelt Avenue Shoppette (1956), Mt. Rose Avenue and Hill Street (1962), Emigsville (1966), Richland Avenue (1968), Queensgate Shopping Center (1975) and York Haven (1978).

In 1979 the bank withdrew its membership in the Federal Reserve System and became a state chartered institution. The official name of the bank was changed from the Drovers & Mechanics National Bank of York to the Drovers & Mechanics Bank. However, all bank depositors' funds remained insured by the Federal Deposit Insurance Corporation for up to $100,000.

Branches continued to open, including Memory Lane in 1981 and the Westgate Branch in 1983.

In April of 1987 the main offices of Drovers at 30 South George Street underwent another renovation. This $1.5 million project involving two floors of approximately 18,000 square feet was completed in October 1988. The building's new facade was designed to coincide with that of the new five-story office building erected on the site

The Drovers and Mechanics Bank gained a new building during the 1960s, located on the historic site at 30 South George Street, York. The bank displays a mural by York artist, Herb Leopold.

The Drovers Bank entrance as it appeared in the late 1920s.

The Drovers Bank headquarters at 96 South George Street, York.

Fulton Financial was a positive step for shareholders, customers, associates, and communities because of the mutual belief that local bankers are best qualified to make the right decisions in the markets where they live and work. The merger also allowed Drovers Bank to offer its customers an expanded array of financial products and services that previously had not been possible. Drovers customers now enjoy access to more than 70 locations and 165 automated teller machines (ATMs) throughout York, Lancaster, Berks, Chester, Cumberland, Dauphin, and Montgomery counties, all due to its partnership with Fulton Bank and its affiliates. The merger was completed with a smooth operations transition that took place in August 2001.

which previously served as the customer parking lot for its main office.

Expansion continued as the South York branch, located inside the Giant Store, opened in 1990, followed by a full-service facility in Cape Horn in 1992. Two other Giant Supermarket branches were opened in East York and West Manchester in 1994.

The five-story office building at 96 S. George Street, located adjacent to the main office in downtown York, was purchased by Drovers in 1994 to provide for future expansion. The fifth floor was remodeled, and on January 4, 1996, the executive offices of Drovers Bancshares Corporation were moved to this location.

A shared facility housing a Tom's convenience store and a full-service branch was opened in Dover in 1996, and the Penvale office, a second convenience store location, followed in 1997. The Shrewsbury office opened in 1998, and the Hellam and Dillsburg Branches opened in 1999. In continuing with Drovers Bank's expansion strategy, a relocation of the current Memory Lane location was completed in May 2000.

In May 2001 Drovers shareholders approved a merger between Drovers & Mechanics Bank and Fulton Financial Corporation, becoming Drovers Bank, a division of Fulton Bank. The affiliation with

The recently built Cape Horn Branch, which is a model of the present Drovers branches.

In August 2002 the Cape Horn Office was relocated to a new facility at 3191 Cape Horn Road, in the new Windsor Commons Shopping Center in Red Lion.

The growth of Drover's Bank can best be attributed to its excellent leadership, which began with the first president of the bank, Mr. Nathan F. Burnham. Succeeding Mr. Burnham were Mr. Israel F. Gross, Mr. Samuel Lichtenberger, Mr. Jacob Beitzel, Mr. James Glessner, Mr. George Jordan, Mr. A. W. Girton, Mr. Richard M. Linder, Mr. A. Richard Pugh, and its current President, Mr. David W. Freeman.

D. E. HORN & COMPANY/PENNFIELD CORPORATION

In 1919, David E. and Ernest O. Horn, sons of a York, Pennsylvania flour miller, established a business partnership. With $500 in cash and a $2,000 loan from Western National Bank, these 3rd-grade-educated entrepreneurs began making animal feed and flour deliveries with their first delivery vehicle, a horse-drawn wagon.

At the ripe old age of 21, the eldest brother, David, was manning the business from the "inside" while his 19-year-old brother Ernest was the designated "outside" guy. Success was hard earned by the two young brothers as they worked virtually round-the-clock at their Roosevelt Avenue and Philadelphia Street location.

As the business grew, sales calls and deliveries were expedited by the purchase of a used Model T Ford pickup. Continued hard work, excellent service, and quality products allowed the brothers, known for their integrity, to expand the business by opening a branch retail store in nearby Red Lion, Pennsylvania.

Sometime in the early 1920s, the business partnership became a dealer representative of the nationally recognized Ralston Purina Company. Representing an industry giant like Ralston Purina allowed the brothers to operate their own

D. E. Horn Co., Purina dealer, circa early 1920s.

Left to right: Ernest and Dave Horn, business partners, circa 1920.

business and learn from an animal feed industry pioneer and leader. Before long, the Horn brothers were warehousing livestock feeds and flour in as many as four different locations around the York area.

While Dave and Ernest seemed to be all work and no play, each of them found time to marry and start their own families. From boyhood on, Ernest always possessed a love for agriculture and farm production of livestock and crops. His fondness for farming was even reflected in his choice of brides. Ernest's young wife, Ethel M. Lauer, was the daughter of a farmer from the rural community of Dover, Pennsylvania.

As the "Roaring '20s" were nearing their end, Dave and Ernest purchased Hoke's Mill, located in the southwest rural area of York, along present day Indian Rock Dam Road. This water-powered grist and flourmill was a two-story structure built prior to the existence of the dam that would be later constructed at "Indian Rock."

Although the effects of the Great Depression

played a major role in both the business and personal lives of Dave and Ernest, the two continued to make ends meet. Unfortunately, a brief time later, in 1933, a major flood literally forced the two brothers to move their milling operation from the first floor of their mill to the second floor. Needless to say, business was interrupted, but customers did not go long without the high quality products and services they had grown to expect from the Horns.

In spite of significant adversities, a major flood and a nationwide economic depression, nothing seemed to break the entrepreneurial spirit of the Horn brothers. Shortly after cleaning up from the flood damage at the Hoke's mill location, Dave and Ernest purchased property at the corner of Lincoln and West streets inside the York city limits.

Their next major endeavor occurred in 1935, when they constructed their first animal feed manufacturing facility on the recently acquired Lincoln and West Street property. This feed mill would eventually be regarded as the cornerstone of D. E. Horn & Company, Inc., manufacturer of Hornco brand poultry and livestock feeds.

The business was enjoying a great deal of success, but nonetheless, this expansion was regarded as monumental for the time. In fact, there were those who implied, "Dave and Ernest are digging their own graves."

A history of D. E. Horn & Co., Inc. would be incomplete without a closer look at the personal lives of the founding brothers. A noteworthy point at this time is the origin of the company name. The *D* and *E* in D. E. Horn are the first and middle initials of David Eugene Horn; and not, the first initials of David and Ernest.

Dave's family included his wife Hattie and their two daughters, Mildred and Marie. Neither Mildred nor Marie ever expressed an interest in their father and uncle's business.

On the other hand, Ernest's family was completely opposite of Dave's in many respects. Ernest and Ethel had two sons, Ernie, Jr., and Donald. Unlike their cousins, Ernie, Jr., and Donald were both interested in their father and uncle's business.

Because Ernie, Jr. was 15 years his brother's senior, his entry into the business was almost a decade before his younger brother, Don. After graduating from William Penn Senior High School (M'42-midyear), Ernie, Jr., served a three-year stint with the U.S. Army and studied briefly at York Collegiate Institute. In 1947 he joined his father and uncle in the family business.

The decade of the '50s had just begun when Dave, Ernest, and Ernie, Jr., decided to expand and modernize the Lincoln and West Street feed mill. The science of animal nutrition and feeds was advancing exponentially and the Horns were committed to keeping their customers at the forefront of animal feed technology.

One of Pennfield's four modern feed mills.

Left to right: Ernest, Ethel, Hattie, and Dave Horn, circa 1961.

In 1956, after graduating from William Penn, Ernest's youngest son, Donald, joined the business. In 1961, a farm research facility was built to test "scientific" poultry feed formulations. Just prior to Dave's death in early 1964, he, Ernest, Ernie, Jr., and Donald began talking to another family-owned feed company about possible joint ventures. Those talks resulted in two such transactions over the next three-to four-year period.

In 1971, the Horns and their Lancaster, Pennsylvania partner, Miller and Bushong, combined forces to form a new company, which they named Pennfield Corporation. The new company with a long history continued to grow and expand through the '70s, however, in 1982, just a few years prior to the deaths of both Ernest and Ethel, the Horn family assumed complete ownership of Pennfield.

Today, Pennfield has evolved into a diversified consumer foods and agricultural products company serving customers throughout the Mid-Atlantic and Northeast regions. Headquartered in Lancaster, Pennsylvania, Pennfield employs more than 500 associates in nine locations.

The company is still owned by the family of Ernest and Ethel Horn. At present, Ernie, Jr., is retired and Donald serves as chairman of the board. Five of six grandchildren are involved with the business. The first of five great grandchildren has begun fourth generation involvement in the business. For more about modern-day Pennfield, log on to www.pennfield.com.
Dedicated in memory of:
Ernest O. and Ethel M. Horn.

MOREX CORPORATION

This is the story of a German-based decorative ribbon company, the "More Exclusive Ribbon Company," the fastest growing decorative ribbon company in the United States.

Morex Corporation was founded in 1990 by three German businessmen. One of the founders was Volker Pattberg. Pattberg was interested in expanding his business of ribbon manufacturing to the United States. His company, C. E. Pattberg GmbH & Co., was founded in Hattingen, Germany in 1893 and is one of the top three ribbon manufacturers in Germany. He envisioned changing his company from a small trade company into a world-

Volker Pattberg, founder and shareholder of Morex Corporation.

wide trading company. Like generations before him, he found himself looking to America in search of a new and exciting opportunity. The decision to base the company in York, Pennsylvania was due to the sponsorship of European companies by the city of York and the Commonwealth of Pennsylvania. When deciding on a name for the company, the founders chose Morex, a hybrid of "more exclusive."

Morex faced many business challenges in the first year. The most daunting was a lack of leadership. The partners resided in Germany and found it difficult to run a company effectively without supervision. Two of the partners decided to abandon the business venture, but Pattberg believed the company would succeed and began searching for another partner. In Markus

Markus Grunewald, president and majority shareholder of Morex Corp., is a native of Wuppertal, Germany.

Grunewald, Pattberg found a new partner to share his vision. He was a native of Wuppertal, Germany, with a master's degree in information systems and had been working as a consultant for the C. E. Pattberg GmbH & Company. Grunewald first visited Morex in 1991 and found the central Pennsylvania region to be similar to that of his homeland. The region was rich in German heritage, and he immediately felt at home. After analyzing the business and researching the American market, he was anxious to follow in the footsteps of the German immigrants

who went before him in pursuit of the American dream. He purchased 30 percent of the Morex shares using his life savings and a bank loan, and became president of the company in 1992. Pattberg and Grunewald restructured Morex as an affiliate of the C. E. Pattberg GmbH & Co. and developed a business plan reflecting their management principles. After moving to York in 1993, Grunewald became the majority shareholder of Morex, holding 51 percent of the company's shares while C. E. Pattberg GmbH & Co. held the other 49 percent.

Morex Corp. is located in the city of York at 220 North Belvidere Avenue. It has its century-old roots in the Westphalian town of Hattingen, Germany, where its parent company continues to thrive. Morex has enjoyed a decade of continuous growth since 1992. The success can be attributed to Grunewald's leadership, direction, and vision. The company recently earned the distinction as the fastest growing decorative ribbon company of the new millennium in the United States by increasing annual sales in excess of 25 percent. When

Morex's 55,000-square-foot facility is located in York, Pennsylvania.

reflecting back on the company's earlier years, Grunewald remembers struggling to succeed. During that period, there was no time for managing, only time to dig in and get the work done. Now he has the time to travel to various cities across the country to showcase Morex's exciting and exclusive decorative ribbon line. He enjoys the challenges of management and business and is pleased with the success of the company. He considers one of his greatest business accomplishments to be the development of an alliance between business partners from around the world with Morex. This strategic negotiation has resulted in a strong competitive advantage for Morex in the domestic market. The company employees 45 full-time employees in a 55,000-square-foot facility and has 40 sales representatives throughout the United States. Morex has an affiliation with DaVinci Artfleur in Haan-Gruiten, Germany; Kuny in Kutingen, Switzerland; and Vaban Bandfabrik in Breitenbach, Switzerland.

Morex's focus is on the production and distribution of fine quality decorative ribbon for the North American market. The company offers the most extensive line of European ribbon fashion and design available in the United States. The majority of the ribbon marketed by the company is imported from its parent company in Germany. Morex also purchases ribbon from companies in the United States, England, Switzerland, Italy, France, Brazil, Japan, China, and Taiwan.

Morex's production involves the re-spooling of ribbon from 1,000- to 6,000-yard spools. Using semi-automatic spooling machines programmable to measure yardage, Morex's production personnel converts these bulk spools into smaller, sellable units such as nine feet, 25 yards, 100 yards, or any length the customer requires. A variety of curling ribbon, French-wired fabric ribbon, sheers, double-faced satin, cord and printed ribbon is sold to

The Morex employees are an integral part of the company's success.

national gift wrap distributors and companies, florist wholesalers, and larger retailers in the United States and Canada.

Morex also produces spooled ribbon for sale under a private label. Each of these customers in turn sell directly to retailers such as American Greetings, florist wholesalers, A.C. Moore, and Ben Franklin Craft stores, as well as local gift and party supply shops.

Grunewald designed an organizational structure and layout for Morex to optimize operations and increase efficiency and productivity. The organizational chart was created to provide an overview of the company's structure for management and employees to reference. It defines the levels of management, the goals and focus of each department, and the role, responsibilities, and duties of each employee. The layout of the facility was designed to ensure a smooth flow of materials from start to finish.

Morex carries more than 500 styles of decorative ribbon in hundreds of colors at its facility. Morex stores raw and working materials, as well as finished products in its

Morex exhibits annually at numerous craft, floral, gift, and packaging tradeshows in the United States.

Morex showcases its gift wrap and party ribbon fashion line.

Morex warehouses over 20,000 different finished products at its facility.

warehouse facility. This allows the company to remain competitive by offering more than 20,000 different finished products in stock, minimizing delivery time, and enabling its customers to reduce their own stock capacity. Morex continues to expand its product offerings to meet the needs of its customers.

Markus Grunewald credits the success of Morex to the support of its parent company, C. E. Pattberg GmbH & Co.; the Morex employees; its focus on being first with the customers in quality, service, and price; and the fact that the shareholders reinvest all profits back into the company. C. E. Pattberg GmbH & Co. provides valuable insight on trends, research, product development, and presentation concepts as well as providing Morex with an up-to-date and trend-setting decorative ribbon collection. Customer service is a priority at Morex. The staff of the marketing and customer service departments is dedicated to its customers. They show customer dedication by always going the extra mile to provide the best service and solutions. The Morex employees are an integral part of the company's success. Each employee is considered a vital member of the team and is encouraged by an open-door policy to offer ideas for improving operations throughout the plant. Morex's employee philosophy is based on the following principles: hire qualified individuals for the position; involve and motivate employees and help them strive for success; consider all contributions to the team important; allow the company's growth and stability to be determined by its employees; and believe an organization improves performance when its people improve performance.

Morex is dedicated to its community and shows its support by contributing to programs such as Tennis for Kids and by sponsoring local tennis tournaments. Morex also donates between 5,000 and 20,000 yards of ribbon annually to non-profit organizations.

As a company leader, Grunewald continually looks to the future. He has developed a long-term business

The artistic flair of Morex's marketing team is apparent in this design for its spring ribbon fashion line.

plan to achieve $100 million in annual sales by the year 2030. He is confident this goal is achievable in a $600 million market. He hopes to achieve this goal by examining newly available technologies and introducing progressive machinery and technical equipment to the company. He plans to change Morex from a distributor into a manufacturer that will produce decorative ribbon from start to finish at a new facility. For now, he will focus on optimizing operations at the current location and develop new strategies and concepts for marketing Morex's decorative ribbon line.

Additional information on Morex Corp. is available on its website http://www.morexcorp.com. Additional information on C. E. Pattberg GmbH & Co. is available on its website http://www.pattberg.com.

YORK COUNTY HERITAGE TRUST

The York County Heritage Trust was created in 1999 from a merger of the Historical Society of York County and the Agricultural and Industrial Museum of York County. In 2000, the Fire Museum of York County also joined the Trust.

The history of the Historical Society of York County began in 1895 when an assembly of concerned citizens met and decided to collect, preserve and interpret the history and culture of York County. The society's original focus was the development of a library to serve as a repository for the county's genealogical resource material. By 1900, a growing collection of artifacts led to the opening of a museum. In 1958, the society moved to its present location at 250 East Market Street. Today this site houses the York County Heritage Trust's Historical Society Museum and Library.

In 1966 the Historical Society of York County acquired the Golden Plough Tavern (circa 1741), the General Gates House (circa 1751) and the Barnett Bobb Log House (circa 1812). During this same period, the society acquired the Bonham House (circa 1875). These historic sites are furnished and interpreted to their times and provide

The Industrial & Agricultural Museum courtyard features a bronze statue celebrating the worker, by York County artist Lorann Jacobs.

Th York County Historical Society Museum & Library is located at 250 East Market Street.

a window to a century and a half of life in York.

The history of the Agricultural and Industrial Museum began with a group of individuals whose focus was directed toward the agricultural and industrial heritage of York County. In 1991, after two years of preparation, a museum opened in the old Eastern Market House (circa 1886). In 1992 the Agricultural and Industrial Museum acquired an industrial complex consisting of six buildings (circa 1874 to 1955). Several

of these buildings were renovated to house their artifact collection and are now a part of York County Heritage Trust's Industrial and Agricultural Museum.

The Fire Museum of York County was formed by active and retired firefighters. Set inside the Royal Number 6 Fire House (circa 1903), the museum depicts the unique history of York County's firefighting men and women.

The York County Heritage Trust also provides tours of the replica Colonial Courthouse (circa 1976) that is currently administered by the York Bicentennial Commission. The original structure was constructed in 1754 and witnessed the adoption of the Articles of Confederation during Congress' stay during the winter of 1777-78. Currently, plans are underway for the Bicentennial Commission to also become a part of the York County Heritage Trust.

Today the York County Heritage Trust maintains three museums and four historic sites that preserve and present 300 years of York County's rich and diverse history.

NORMANDIE RIDGE
SENIOR LIVING COMMUNITY

Normandie Ridge Senior Living Community offers an array of services including residential living, assisted living (a.k.a. personal care), nursing care, speech therapy, occupational therapy, physical therapy, massage therapy, and pharmacy services to the people of south central Pennsylvania. Originally opened as York United Methodist Home in 1992, the name of the community was changed to more accurately reflect the organization's mission, vision, and values. Since its inception, the community has been owned by Albright Care Services.

Albright Care Services originated in 1916 in Lewisburg, Pennsylvania and is not-for-profit and affiliated in faith with United Methodists. Its rich history as a United Methodist organization has helped guide it through the years. A board of trustees governs the corporation, which meets quarterly and establishes policy and long-range planning for the organization. The corporation also owns RiverWoods, a similar senior living community in Lewisburg, Pennsylvania, and manages Warrior Run Manor, an apartment building in Watsontown, Pennsylvania, which is approved by the United States Department of Housing and Urban Development.

Built on 27 acres in West Manchester Township, Normandie Ridge is conveniently located along Kenneth Road just north of Route 30. Numerous resources are close by including physicians, restaurants, golf courses, movie theaters, and shopping, to name a few. A contributor to the local economy, Normandie Ridge has over 150 full and part-time employees in various departments including nursing, housekeeping, maintenance, food service/catering, human resources, accounting, therapy, marketing, and administration.

Construction of Normandie Ridge's newest addition, Manchester Court and Commons, was completed in October 2002. The Court and Commons boasts 73 beautiful residential living apartments along with a

Numerous events are held throughout the year, inviting the public to see the many choices Normandie Ridge offers.

community center. Four additional apartments serve as hospitality suites for visiting families, friends, and out-of-town guests. Manchester Commons offers a dining room, chapel, library, creative arts center, wellness center, fitness center, heated indoor swimming pool, whirlpool, beauty salon/barber shop, general store, café, woodworking shop, banking services, access to personal computers and educational classes. The Court and Commons are all under one roof, a feature appreciated during the winter months.

Construction of Manchester Court and Commons at Normandie Ridge was completed in October 2002. The addition boasts (right) 73 apartment-style homes, four guest suites, and an array of amenities.

Manchester Court and Commons enhances the life-style choices available to seniors in the York area. Alternatives to the apartment style homes are the Garden Cottages. The cottages are available in one and two bedroom floor plans and some feature garages. Residents may choose to plant flowers or vegetables around their cottage. Parking is available in front of each cottage, providing easy access when returning from a day of shopping. Several financing options are available to suit individual needs for persons interested in either Manchester Court and Commons or the Garden Cottages.

The Nursing Care Center has 64 beds available and offers both skilled and intermediate nursing care. Residents pay a monthly room and board charge plus fees for any additional services utilized for their care. The nursing care center is both Medicare and Medicaid certified.

The Assisted Living Center is home to residents who need help with daily living activities but do not require 24-hour care. Residents pay a monthly fee for room, board, and services.

Carol B. McKinley, executive director, strongly believes in the commitment and dedication of every

Normandie Ridge employee. "Our Christian-based ministry continues to grow because of the efforts and dedication of countless individuals. Employees receive clinical and hospitality training on a regular basis. Caring for our nursing and assisted-living residents is challenging and very rewarding—it's a team approach."

Dr. Pawan Arora serves as medical director of the community and has a full-time primary geriatric care practice in Pine Grove Commons, Leader Heights.

A vital part of Normandie Ridge and Albright Care Services' history is its benevolent and charitable work. Charitable care specifically addresses the needs of individuals who have depleted their financial resources and have no available family to turn to for help. Through the help of Albright Care Services' Charitable Care Fund, administered by the fund development office, Normandie Ridge has never asked a resident to leave due to inability to pay.

Albright Life Learning Institute (ALLI), the continuing education department of Albright Care Services, is beginning to increase the number and types of classes offered at Normandie Ridge. ALLI was established to fulfill the educational needs of staff and residents as well as other professional organizations and the general public. Continuing education is becoming more popular nationwide as older adults seek

educational opportunities. One of ALLI's unprecedented training programs is the Geriatric Certified Nursing Assistant program. This specialty program designed exclusively for certified nursing assistants (CNA) working in long-term care consists of 192 hours of intensive classroom and clinical study. The training is part of the Albright CNA career ladder where nursing assistants working at Normandie Ridge may expand their nursing careers.

Normandie Ridge is accredited by the Joint Commission on accreditation of Healthcare Organizations (JCAHO). JCAHO accreditation standards far exceed federal and state requirements. By achieving accreditation, Normandie Ridge is part of a select group of Joint Commission accredited long-term care organizations having received this honor nationwide. Normandie Ridge is

Many residents of the Garden Cottages at Normandie Ridge enjoy flower gardening.

also a member of Pennsylvania Association of Non-Profit Homes for the Aging and the American Association of Homes and Services for the Aging. The Nursing Care Center is examined and certified annually by the state of Pennsylvania.

Another effort continually underway at Normandie Ridge is involvement in the local community. This is accomplished through hosting special events including food festivals, sponsorship of outdoor musical concerts, and public speaking engagements. Normandie Ridge's Auxiliary also plays an active role with such events as hosting the annual anniversary celebration every October. The celebration is a combined effort among the Auxiliary and Normandie Ridge staff. The Auxiliary is a very popular and special group, donating proceeds from the celebration towards items that enhance the quality of life for nursing care and assisted-living residents.

Normandie Ridge's leadership in the senior living industry is contributing to the growth, prosperity, and integrity of the greater York area. The hard work of its employees and volunteers and the loyalty from residents and families contributes to its success and paves the way for growth in the future.

PEDIATRIC HEALTH ASSOCIATES, P.C.

Pediatric Health Associates, P.C., traces its roots to November 1977, when Philip W. Eppley, II, D.O., came to York to become chairman of the Department of Pediatrics at Memorial Hospital. Dr. Eppley's initial practice was to provide inpatient pediatric and newborn care at Memorial Osteopathic Hospital.

The move to York was easy for Dr. Eppley, as he was a native of the city, and his immediate family was still living here. Dr. Eppley grew up on a farm in the Leader Heights area and went to Dallastown Area High School, graduating in 1964.

He then earned a Bachelor of Science from Albright College in 1968, and afterwards went to the Philadelphia College of Osteopathic Medicine, graduating in 1972, with his D.O. degree. He completed an internship and pediatric residency at the Oklahoma Osteopathic Hospital in 1975, and then returned to Pennsylvania to work with Dr. Harold Finkel in Lancaster, Pennsylvania, until his move to York in November 1977. The initial office was at 1794 Third Avenue and later moved to 1787 Fourth Avenue in 1978.

Later that same year, Dr. Eppley was joined in the practice by Thomas P. Bride, D.O., and the practice was then known as Eppley-Bride Pediatric Associates. In 1980, David M. Yakacki, D.O., joined the twosome, and in 1982 a branch office was opened in New Freedom— which later moved to Shrewsbury, where it remained until 1999. At that time, the office site was sold to Pediatric Care of York. The doctors joined the medical staff of York Hospital in 1983. Dr. Bride left the practice in 1985 to pursue a career in anesthesia, and Dr Yakacki left in 1999 to remain in the Shrewsbury area.

Dr. Eppley was instrumental in starting the first pediatric clinic at Memorial Osteopathic Hospital in 1978, and that clinic has evolved into the clinics for family practice, obstetrics and surgery at the hospi-

The office of Pediatric Health Associates, P.C., at 2860 Carol Road.

tal. The clinic serves low-income, Medical Assistance and self-pay patients in the community. The clinic is also an integral part of young doctors' training in how to serve the community.

In the early days, Dr. Eppley felt that education and community involvement were important ways to contribute to the York community. He was a physician advisor for the Concerned Citizens for Epilepsy from 1977 to 1982, and the Society for Juvenile Diabetes Research from 1978 to 1981. In addition, he was selected to serve on the Health Advisory Board of the March of Dimes from 1978 until 1990, and, also in 1978, served on the Board of Directors of the York Health Corporation, on which he still serves today.

The initial practice concentrated mostly around hospital care, but as insurance companies and HMOs were stressing more outpatient care and less hospitalization, the prac-

tice had the vision to emphasize more of the outpatient side of practice, too. The HMOs were also instrumental in helping families to have access to pediatricians as their children's primary doctors.

The current office at 2860 Carol Road was opened in December 1987, and the practice was called Pediatric Health Associates, P.C. The land for the building was purchased from Jim and Nina Mulay, grandparents of a family served by the practice.

Dr. Eppley constructed the current building of 4,960 square feet, used 2,680 square feet for the pediatric practice, and rented the remaining space to Pediatric Surgery, Limited, and the Square D Company. In 1998, Pediatric Health Associates, P.C., took over the entire building, as the practice had

216

The physicians and staff at Pediatric Health Associates, P.C.

grown and needed to expand. In the spring of 1999, they sold the Shrewsbury office to better concentrate on enhancing patient care in one location.

Pediatric Health Associates, P.C., exclusively treats children—from newborns to young adults. They offer a full range of pediatric care, from birth through the early twenties, which includes well-care, educational guidance, and the care of ill children and minor injuries. Infants can be seen in the nursery and followed later until they go to college, move from the area, or start their own families.

The mission of the practice is to work with parents and help them raise their infants, children, teens and young adults to grow happily, healthily and safely. Everyone at Pediatric Health Associates, P.C., sincerely likes children and enjoys the work of caring for children.

Pediatric Health Associates, P.C., has provided care in the York community for over 25 years and

offers care for each individual child in a friendly and caring office environment, designed just for children. The practice feels that there is nobody better than a pediatrician who knows about children's health, growth and development, and childhood diseases, and who understands their behavior.

In the practice, there is a strong commitment to patient and parent education, believing that parenting can be more fun and more effective if parents are informed and prepared. The doctors believe that they are there to help parents in the raising of their children, so they will provide guidance and advice—but will also respect parents' feelings and opinions.

The doctors wish to be a part of a child's life, not only as a guardian of the child's health but also as a guide and resource that the parents can count on. This is a developmentally-based practice that will advise

and inform parents about what to expect at each age and about what is normal. In that way, they hope to prevent problems. They believe that an informed parent or patient is a valuable ally in their attempt to provide the best in health care.

At the current time there are three pediatricians: Philip W. Eppley, II, D.O.; Melencio C. Ventura, Jr., M.D.; and Gail S. Hertz, M.D., I.B.C.L.C. Ann M. Summers, C.R.N.P. is also part of the team. Dr. Ventura joined the practice in 1994, and Dr. Hertz joined in July 2000, while Ann Summers has been with the practice since 1992. All of the providers work together closely to provide their patients quality pediatric care in a "kid-friendly" environment.

The pediatricians who work at Pediatric Health Associates, P.C.

PENN STATE YORK

With more than 2,000 students and a wide range of educational opportunities—including six associate degree programs, seven baccalaureate degree programs, and a focused master's degree in teaching and curriculum—Penn State York has grown to be an important part of the York community.

Penn State first offered educational opportunities in York in 1926, when a program in accountancy was conducted by the engineering extension for a group of citizens at the newly built York YMCA. The professors traveled from State College to York each week to teach.

In 1939 as the land grant Institution of the Commonwealth, the federal government designated Penn State to conduct the engineering, science, management, and defense training programs. Classes met at the William Penn Senior High School. Fourteen men—the first graduates—completed the program in the summer of 1941. The next class began in February 1942 (a polio epidemic in the York area caused classes to be cancelled during the fall of 1941). By this time, our nation was at war, and because of the large numbers enrolled, classes were held at both William Penn and York Junior College through June 1945. By the spring of 1946, several thousand Yorkers had completed, or were in the process

Edward M. Elias, one the founders of Penn State York, watches as construction progresses on the first campus building.

of completing, their programs of study. These academic programs were conducted on a part-time basis, requiring five years to earn a diploma in one of several majors.

The returning veterans, in addition to those already in the program, brought new pressure on the University to accelerate the programs. In 1949, a one-year, full-time day technical program offering a diploma to its graduates was instituted. York campus dates its official beginning from this time. By the fall of 1950, the York center consolidated both its day and evening operations into the Wilson Elementary School on Carlisle Avenue. This building was leased to the University by the School District of the City of York.

Also in 1950, Edward M. Elias was the first full-time employee and faculty member at what was known as the Penn State General Extension Center in York. At that time the center served 25 daytime and 300 evening students.

The York center remained at Wilson until the fall of 1953 when it was moved into the Shiloh Elementary Building. An important program change took

place with the initiation of the two-year associate degree programs in Engineering Technology. The two programs originally offered were Electrical Technology and Drafting and Design Technology, the forerunners of today's Mechanical Engineering and Electrical Engineering Technology programs.

Elias, considered one of the founders of the campus, was always a proponent of the York campus' need for a permanent facility. He saw that goal begin to become a reality in 1956, when the school's advisory board provided funds for the purchase of eight acres of land on Edgecomb Avenue.

As enrollment increased, a two-story, 100-by-75-foot classroom-laboratory-administration building

Springtime at Penn State York.

was constructed. In 1959 the York center officially became the York campus as part of a general University reorganization which established the Commonwealth Campus System or Commonwealth Educational System.

Elias served the campus until 1985, having helped bring Penn State York from a part-time extension program that rented space in old elementary schools to a complete undergraduate campus.

Anticipating an increase in college students due to the arrival of the "baby boom" generation, the

Engineering students get hands-on experience in the early years at the campus.

Penn State York Advisory Board conducted a local fund-raising drive to add a classroom wing. In 1966 the new facilities were opened, and a limited bachelor's program was offered in engineering and science. By 1968, the first two years of almost all of the University's baccalaureate degree programs were available at the York campus.

Construction took a giant step forward when the General State Authority and the federal government provided funds to build a much-needed library, science wing, and gymnasium. Groundbreaking occurred in early 1969, and the buildings were dedicated and in use by the fall of 1970. A $750,000 capital fund-raising effort provided the money to construct the student center (now the Joe and Rosie Ruhl Student Community Center) adjacent to the gymnasium in 1976. This construction completed the core campus buildings.

Associate degree programs were expanded with the addition of Letters, Arts, and Sciences in 1968, Computer Science in 1970, and Business Administration in 1986. Associate degree students were now able to transfer to some baccalaureate programs and complete their degree requirements in two

Faculty members enjoy taking classes outside when weather permits.

Penn State York has grown to more than a 50-acre campus offering a wide range of programs. Photo by Wyatt McGuire

additional years.

Penn State York's partnerships in the community, and work with the city of York, helped bring about growth in the size of the campus. In 1990, a generous donation of 34 acres of land by the city of York increased the campus size threefold, bringing it to more than 50 acres.

In June 1991 the campus dedicated another new facility, a computer and bookstore building (Information Sciences and Technology Center), the result of another community fund raising effort, which exceeded $2.1 million. The new building centralized and consolidated all campus computer facilities, provided improved faculty office and support spaces, and opened a new and modern bookstore to serve the campus and community.

In 1994, the Focused Master's in Education degree in Teaching and Curriculum began in York through a partnership with Penn State Harrisburg. The program, built with the input of teachers and district superintendents, provides a course of study designed to enhance the skills of K-12 teachers in York County. Through this program, teachers learn the latest research, theory and practice; integrate current theory and research into the classroom; prepare to meet new Pennsylvania Department of Education regulations; pursue professional development goals; address their district's staff development and strategic planning goals; and learn to manage change effectively. Currently, the program boasts an enrollment of 447 teachers and 260 teachers have graduated and earned their degrees. The success of this program has helped change the face of education in York County.

On July 1, 1997, Penn State's

Students enjoy the opportunity to pose with a replica of the Nittany Lion shrine. Photo by Wyatt McGuire

Commonwealth Educational System (the administrative unit previously responsible for oversight of the University's campus system) reorganized to better meet the educational needs of Pennsylvania residents, particularly those residing in communities in which the campuses are located. One of the reorganization's outcomes was the creation of the Commonwealth College, which consists of twelve Penn State campuses, including York. Historically, the campuses offered associate degrees—and the first two years of a baccalaureate education to students who were expected to complete their degree at University Park. With this reorganization, campus locations, through the Commonwealth College, were allowed to begin offering baccalaureate degree programs, in addition to their traditional course offerings.

The Bachelor of Science in Business, the campus' first four-year degree, was initiated in the fall of 1997. An associate degree program in Human Development and Family Studies was also put in place. The Bachelor of Arts in Letters, Arts, and Sciences was launched in spring 2001, and by fall 2001, the campus added new bachelor's degree programs in Information Sciences and Technology, Electro-Mechanical Engineering Technology, and Communication and Arts and Sciences. In spring 2002 the campus launched a new bachelor's degree program in Science. The Bachelor of Arts in English started in the fall of 2002 bringing the total of four-year degrees students can complete at Penn State York to seven.

Throughout the years, Penn State York has continued to provide training and education for the local manufacturing community which dates back to its original beginnings in York. The campus works with local business and industry to provide on-site credit and noncredit courses at Harley-Davidson Inc., Starbucks Corp., Tyco, Susquehanna Pfaltzgraff, Honeywell, United Defense, York International Corporation, Snyder's of Hanover and Wellspan. Numerous business and industry partnerships have been formed throughout the years with the campus leading the way with educational opportunities.

Penn State York is actively involved in community outreach, economic development and outreach to community youth and public education. Whether it's a program for middle and high school students or seminars and workshops for child care workers, Penn State York is dedicated to working with the community.

Flags fly on the campus representing the homelands of students, faculty and staff, including Spain, Turkey, Russia, Japan, Thailand, Zimbabwe, Italy, Canada and Vietnam to name a few. The flags symbolize the pride Penn State York takes in the ethnic heritage of the campus and a commitment to provide an environment where all opinions are valued and respected.

The campus enrolls more than 2,000 students in credit courses, ranking York the largest in enrollment of the twelve campuses in the Commonwealth College. In addition to those students taking credit coursework, the campus also serves 6,000–7,000 annually through continuing education services in both York and Lancaster.

Penn State York has planned a performing arts center and a new library building to be in place in January 2004. This $11.9 million facility will be an asset to the campus and community.

Penn State York's Performing Arts Center/Library is planned to open in 2004. Artist's rendering by Murphy & Dittenhafer, Inc.

JLS AUTOMATION

Joseph L. Souser was a manufacturers' representative for power transmission equipment when he and his wife, Polly, founded JLSouser and Associates in 1954. In the years that followed, he represented from six to ten manufacturers at a time in the middle Atlantic states: Pennsylvania, Virginia, Maryland, Delaware, New Jersey, and the metropolitan New York area.

"He was very much a people person," says son, Craig, president of the company today. "He instilled integrity and the concept of an honest day's work for an honest day's pay, providing what customers want and making them glad they worked with you."

When Joe died in 1976, Polly took over. She hired a sales representative, and Craig helped while attending Lehigh University. He graduated in 1980, took over the sales responsibilities, and, in 1986, succeeded his mother as president.

During the '80s, the company's focus shifted. Electronic controls for AC motors was the developing technology. JLS expanded its product range to include variable frequency drives and built a significant following providing application engineering assistance.

JLS recognized the importance of the servomotor in industrial automation. It worked with several manufacturers before becoming, in 1987, a representative of Indramat, then—and still—a world leader in motion control equipment.

By 1991, JLS noted more companies outsourcing, and began offering systems engineering. Soon, it was providing customers with turnkey engineered systems and field service to support them and other installed JLS products.

As staff and demand grew, the company moved into ever larger quarters. In 1991, with a staff of five and a need to stage products and equipment, JLS moved from 458 W. Market to 402 Wheatfield and a separate shop facility. In 1994, it relocated its ten employees to 1285 E. Princess. It added an engineering department and computer network. About a year later, it moved once again, this time to the Prospect Commerce Center, and made a commitment to Star Linear Systems. In 1996, it formed JLS Robotics, a subsidiary to capitalize on opportunities for Custom Gantry Robots.

In 1998, with a staff of more than three dozen, JLS built its current integrated facility at 3495 Industrial Drive in York. It was planned to handle expansion; little more than half of its 40,000 square feet was needed immediately.

Today, JLS is still a middle Atlantic manufacturers' representative, but also a distributor and integrator for its affiliates. It offers electrical, mechanical and software engineering; field service; training; panel fabrication; cable assembly; and mechanical assembly. It has its own representatives nationally for its systems group, which designs and installs printing press drive and control systems—and it builds and integrates gantry robotic equipment. It serves, in addition to printing, machine tool, packaging, plastics,

Corporate headquarters of JLSouser & Associates, Inc.

food, corrugated box, and other industries.

"We take care of our customers and our employees," Craig Souser says, noting its programs to encourage employee health and development. As a nationally recognized leader in implementing advanced technology for machine and motion control, it attracts talented individuals and is committed to retaining and motivating them.

"Our assets are people," says Souser. "They tend to stay with us. We've had a number of people who tried other opportunities and came back. We value our employees and customers, and support them every way we can. We recognize that, at the end of the day, the one thing you have left is your reputation."

Even though he might not recognize his company today, Joseph Souser would certainly recognize that sentiment.

The company changed its name to JLS Automation in 2002, to better reflect the nature of its business.

QUIGLEY MOTOR CO., INC.

They quickly gathered the team to get everyone to Kosovo before the rains came. All the bombing had torn up the roads, and the mud was almost impassable. The advance people notified headquarters that with all the evidence the scientists needed for the war tribunals, they needed larger vehicles; the Hummers just wouldn't carry everyone.

In America, a big black van, part of a motorcade, follows the president of the United States. (It's just one of several that are used by the the Secret Service detail accompanying him.) The White House Communication Vehicle always goes wherever the president goes, regardless of the weather.

Up in Yellowstone National Park, everyone is very quiet, totally immobile. It's early in the morning and the indicators are good that the pack of wolves living there will make their appearance. Never before has the opportunity presented itself to capture on film such beautiful creatures in their natural habitat. Weeks of preparation went into arriving at this remote location—with all the gear and support needed to produce this documentary on the life of the American Timber Wolf—and Kennan and Karen Ward pulled it off.

Finally, on a dangerous mountain

A true oceanfront beach house.

A go-anywhere 4 x 4 Sportsmobile camper.

road covered with snow and ice, an ambulance spots a car accident. The rescue squad knows that they have little time to administer life-saving techniques with any chance of success. They have to hurry. As they make their way through the mountains, they forge their own path, because the grader hasn't been through, yet.

All four of these scenes have one commonality: Quigley Motor Company. Located in York, Quigley is the oldest, largest, and most successful manufacturer of high-quality, four-wheel-drive conversions for full-sized vans and "cut-a-ways" in the world, with over 10,000 of its unique drive systems sold. Quigley also manufactures and installs Right-Hand Drive (RHD) conversion systems for GM full-size vans and cutaways for export to any of the 56 countries in the world that require RHD.

When William "Bill" Quigley opened for business in 1966, his primary source of income came from new and used truck sales and rentals. As his reputation and business started to grow in the early 1970s, he began to sell recre-

ational vehicles, as well. Selling RVs enabled Quigley to get in on the ground floor of the emerging "custom van" craze then sweeping North America. His van conversions turned utilitarian trucks into exciting vehicles that featured plush interiors and eye-catching exterior designs that were literally one of a kind.

But many customers wanted full-sized vans that were more than fair-weather vehicles. They desired vehicles that could go anywhere on or off the road, regardless of the weather.

In 1975 this inspired Bill to have his oldest son Mike engineer a unique four-wheel-drive system, an engineering feature then unavailable from Ford or General Motors. Since its first 4 x 4 conversion in 1975 when they developed the "Quadra-Version" four-wheel drive system, Quigley has used its innovative "duo-strut" torque rod system to locate the front axle. One of the characteristic features of the system is that it retains the coil spring suspension within the O.E.M. frame structure. This design has been a standard feature on all converted full-sized Ford vans. The inclusion of the "duo-strut" system makes Quigley a pacesetter in the O.E.M. four-wheel-drive field. Over the years, this same design has been adopted by Jeep (in 1985) and Dodge (in 1994) for use on their 4 x 4 Ram trucks. With the new GM van debuting in 2003, Mike Quigley and his team have developed the Independent Front Suspension (IFS) to make it one of the most exciting products on the road. The van now has a more car-like ride, and it will fit in an underground parking garage.

On the component side, in Quigley's desire to provide the safest, highest quality product, it adheres to all applicable Federal

The Quigley plant with some of the hundreds of FedEx 4 x 4 vans.

No snow days off when your bus has 4 x 4.

1989, Quigley again pioneered an untapped market segment. It created right-hand drive for General Motors on the full-size van, cutaway, Suburban, and pickup truck. General Motors—trucks and SUVs equipped with Quigley's RHD conversion have attracted customers in the United Kingdom, Africa, the Far East, Australia, and New Zealand. Today, Quigley Motor Company is an authorized up-fitter for General Motors to design, build, and install RHD.

It is because of Quigley's demand for excellence that it has been successful in all of its engineering reviews with Ford Motor Company's Modified Vehicle Engineering (MVE) Division. These high marks were needed for Ford to agree to not only bring new, untitled, vehicles to the Quigley facility, but also to pick them back up for delivery to any of the Ford dealers in the country, just like a new car. A similar plan is in place on the GM units as well.

The Quigley Story is a family story, a story of what one man did, with God's help, to feed not only his immediate family, but his extended family as well—the people that work for him. It is a true success story of the indomitable spirit of the people in and around York.

A Quigley 4 x 4-equipped motor home at the Arctic Circle in February 2000.

Motor Safety Standards (FMVSS) and all parts are manufactured to their design and in accordance with SAE (Society of Automotive Engineers) specifications.

The Quadra-Version van conversion features a comfortable ride and prodigious off-road capabilities. For both business and play, the Quigley 4 x 4 quickly earned a reputation for "making the impassable possible" as Bill Quigley would often say.

Armed with a well-received product and a clearly defined market niche, Quigley began to aggressively grow the business. And grow it he did. Fitting full-sized vans with Quigley's "Quadra-Version," 4 x 4 system became the company's main business activity throughout the late 1970s and 1980s.

Initially, the lion's share of Quigley's business was with the non-commercial buyer, the outdoor sportsman, the boater, and the weekend car racer. But soon the virtues of the Quigley product line became known to a new buyer—the commercial and ambulance markets. In addition to providing the platforms for ambulances and mobile telecommunications trucks, Quigley has also sold vehicles to some of the most famous names in American business: Fed-Ex, AT&T and Haliburton Service Corporation. There are also Quigley "Quadra-Version" vans serving with the ATF, FBI, Secret Service, and the CIA. They have attained a level of engineering excellence that now has them listed as an option in the Federal Standards, available to any government agency ordering through the General Services Agency (GSA).

Through the '90s Quigley Motor Company continued its transformation from a small "car lot" into a vehicle manufacturer with global sales and world class capabilities. The capabilities of Quigley's "Quadra-Version" system on a full-sized van positions the Quigley as the ultimate SUV of choice for all seasons and all terrains.

The "Quadra-Version" conversion, however, is only part of the Quigley story. In

RED LION BUS COMPANY
AND RED LION TOURS & TRAVEL

Ci gar (si gar'), n. a cylindrical roll of tobacco leaves cured for smoking.

Why would a bus company history begin with the definition of a cigar? The year is 1939 in the small central Pennsylvania town of Red Lion. Blessed with rich soil and an ideal climate, many area farmers grow tobacco, and the cigar manufacturing business is flourishing. In such a sparsely populated location, there is little demand for public transportation—or so it seems to everyone but a local automobile dealer, Alvin Fauth.

Burdened with a bus he had to repossess—because the previous owner was unable to make payments—Mr. Fauth decided to recoup some of his loss by transporting workers to and from the many local cigar-making enterprises. It worked! In an age when few people owned cars, potential customers were quick to realize the benefits of this service, and the Red Lion Bus Company was born.

In the early 1940s, the operation grew to three buses when students were transported to Red Lion Schools. During this period, students paid their own way, purchasing a monthly ticket.

Bruce Runkle, who had been driving for Mr. Fauth, purchased the company in 1946. During this year,

Ford bus, circa 1939.

School bus, 2002.

the school district started paying for student transportation, and Mr. Runkle added four more buses for carrying students and workers. He realized that a new need for his services was about to emerge, when the various county school districts started consolidating. From that point on, the company's growth in school bus operations flourished as consolidation continued.

In the 1950s, the company began to offer charter service, initially using school buses. A few motorcoaches were then added to the fleet—and, in 1964, the World's Fair in New York provided a major attraction destination for company tours. Since that event, motorcoaches have comprised a significant segment of the company fleet.

In 1972 the Warner family acquired Red Lion Bus Company. Earl Warner had spent his career in the dairy business, with his brothers Jesse and Donald. That company, Warners Dairy, was sold, because the industry was experiencing a wave of consolidation of smaller companies into larger ones. Looking for a new business interest, Earl became the principal backer for the acquisition of Red Lion Bus. His sons, Dennis and Floyd, took on the responsibilities of company operations.

Also in the 1970s, the energy crisis led to the popularity of motorcoach tours and group charters. People were looking for alternatives to the car for vacations and recreational travel. Red Lion Bus was there to help. Additionally, it acquired three school bus companies in the 1970s and 1980s. Meeting the demands of growth demanded larger facilities and so a new complex was completed in 1978, which included the main office, fleet maintenance building, fuel facilities and parking for all vehicles. This facility was constructed at 110 East Walnut Street, Red Lion, and is the company's main operations base today. Two satellite locations are also used as bases for school bus operations in York County. These are located at Stewartstown and Delroy. The company has contracts with four school districts to provide student transportation services.

In 1982 Red Lion Tours, Inc., was established by Dennis and Floyd to specialize in escorted motorcoach tours and tours for groups. Within a few years, this role expanded to become a full-service travel agency. By 1985 Red Lion Tours had acquired Ridgeway Tours of Lancaster, a highly respected travel agency and tour company founded by Oliver Shenk in 1920. Today, Red Lion Tours, Inc., is known by the business name of Red Lion Tours & Travel, reflecting its role in providing a broad range of tour and travel services.

In 1991 Floyd Warner decided to pursue another career opportunity, and he resigned from the Red Lion Bus Company Group. Dennis then acquired Floyd's interest in the companies, becoming the sole owner. The Red Lion Bus Company Group currently consists of Red Lion Bus Company; Red Lion Tours & Travel; EDW, Inc.; and EDF Associates. EDW, Inc., provides fleet maintenance and other services primarily to Red Lion Bus Company, and operates an auto service and

Prevost Coach, 2002.

repair center. EDF Associates is a proprietorship, which owns and maintains all buildings and properties involved in the operations of the group.

In 1995 a new phase began in Red Lion's history. Dennis' wife, Sandra, joined him in the operation so that they would have more balance in their business and personal life. She progressively assumed more responsibilities each year and is currently the general manager of Red Lion Tours & Travel. She is also the secretary/treasurer of all Red Lion companies, and in that capacity, has management oversight for financial and general office functions.

Dennis and Sandy have forged a

management arrangement—which functions essentially as a partnership—in their business life, and it works! They note with humor, however, that the original objective of having Sandy help with the business so that they would have more personal time never materialized, since she has continued to take on additional responsibilities. Although the company's intensive customer service environment is an ongoing challenge, they get a sense of satisfaction and accomplishment from Red Lion's whole team of approximately 185 employees. The operations throughout central Pennsylvania and Maryland involve a fleet of 20 motorcoaches, 110 school buses, 16 vans, service vehicles and supervisor vehicles.

Red Lion continues to believe that a commitment to quality is the essential constant in a changing world. With this view, they see three categories of people who are vital parts of the mission: employees, customers, and potential customers. The employee team will continue to provide excellent service and value to its customers, and this reputation will induce potential customers to continue to come in the future.

Main facility at 110 E. Walnut Street, Red Lion, Pennsylvania.

SESAME PERSONNEL & SESAME TEMPS INC.

Large enough to be a leader in the community and small enough to give personalized service.

Sesame Personnel was a small employment agency servicing the local York area when, on March 1, 1976, Lois Gable purchased it. At the time of purchase Sesame had three employees, a receptionist, a placement counselor, and Lois. Lois felt with hard work and determination she could succeed in making it a viable agency. However, Lois' road would not be an easy one.

Before Lois could purchase Sesame, she would have to overcome one very large hurdle. While York was an excellent town to support employment services, the business climate in York at this time was not equally as supportive of a young woman looking to own and operate her own company. As Lois visited banks and requested a business loan, she quickly learned that "the Old Boys Network" was not inclined to issue a loan to a single woman unless she had a spouse or family member to co-sign, and Lois refused to have her parents sign bank papers. But despite this obstacle, Lois managed to get a toehold. By meeting and talking with businessmen in the area, she gained the support of a gentleman who verbally backed her to the banks.

At purchase, Sesame was a local agency focused on local companies and filling their full-time job openings. After Lois established Sesame even further in this arena, she grew Sesame to be specialized in job placement at three distinct levels. Lois represented these levels by dividing Sesame into three separate entities.

The first was Sesame Personnel. This division would handle full-time placement for York County. Included in full-time placement are office services and management positions. Some examples of jobs in this area are typists, computer operators, office managers, file clerks, pharmacists, chefs and engineers.

Lois P. Gable is the owner of Sesame. Lois came from a solid middle-class family with a strong sense of community commitment. Her parents, Reverend and Mrs. Walter H. Gable, instilled values, honesty, and integrity in their children. When he was 21 years old, Reverend Gable set up a small barber shop in his father's tool shed on his father's farm. Over the years this grew into a barber supply business. It seems this entrepreneurial spirit was passed on to his daughter.

The second division Lois created was Sesame Temps, Inc. This group would handle placement in all of the same categories as Sesame Personnel, but only for temporary positions. In addition, because York was (and is) such a large manufacturing city, this group would handle many positions considered light-industrial or labor positions.

The last of the Sesame entities would be SP Tech Search, a nation-wide search firm for high-end placement. This group would handle upper-level management and professional positions throughout the United States. This group would also handle professionals following a specific career path, such as engineering or computer technology.

Sesame still maintains these same operational groups, allowing the company to stay heavily in-volved in job placement at all levels. The only significant difference is that while six Sesame direct recruiters once handled National Placement, it is now handled through a network of placement services throughout the United States.

Another way in which Sesame has been better able to serve its clients is by joining industry specific organizations, as well as community-based organizations. These relationships allow Sesame to remain in touch with the current placement market, as well as the job market as a whole.

Sesame succeeds in business where so many others fail, because they feel equally that the client company and the temporary hire are people and not just a sale. The people at Sesame believe in a smile and a friendly hello as you enter their offices. They also believe in the importance of a live person answering the phone, rather than the electronic systems so many companies have come to rely on. These basic business values are highly respected by those in the York community.

In turn, The York community is very important to the people at Sesame. Local placement dollars spent at Sesame stay in the community. Money does not just pass through the area to another city. It stays there to help build a strong community. Some causes Sesame contributes to regularly are: The Family Assistance Fund, The Farm and Natural Land Trust, Bell Socialization, Big Brothers/Big Sisters, The Firefighters Association, Guiding Eyes for the Blind, Junior Achievement, The Martin Memorial Library, The Strand-Capital Performing Arts Center, The Girl Scouts, The York Rescue Mission, The Salvation Army, The York County Food Bank, and several scholarship funds.

Also a tremendous contribution to the community was Lois' involvement in developing the IRC Unit at Memorial Hospital. Workers compensation accidents were few and far between in the early days of Sesame, but as permanent jobs lessened and the temp industry took over, workers comp accidents became a real issue. While real accidents are always present, a great many fake accidents were being claimed as well. Knowing she was in the employment industry, Michael H. Hady III, vice president of business development for Memorial Hospital approached Lois to find out what Memorial could do to help. She told Mike that a group of doctors who had an understanding of the temp business, as well as the ability to identify fake injury claims would be the answer, and so the Industrial Resource Center (IRC Unit) of Memorial Hospital was born. In addition, Sesame created its own safety committee, which set standards for client companies of Sesame. Now, before a company is ac-

On the left: Karen Foltz, designer, B.S. in Accounting is the accounting manager, and Tammy Wilson, CPC, CTS, is the operations manager. Together they have over 20 years working together ar Sesame.

Front row, left to right: Tammy Wilson, Lois Gable, and Karen Deisinger. Middle row, left to right: Lyndsay Fry, Rachel Grebe, and Elena Damrauer. Third row, left to right: Krista Shorts, Annie Kohler, Beth Wilson, Lynn Snook, and Jen Zeisloft. Back row, left is Brain Shorts and Nate Pritchard.

cepted as a Sesame client company, they are screened via a walkthrough conducted by a member of the Sesame Safety Committee. If a company is found to be unsafe and unconcerned with the safety of their employees, the company is rejected by Sesame.

Each year Sesame has a March of Dimes picnic for client companies. This event raises money for the March of Dimes, as well as gives the client companies the opportunity to sit down with each other and talk about what is happening in the community and nationwide. To further their commitment to be a personal company and not just the "big boss," twice a year Sesame has a picnic for those on the temp payroll. The temps thoroughly enjoy this respite from work and enjoy talking to each other and the Sesame staff.

Sesame's offices are on Market Street in York. Sesame is still a viable business in York today.

SUSQUEHANNA PFALTZGRAFF CO.

The companies that form Susquehanna Pfaltzgraff are separate businesses with different markets, objectives, and goals, but they share a single corporate philosophy. The Pfaltzgraff Co., Susquehanna Radio Corp., Susquehanna Communications, Susquehanna Data Services and Susquehanna Real Estate are all part of a company whose name stands for quality products and services. Their history reflects the changing needs of a changing nation, and their development is a tribute to the entrepreneurs of yesterday and today.

The Pfaltzgraff Co.

The roots of Susquehanna's oldest business go back to the one-man pottery run by Johann George Pfaltzgraff, who settled in York County, Pennsylvania, in the early 1800s, and who was the great-great grandfather of Louis J. Appell, Jr., chairman of Susquehanna Pfaltzgraff. Today, Pfaltzgraff is not only the oldest part of Susquehanna, but also the oldest pottery manufacturing company in the United States. With a strong emphasis on design, quality and customer service, Pfaltzgraff has grown from that first rural pottery to become a leading American manufacturer of ceramic dinner-

Susquehanna Radio's WSBA-AM and its sister FM station, WARM-103, are headquartered just east of York, along Route 30. The station's promotional vans are a common sight throughout the listening region, for special events and remote broadcasts.

ware and related tabletop products. To offer a total, coordinated look, Pfaltzgraff imports glassware made to the company's strict specifications, and licenses its designs and brand name to other high-quality manufacturers of products for the home. The majority of Pfaltzgraff ceramic production takes place in York County, with an additional facility located in Nogales, Mexico. Pfaltzgraff products are distributed through more than 70 Pfaltzgraff-operated retail stores and four clearance centers, as well as major department stores, mass merchants, gift and specialty stores, and through its own direct mail catalog and Internet site.

Susquehanna Radio Corp.

Susquehanna Radio is a communications company whose core business is radio broadcasting, but which also creates and provides a wide variety of marketing and lifestyle products and services for both its listeners and clients. Susquehanna has grown to become one of the 11 largest radio group broadcasters in the nation.

The first station in the Susquehanna portfolio was York's WSBA-AM, founded in 1942. Today, the company owns and operates 33 AM and FM radio stations na-

The Susquehanna Commerce Center was constructed on a long-abandoned industrial site in the City of York, and is a key element in the revitalization of the downtown area. Over 600 people will occupy the campus, which will be home to more than a dozen professional, engineering, communications and technology firms.

tionwide, most of which are located in large and highly competitive markets throughout the United States. These include: San Francisco, California; Dallas, Ft. Worth and Houston, Texas; Atlanta, Georgia; Cincinnati, Ohio; Indianapolis, Indiana; York, Pennsylvania; and Kansas City, Kansas. Each of the stations shares the Susquehanna philosophy of producing a high-quality information and entertainment product by talented people, both on and off the air, and providing creative, effective solutions to clients' marketing objectives.

As a leading broadcaster, Susquehanna Radio Corp. maintains a strong and visible presence in the business through active participation in numerous industry and trade associations. The company has been a vocal proponent of a variety of marketing, sales, financial management, regulatory and technical initiatives over the years, and many employees continue to work in such endeavors.

Susquehanna Communications

This broadband services provider operates advanced networks in five states, serving over 200,000 customers. The company name was changed to Susquehanna Communications in 1999, to reflect its change from a traditional cable television company to a provider of interactive, digital communications products. In 2000, the SusCom brand was introduced for consumer marketing, based on its frequent use and familiarity to customers. With over 35 years in the business, SusCom has grown to be among the top 20 cable and broadband companies in the United States.

The company has long been a leader in delivering cutting-edge technology. SusCom customers in every location can enjoy advanced digital video services, including digital cable and interactive games. Consistent with this tradition, SusCom plans to offer high-definition television (HDTV) and video-on-demand (VOD) in the near future. SusCom's leadership role has carried over to the growing high-speed data services market. Customer demand for cable modem service has been strong and consistent. In the near future, the ultimate connection to the Internet will be available to virtually all of SusCom's customers. Digital telephone service is on the horizon, as SusCom continues to bring the newest digital communications products to its customers.

SusCom is ideally positioned to maintain its industry leadership. Advanced hybrid fiber optic and coaxial networks are in place or under construction in nearly ninety percent of its service areas, and will be fully deployed within the next two years. These are the high-capacity broadband networks that will allow SusCom to achieve its goal of being the premier provider of video, data and voice services to consumers and businesses in the communities it serves. This is more than a mission statement; it is a commitment that SusCom has delivered on every day since its inception—and will continue to deliver on in the future.

Susquehanna Data Services
Created in June 1996, Susquehanna Data Services, Inc., operates

two divisions: BlazeNet and Susquehanna Technologies (SusQtech). The company was created to provide Internet access, web development and other Internet-related services to businesses and consumers. Susquehanna Data Services also seeks to support the Internet-related activities of other Susquehanna subsidiaries. Following is the area of concentration of each individual business:
• BlazeNet provides Internet access, hosting, Local Area Network ("LAN") and Wide Area Network ("WAN") design and implementation and consulting to business customers. Dial-up Internet access is also available for consumers.
• SusQtech offers web design and custom application development, e-commerce and system integration to commercial enterprises and associations throughout the United States. SusQtech is a Microsoft Gold Certified Partner in E-Commerce.

Susquehanna Real Estate
In February 2002, Susquehanna Real Estate became a new business within the Susquehanna Pfaltzgraff Co. Formed originally in December 1981 as a corporate division of Susquehanna Pfaltzgraff, the Real Estate group was responsible for all real estate support services,

Pfaltzgraff designers drew upon the famous peach orchards and vineyards of York County, Pennsylvania, to create Orchard, a richly colored celebration of the bounty of the local harvest.

including facility design and construction, for operating entities of the company.

Today, Susquehanna Real Estate continues to carry out its original responsibilities. Activity has grown, however, to include commercial and residential project development in both new construction and restoration projects, as well as active involvement in fulfilling Susquehanna Pfaltzgraff's commitment to the community. This is achieved through successful investment and redevelopment projects that support the preservation and advancement of downtown York.

As a family of businesses, Susquehanna Pfaltzgraff is also a family of individuals who makes these businesses thrive. Susquehanna Pfaltzgraff is an employee-owned company through its Employee Stock Ownership Plan (ESOP) that is committed to the welfare of its business enterprises, its employees, its customers and to the communities in which they work and live—in York, Pennsylvania, and nationwide.

TIGHE INDUSTRIES, INC.

Dance recitals, gymnastics schools, cheerleaders, and drill teams—all are as American as apple pie. Yet many of the garments for each are designed, manufactured, and marketed by a York County, Pennsylvania company with a truly global focus.

With sales representatives in Japan, the United Kingdom, Ireland, Iceland, Germany, and Australia, that York County company—Tighe Industries—has become a world leader in producing dance costumes and gymnastics apparel.

Tighe Industries stands out in what traditionally has been a cottage industry. Started in York in 1945 as one of the first ready-made dance recital costume companies, Curtain Call Costumes established a reputation for high quality ballet costumes. From 1945 to 1969, Curtain Call was the family business of Mr. and Mrs. Herman Harrison of York. The Harrisons ran a small operation, employing about 15 people to make costumes for students performing in spring dance

Curtain Call Costumes, a division of Tighe Industries, has outfitted millions of dancers around the world.

recitals. The business was seasonal, lasting from February to June, and the costumes were ordered by mail from a catalog the company distributed. During these two founding decades, the company's growth was modest, employing 13 people and servicing a small regional market.

Leroy King, Jr., and his mother and father, Eleanor and Leroy King, formed a partnership and bought Curtain Call's assets and equipment in 1969. They moved the entire operation into their sewing contracting company, King's Sportswear, in East Prospect, Pennsylvania. The younger King took charge, investigated his market and his competition, and set forth to create a growing company that would live by a continuing standard—to create garments of quality and to provide honest and reliable service to customers.

King's goal was firmly rooted in the adage, "The show must go on." His customers each had up to 350 students performing in recitals, and he knew that when the curtain went up, his costumes had better be there. His endeavor to meet the needs of his clients and to make the company grow was successful. In

1969, Curtain Call manufactured 5,700 garments. Three years later, the company was incorporated as Curtain Call Costumes, Inc. By 1975, Curtain Call moved into its own manufacturing facility in Yorkana, Pennsylvania.

King then diversified, founding Alpha Factor Gymnastics to produce and distribute competitive gymnastics apparel in 1978. He then purchased Gantner Swimwear in 1979. Tighe Industries, Inc., was soon formed as the parent company for the gymnastics, swimwear, and costume divisions. In 1981, Tighe Industries built the 74,000-square-foot East Prospect manufacturing facility that still serves as the company's primary production facility. The purchase of another facility in Emigsville, Pennsylvania, and a 122,000-sqaure-foot warehousing/distribution center in York that also houses Tighe Industries' corporate headquarters, soon followed.

First certified as a Class A manufacturing company in 1996, Tighe Industries continues to search for and implement new strategic initiatives to keep the company competitive in a global marketplace. State-of-the-art production,

Tighe Industries' Curtain Call Spirit division has made inroads into professional sports, outfitting cheerleading squads for teams such as NBA's Cleveland Cavaliers.

nized globally. Alpha Factor is a familiar and reliable name in the world of gymnastics. Leading gymnasts wear Alpha Factor leotards and warm-up suits in local, state, intercollegiate, national, and international competitions. Olympic medalist Nadia Comaneci was seen warming up at the 1980 Olympics in Moscow in a suit manufactured in York County and given to her a year earlier. In 1996, millions of Americans witnessed the dramatic gold medal efforts of the U.S. National Team as well as Russian gymnasts in uniforms produced by Tighe Industries through a strategic partnership with Reebok.

Tighe's Gantner Swimwear line has been featured in *Seventeen, Cosmopolitan,* and *Good Housekeeping* magazines. It continues to be a staple, particularly for the Misses market, and is distributed through Tighe's retail stores, located in Pennsylvania, Virginia, and Florida.

The growth of Curtain Call Costumes has consistently increased since its entrance into the dance world nearly six decades ago, to become today's largest manufacturer and marketer of dance costumes. Nonetheless, clients continue to receive the same honest, personalized service they did in the 1940s. Curtain Call's client list is long and diverse, consisting of dancing schools, recreation

departments, high school and college majorette corps, dance companies, even Disneyworld, and the state pageants for the Miss America competition. Specialized lines like Curtain Call Spirit have made tremendous inroads into the world of professional sports, outfitting cheer-leading squads for teams like the NBA's Dallas Mavericks and Cleveland Cavaliers and the NFL's Philadelphia Eagles and Buffalo Bills. Tighe Industries has also provided the costumes for the extravagant Orange and Sugar Bowl halftime shows.

Each of the 420 Tighe Industries associates is up to the constant challenge of maintaining his or her status as a superior employee in a world-class company in a worldwide marketplace. Leroy King, Jr., credits the "dedication and pride our people take in performing their work," he says. "All of our employees make the old American ideal 'caring about their work' their way of life."

Gymnasts from all over the world, as well as Olympic teams, have competed in garments designed and produced by Tighe Industries' Alpha Factor division.

inventory, and delivery systems are continually improved through an associate input and feedback program that places an emphasis on the experience and expertise of every highly valued employee. Tighe Industries has also recently entered the electronic marketplace with an Internet site showcasing its varied product line. A business-to-business e-commerce system is currently in the process of development to allow dance teachers and gymnastics coaches around the world to search, view, and purchase garments on-line at www.tighe.com, a natural step for a direct marketing company famous for comprehensive customer service.

Each division of Tighe Industries has established a name and unique quality since originating that has been, and continues to be, recog-

UNITED DEFENSE GROUND SYSTEMS DIVISION

Nestled among farmland just west of York is one of the most efficient defense-oriented facilities in the country. United Defense's Ground Systems Division in York has been providing ground combat systems to the U.S. and Allied militaries since 1948.

In 1940, J. L. McLaughlin and Truman Bowen merged their construction and automobile businesses, respectively, and set up shop as Bowen McLaughlin in Arizona. Less than a decade later, the company won a U.S. Army contract to recondition 1,300 World War II M4 Sherman tanks, which were being stored at the Letterkenny Army Depot in Chambersburg, Pennsylvania. To fulfill the Army's contract, Bowen McLaughlin sent 22 men to York, Pennsylvania to refurbish the old McGann Plant on Kings Mill Road for the remanufacture of military vehicles. The facility was renamed Bowen McLaughlin-York (BMY). The new plant was located 60 miles from Letterkenny and was close to steel mills and East Coast shipping

ports. BMY was also located in an area known for an abundance of skilled workers and craftspeople, and the company was looking to hire them to work on the M4s.

After completing its first set of contracts to recondition tanks for the Army, BMY designed and developed the M74 Tank Recovery Vehicle. Following the initial development of the M74, the company developed and delivered the M88 Tank Recov-

The M2A3 Bradley Fighting Vehicle, manufactured in York, is the world's most advanced infantry system.

ery Vehicle to an enthusiastic U.S. Army customer. United Defense continues to manufacture the successor to the original M88 vehicle today, known as the HERCULES.

With the company's continual growth, BMY relocated from urban York to a site just west of the city, near Bair, Pennsylvania. In 1967, Harsco Corporation of Camp Hill, Pennsylvania bought BMY. Throughout the 1970s, BMY continued to fulfill U.S. Army contracts while also expanding into international markets.

In 1994, Harsco combined its BMY Combat Systems Division with FMC Corporation's Defense Group, based in California, to form United Defense, LP. Three years later, the Carlyle Group purchased United Defense, and in December 2001, United Defense became a publicly traded company on the New York Stock Exchange (NYSE: UDI).

Today, United Defense is a worldwide leader in the design, development and production of combat vehicles; artillery; naval guns; missile launchers and precision munitions and non-nuclear ship

Four employees work on reconditioning an M4 Sherman Tank, one of the first U.S. Army contracts won by Bowen McLaughlin that brought company operations to York, Pennsylvania.

repair, modernization and conversion. United Defense strives to protect freedom worldwide by serving the security needs of the U.S. Department of Defense and its Allies by providing customers with a broad line of products, new technologies, and cost-efficient manufacturing capabilities.

York is headquarters to United Defense's Ground Systems Division, which focuses on outstanding customer service from initial design, development, and system integration to pre-production and test, continuing throughout, manufacturing and production, and worldwide life cycle support.

United Defense has developed an extensive library of physics-based computer models that allow for rapid design, virtual testing, and production of new systems. The company continues to develop technologies relevant to future military systems such as hybrid-electric drive, band track systems, advanced crew cockpits, advanced survivability technologies and advanced armaments.

The M88A2 HERCULES Improved Recovery Vehicle was designed in York, and continues to deliver safe recovery capabilities to soldiers and Marines.

The United Defense (then BMY) plant on Bairs Road in 1978.

The dedicated employees of United Defense in York design, remanufacture, assemble and test vehicle systems such as the most technically advanced infantry vehicle in the world, the M2A3 Bradley Fighting Vehicle, the M88A2 HERCULES improved recovery vehicle, and the M109A6 Paladin self-propelled howitzer.

Other products manufactured by Ground Systems Division are Assault Amphibious Vehicles (AAVs), the M992A2 Field Artillery Ammunition Support Vehicle (FAASV), Multiple Launch Rocket System carriers, the M9 Armored Combat Earthmover (ACE) and other variations of the Bradley. To meet changing customer needs, the York facility is developing new manufacturing capabilities such as the production of structural composites for combat vehicles.

United Defense's manufacturing, prototyping and engineering quality systems are ISO 9001 certified. Safety is a core value of the company, and in 2000 the York plant received the Pennsylvania Governor's Safety Award for outstanding safety performance. Later the same year, employees set an all-time site safety record of 3.3 million hours worked at the facility without a lost-time accident.

United Defense is actively involved in the local community. In addition to an annual United Way Campaign conducted in conjunction with the United Steelworkers of America's Local 7687, United Defense also supports and contributes to educational activities, local associations, historical societies, the arts and veteran affairs.

United Defense offers employees opportunities for personal and career growth through a variety of training programs. United Defense also provides a tuition reimbursement program to encourage employees to participate in training and continuing education relative to their jobs within the company.

United Defense and its employees in York continue to develop new technologies and capabilities for the 21st century, while providing the best combat systems for the men and women of our nation's Armed Forces who have answered the call to defend freedom and liberty worldwide.

WARNERS MOVING AND STORAGE

Warners celebrate 100 years of service.

Wallace B. Warner was known throughout the county as the best among all teamsters. As a boy, his job was the hauling of building materials from county seat to the masons and carpenters of his neighborhood. The hours were long, and the work was hard. Someday he dreamed he would have a business of his own, where he could use horses. It would be a milk route, and he could then drive a horse and buggy in style. One fall morning in the year 1903, Wallace Warner, then 19, woke with a determination to carry out his dream. After breakfast, he went to the stable, where he hitched the mare to the family buggy. He drove by the springhouse, loaded a can of milk, placed a tin dipper on the seat beside him and departed down the lane. Wallace was now driving his first milk route—a milk route of his very own—one destined to grow and become a thriving dairy in the community of Red Lion, Pennsylvania.

Wallace married Jennie Hildebrand in 1901. They had four children, Earl, Jess, Donald and

Founders were Mr. and Mrs. W. B. Warner.

Virginia. His first two loyal helpers were his small sons, Earl and Jess. With the advent of the glass milk bottles, came more work for the Warner family. Long hours were spent in the kitchen scalding and scrubbing hundreds of bottles, filling them by hand and pressing on the cardboard caps one at a time. By 1924, the nurtured business was not large—but did have a solid foundation upon which an enterprise of any proportion could be built. Thus in 1924, Earl and Jess Warner guided the course of the business, and a complete dairy plant was established at First Avenue and Franklin Street in Red Lion. A new era began.

W. B. Warner & Sons was formed in 1932. Earl and Jess realized their goal of building a fine modern dairy, reached through sound development. So, by 1935, there was the installation of a larger ice-cream department and complete dairy store. Don Warner, the youngest son, gave up a promising career in music to become partner in 1937. Now, the family circle was complete, and the dream continues.

The Ice Cream Field, a national monthly publication featured the Warner's Dairy in its December 1952 issue. It tells of Warner's production, which, at that time, ran 400 dozen novelties and 300 gallons of bulk a day. Yet the firm sold within a seventy-five mile radius of the plant at Red Lion and held its own against major Philadelphia competition in sales of both milk and ice cream. When asked how they did it, Don Warner, then sales manager, said, "Easy. Just start with a quality product and then go out and do a top-notch selling job." The Warners maintained two airplanes with their own airport. The planes were used for several purposes: to tow advertising banners, to respond to emergency service calls for dealers and for rush deliveries. Earl, Jess and Don were pain-

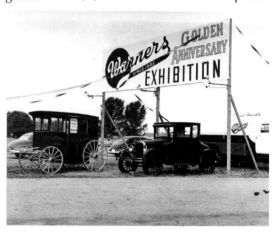

The golden anniversary celebration with a 1903 milk wagon.

stakingly aware of top quality and were real trailblazers when it came to promotion.

On Saturday mornings, The Warners sponsored a program of musical favorites over the air played by Don Warner himself on the organ. Through the years, the firm followed a policy of getting acquainted with the folks of the community. For example, they provided their airfield for local functions. When the Red Lion Golden Jubilee was held on Warner's farmland, Don Warner flew both Miss America of 1954,

Don Warner playing the organ on his weekly radio and television show.

Evelyn Ay, from her home in Virginia, and Aunt Jemima, the pancake queen, to their town to take part in the celebration. Warner also flew the Red Lion Troubadors, a trio of talented young trumpet players to New York to be contestants on the Ted Mack TV show, one of the most popular programs at the time. Their plane was used for humanitar-

A 1926 G.M.C. truck in York's annual Halloween Parade with Don Warner at the organ.

ian causes as well. When the borough chief of police was seriously ill, Don was given permission to land at McGuire Air Force Base to pick up his son, who was stationed there to fly him home to be with his father.

In 1943 the Warners purchased Miller Motor Freight from an estate, and the Warners Moving & Storage Company was started. This purchase consisted of trucks, men who were trained to handle furniture and

Warner Moving and Storage warehouse and company plane.

I.C.C. and P.U.C. operating rights. By purchasing this fleet of tractor trailers, it contributed to the efficiency of their truck repair shop. Customers of the dairy asked, "Why trucks when you are in the dairy business?" They answered, "Well, we can't bring the cows to your door; we use trucks to get the milk to you."

The Warner family proudly celebrates 100 years of service. Plans for the company's 100-year celebration are now in progress. Four generations of Warners have contributed to the development of this story—starting with Wallace B. Warner, then his sons Earl D. Warner, Jesse B. Warner, Donald M. Warner and daughter Virginia Warner Tietbohl, who managed the Dairy Bar & Restaurant. Donald H. Warner, son of Donald M., took over the company in 1993. He runs the company today. Fourth-generation Steven P. Warner, son of Donald H., assists his father in the running of the moving and storage business.

YORK HOSPITAL/WELLSPAN HEALTH

On a cold day in January 1880, a group of York businessmen met to deal with a serious problem. The city's population was growing rapidly and the need for a hospital was becoming urgent.

To respond to the need, Samuel Small and other Yorkers created the York Hospital and Dispensary Association. Small contributed a three-story dwelling on West College Avenue "for the medical and surgical treatment of the sick and injured." Then he and others raised $70,000 to convert the structure into a hospital to serve York.

The first facility was modestly furnished, containing 12 wrought-iron bed frames with headboards and mattresses purchased for $98. In 1885, Dr. George E. Holtzapple treated a patient with pneumonia at the York Hospital and as part of this treatment, fanned the fumes rising from the liquid in an oak bucket toward the patient. Those fumes were oxygen, and Dr. Holtzapple used it that day for the first time in recorded medical history.

The services offered by the hospital continued to grow. Affiliations with the York Collegiate Institute provided educational opportunities—the York Hospital Training School for Nurses was opened; an ambulance service was begun in

1896; and the first hospital clinic was opened in 1903.

The institution's name officially became York Hospital in 1925 and a 20-acre tract of land was purchased on the southern edge of the city. Through a countywide effort to raise money, a new facility was completed and opened in September 1930.

By the early 1950s, York Hospital had outgrown its original building. The South Wing was added and expansion has occurred several times since.

The 1960s and 1970s saw a number of medical advances. York Hospital, always a leader in technology, opened its Cardiac Diagnostic Laboratory in 1967; purchased a linear accelerator which used x-ray therapy to treat cancer patients in 1973; acquired its first computer in 1975; performed its first open heart surgery in 1975; and purchased a Computerized Axial Tomography (CAT) scanner in 1978.

The York Hospital and Dispensary was established in 1880 in response to community need.

In the 1980s, there was a shifting emphasis from inpatient care to outpatient care. As a response to that trend, construction began in 1986 on Apple Hill Medical Center, the first free-standing ambulatory center in the county. It was designed to provide easy, one-stop shopping for outpatients and featured a wide range of services, including physician offices, diagnostic services, a pharmacy, rehab center, blood donor center, and a surgical center. Apple Hill Medical Center opened in March 1988. Laboratory services and diagnostic centers also were expanded throughout the area during the late 1980s and 1990s.

A growing and aging population, however, was also exerting pressure on York Hospital's capacity. In late 1989, York Hospital announced plans for a $50 million expansion, known as the Century Project. The goal was to expand some services and create space to fulfill the future health care needs of the York community. The project featured a larger

Always a leader in bringing new technology and medical procedures to the community, York Hospital performed its first open heart surgery in 1975.

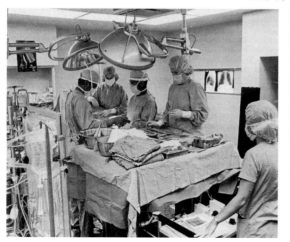

Emergency Department, more intensive care beds, and expanded Labor and Delivery and Maternity. The project was completed in October 1993.

The rise of managed care and the creation of integrated healthcare delivery systems were two of the major developments of the 1990s. Managed care, which encouraged employees to use selected doctors and hospitals which were able to demonstrate value and quality, became a major factor in the way healthcare was delivered. To increase efficiency, there was a national movement from hospital-based healthcare to an integrated delivery system, where people were able to receive a seamless continuum of care, regardless of the nature of their illness or site of care.

York Hospital Foundation (the parent company of York Hospital) took a number of steps in response to these two major developments. It collaborated with physicians, and businesses to create the York Health Plan, which later became South Central Preferred. It offers an alternative to commercial insurance for self-insured employers. South Central Preferred covered more than 68,000 individuals in 2002.

The Medical Group was formed to improve access, attract more

WellSpan Health is known for its outstanding patient care.

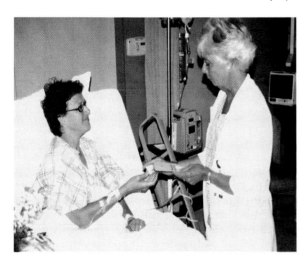

York Hospital's high quality and cost-efficient care began to attract national attention in the late 1990s. York Hospital was named one of the 100 top hospitals in the nation from 1997-2000.

primary care physicians to the area, and provide care to underserved areas. Medical Group physicians were employed by the York Hospital Foundation. By 2002 the Medical Group consisted of 40 offices and 165 physicians.

Reflecting the evolution of the organization and the way healthcare services were delivered, the York Hospital Foundation changed its name to York Health System in January 1995. York Health System was comprised of York Hospital, York Health Plan, York Health System Medical Group, York Health Care Services, York Apothecary, and Apple Hill Surgical Center. VNA (Visiting Nurse

Association), a provider for home health, hospice, and private duty services for patients, affiliated with York Health System in 1997.

In June 1998, York Health System and Gettysburg Hospital announced their affiliation and that they would form a regional healthcare delivery system covering York and Adams counties and northern Maryland. Through the affiliation, communities were better served with improved quality of care by sharing best practices and care management. It also improved access as well as continuity and coordination of care throughout the region.

Eighteen months later, York Health System and Gettysburg Hospital unveiled a new name and logo for its integrated health system—WellSpan Health. The name and identity implied a breath of services, quality of care, and a strong and healthy community.

Also in the 1990s, there was a growing emphasis on community health. People began to broaden the definition of health to include one's social and physical environment. A six-month long community health assessment was initiated in late 1993. It was used to identify and prioritize the health needs of York County.

The assessment identified eight major concerns and community leaders came together to discuss and prioritize those concerns. As a result, the Healthy York County Coalition was formed and numerous task forces were created. Several years later, a similar organization—Healthy Adams County—was formed.

In March 1999, HealthConnect, a state-of-the-art mobile health van which provides free healthcare services to the uninsured, hit the road.

It was made possible through the financial support of the York Health System Auxiliary, Harley-Davidson Motor Company and its Tyson Lodge 175 I.A.M. employees and the Young Women's Club of York.

Rapidly growing computer technology and the increased demand for data were major factors impacting healthcare in the 1990s. To enhance its position as a regional healthcare provider, WellSpan Health implemented new information systems focused on four areas: clinical, finance, managed care, and physician practice management.

PowerChart, a computer program that allowed clinicians to easily access a patient's clinical information from a computer workstation, was introduced. It initially featured lab and text radiology results and was the beginning of an electronic medical record.

In 2002, WellSpan Health was named one of the 100 Most Wired health systems in the United States by Hospitals and Health Networks. The study measured healthcare systems on their use of Internet technologies to connect with patients, physicians and nurses, payors, health plans, and employees.

York Hospital's high quality and cost-efficient care began to attract national attention in the late 1990s.

York Hospital was named as one of the Top 100 Hospitals in the United States for 1997 and 1998 by HCIA Inc. and William Mercer, Inc. It also was named to the list for 1999 and 2000. York Hospital continued to receive national recognition as it was named among the Top 100 Cardiovascular Hospitals and the Top 100 Hospitals for ICUs in 2001. WellSpan Health was recognized as one of the Top 100 integrated healthcare networks by SMG Marketing Group, a Chicago-based company.

Recognizing the changing healthcare needs of the community, WellSpan Health opened the Center for Mind/Body Health in 1999 and the WellSpan Midlife Center at Apple Hill Medical Center in 2001.

The Center for Mind/ Body Health provides complementary medicine services such as acupuncture, massage therapy, Yoga, mediation, and guided imagery. The WellSpan Midlife Center focuses on improving women's healthcare throughout menopause.

In March 2001 an initiative to develop York Hospital's South George

Apple Hill Medical Center, designed to provide easy, one-stop shopping for outpatients, opened in 1988. It was one of the first freestanding ambulatory centers in the country.

Street campus with new and updated facilities was announced. The project, with construction cost of $65–$75 million, was designed to increase the number of inpatient beds and private rooms, improve access to the hospital, and assure that specialized services such as cardiovascular and ob-gyn had the necessary facilities to continue to provide excellent care and enhance clinical support areas. The project included the construction of a six-story patient care tower, the demolition of the Education Building, and the creation of the Robert L. Evans, M.D. Medical Education Pavilion.

For more than 120 years, York Hospital and WellSpan Health have worked to meet the healthcare needs of the community. To do so has required having a vision of the future, being able to adapt and change, and holding firm to an unwavering commitment. WellSpan Health continues its pledge to assure the community has the access to a quality healthcare system and that, regardless of the challenges ahead, the healthcare needs of the community will continue to be met.

HealthConnect, a state-of-the-art mobile health van which provides free health care to the uninsured, travels to several sites throughout York and Adams counties.

MARTIN MEMORIAL LIBRARY

Halloween night 1935 was a night to remember for those who gathered in the newly constructed Martin Library to celebrate the achievements at hand. Thousands of prospective library cardholders arrived to participate in the pre-opening celebration. One staff member called the scene "bedlam" and noted that many of the visitors were in costumes, giving the scene a surreal atmosphere. Martin Library has since sustained, and indeed surpassed, the excitement of that celebration.

Today, people ask if libraries will survive, as emerging technology makes information more accessible to the public. Martin Library has no interest in merely "surviving"—instead, it will thrive as a premier player in the information utility that the York County Library System has become.

Never losing sight of the fact that the first word in the term public library is "public," all of York County's libraries aim to help people learn for a lifetime. Together, the libraries supply answers for living and knowledge for life. York County's 125,000 library card-holders now have free access to an extensive variety of materials, which include an up-to-date collection of books, books on tape, books on CD, large print books, Spanish-language materials, videos, DVDs,

Martin Library, located on the corner of Market and Queen Streets in downtown York, is rich in historical and architectural significance. Expansion into the neighboring brownstone will feature a three-story atrium to connect the two buildings.

computer databases and Internet access. Approximately 200,000 visitors take advantage of Martin Library's resources and services each year.

Martin Library's partnership with the York County Library System enables its users to access the library's catalog and databases from their homes and offices. The York County Library System's newest endeavor is the Virtual Library, an online answer desk staffed by a reference librarian 24 hours a day, seven days a week.

Martin Library offers programming for people of all ages and interests: Born to Read gives babies a gentle introduction to the library and teaches caregivers how to foster a lifelong love of reading; the statewide Summer Reading Club reaches approximately 6,000 children with Martin Library cards each year; structured programs in the ten-station children's computer lab supplement traditional and home-school curricula; junior book discussion groups help students develop reading comprehension and basic literary analysis skills; and adults can enjoy humanities programs, book discussion groups, and instruc-

tional seminars. Martin Library also houses the Grants Resource Center and hosts grantwriting workshops for nonprofit organizations. By partnering with, and providing services to, over 40 businesses and 120 non-profit organizations, Martin is able to reach beyond itself and connect people in a wide-area network.

The community has invested in Martin Library twice since its establishment, and plans are set to break ground in the summer of 2003 for its third addition. Plans to renovate the existing building and expand into the neighboring brownstone include a three-story atrium and a new teen center. The expansion will enable Martin Library to serve in a greater capacity as a cultural center for the city of York.

The traditions that York's Martin Library has established will remain intact indefinitely—while the library's vision is to keep the door open to knowledge and information, as it enhances current standards and embraces new technologies.

In the year 2002, York County residents spent 5 million hours reading books from Martin Library.

YORK INTERNATIONAL CORPORATION

The history of York International is a story about technology and engineering.

Like all of us, York developed its principal personality traits early in life.

From its start, York focused on technology and engineering initiatives that benefit people—preserving food, providing comfort to stay healthy and productive, and finding ways to make systems smaller and more energy efficient.

The York of today was formed by such signal events as being the first company to commercialize ice making for food; fully air-condition an office building; invent the first successful room air conditioner; design equipment that used the breakthrough coolant, freon—and, in recent years, engineer systems utilizing environmentally friendly refrigerants.

York's adventurous spirit was evident early when the company made its first foray beyond U.S. shores, selling products in Japan in 1898. By the 1920s, York was actively building a market in China, and the company was instrumental in the growth of the dairy industry in En-

The warm winter of 1890 gave impetus to the popularity of refrigeration. (York built its first ice machine in 1895).

gland, supplying refrigeration systems to numerous businesses.

Today, York employs over 23,000 people, sells products in over 125 countries, has manufacturing operations in 10 countries, and achieves a majority of its revenue from international business.

History tells the story. It was the fall of 1874 when six men, eager to vent their curious minds and inventive aptitudes, pooled their meager resources to form the York Manufacturing Company in York, Pennsylvania.

York's future arrived in 1885 when the company built its first ice machine for a customer in Mississippi. Commercial ice making was slow to grow, because people were confident they could continue harvesting and storing ice from frozen rivers and lakes. A warm 1890 winter crushed that tradition—and, by summer, York was working three shifts making ice machines.

York's decision to focus on one core business dates to 1897, when Thomas Shipley, general manager, sold or discontinued all product lines except ice making and refrigeration. The company has grown from that strategic move ever since.

The original plant and office building of York Manufacturing Company in 1885, and York International Corporation logo today.

The birth of air conditioning can be traced to 1903 when York installed a large system for dehumidifying blast furnace air in a plant being operated by Carnegie Steel Company. It was the first link between refrigeration and industrial air conditioning.

Cooling for comfort was everyone's wish by the end of the 19th century and it became a reality as early as 1914, when York air conditioned the Empire Theatre in Montgomery, Alabama. In 1923 York completed the first air-conditioning of an office building, the San Joaquin Light and Power Company, in Fresno, California. Yet another first for York was the first completely air-conditioned hotel in the U.S., the St. Anthony Hotel in San Antonio, completed in the late '20s. Eight years later, York became the little company that could, when it won a milestone contract from DuPont against bigger competition to design equipment using the new freon refrigerant. The know-how to air-condition large facilities was

Original 200 TR Ice Machine

A drawing of a 200-ton ice machine manufactured in the late 1800s in York.

now at hand, and York responded with complete cooling systems for the B & O "Colombian" cross-country train—the first fully air-conditioned train—and for the U.S. Capitol building in Washington, D.C.

London became York's first European address in 1923. A branch operated in Manchester a year later, and the company was fabricating evaporators, surge drums and other equipment, again in London, in 1927.

The late '20s brought a breakthrough by York that was to revolutionize home comfort—the single room air conditioner. It weighed 600 pounds. Contrast that with a York whole-house cooling unit today, weighing around 200 pounds. With the home market moving slowly, the company concentrated on installing air conditioners in commercial establishments. These units incorporated important technological developments, including

It's full speed ahead for the 50-km English Channel Eurotunnel, cooled by York equipment. The system cools 54 million gallons of water through its 150-mile network of chilled water pipes.

high-speed, lightweight compressors using freon or ammonia.

Meanwhile, in England, a York refrigeration system at the Express Dairy Company helped make milk pasteurization a reality. This dairy grew to be the largest in the world at the time, continuing to rely on York refrigeration. By 1936, York air conditioning was cooling guests in the Great Hall of the Grosvenor House in London. More than 1,000 York air conditioning installations were functioning across France by 1940.

Commercial development was put on hold in the early 1940s as York joined the war effort, installing refrigeration equipment at sites ranging from headquarter operations to strategic outposts and the front lines, and working on such high-stakes projects as the Manhattan Project and aircraft test chambers.

Non-Stop String of Developments. The story of York continues as one of product development and engineering accomplishment. The company's first automatic ice makers for hotels, restaurants and hospitals made their debut in 1948. Hermetically sealed cooling circuits for room air conditioners were brought to market two years later. Industrial ice makers enjoyed strong sales in the early 1950s. Improved heat pumps for year-round comfort were unveiled about the same time. The first single-stage, high-speed centrifugal refrigeration compressor was introduced in 1954.

In the 1950s and 1960s, York was installing major "Big Air" conditioning systems in larger buildings. It supplied a 10,000-ton TurboMaster system to the Kennedy Space Center in 1965 and installed the world's largest water-cooled air conditioning system at the World Trade Center in New York City in 1968.

Through the years, product innovation has become the hallmark of York. In 1972, it developed the TurboGuard compressorless purge system that warns operators of a possible leak. The world's largest Packaged Air Cooled Reciprocating Liquid Chiller was unveiled in 1976. In 1979, York introduced the Turbo-Modulator, the first practical

The Hong Kong Exhibition Center and most of the buildings of the Hong Kong skyline are cooled by York equipment.

electronic, variable-speed control for centrifugal chillers.

These achievements were closely followed by a driveline retrofit package, providing a low-cost alternative to centrifugal chiller replacement. As environmental concerns rose, York moved quickly, bringing out a new line of CFC-free chillers in 1988, and was the first to develop a broad range of chillers compatible with the new environmentally friendly refrigerants.

This product innovation continued into the '90s with York introducing technologically superior new products, allowing the company to differentiate itself from the competition and penetrate new markets. Customers received key benefits such as higher system efficiencies, better reliability, lower noise levels and environmentally friendly system options.

Business strategy also has helped shape the York of today. The company was acquired by Borg Warner in 1956. The resulting infusion of capital funded many of the pioneering technological developments. York was "spun off" from Borg Warner in 1986, taken private in a 1988 leveraged buyout, and became a public company once again in 1991.

A refrigeration machine from the late '20s —early proof of York's commitment to engineering expertise.

Growth-minded York acquired numerous businesses in the '80s and '90s that fit with the core heating ventilation, air conditioning and refrigeration operations. The acquisition of Frick Company in 1987 and Sabroe A/S in 1999 resulted in York becoming the recognized world's leading supplier of industrial refrigeration equipment. Maintaining this leadership position, and continuing product development, best describes the company's legacy.

Recognition of York as an international industry leader is documented by its winning a large number of landmark projects throughout the world, such as the English Channel Eurotunnel, the British Houses of Parliament, the Kremlin, the Sydney Opera House, the Pompidou Centre in Paris, and the Kuala Lumpur Civic Centre in Malaysia— the world's tallest building.

Meeting the opportunities ahead. York is just hitting its stride. The timing couldn't be better, because there are opportunities to provide complete products and services—York's strength.

As one would expect, a company that has been in business for over 125 years has an enormous opportunity to provide service for its installed base of products. York has been emphasizing the importance of taking care of its customers after the sale is made, from the time technicians traveled in horse-drawn wagons. Contrast those times with today's modern, fully equipped service vans and instant ordering of parts through wireless technology. Aftermarket service technicians lead the way as the company ensures that customers receive the attention they deserve.

Growing use of air conditioning and refrigeration is challenging the

Hotels around the globe rely on York air-handling and conditioning systems to provide comfort cooling, as well as indoor air quality.

industry to develop higher efficiency systems. Industries such as electronics and plastics require enormous amounts of cooling. Emerging nations around the world are strengthening their economies, building processing plants and, in sum, upgrading their lifestyles. World population continues to rise.

York's history will serve the company well in leading the industry in developing solutions to take advantage of many opportunities.

York has compiled a rich base of experience in building its future. Experience has taught York how to advance technology in making better products and how to please customers through excellent service.

If history is prologue, then York has much to look forward to.

Eastern Europe presents opportunities for the future. The Kremlin is one of many York applications in this region.

SELIGMAN, FRIEDMAN & COMPANY, P.C.

A World War II and Korean War veteran and a Penn State graduate was named an honorary 50-year member of the American Institute of Certified Public Accountants in 2002. Murray D. Friedman, founding partner of Seligman, Friedman & Company, P.C., has managed to achieve several milestones in his lifetime.

Seligman, Friedman & Company, P.C., a regional certified public accounting and consulting firm, has been serving the York County community for over 50 years. It was through the vision of Murray D. Friedman that the firm has grown to three offices covering central Pennsylvania, with over 75 employees.

The mission of Murray D. Friedman, and the staff of Seligman, Friedman & Company, is to provide sound traditional accounting advice and other financial services of the highest standards and quality. This mind-set has made Seligman, Friedman very successful for the last fifty years. The staff is innovative and is guided by a principal purpose—to increase the profitability and net worth of its present and future clients.

The history starts with Charles S. Seligman, C.P.A., who began a firm in 1950 in York. In 1956, Murray D. Friedman joined Charles Seligman and was named managing partner. Under Murray's leadership the firm grew, and, in 1973, an office was established in Harrisburg.

Murray's networking reached beyond York County. He maintained many of his Penn State connections throughout the years. As part of his vision, in 1994 a State College office was established through mergers with Levy and Blumenthal, Piper & Company, and Calvin J. Wagner, C.P.A. Murray knew that the similar cultures and philosophies of these firms would make for successful mergers.

Under Murray's direction in 1988, Seligman, Friedman & Company was admitted to membership in Accounting Firm Associated, Inc.

Murray D. Friedman.

(AFAI), which is now called CPAmerica, International. This membership gives Seligman, Friedman & Company, national and international support and resources, without losing the close personal touch of a regional firm.

As the years progressed, so did the accounting industry. Murray Friedman encouraged the accounting staff to achieve other certifications to better service their clients. In addition to preparing tax returns and accounting and auditing services, the firm now has employees certified to handle business valuations, estate planning, non-profit and governmental audits, and forensic accounting. A subsidiary was formed to handle all the financial, college, retirement planning, and asset management services called SFC Asset Management, Inc. In October 1998, the firm purchased Krauss and Pasternack, a human resource and employee benefits consulting firm in State College. With these additional services, the firm continues to provide a full range of financial and business consulting services to their clients.

Murray also has a strong commitment and dedication to York. As a result, it is the firm's policy to give back to the community. Murray encouraged the staff to join various organizations and hold board positions. He was a leader by example, having served on various organizations. Within the past year, Murray Friedman has been involved with the creation and successful fund-raising for the World War II Memorial statue, which now resides in the square of downtown York that honors all WWII veterans.

Although Murray is no longer an active partner of the firm, his vision and dedication to York County and their clients is part of the Seligman, Friedman & Company culture.

York partners, left to right: Arthur Full, Claire Weaver, Robert Freed, managing partner, and Edward Waltemyer (missing from photo is John Cardello).

BROWN'S ORCHARDS & FARM MARKET

The transition from the humble beginnings that marked the start of Brown's Orchards & Farm Market represents one of the finest examples of growth and entrepreneurship in York County. A family business from its inception, the Brown tradition is still going strong.

When the York Safe & Lock Company closed its doors one last time in 1948, factory foreman Earl Brown knew he wanted to try something new. He and his wife, Margaret, decided to take on a significant risk: they bought a relative's 35-acre fruit and poultry farm in rural Loganville. Although they had raised turkeys in their backyard on Pine Street in York City, farm life was new to them and presented some very real challenges.

Together, they persevered and learned the secrets of successful fruit growing from orchard sales reps and the Penn State Extension Service. Their three sons—Stanley, Roger and Richard—learned along with them.

It was the oldest, Stan Brown, who took to the land and the business as a lifestyle. While Roger and Richard pursued careers in dentistry and banking, Stan married Nona, an elementary school teacher, and, following college and a stint in the U.S. Army, began raising fruit, vegetables, and a family as well.

The original roadside stand, shown here as it was in 1953.

Founders Margaret and Earl Brown in 1969.

Both Stan and Nona shared another passion—community service. "There's nothing as good as the feeling of knowing that you've helped someone," says Stan. Through the years, the Brown's involvement has taken many forms, but they don't point out each act of generosity. Their focus is on customer service, and they take a genuine interest in their customers. As a natural outgrowth of this concern, they offer free seminars on nutrition and gardening to help the community learn and grow.

Their philosophy has turned their small farm-stand operation into a full-fledged farm market and a spread encompassing 150 acres. The first move toward the beautiful store they have today was enlarging the roadside stand—several times.

A new generation enjoys the legacy. Of Stan and Nona's three children—Scott, Linda and David—it was Scott who chose the growing, family fruit business long-term. As more land was added in the 1970s, Scott joined Stan and Earl at the farm—yet, their other children played a vital role in the Brown's story, too.

In 1979, when Linda was a teenager, she began baking zucchini breads and cherry puddings, and customers were soon standing in line for them to come out of the Brown's oven. By 1982, in their basement, Stan and Nona were making what is now a hallmark in York gift-giving, Brown's gourmet gift baskets. Their son David, now a computer consultant, introduced the computer to the family business.

For the whole family, then, 1986 was a momentous year for the Browns. With demand for their fresh produce and baked goods continuing to grow, the Browns built a 2,500-square-foot market just south of their first roadside stand. Unfortunately, the old landmark burned down in an electrical fire that same year. Earl and Margaret lived to see the new store's success, under the vision and leadership of Stan and Nona.

Today, a new generation of Browns—chiefly Scott and wife Brenda—is poised to lead Brown's Orchards & Farm Market into the future. Scott is the grower who manages its large orchard operation, and Brenda acts as office administrator and personnel manager, and works closely with Stan in many facets of the market operation.

The Browns feel that all of their dedicated employees are the very "core" of their farm market. Among the store's 120 employees (the number swells considerably during holidays) are other Browns. Grandchildren Mandy and Travis Brown work at the market as well and were there to celebrate in the year 2000, when Brown's opened its present market, encompassing a spacious 7,000 square feet.

Growth leads farm market into new areas. Today the secret of success for Brown's Orchards & Farm Market is not only its fresh fruit and vegetables and its popular full-fledged bakery—they sold over 3,500 pies this past Thanksgiving—but also its variety. With a seemingly unerring feel for what customers want, Brown's continues to add items and services that sell.

In its new market, there is a full-service deli where customers order salads, meat and cheese, as well as custom-made sandwiches to go. A new candy stand features delectables from Fitzkee's, a local candy maker, along with Brown's home-made fudge. In the gift and gardening areas, a new floral room and greenhouse have been added, and a wider gift selection awaits browsers in search of ideas. Just past the original Americana-style mural in the Fruit Room, the congenial staff at Brown's expanded gift-basket counter offers a wide variety of services to customers.

Incorporated into the design at Brown's is wheelchair accessibility, giving the store a spacious feel. There's even an outdoor ice-cream pavilion that features hand-dipped ice cream, hot dogs and peach sundaes, for starters.

The newest venture by Brown's is its first cookbook, *Cooking in Brown's Country*, featuring area cooks' favorite recipes. Along with its new features, the market continues to hold well-attended seasonal festivals throughout the year.

The market's success is reflected clearly by its popularity—it is a destination in itself. Located just 8

The Browns: Nona, Stan, Scott, Brenda, Mandy and Travis in the fruit room.

miles south of York on the old Susquehanna Trail, Brown's sees an average of 1,300 customers each weekday, and 2,500 stop by each Saturday or Sunday. Visitors travel regularly from Maryland, Virginia and much farther afield.

Brown's success can also be seen in how it is recognized and honored by the community. The list of awards it has received is impressive—the prestigious State Horticultural Association's Grower of the

Year, Master Farmer Award, York's Top Local Produce and Bakery, York County Chamber of Commerce's Small Business of the Year, and Farm Family of the Year, among others.

Brown's Orchards & Farm Market, through hard work, customer service, good business instincts and strong family ties, has proven that it is here to stay—and will continue the legacy in York County for generations to come.

For more information, their website is www.brownsorchards.com.

A commissioned sketch by Hartman Graphics depicts the expanded market in 2000.

ESAB WELDING & CUTTING PRODUCTS

When Edward J. Brady founded the Alloy Rods Company in York, Pennsylvania (1940), he probably had no idea that his business would one day become part of ESAB—the world's largest welding and cutting products company. Alloy Rods started in a small building located on East Prospect Street producing stainless steel welding electrodes under the trade name "Arcaloy."

Alloy Rods grew rapidly during the years of World War II, as Arcaloy electrodes were used extensively for the manufacture and repair of armored vehicles. The company expanded its facilities further in 1946, moving to a newly constructed plant in West Manchester Township. Then in 1969, Alloy Rods moved to an even larger plant/office complex in Hanover, Pennsylvania where the business still operates today. Alloy Rods became well recognized worldwide for industry leading products such as Arcaloy stainless steel electrodes, Atom Arc low hydrogen electrodes, and Dual Shield flux cored wires.

An interesting development took place for Alloy Rods in the mid '50s, one that "foretold" a business relationship that would come into being many years in the future.

Aerial view of ESAB Hanover research, testing and manufacturing facilities.

Covered electrode products manufactured at the ESAB Hanover facility.

During the hectic years of World War II, more than 2,500 liberty ships were constructed to support the War effort. These ships were welded instead of riveted. The welding process carried a much higher rate of productivity, but serious problems developed later when welds began to fail at sea, and many ships were lost. Subsequent investigations into the cause of these weld failures identified hydrogen in the weld metal as the primary factor. This in turn led welding electrode manufacturers to seek development of welding electrodes with low hydrogen properties—and the first company to succeed was ESAB in Sweden.

When Ed Brady learned of ESAB's low hydrogen electrode, he contacted their president, Walter Edstrom, and arranged for a personal meeting in New York City. This meeting produced a license agreement between ESAB and Alloy Rods and led to the introduction of the Atom Arc

product line in 1957. When the two men signed that agreement (which they accomplished without a single lawyer) they had no idea that some 40 years later Alloy Rods and ESAB would be part of the same global company.

Before that would happen, however, Alloy Rods was acquired by Chicago-based Chemetron Corporation in 1961, becoming part of Allegheny Ludlum Industries in 1977. After a period of private ownership by its management and salaried employees in the mid '80s, Alloy Rods became part of ESAB in 1990.

ESAB's history is one of the most impressive and interesting in the welding industry. The company was founded in Gothenburg, Sweden in 1904 by Oscar Kjellberg, the man who invented the coated stick welding electrode. That invention created great interest with European manufacturers and a major breakthrough occured in 1920 when Lloyd's Register of Shipping approved the stick electrode welding process for ship construction. In fact, the first all welded ship to be certified by Lloyds was aptly named "The ESAB IV." For his pioneering work in welding technology, Kjellberg received a gold medal from the Royal Swedish Academy of Engineering Science.

From its original base in Sweden, ESAB expanded rapidly throughout Europe, then into Latin America, North America, and Asia. The fuel for this steady growth was—and still is—product innovation. In addition to its invention of the coated stick electrode, ESAB companies developed the first oxy-acetylene welding process, the first submerged arc welding equipment, the "Heliarc" TIG process, the Dual Shield flux cored welding process, MIG/MAG process, plasma cutting, narrow gap welding, friction stir welding, laser bevel cutting—and many other significant product and process innovations. These products and processes are used extensively today in such industries as shipbuilding, automobile production, farm and construction equipment, power plant construction, bridge fabrication, gas/oil pipelines, etc. The world today depends on welding to make possible the products used every day and ESAB truly is the global leader in welding and cutting technology.

Above: Artist's depiction of ocean oil rig.

Below: P & H heavy earth mover.

With worldwide sales of approximately $1 billion, ESAB employs over 7,500 people. The ESAB Hanover facility has 375 employees involved with manufacturing, marketing, research, and other key business activities. ESAB Hanover people work closely with their counterparts in other ESAB facilities around the world, making the Hanover operation a truly global business entity.

Although the welding industry is of critical importance to the global economy, most people are just not aware of this. In the U.S. alone, welding has an annual economic impact of $37 billion. Most products we use and rely on every day were touched by welding in one way or another—and wouldn't be here without welding. But, as important as welding is to daily life, the U.S. welding industry is facing a major crisis.

During the next 10 years, more than half of all people in the U.S. welding industry will retire—and there simply aren't enough young men and women entering the industry to replace them. If U.S. manufacturing companies cannot find a sufficient number of welders, welding technicians, welding engineers, and other welding professionals— they will have to transfer their manufacturing operations (and ALL the jobs associated with them) to another country. That's not just bad for the welding industry—it's bad for the entire economy.

As a result of this shortage, outstanding "Gold Collar" welding career opportunities can be established with two years or less of formal post high school education. Specific career opportunity information can be obtained from The American Welding Society at www.aws.org.

Ed Brady was very proud to see the welding products company he founded become part of ESAB in 1990. He would be even more proud today to see how ESAB people, products, and technology continue to lead in the world of welding.

GENT-L-KLEEN PRODUCTS, INC.

Back in 1949, C. E. (Bud) Strickler, Jr., the founder of Gent-L-Kleen Products, Inc., started manufacturing waterless hand cleaner using homemade production equipment in the basement of his home in the Shiloh area of York County, Pennsylvania. What started as a part-time business has grown into a major hand cleaner manufacturer. Gent-L-Kleen's most well-known products continue to be heavy-duty hand cleaners used by garage mechanics, service station attendants, factory workers, construction crews, painters, and others who need a reliable, professional product for removing the most difficult soils.

Bud was working full-time as a floor hand at the New York Wire Company. Although he went no further than the 7th grade in school, his business sense told him the time was right for a new, innovative hand cleanser. With the help of a grade-school friend, he started his part-time manufacturing operation. Sales the first year were $800. He called his product "Strick" and sold it to garages and service stations in the York area.

C. E. Strickler, Jr. (right), founder of Gent-L-Kleen, and his wife, Betty, who also worked for the company before their retirement in 1994.

The original Gent-L-Kleen® formula line as manufactured today.

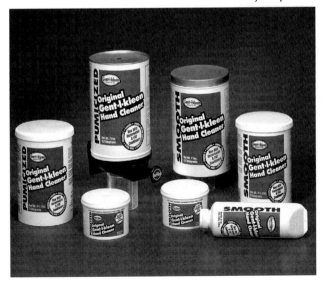

Strickler had made major improvements to his product in 1952 to enhance its cosmetic qualities, so he changed the name to "Gent-L-Kleen." He also made his first major purchase, a second-hand Readco vertical mixer that could mix 19 gallons (or 132 pounds of hand cleaner) in each batch. Deciding to devote all of his energy to the manufacture and sale of his waterless hand cleaner, Bud went into business full-time on August 11, 1953. In 1955, Bud and his family moved to a new home in Shiloh where he continued the operation

in that home's basement. During the day, Bud traveled around the region calling on customers and selling product from the back of his station wagon. Nights and weekends were spent making and packaging the product along with the help of his brother, Raymond.

Though relatively small compared to the giants in the soap industry, Gent-L-Kleen continued to grow, year after year. Strickler began to use manufacturer representatives to market the product across the country. A sales manager, William (Mac) Makibbin, joined the company as president in 1957 and the business was incorporated in December 1959. During his 13 years at Gent-L-Kleen, Mac was responsible for the increase in sales from $25,000 in 1957 to over $350,000 upon his retirement in 1970. Today the company's annual sales are in the millions with product sold throughout the United States and over 20 foreign countries.

Having moved and expanded in size twice to meet production demands, a new, 40,000-square-foot plant located just off the I-83 Emigsville exit was completed in 1977. This new facility greatly increased Gent-L-Kleen's production and warehouse capacity and office space for their 15 employees. The operation is still run from this facility using off-site, leased warehouse space as needed and employing a second shift to meet customer demands.

Bud Strickler's eldest son, James (Jim) E. Strickler, joined Gent-L-Kleen full-time after completing his college education in 1970. Becoming increasingly active in the

Growth has been the key to the Gent-L-Kleen story. The production capacity in 1949 was 210 pounds per hour as product was mixed in a crock using a bed slat as a paddle. Today's capacity is 6,000 pounds an hour or 144,000 pounds daily using modern mixing and filling equipment.

Gent-L-Kleen's product line has also grown. In 1959 the company engineered and began producing a highly efficient and economical push-button dispenser to dispense gel products like their original Gent-L-Kleen® Hand Cleaner. In 1977 Grime Grabber® Hand Cleaner, another gel product, was added to the line. More aggressive, gritty versions of these hand cleaners, Pumicized Grime Grabber® and Pumicized Gent-L-Kleen®, soon followed. The first lotion hand cleaners were added in 1987.

A major product introduction occurred in 1999 with the addition of Gent-L-Kleen's Dispenser-Mate® 5000 Dispensing System. Protected by over 12 U.S. patents, this unique system uses a reservoir dispenser that mates with a custom, 4-liter refill holding lotion or liquid product. Dispenser-Mate®'s no-waste design has revolutionized the way lotion hand cleaner and soap is dispensed.

Today Gent-L-Kleen manufactures more than twelve varieties of hand cleaners, two hand soaps, and Power Wipes® Hand Cleaner Towels. They also market Skin Armor™ Barrier Foam, used to help shield skin from hazardous substances and soils; and a concentrated powder car and truck wash. Products are manufactured and packaged for other companies, such as International Truck and Engine/Navistar, as well as under Gent-L-Kleen's own labels.

Gent-L-Kleen believes that customers are their business. That is why their motto remains, "Skilled hands deserve the very best!"

Filling line in old plant on Derry Road in Shiloh, circa 1970.

Gent-L-Kleen's Dispenser-Mate® 5000 Dispensing System shown with GLK-55™ Solvent Free Heavy-Duty Hand Soap introduced in 2001.

company, Jim became president in 1994. In the same year, Bud and his wife Betty retired from the company, turning full control over to Jim who had also become part owner by this time.

Two of Bud and Betty's other children are very active in the business and are also part owners. Jeffrey (Jeff) Strickler is the corporate treasurer and vice president of operations, having started with the company in 1978. Jill Meckley, the corporate secretary and administrative assistant, reports to Jim. Jill began working for the company in 1977. Jim and Jeff's wives are also employed by the company.

HAMME ASSOCIATES

Creative architectural design and engineering for every need and demand.

In 1900 Mr. John B. Hamme opened an office in the city of York, Pennsylvania for the pursuit of the profession of architecture. His practice continued uninterrupted until his virtual retirement in 1945, at which time his son and partner, J. Alfred Hamme, assumed full responsibility for the administration of the firm. After a lengthy period of service as a sole proprietorship, the firm was reorganized in 1963 as a partnership with Mr. Hamme and various associates. At that time, the firm was known as J. Alfred Hamme and Associates, with Walter M. Zarfoss, Clifton B. Barnhart, George Roth, John Gilbert, Stanley C. Snyder, W. Stanford Baer, and Baird P. Krecker as associates. The firm continued to operate in that manner until the death of Mr. Hamme. The name was then changed to Hamme Associates. In 1992 the firm was again reorganized with John Gilbert and Barry L. Harding, registered architects, assuming responsibility in all operations of the company.

Since the founding of the firm at

The York County Area Vocational-Technical School, York.

the turn of the century, Hamme Associates has produced significant architecture by combining talent, creative ability, practical knowledge, and understanding of the building process—combined with over 100 years of experience. This firm has the ability and know-how to design and engineer buildings as modern as today—and as forward-looking as tomorrow.

Since the success of a firm is measured by the character, training, and personality of its personnel, years of successful experience is the touchstone that, more than any other factor, assures the owner of a successful building investment. Its

The J. E. Baker Company building, York.

Snyder's of Hanover corporate office building, at 1250 York Street, Hanover.

staff of specialized consultants, architects, and engineers offers this experience.

Hamme's operation is amply qualified to carry through on any project, large or small, from rough site to finished building, with the same exacting attention to every detail that has earned it the increasing respect of clients since the turn of the century. During its many years of active architectural practice, the firm has earned a professional reputation of which, with all humility, it is justifiably proud. To those clients already familiar with the firm and its methods of operation, the unqualified opinion is that its success is because of continual effort to give them, the clients, regardless of their project's size, full and complete service. Each member of the firm shares the belief that all architecture and engineering must be done on an individual basis. All members believe that mass production and assembly line methods cannot be defended—and that only by close attention and complete investigation of a client's problem can the client receive the type of service to which the payment of his fee entitles him.

Although the office of Hamme Associates has a varied background in architecture, the majority of commissions have been for churches, grade schools, and institutions of higher learning. Among the hundreds of churches designed by this office, many denominations are represented by structures located in Pennsylvania, Maryland, West Virginia, Virginia, New York, New Jersey, and the District of Columbia.

With commercial and industrial design, Hamme's work includes office buildings, shopping centers,

Church of the Abiding Presence, Lutheran Theological Seminary, Gettysburg, Pennsylvania.

Natatorium, Dover Intermediate School, Dover, Pennsylvania.

hotels and motels, supermarkets, convenience stores, banks, manufacturing facilities, warehouses, distribution centers, auto dealerships, retail and commercial spaces, and historic preservation buildings. It has also completed public projects for state, county, and local authorities.

Basic to its philosophy of operation is the belief that, as trained professionals, exacting attention must be given to every detail of construction—from schematic to contract drawings—in order that the end result will be a building sensibly and economically planned, intelligently engineered, and aesthetically satisfying.

Hamme Associates has enjoyed a healthy growth based on a conscientious endeavor and single-minded purpose to render superior service. It is justly proud of this record and intends to continue its practice with the highest type of creative design consistent with sound construction and integrity to every client.

HOFFMEYER & SEMMELMAN

William F. Hoffmeyer, Esquire, was admitted to the practice of law in the Commonwealth of Pennsylvania in 1962 after receiving his A.B. from Franklin & Marshall College and his J.D. degree from The Dickinson School of Law. His first staff person consisted of one part-time secretary and one of the first telephone-answering machines on the market.

In 1974, after continuous growth, the name of the law firm was changed to William F. Hoffmeyer & Associates.

In 1982, having grown to a staff of sixteen, including paralegals, attorneys and support personnel, Karen L. Semmelman, Esquire, joined Attorney Hoffmeyer in partnership to form the law firm of Hoffmeyer & Semmelman.

Attorney Semmelman received her B.S. degree, magna cum laude, in 1975 from York College of Pennsylvania and her J.D. degree in 1979 from The Delaware School of Law.

William F. Hoffmeyer, Esquire.

Karen L. Semmelman, Esquire.

James G. Keenan, Esquire, became a partner in November 1998. Attorney Keenan received his B.A. degree in 1978 with a major in social work and criminal justice from Salisbury State College; his master's degree in social work, with a concentration in juvenile and criminal justice, in 1980 from Howard University School of Social Work; and his J.D. in 1987 from Howard University School of Law. He worked for several years prior to law school as a social worker in the emergency room of Washington, D.C. area hospitals.

David C. Schanbacher, Esquire, became a partner in January 2000. Attorney Schanbacher received his B.A. degree in 1983 from Shippensburg State College and

his J.D. degree in 1986 from Duquesne University School of Law. He was an academic All-American football player and graduated from the Federal Bureau of Investigation Academy at Quantico, Virginia in 1986. He also worked as a special agent for the FBI.

The principal office of the law firm is located at 30 North George Street, York, Pennsylvania, with a branch office at 73 Forrest Avenue, Shrewsbury, Pennsylvania.

The firm's staff is comprised of approximately twenty-five individuals, including seven attorneys, support professionals and supporting staff. The firm has extensive experience in all phases of family law, real estate law, estate planning and wills and general civil practice. Five of the attorneys devote all, or substantially all, of their practice in the family law area, and two of the attorneys devote most of their practice to real estate and accompanying civil practices.

The firm's principal place of business is a four-story building extending one-half of a city block. It contains a number of conference rooms and offices, a mediation room, an extensive library and a health club for the benefit of the staff.

The nautical decor of the offices provides a comfortable and relaxing environment for the client, as well as serving the needs of the law firm. The decor is so unusual that it was recognized in the October 1995 edition of the *American Bar Association Journal* in an article written by Barbara L. Morgenstern. In her article, Ms. Morgenstern stated that clients who visit the law firm of Hoffmeyer & Semmelman stroll through offices that feature ship wheels, original hatch covers that are finished into tables, brass portholes, netting, lobster traps, original Pennsylvania Dutch barn beams, a canoe hanging from the ceiling, a waterfall, displays of sea shells and ship models and an atmosphere that dispels the feeling of trepidation and concern over the results of their visit that the typical client feels when entering a law office.

Attorney Hoffmeyer has lectured extensively as an adjunct professor in the paralegal program at the York Campus of Pennsylvania State University and at York College of Pennsylvania, in numerous courses in real estate and related fields for the Pennsylvania Bar Institute of the Pennsylvania Bar Association, the Pennsylvania Bankers Association, the Pennsylvania Land Title Institute and various paralegal and realtor organizations. Further, he has served as author, lecturer and course planner of numerous courses in the unauthorized prac-tice of law field for the Pennsylvania Bar Association as the Chair and Co-Chair of its Unauthorized Practice of Law Committee. He is the author of *The Abstractors Bible, Pennsylvania Real Estate Installment Sales Contract Manual, The Pennsylvania Real Estate Settlement Procedures Manual, Contracts of Sale for Real Estate* and *How to Plot a Deed,* all published by Cherry Lane Publishing Company, and *Law Offices That are Different,* published by ALI/ABA. Attorney Hoffmeyer is past president of the East York Lions Club and the York County Shriners Club.

He is listed in *Who's Who in the World, Who's Who in the East, Who's Who in American Law* and *Who's Who in American Education.* His areas of practice include real estate and zoning law; business, partnership and corporate law; estate planning; and decedents' estates. He also acts as an expert witness in litigation concerning real estate matters throughout the Commonwealth of Pennsylvania. He was only

James G. Keenan, Esquire.

the sixth recipient of the Pennsylvania Bar Association's medal, when it was awarded to him in 1997, for his work concerning the prevention of the unauthorized practice of law.

Karen L. Semmelman has lectured and written extensively in the family law area and the paralegal program for the Pennsylvania State University, York Campus; the York County Bar Association; the Pennsylvania Bar Institute of the Pennsylvania Bar Association and the Pennsylvania Trial Lawyers Association. Attorney Semmelman has served on numerous boards of directors for nonprofit organizations in the York County area, as well as serving as chairperson on numerous committees for the York County Bar Association and as committee member for many Pennsylvania Bar Association committees. Her area of practice is exclusively in the area of family law, divorce, custody, support, adop-

tion, pre-nuptial agreements and custody mediation.

The office of the law firm of Hoffmeyer & Semmelman is located in the heart of the York, Pennsylvania's historic district, directly across the street from the new courthouse, in the same block as the Stand-Capitol Cultural Center, and adjacent to the Central Markethouse, a significant historical structure of great beauty. The office building itself served, among other things, as a cafe and restaurant, as well as an early version of a sports bar at the turn of the century. (Some old photographs show a number of hunters standing outside the cafe with a large number of pheasants and other animals, which they had evidently taken during the hunting season.) The rear portion of the building, a four-story warehouse, contained a candy factory, candy store, restaurant supply and related business, as well as a sewing factory and an office supply business, before the building was converted into its present use as the law offices of Hoffmeyer & Semmelman.

David C. Schanbacher, Esquire.

MEMORIAL HOSPITAL

Memorial Hospital, formerly known as West Side Osteopathic Hospital, opened its doors to patients in 1945. A group of local physicians and business people had a vision to open a new community-oriented hospital with a family-like atmosphere to serve York residents. The following founders achieved their dreams by opening the 12th osteopathic hospital—which was accredited by the American Osteopathic Hospital Association—in Pennsylvania: Grover Artman, D.O.; Lester Bentz; Paul Brown, D.O.; Edward Fitzgerald; Clarence Frey; M. Carl Frey, D.O.; Roy Kammer, D.O.; Ernest Markey, D.O.; James Mullan, D.O.; Philip Smith, D.O.; Keanneard Steigelman, D.O.; Rachel Witmyer, D.O.; Paul Woolridge, D. O.; and Barclay Zeigler, D.O.

West Side Osteopathic Hospital was located at 1253 West Market Street in York, beside the York Fairgrounds. During the early years, the hospital experienced steady growth in all service areas. Services provided then included radiology, obstetrics, surgery, emergency care, pediatrics and laboratory.

In addition to providing patient care, the hospital was also a place for teaching interns. The first two interns began at Memorial on Novem-

Memorial Hospital today.

ber 6, 1946. Today, Memorial boasts a nationally recognized medical education program for medical students, interns and residents. Students and physicians who graduate from the program go on to practice both in York and at hospitals throughout the country.

After serving the York community for 11 years, the facility no longer physically met the needs of its growing patient population. The building was in need of many repairs and was not originally designed to meet the needs of patient care. Thus, plans to build a new hospital began.

On February 28, 1956, a 12-acre site on South Belmont Street in Spring Garden Township was purchased for $45,000. The Spring Garden Township land was purchased

because of its proximity to the soon-to-be constructed Interstate 83. Other factors that led to the acquisition of the land included local population trends, adequate off-street parking availability at the site and the quiet, peaceful surroundings of the Elmwood neighborhood.

Construction of Memorial's new $2.3 million hospital was completed on February 7, 1962. It was the first new hospital in York County in 30 years. The state-of-the-art facility featured the latest technology in surgical services, obstetrics, laboratory, emergency services and radiology. The new hospital treated record-breaking numbers of patients. During the first year of operation, 2,500 patients were treated in the emergency room; 8,016 inpatients were seen; 5,981 outpatients were examined; 1,530 radiology treatments were performed; 1,627 fluoroscopic examinations were completed and 42 radium treatments were administered.

Throughout the years, Memorial Hospital has recognized the community's needs and responded by expanding the services provided. In 1980, Memorial Hospital opened the first advanced life support unit in York County to improve pre-hospital services for York County's emergency patients. Memorial founded the Industrial Resource

Memorial Hospital's Family Birth Center, renovated in 1998, features single labor, delivery, recovery and postpartum (LDRP) rooms for new mothers. Mothers stay in one room during their entire hospital visit.

Center (IRC) in 1985 to service York County's employers and employees. The IRC currently serves over 500 York County companies' industrial medical needs through pre-employment physicals, drug testing, physical therapy, ergonomic consultations and the treatment of other work-related injuries. Memorial Hospital recognized a need in the community for home health services and hospice care. They responded by opening HomeCare of York in 1987 and White Rose Hospice in 1991. In 1989, an ambulatory surgical facility called the Surgical Center of York was built. Last year, the medical staff of 119 physicians performed 4,535 procedures at the center. In 1992, Memorial Hospital acquired the assets of Susquehanna Counseling to serve the county's mental health issues. In the mid-1990s, Memorial Hospital opened several primary care physician offices. In 1998, the hospital's obstetrics facility was completely transformed to meet the changing expectations of new parents. Five labor, delivery, recovery and postpartum (LDRP) rooms were built in the new obstetrics wing now re-

An aerial view of Memorial Hospital (right) at its original site on West Market Street in York. The hospital was located beside the York Fairgrounds.

Memorial Hospital's Heart Center opened in 1999.

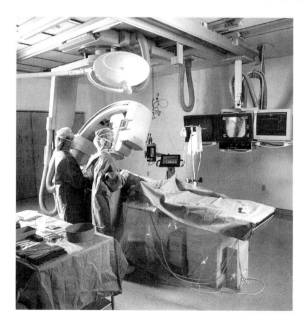

ferred to as the Family Birth Center. In 2001, 704 babies were born in the Family Birth Center. In 1999, a cardiac catherization lab, the Heart Center, was opened to diagnose and treat the growing number of patients with heart problems. Greenbriar Medical Center opened in 2000 to provide outpatient laboratory and radiology services to residents in Western York County. Most recently, Memorial opened the Breast Center—a facility dedicated to preventing and detecting breast cancer.

Memorial Hospital not only focuses its efforts on treating patients, it also concentrates on the prevention of future illnesses and injuries. Memorial Hospital educates thousands of York County residents each year through classes in nutrition, first aid, CPR, smoking cessation, violence prevention and other topics.

Memorial Hospital has consistently grown over the years in all aspects of the organization. In 2001, Memorial had over 250,000 patient encounters with York County residents who turned to Memorial Hospital for their health and wellness concerns. The medical staff has expanded from an original staff of eight physicians to over 250 today. Memorial Hospital is one of the largest employers in York County with a total staff of nearly 1,000 people.

Though technology and services have changed, Memorial's philosophy has remained the same since it opened in 1945. Memorial Hospital remains a family-oriented hospital committed to enhancing the health and well-being of the York community. Its staff contributes over 12,000 hours of service to the community through volunteerism, and its associates are active members of many nonprofit agencies. In addition to community service, Memorial Hospital contributes financially to other local nonprofit agencies.

As Memorial Hospital looks to the future, the York community will remain its focal point.

READCO MANUFACTURING, INC.

The Read Machinery Company was founded in 1906 by Harry Read, and the original plant was located in Glen Rock, Pennsylvania. In 1921 the Glen Rock facility was destroyed by fire and the company moved to its present facilities at 901 South Richland Avenue in Spring Garden Township.

Originally the company manufactured products for the baking industry including: ovens, proofers, coolers, conveyors, flour handling equipment, and dough mixers. In 1923 the company expanded its product line to include mixing equipment for the chemical process industries.

In the spring of 1938, with the beginning of World War II, Read Machinery Company became involved in production activities to support the war. Utilizing its mixing technology, the company worked with the government on powder mixers for the production of explosive smokeless powder. The company was the first manufacturer to receive the award to produce these mixers for a government arsenal, and in 1938 it was awarded a contract to manufacture 60mm trench mortars and mounts. For several years during World War II this plant produced 50 percent of the 60mm trench mortars manufactured in the United States. In 1941, Read Machinery Company started manufacturing 105mm high explosive shells and constructed additional buildings at its location. At one point the production of these 105mm shells was at the rate of 50,000 per month.

In 1942 a new powder-cutting, small-arms machine was designed and built by Read Machinery Company for loading in shell and bomb plants. The following year, it started manufacturing some of the process equipment used in manufacturing the atomic bomb.

During this period, the company was called upon to assist the Quartermaster Corps in planning, engineering, and laying out complete bakeries for army camps all over

World War II Portable Bread Dough Mixers built by Read Machinery Co.

the country. In addition to the larger baking facilities, the company developed an entirely new line of field bakery installations. The manufacturing process occupied the entire production capacity of the company.

After the war, the company turned its attention to their regular line of products, which included flour handling equipment, sugar handling equipment, horizontal and vertical dough mixers, automatic proofers, roll dividers, water coolers, and other bakery equipment. Along with its continuing leadership position in the bakery equipment business, Read Machinery Company developed a reputation for quality and superiority in the Sigma Blade mixer and ribbon blender businesses. More and more of its business moved from bakery equipment to the mixing machinery business as the company progressed through the years.

In 1957 the company purchased the assets of the Standard Stoker Company out of Erie, Pennsylvania and began producing screw con-

veyors for transporting coal to the engines of locomotives.

In 1959 the company was sold to the Capital Products Corporation out of Harrisburg, Pennsylvania and became known as Read Standard, a Division of Capital Products. With this change, the company began manufacturing metal window and door frames and metal street light poles. Also during this time, the company purchased the assets of Unique Welding out of Brooklyn, New York and started manufacturing automatic welding equipment. The company produced large welding positioners for very large vessels. One assembly was for the welding of the turbines for Grand Coulee Dam in Washington State.

In 1960 the company developed the first of several patents for the production of continuous mixers, which were considered revolutionary at the time. These patents became the basis for machinery being produced for customers of today.

In 1963 the company was sold to a group of local investors who changed its name to Read Corporation, and was again resold in 1968 to Teledyne Incorporated, a large conglomerate, and renamed Teledyne Readco.

In 1972 the company developed a design to allow for the construction of high-rise buildings by pouring concrete into portable metal wall molds called Porticos. This process revolutionized the building industries by shortening the pouring and setting time to days instead of weeks. The first structure that was built using this technology in the United States was the Fenwick Towers building in Fenwick, Delaware.

In 1996 the company was again sold to a group of private investors and became Readco Manufacturing, Inc., a division of Readco Holdings.

The company's product line today is concentrated in the area of mixing and blending machinery. The main product line is the Continuous Processor, a twin-shaft, co-rotating continuous mixing machine used in the chemical and food industries. The Continuous Processor is used by many of the Fortune 500 companies to produce large quantities of product all the way from rocket fuel to chocolate. The companies involved include General Electric, M & M Mars, Hershey Foods, Dow Chemical, Dupont, US Gypsum, and General Motors. The company also produces a powder blender called the Containerized Batch Mixer, which is used to blend dry powders used primarily in the cosmetics, color, and plastics industries. Major customers include Estee Lauder, General Electric, and Colorcon. The third product line is United Equipment Technologies, a company purchased by Readco in 2000. With this acquisition, Readco now designs and manufactures batch liquid tank mixers.

Readco has also provided the academic field with support over the years. The company has provided laboratory models of the Continuous Processors to Penn

State University in State College, Pennsylvania. One unit is in the Center for Innovative Sintered Products and the other is at the Center for Food Manufacturing. Also, the company has units installed at the University of Delaware and Purdue University. Every year the company also provides training for the continuous production of chocolate in association with the Pennsylvania Manufacturers Confectionary Association and Wolfgang Candies, York, Pennsylvania.

In addition to domestic production by Readco, the company has two manufacturing licensees, one in Osaka, Japan and the other in Paris, France, who have manufactured the Continuous Processor for

One quart to 40 cubic feet CBM units built by Readco.

25 years. The Continuous Processor has been distributed worldwide through a combination of the three company locations.

In the present day, Readco Manufacturing, Inc., utilizing all its history and expertise, produces equipment that is innovative and productive for today's changing manufacturing world. Many of the products used today are produced on Readco mixing equipment.

Readco's fifteen-inch Continuous Processor.

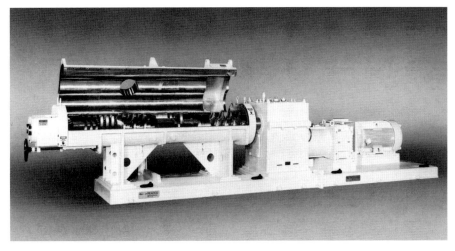

RED LION ANTIQUE CENTER

The town of Red Lion, which was incorporated in 1880, was primarily settled by German immigrants. What began with a population of 241 has grown to 6,149 residents, according to the 2000 Census.

It has been said that Red Lion was "built with cigars." The town owes its fame, reputation, popularity, growth, and prosperity to the cigar business. By 1907 it also became known for its furniture manufacturing with the establishment of the Red Lion Furniture Company. From these roots, Red Lion has continued to grow into the multi-business community that exists today.

The Red Lion Antique Center building, constructed in 1929 and located on South Main Street, was first operated by A. Scott Frey as a cigar business. Soon after, several car dealerships, including H. G. Barnhart, Sterner's Chevrolet, and Strawbridge Sales, moved in. Over the years, the different additions increased the building size to 17,000 square feet.

One day in 1995, Tina and Ben

A view of the inside of the Red Lion Antique Center, with some of the merchandise that they sell.

Fishel happened to be driving by the large, older building which was for sale at the time. Ben said, "There ought to be something we could do with that building," and Tina responded, "It would make a great antique mall." She bought the building within a few weeks, and the Red Lion Antique Center was born.

Tina Fishel, a native of Jersey Shore, a small town in Lycoming County in upper Pennsylvania, felt right at home when she moved to the small town of Red Lion. She came to the area in 1982 to marry Ben Fishel, part owner of Fishel Chrysler Jeep, a well-known, family-owned York County business located on Cape Horn Road. Tina was 33 years old when she started Red Lion Antique Center. Prior to that, she had been a cosmetologist for 12 years. The career change was quite a switch, but Tina has

A picture of Sterner Chevrolet in 1946, when it operated out of 59 South Main Street, where the Antique Center exists today.

always tried to be a hard worker. Her father often told her, "You don't get anywhere in life without working hard for everything you want."

The doors of the Red Lion Antique Center opened on Friday, October 13, 1995. Tina always thought that if she could survive Friday the 13th, she could survive anything. The business grew from five dealers on opening day, to 25 within a six-month period, and over 40 strong today.

The Antique Center occupies 7,000 square feet with plans to expand into the lower level in the near future. The repair garage area in the basement is currently rented for repair and inspection of automobiles and motor homes.

The day-to-day business of this multi-dealer co-op is always a challenge. Spaces are rented to dealers by the month. The dealers set up and display their antiques and collectibles with their own unique style. Dealers do not have to be present at the time of the sale. Red Lion Antique Center's basic responsibility is to sell the items, collect the money, and disburse it to the dealers, but it goes much further by providing advertising and presenting a pleasant shopping atmosphere.

The Red Lion Antique Center has no employees, just wonderful dealers who personify the meaning of a co-op: a willingness to work with others, marked by cooperation and effort.

"Being open during advertised hours is one of the keys to success for the Red Lion Antique Center. It can really damage a business if a customer drives miles to get to a shop and finds it closed," said Tina. A business-person needs to be there ready to greet the customer with a smile. Every shopping experience

should be a memorable one, from the coffee and snack area to the witty personalities that Tina and her dealers bring to the co-op. Their goal is for the customer to want to come back time and again.

It is fascinating to watch the collecting trends from month to month and year to year. One month 1950s kitchen items may be hot, and the next month Victorian settees may

The Red Lion Antique Center today at 59 S. Main Street, Red Lion, Pennsylvania.

have the edge, making it a very interesting business to be in.

Tina and Ben are never far from the history of York County. They live in a 1780s log house that they had relocated from the East York area known as Camp Security, a Revolutionary War encampment. The house was rebuilt to its original state at its current location in Southern York County, Pennsylvania. An addition was added using fieldstone from a York County barn built in 1880.

Just like anyone in a small community, Tina likes contribute to her community. She has served as the president of the Red Lion Area Business Association as well as being a member. She is also a member of the York Chamber of Commerce, the York County Convention & Visitors Bureau, and the Southern York County Driving Tour.

Tina finds her work at the Red Lion Antique Center most rewarding. It is a wonderful feeling when a customer finds that special item—whether it is the teddy bear she had when she was 3 years old, or the chrome kitchen set on which grandma always served Sunday dinner. Part of the reward is the smile that comes to each person's face. That is what this business is all about!

Tina and Ben's log house built in 1780.

D.F. STAUFFER BISCUIT COMPANY, INC.

In 1871 David F. Stauffer, the son of a Mennonite minister, took over the cake and cracker business that had been founded back in 1858 by Jacob Weiser. When Stauffer entered his new venture, five barrels of crackers were considered a good volume of production per day. The delivery of the crackers was done by wheelbarrow, often by Stauffer himself.

Today, D.F. Stauffer Biscuit Company is a multimillion-dollar corporation, distributing its products nationwide and employing over 700 people, in five manufacturing plants across the country. The primary products have not changed much from crackers and pretzels to cookies and it's signature item—Animal Crackers. The business remains family-operated by the Stauffer's and is still dedicated to a tradition of quality that dates back over 130 years.

The D.F. Stauffer Biscuit Company, originally located on South George Street in downtown York, built the building show to the right around 1910 at 21 W. Princess Street, and became an incorporated business in 1913 with no more than 25 employees. At the time of incorporation, D.F. Stauffer brought his four sons into the business with him—Calvin, Harry, William, and D. Preston.

After the founder's death in 1921, his eldest son, Calvin, assumed the presidency. Calvin Stauffer led his family's business into a period of growth that would see the company become the leading supplier of cookies, crackers, and pretzels in the York area.

David E. Stauffer, Calvin's son, took over the leadership of the company in 1955. By 1960 the firm had outgrown its downtown York facility and relocated to a new plant with 65,000 square feet located at 360 Belmont Street in the Elmwood section of York. At the time of the move, the business was producing cookies, crackers, and pretzels on two oven lines and one marshmallow enrobing line.

In 1964 third-generation Stauffer, Neil P., son of D. Preston, was elected to the position of president. In 1982 a fourth-generation Stauffer, David E. Stauffer, Jr., was elected to the presidency after the retirement of Neil P. Stauffer. Not too long after David E., Jr. became pesident, a fifth generation of Stauffer's joined the company, Rodney C. Stauffer, now executive vice president of sales and marketing. David Scott Stauffer was named COO.

In 1990 the Stauffer family partnered with the Meiji Seika

The manufacturing facility opened in 1910 and operated until 1960 located at 21 W. Princess Street.

Kaisha Limited, the largest manufacture of confectionaries in Japan, this partnership allowed the Stauffer family business to expand worldwide. Over the past 12 years this partnership has acquired three cookie companies; the Farnsworth Cookie Company in Cuba, New York, the Fleetwood Snack Company in Blandon, Pennsylvania and in 1999 they acquired the Laguna Cookie Company in Tustin, California.

Today the D.F. Stauffer Biscuit Company operates four manufacturing plants on both coasts of the United States. They are one of only four national companies to have the ability to do this. In total Stauffer has over 500,000 square feet of manufacturing and warehousing.

In 2002 the company moved its Tustin, California plant to Santa Ana, California where it opened a 217,000 square-foot state-of-the-art facility to establish itself as a major cookie and cracker manufacturer both nationally and internationally. Today, the company sells

D.F. Stauffer, seated in the center (with beard, coat and tie), is seen with his employees in this 1879 photograph taken at the site of his first bakery operation at 21 W. Princess Street, York.

In 1898 D.F. Stauffer's delivery wagon delivered crackers and other baked goods to Yorkers.

its cookies and crackers to Mexico, Canada, United Kingdom and Japan as well as all 50 states; these items are specifically formulated to the needs and requirements set.

Corporate headquarters of the D.F. Stauffer Biscuit Company is still located at Belmont and Sixth Avenue in York, with a regional office located in Santa Ana, California.

Today the company concentrates on developing its private label business in short-run, specialized types of cookies and focuses on segmented businesses. The company has established a reputation as a quality and a specialty house. The Stauffer's have the equipment and the experience to make virtually every kind of cookie imaginable, pleasing cookie/cracker-lovers everywhere. The equipment may have changed, but what will never change is their Animal Crackers, which look and taste the same as D.F. Stauffer made them 130 years ago.

YORK BARBELL COMPANY

Founded in 1932, York Barbell Company has been a legendary part of weightlifting history since the first designs of the York barbell. Eventually, York Barbell became the standard at the Olympic games and countless international competitions—and is now a world leader in fitness and sports performance training.

The success of the company began through the efforts of its late founder and president, Bob Hoffman. Born in 1898 in Tifton, Georgia, Hoffman was often sickly as a child, once almost dying from a double blow of typhoid fever and diphtheria. Things changed, however, and he went on to become one of the greatest athletes in the Pittsburgh area.

Hoffman won many marathon races, but his greatest success was in rowing, competing as an oarsman in the 1915 National Champion "Eights," National Quartermile Championship and the 1925 World Championship.

A veteran of World War I, Hoffman began experimenting with

The York Barbell Strongman was repaired in 2002, after being damaged in a severe wind storm.

York's Olympic Elite Certified Barbell Set sits in the lobby of York Barbell in front of a photograph of the legendary York Barbell Club.

boxing while in the service. He became an amateur boxer of above-average repute, sparring with greats such as Gene Tunney and George Carpentier. After the war, he settled in York and formed the York Oil Burner Company using his own limited capital. His own personal incentive program helped to build the business. In the early days, Hoffman would often travel with just enough money for a sandwich, so if he did not sell a burner, he could not get home.

His interest in athletics never waned, and he decided to sponsor the York Oil Burner Athletic Club weightlifting team, the forerunner of the famous York Barbell Club, the national weightlifting champion for over 50 years. In conjunction with the creation of the York Barbell Company in 1932, Bob Hoffman began to publish *Strength and Health*, a magazine devoted to the sport of Olympic weightlifting and to the principles of physical fitness for people in all walks of life. In the 1940s, Hoffman's company branched out into the health food business by developing vitamins and supplements, and included the introduction of a line of Hi-Proteen™ products.

Hoffman used his status as publisher and editor-in-chief to become a leader in teaching what he called "the ways of health." He authored 64 books and wrote thousands of articles.

Bob Hoffman and his York Barbell Company became synonymous with philanthropy, in addition to business and athletics. Through Hoffman's sponsorship, United States weightlifting teams have competed in numerous worldwide championships. Later, Hoffman found yet another athletic devotion and began actively promoting softball and power lifting on local, national and international levels.

A resolution in 1971 by the International Weightlifting Federation Congress proclaimed Bob Hoffman to be "The Father of World Weightlifting"—and, befitting this honor, U.S.A. Weightlifting approved the site of the official U.S.A. Weightlifting Hall of Fame. This 34,000-square-foot facility contains an extensive collection of weightlifting memorabilia honoring athletes from around the world who have contributed to the sport.

It was with great sadness that the world learned of Hoffman's death on July 19, 1985. He died at the age of 87 and was buried in Mount Rose Cemetery in York. His death had a major impact in the fitness world and even prompted ex-president Richard Nixon to proclaim his admiration for Hoffman. "As vice-president and later as president, there is no one for whom I had greater respect and affection," Nixon said.

After Hoffman's death, York Barbell continued its highly visible role in the sport of weightlifting and general fitness for the next 12 years until 1997, when it began an age of renaissance under new ownership. York has undergone a period of rebirth since its acquisition by Susquehanna Capital, a local holdings company with a diverse portfolio and history of managing successful companies. With the resources and experience of Susquehanna Capital's management team, York has become one the most respected and versatile companies in the industry.

As a true market leader, York is now not only a barbell manufacturer, but also a dominant player in three very distinct product lines—retail, high-end home fitness and the most elite sports performance and weight-training equipment in the world.

Its retail strength continues to grow as the company's reputation surges through the industry. Through

A statue of Bob Hoffman outside of the York Barbell corporate headquarters.

the guidance of Susquehanna Capital's management team, York products are sold in more retail and sporting goods stores than ever before. Its impressive vendor list includes Kmart, Sears, Target, and Meijer's—as well as Dick's Sporting Goods, The Sports Authority, Gart Sports, Dunham's and numerous others. York's performance has been so phenomenal, that Target Stores presented it with their Vendor Award of Excellence, due to unwavering dedication to leadership, service and quality.

As York continued to flex its retail might, the company also broke into the elite sports performance training industry with a brand new product line, the Sports Performance Series. This tank-like equipment took the industry by storm with incredibly beefy structural steel frames and unparalleled bio-mechanical design. Only a few years after its development, you can now find York Barbell Sports Performance Series equipment in the weight rooms of numerous teams throughout the world, including the

NBA, NFL, MLB and NHL, as well as Elite Division 1 universities. Sports Performance Series is the equipment of choice for teams such as the L.A. Lakers, Boston Bruins, Washington Redskins and San Antonio Spurs, as well as Penn State, Vanderbilt University and countless others. York racks, bars and plates are considered, by many, the best strength-training equipment in the world.

Now on the heels of the millennium, York Barbell continues to increase its role in the fitness industry and its mission to bring health and fitness to anyone who desires to feel and look better. While it is difficult to predict the ways in which the fitness industry will grow and change, it is certain York Barbell will continue its legendary heritage. York is a company that will remain on the fitness forefront and surpass all expectations by providing innovation, leadership and world-class service.

YORK HEALTH CORPORATION

As the York Charrette was being planned, one principal work group focused on the health care needs of the county and the types of responses that might address those needs. Their sessions were wide ranging initially, but quickly became centered on the need for primary healthcare services, such as pre-natal care, well baby care, immunizations, and treatment of acute illnesses. While these services were being provided at the three hospitals in the county, and, to some extent, the city and state health departments, the group cited the problems of access and cost that were associated with those existing sources. Consensus began to develop that community health centers, in the city and throughout the county, would be a tangible response to the need.

As the health work group continued to meet, participants asked the next question: Who would make community health centers happen after the Charrette had completed its work? Various options were considered. Perhaps the hospitals or the medical societies should undertake such an effort. What about city and county government? Were they

York Health Corporation's mission statement is to provide compassionate and comprehensive health services to people seeking accessible and affordable quality care.

the logical organizations to be charged with this undertaking? In considering each of these options, and others, doubts were always raised as to whether any other organization would be willing to accept a charge or "hand-off" from this Charrette work group. A galvanizing moment occurred toward the end of the week, when one of the members of the group said, "It appears that if it's going to happen, *we* are the ones who will have to make it happen!" There was immediate agreement, and those present quickly dubbed themselves "The We Group"—at first somewhat in jest, but the name stuck! When the

The 132 S. George Street office is one of four York Health Corporation offices in York County. Others are located at the Hannah Penn Middle School and in Hanover and Lewisberry.

Charrette ended, what had begun as a loosely knit discussion group had evolved to become a planning team for a community health center.

In the weeks following the formal end of the Charrette, the We Group met regularly and recognized the need for an organizational structure to move the effort forward. They decided that incorporation, as a not-for-profit corporation would be an appropriate next step to take. One of the interesting aspects of this action was the selection of the first board of directors. After several options were considered, the group decided to open board membership to anyone who chose to serve, and the first board was in place. The We Group acknowledged that a more descriptive name was needed for the new corporation. Without losing their focus on community health centers, they also saw merit in embracing a broader vision that could serve the county for years to come. A vision statement was adopted that identified the mission of the corporation in terms of bringing about needed improvements in healthcare for York City and York County. In searching for a name to reflect that

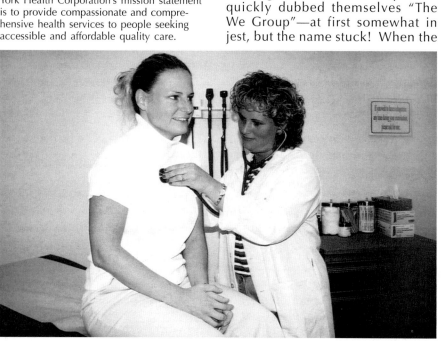

vision and mission, it was decided that the simplest name said it all, and thus was born the York Health Corporation.

The first board of directors set two broad measures of success—service to the under-served and making community changes that improved the healthcare system. What is the York Health Corporation's record? After several years of minimal federal support, in 1975 the Corporation became a federally qualified health center, providing the vehicle to serve the under-served with financial support for uncompensated care. Since 1970, according to staff estimates, physicians, mid-level practitioners, dentists, nurses, and social workers have provided some 800,000 visits to patients. It expanded from a downtown, drop-in center to a network with four sites, a substantial HIV clinical and social service care system, and a model nurse home-visiting program for first-time, at-risk mothers in the city of York. In the early 1970s, it hired its first mid-level practitioner and has continued to use these important healthcare providers throughout its existence. It has provided a vehicle for physician and dental loan repayment in the city of York by having it designated as a Health Professions Shortage Area. Many existing practitioners in the York community started in this county through this vehicle.

In 1983, the Corporation moved to its main site and added primary dental services. In 1985, at the request of a local hospital, it became a free HIV counseling and testing site. In 1991, it applied for and received its first HIV clinical services grant. In a collaborative vein, the Corporation provided medical direction for the York City Bureau of Health. In time the Corporation provided the Bureau several of its mandated physical health services. In 1996, in collaboration with the city school district and a local hospital, it opened a satellite community health center in the district's largest middle school. Though a

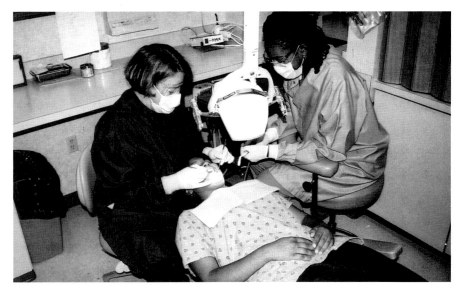

significant service for the students, it is open to family members and community residents. In 2000, it added dental services at this site.

Due to rapid service growth and community need, its Hanover site has gained local support. The area hospital has begun to seek grant support and has offered additional assistance to allow this site to increase hours and services.

What does the future hold? Current projects include facility enhancements, increasing services, participation in the local healthy

Along with medical and dental offices, York Health Corporation also has an extensive Social Services program.

Since 1970, according to staff estimates, physicians, mid-level practitioners, dentists, nurses, and social workers have provided some 800,000 visits to patients.

communities movement, research and actions to diminish local healthcare disparities, participation with other county agencies to discourage tobacco use, and an incipient project to examine ways to improve healthcare to seniors.

The York Health Corporation has not completed its tasks. Its original goals are still valid—it still seeks to address community and personal healthcare needs. Today, its message is the same: citizens can make the difference.

SIMMS MACHINERY, INC.

Originally incorporated in Annapolis, Maryland in 1972, the company was a one-man manufacturer's rep organization consisting of Gordon Simms. His Winnebago "BRAVE" was a "rolling office," traveling around the northeast to various woodworking factories, showing samples of new techniques, material and equipment.

Years before this period of time, Simms visited his mother's aunt and husband, north of York on Canal Road, when he was six years old, at the time of World War II. He recalls trips to the central market and chatting with the regulars at Motter's corner at Canal and Bull Roads. These were pleasant memories that, quite likely, lured him to return to stay many years later.

After college, Gordon Simms went to work for the family hardwood plywood manufacturing company in Jamestown, New York. With his small family, he was assigned to open up a new sales office in the Midwest and moved to Kalamazoo, Michigan in 1962. Stationed there, he called on office furniture, kitchen and millwork manufacturers in the Midwest, who were opening up new accounts. One, in particular, became a good volume account and was managed by Leigh Bench, who was later to become president of Yorktowne Kitchens in Red Lion, just south of York.

Returning to the Jamestown factory, Simms got seriously involved with manufacturing, quality control, methods and materials, attending various seminars in the industry and attending the yearly IWF machinery show. Soon, he was named plant manager for a new, solid lumber rough mill—the first of its kind in the northeast. Working with consultants from North Carolina, the plant was laid out and set up in three months. During this time, Mr. Simms developed and made a production model prototype of a "cut and fold" machine to produce a sixteen-inch square table top, which was two inches thick—from a quarter-inch-thick piece of ply-

Gordon Simms on the right, and Bill Simms at a trade show.

wood, which was twenty-by-twenty inches, in less than two minutes.

The company was sold, and the new owners assigned Mr. Simms to develop new products with his machine at a cabinet factory in Baltimore, Maryland. He started Simms Machinery, Inc., in Annapolis, and one of his first customers was Mr. Bench in York, Pennsylvania.

Several years later, Simms and his family moved to York County. The Pennsylvania Simms Machinery, Inc., was incorporated October 1, 1993, in York. Growth has been slow and steady, with son Dan Simms joining the company. They decided to concentrate on one special machine made in Italy to rapidly assemble wooden frames.

Their first machine was sold to Mr. Bench who had started a pre-hung door shop in Maryland. The machine is now used in over two hundred door shops scattered across the United States.

In 1994, the senior Simms developed a high-strength, solid, high-

pressure laminate computer keyboard platform, a quarter-inch thick, which was an improvement over the vinyl wrapped three-quarter-of-an-inch particle board used at that time. Kiika International, LLC, was started as a division of Simms Machinery, Inc., and son Bill Simms came on board to manage the division, which operates from the same facility in east York.

Kiika manufactures articulating computer keyboard platforms and mouse decks of the thin material, which has become the standard material for platforms in the industry today. Customers are both other manufacturers and office furniture dealers.

York has been great for the three Simms families and the two businesses. This area has such a wide variety of manufacturers, that it finds that it can outsource many of its components from local people. Both sons, with their wives and children, live in York County and are active in local affairs and church. York is ideally located for its proximity to major markets, and it plans on growing both entities right here.

The intersection shown here at North George and Philadelphia streets in the 1930s, has always served as one of the city's busiest sites. The Strand Theater seen at left became the keystone of the Strand-Capitol Performing Arts Center in the 1980s and the spot where Hotel Penn, at center right, once stood was chosen in the 1990s for the county's new Judicial building. The sign painted on the Hotel Penn offers "Free Night Parking." The Milner, a competing hotel across the street, advertised free laundry service for guests, and rooms for $1 a day. Courtesy, The York County Heritage Trust

A TIMELINE OF YORK COUNTY'S HISTORY

1608 Explorer John Smith confers with group of natives where the Susquehanna River enters the Chesapeake Bay.

1660-1670 Native Americans occupy sites in present-day York County, the Byrd, or Lower Leibhart site, and the Oscar, or Upper Leibhart, site.

1682 Charles II grants land in New World to William Penn as payment for debt to Penn's father. Penn arrives here in October.

1719-1720 John Griest and others settle on west side of Susquehanna at Kreutz Creek (without permission). Others settle near "river" called the Codorus.

1729 First authorized settlement at Kreutz Creek.

1732 Temporary line establishes border between Maryland and Pennsylvania and York County's southern boundary.

1736 Thomas Penn grants licenses to about 50 immigrants to settle in Springettsbury Manor. Homes are built here and surrounding areas.

1741 Penn's heirs authorize laying out of town named York after surveyor's English home. First "public house" licensed. The Lutherans, Reformed and "Romanists" apply for church lots.

1743 First bridge west of Susquehanna built across Codorus.

1749 York County is established from western portion of Lancaster County with *York town* as county seat. First county election is marred by riots. Election overturned. First settlers, mostly "Palatines," from Rhine River region of Europe joined by English Quakers and Scotch-Irish Presbyterians who prefer the northern and southern sections of the county.

1752 First markets are held under open skies in Centre (now Continental) Square.

1756 First Courthouse opens; first prison erected.

1758 Indians kidnap teenager Mary

This eight-plate stove, decorated with tulips and other "Pennsylvania German" icons was made at a furnace located on Furnace Creek in Manheim Township about four miles south of Hanover. At one time it was called the Mary Ann Furnace and one of its owners was George Ross whose name is emblazoned across the front plate. Ross was a lawyer and a signer of the Declaration of Independence. The furnace opened about 1762 and closed about 1811. Courtesy, The York County Heritage Trust

Jemison from her home on the nearby frontier.

1765 York Fair is held under Penn charter; surveyors Charles Mason and Jeremiah Dixon running a permanent boundary line to separate Pennsylvania from Maryland.

1772 The Sun Fire Company is formed in York; the Hand-in-Hand Company already has a "water wagon" in service here.

1774 Meeting held in York "to consider the distressed state of the inhabitants of Boston." First military unit formed under commander James Smith, future signer of the Declaration of Independence; Hanover is determined to be part of Pennsylvania, and therefore, a part of York County.

1775 Catholics build a "mass house." The York town Riflemen reach Cambridge; men see action at Bunker Hill.

1776 Colonel James Smith serves on the committee of three (with

Thomas McKean and Benjamin Rush) to write resolutions declaring independence from Great Britain. Smith signs the Declaration with his compatriots.

1777-1778 British move toward Philadelphia; The Second Continental Congress moves westward. On September 30, Congress is in York—takes over courthouse. For the next nine months York County is on the international stage. Congress hammers out the Articles of Confederation. Important people come and go, France sends financial support and the Conway Cabal is squashed by Lafayette. A national day of Thanksgiving is organized and news from near and far changes the course of world history. Congress finally receives word the British have left and members pack up and return to Philadelphia. York County's economy has been injected with a new vitality and the community has earned a heightened confidence that sets the tone for the future.

1780 Abolition Act frees 43 slaves living in York.

1781 Articles of Confederation ratified by Congress in Philadelphia.

1787 York town is "erected" into a borough. York County Academy is incorporated.

1791 On Sunday, July 3, George Washington accompanies his host Thomas Hartley to services at the Dutch (German) Reformed Church. Congress puts excise tax on liquor, a blow to York County makers of whiskey and beer.

1796 Solomon Meier starts publications of *Die York Gazette*, the first local newspaper printed in German.

1800 Adams County is carved out of York County's western portion on June 22, leaving York town or York borough the seat of a county with 587,440 acres, 921 square miles,

and 2,503 inhabitants. Population of the county—minus Adams County area—drops to 25,643 from 37,600

1803 Several Negro residents charged with setting fires in town put on trial.

1810 York National Bank is founded as state institution.

1811 William Goodridge, born to a slave in Baltimore, is indentured to York tanner.

1814 Sixty acres annexed to the borough. The York Volunteers defend Baltimore at the Battle of North Point.

1815 The town of Hanover is incorporated

1816 York Water Company is formed.

1817 Flood takes ten lives. The first Union Sunday School organized.

1818 Dorcas Society formed by ladies of the borough to educate children.

1824 William Goodridge, after years of absence, returns to York and Israel Williams gives him a job as barber. Later Goodridge purchases the business on Centre

Capturing ordinary people doing ordinary things was the specialty of Horace Bonham, born in York in 1835 and now recognized as one of America's finest "genre" painters. Bonham often used people from his East Market Street neighborhood as models. Titled *Pluck*, this oil on canvas shows children choosing or "plucking" a puppy from a litter of six. The dogs' mother, also a "resident" of the Bonham neighborhood, looks on. Painting in the collection of the York County Heritage Trust. Courtesy, The York County Heritage Trust

Square from the owner and marries Evalina Wallace. With her help, he becomes a successful entrepreneur, property owner, transportation broker, and leader of the underground railroad.

1825 John Elgar builds the first iron-hulled steamship, the *Codorus*. General Lafayette visits York and offers the toast, "To York, the capital of our country in its most gloomy time!"

1826 John Kline and Jonathan Jessup propagate the York Imperial Apple.

1829 Hanover Jewish population dedicates a synagogue.

1831 A locomotive named *The York* is built by Phineas Davis and

wins competition sponsored by the Baltimore and Ohio.

1835 Bank of Hanover and Trust Co. is formed.

1837 Runaway slave Margaret Morgan and her children, born in York, are captured by Edward Prigg; Prigg brought to trial for kidnapping. He is convicted and appeals case to the Supreme Court.

1838 First regular train from Baltimore arrives. Farmers growing tobacco seed from Cuba. Erection of first schoolhouses.

1840 The second York County Courthouse is built on Market Street, a block east of the Square. William and Evalina Goodridge sell tickets to the exhibition of a Christmas tree at their residence on East Philadelphia Street.

1850 Telegraph line extended from Baltimore to York, then Columbia and Philadelphia. Slate mined in Delta is judged best in the world.

1852 The Reverend John N. Neumann organizes Old St. Mary's Church for mostly German Catholics, and confirms 48 people. (Later, he becomes the first U.S. male declared a saint).

1855 York County Prison built on Chestnut Street. Spring Garden Cornet Band organized.

1861 Locals meet in courthouse after firing on Fort Sumter; adopt resolution to answer Lincoln's plea for soldiers: the Worth Infantry and York Rifles are among the first to fight for the Union.

1862 An Army Hospital is established on the town common; 14,000 men are treated here, including many wounded in Battle of Gettysburg.

1863 June 27 a Committee of Safety meets General Gordon at a farmhouse west of York; arranges terms of Confederate invasion of York. Sunday, June 28, 9,000 Confederate troops occupy York; Troops march toward Wrightsville

This 1915 Sphinx was one of the thousands of automobiles made in York County during a period when York had up to 30 separate automobile assembly plants. In the restored model pictured above Mr. and Mrs. Theodore F. Freed are seen in the front seats while Mr. and Mrs. Howard Campbell enjoy the open air ride in the rear seats. Standing alongside the car in the rear is W.F.O. (Fred) Rosenmiller who has helped to document York's roles as the "Detroit of the East." Courtesy, The York County Heritage Trust

and locals burn bridge to prevent advance to Philadelphia; Tuesday, July 1, Confederates leave York, joining Lee near Gettysburg. In this push northward, Confederates also engage Union patriots near Hanover; 15 are killed and 60 wounded.

1865 On April 21 President Lincoln's funeral train stops here. Within the next few months William Goodridge leaves York to join his daughter in Michigan. The Children's Home is incorporated. York organizes a police force.

1869 The York YMCA is organized.

1873 The York Collegiate Institute opens.

1879 York City Market opens, capped by a 95-foot tower. New group of Jewish immigrants, mostly from Austria and Hungary, settle in York.

1880 York Opera House opens.

1882 A telephone system links 27 stores and offices.

1883 Charter is granted to Anshe Hadas Congregation.

1884 Codorus floods 100 acres and sweeps away all bridges.

1885 Dr. George E. Holtzapple administers oxygen to boy suffering with pneumonia.

1887 York becomes a city. Daniel K. Noell is first mayor of city with ten wards. Edison Light and Power Co. wins contract to light city.

1888 Central Market opens; Eastern Market House opens.

1894 Grier Hersh builds first golf course at his home, Springdale.

1895 Historical Society of York County formed. St. Patrick's Church erected.

1897 Merchants form a Protective Association, a forerunner of the Chamber of Commerce. Silent films are shown in York. First Halloween Parade is held.

1898 A new courthouse is authorized on same site as the old one. Hanover writer John Luther Long gives birth to "Madame Butterfly."

1899 York County communities join to celebrate Sesquicentennial.

1900 Adas Israel Congregation organized in York.

1902 Ohev Sholom Congregation organized. York Hospital acquires site on South George Street.

1904 York Oratorio Society is organized.

1906 The Manufacturers Association organized; 29 industries join first year; showing diversity that becomes a York hallmark.

1907 Congregation Beth Israel dedicates temple on S. Beaver St.

1908 York Visiting Nurse Association is formed.

1909 York Carriage Co. announces plans to make motor vehicles.

1910 Glen Rock State Bank is formed.

1911 West Side Sanitarium opens. Peoples State Bank of East Berlin is formed. The Bon Ton Department Store welcomes shoppers to new showplace in downtown.

1912 Grand opening of new Bear's store; Lehmayer's opens store nearby.

1913 York is chartered as third-class city. A trans-continental highway brings traffic through the heart of York County.

1917 Six thousand Yorkers serve in war. York Haven State Bank is formed.

1918 Influenza hits 6,500 residents.

1920 Prohibition goes into effect. Countless York countians defy the new law by making "bath-tub gin" and brews of staggering concoctions.

1920s Sears opens its new store at 149 West Market Street. Workers making handcrafted automobiles here are offended by cookie-cutter cars produced by Henry Ford.

1925 White Rose Baseball Team brings pennant to York after 5 to 3 win. Group of businessmen raise funds to build the Yorktowne Hotel.

1927 William Penn High, Hannah

Above
York's love affair with baseball was heightened in 1925 when the York White Roses brought the championship pennant home to the White Rose community. This photograph shows the 1932 team taken by well-known photographer C.W. Simon. The team played its last game in 1969. Courtesy, The York County Heritage Trust

Right
Even before the Harley-Davidson company opened an assembly plant in York the motorcycle that bears the name had a strong presence in York. This photo shows an employee of the York Sanitary Milk Co. using a Harley with sidecar to deliver milk and ice cream. The shop housing the local Harley-Davidson dealership, can be seen in the background with glass show windows bearing the company name. Courtesy, The York County Heritage Trust

Penn Junior High School and York Catholic School open.

1928 Self-proclaimed "powwower," Nelson Rehmeyer, is murdered.

1929 Two men and a 14-year old are tried for the murder of Rehmeyer. "Comfort Stations" for men and women are opened under the Square for convenience of Downtown shoppers.

1930 Bank clearings set new high but Depression leaves thousands jobless.

1931 Crispus Attucks Association is formed, offering recreational and educational programs for York's black citizens. Women allowed on York juries. Samuel S. Lewis is appointed Pennsylvania Secretary of Highways.

1932 WORK Radio begins broadcasts from 5,000-watt signal.

1933 Sale of beer resumes on April 7. Devastating flood occurs on August 23 and 24; four covered bridges are carried away; 900 homes and businesses are damaged.

1934 State supervises flood protection project on Codorus—creek bed is lowered. Eighteen plants hit by strikes. Sadie Tassia transforms the Coliseum Theater into the Valencia Ballroom and brings big bands to town.

1935 Martin Memorial Library opens. The Maternal Health Center

Above
George Leader, a popular Democrat from York County, is seen in this photograph published on November 4, 1954 just after he won the gubernatorial election. By law, governors could serve for only one four-year term in that era. During his administration he appointed blacks to important positions and prioritized social issues bringing a new sense of "common wealth" to the state. Courtesy, The York County Heritage Trust

Below
York's "Shoe Wizard" Mahlon Haines built this house in 1948 just off the Lincoln Highway. Haines, a shoe merchant who made a fortune selling shoes at numerous outlets in the United States, offered use of the storybook house to newlyweds for their honeymoon. The guests would arrive to a full supply of food, including beef from the Haines farm nearby. Later this sterling example of roadside architecture became an ice cream shop. Courtesy, The Schintz Studio

Army Services Depot is one of 12 in nation supplying the war. The York Ordnance Depot is important supply center. York Symphony Orchestra organized.

1942 New City Hall is dedicated. WSBA Radio begins broadcasting.

1943 Rabbi Alexander D. Goode is one of Four Chaplains lost in the sinking of a cargo-transport ship in the Atlantic.

1945 As World War II ends, York County counts thousands of citizens who served—371 killed, 822 wounded, 152 reported missing and 192 taken prisoner.

1946 Reorganization of the county school system places pupils from 72 municipalities into 14 administrative units. A consultant reports that the section of Codorus Creek running through the city "resembles an open sewer." Traffic and parking problems plague city.

1947 York voters repeal "Blue Laws" and Sunday movies return.

1948-1949 The municipal pool remains closed while citizens challenge city hall's decision to prohibit Negroes from swimming

is established.

1936 Yorker Tony Terlazzo wins title in Olympic Weight Lifting in August.

1939 New airport opens west of York. Buses replace electric rail cars and trolleys. Fish-kill in Codorus alarms residents.

1940 The 15-point York Plan coordinates manufacturing resources to bring war contracts here. York weightlifters sweep national competition. John Grimek is named Mr. America.

1941 General Jacob L. Devers, commands Sixth Army, along with other assignments in war. Seventeen blacks from York serve in all-black units. The New Cumberland

there. WNOW Radio begins operation.

1949 Telecasts from WGAL TV, Lancaster, reach York. York County's Cameron Mitchell is "discovered." Penn State University begins classes for veterans.

1950 York City population reaches all-time peak at 59,704. County population reaches 202,737. City officials turn many streets to one-way thoroughfares. YWCA opens new headquarters. New housing developments form rings around the city.

1952 WSBA TV goes on the air.

1953 Sixty three countians give their lives in the Korean War; 6,900 sent to battle.

1954 George Leader elected Governor of Pennsylvania. York acquires first "sister-city," Arles, France, continuing camaraderie that began in the Revolutionary War.

1955 York County Shopping Center opens near new development called Haines Acres. Sears closes downtown store and moves to Mall.

1960 Developing highway linking Baltimore, York and Harrisburg dubbed, Interstate 83.

1961 Restoration of Golden Plough Tavern and General Gates House begins.

1964 Jane M. Alexander becomes first woman elected to the Pennsylvania Legislature from York County.

1965 The Pfaltzgraff Company forms the Susquehanna Cable Company.

1966 Ron Everett, later Maulana Karenga, a graduate of William Penn High School founds seven-day celebration known as Kwanzaa.

1967 Peach Bottom Atomic Power Plant opens.

1968-1969 York is one of 200 cities struggling with racial tensions. Riots erupt and Henry C. Schaad, a York patrolman is shot,

dies 11 days later. Lillie Belle Allen from South Carolina is shot to death on Newberry Street while visiting relatives. No one is charged with murders.

1969 York Charrette is formed. York's Eastern Baseball League team plays last game. Climate-controlled York Mall opens with 30 stores under one roof.

1970 J.W. Gitt sells the *York Gazette and Daily*.

1972 Tropical Storm Agnes wreaks

York sculptor Charles Rudy (1904-1986) created some of America's most famous icons in stone, bronze and wood. This grouping is typical of the work he created for the Sun Oil Seaman's Memorial in Marcus Hook and the Memorial at the Flag Pole on Smith Walk at the University of Pennsylvania campus. When he was eight years old he started working with his father, J. Horace Rudy, in his stained and leaded glass workshop and within a year learned to stain and fire glass. Among other large-scale works he supervised 30 sculptors as they cut huge figures of Jefferson Davis, Robert E. Lee and Stonewall Jackson into the side of Stone Mountain, east of Atlanta. Courtesy, The York County Heritage Trust

Above
Former President Nixon visits the Richard M. Nixon County Park near Jacobus in August 1989. Park naturalist Kim Young, wearing white, is shown chatting with the president about park features. Nixon's parents and brother moved to York County to be closer to the promising young politician after he won a seat in the U.S. Congress. Photo by Steve Busch.   Courtesy, Harry McLaughlin

havoc on York County: at least 50 die and property damage reaches billions of dollars.
1974 Bill Goodling takes his father's seat in Congress. Delma River helps found the York Spanish Council. Downtown businesses close, including Peoples Drug Store, Colonial Hotel, Lehmayer's, and Thom McAn.
1975 Mattie Chapman becomes prothonotary, first black woman elected to county office. Bear's Department Store sold to Zollinger's.
1976 Patriot fever sweeps York with Bicentennial activities stimulating love of history. A group of citizens plan to reconstruct the colonial York County Courthouse, seat of Congress for nine months. Strand Theater closes.
1977 Elizabeth Marshall is elected York's first woman mayor. Retail sales for county top $1 billion.
1979 The nation's worst nuclear accident takes place at nearby

Three Mile Island. TMI Unit 2 loses cooling liquid—leading to damage to unit's reactor core. Thousands flee area. Thomas Chatman becomes York's first black chief of police.
1981 Margaret E. Moul sees her dream realized—a home for mentally-alert but physically handicapped individuals. The Weightlifting Hall of Fame opens. Spanish-speaking population estimated between 4 and 5,000.
1986 President Ronald Reagan visits the Harley-Davidson plant to spotlight global competition.
1987 Sheryl Dorney is first woman elected judge in York County.

Labor Union membership numbers more than 25,000.
1988 York Peppermint Patties purchased by Hershey Foods Corporation and moved out of town. Policeman responding to "hostage situation" kills Israel Ramos, 19. Community activists revive concerns about police brutality. The *York Dispatch* is sold to out-of-town company.
1989 York's morning and evening papers discuss a joint operating agreement; with condition that newsrooms remain independent.
1991 Local band, LIVE, records its first album; international tours follow, then cover of *The Rolling Stone*. Agricultural and Industrial Museum of York County opens. Racial tensions erupt in Hanover; Hanover United formed to promote understanding. First fish ladders open to allow migrating shad to return to historic breeding grounds.
1992 Bill Clinton opens his campaign for the presidency in York. York Mayor Bill Althaus becomes head of the U.S. Conference of Mayors.
1993 County prison signs a multimillion deal with the U.S. Immigration Service that brings more than 150 Chinese to York as detainees after their ship, *The Golden Venture*, is wrecked on the shore at Rockaway, New York.
1994 Starbucks Coffee Company chooses Emigsville industrial park for a new bean roasting plant.
1996 Caterpillar, Inc. announces plans to close its York facility laying off 1,100 workers. York Murals Program is kicked off.
1998 The Historical Society of York County and the Agricultural and Industrial Museum merge to form The York County Heritage Trust. AMP Inc. closes its Loganville plants. Goodyear Tire & Rubber Company builds $22 million

distribution center. "Super stores" like Wal-Mart, Target and Kohl's extend growth rings outward leaving older facilities in jeopardy.

1999 York County celebrates its 250th Anniversary with year-long program. Meanwhile, anniversary of 1969 Race Riots brings media coverage, political bickering and cry for justice of unsolved murders.

2000 City population drops below 41,000; County population increases to 381,751. York, Cumberland, Dauphin, Lebanon, Lancaster, and Berks cooperate in Keystone Opportunity Zone and other cooperative initiatives develop. County officials choose downtown site for new $22 million Judicial Center to relieve Courthouse crowding.

2001 Old Smokestack Property becomes site for new business campus. White Supremacists target York. A rally attracts groups for and against the cause. They clash and police make arrests.

2002 Trial for those allegedly involved in the 1969 riots takes place; two convicted while former mayor acquitted. Extremist groups rally again; this time interest is low. Millions of dollars are being invested on construction and improvements in the city and county.

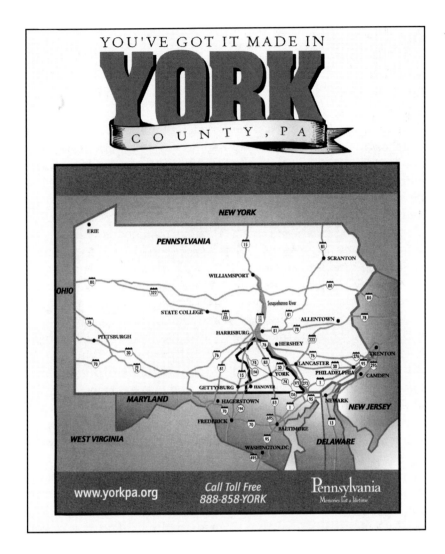

Top
This map showing York County's strategic location was created for York County Parks in one of many efforts to promote the new Rail Trail running 21.1 miles from the Maryland state line with more than ten landmark features before entering the city of York at the reconstructed York County Colonial Courthouse. Courtesy, York County Parks

Right
Bill Clinton, the Arkansas governor, opened his campaign for the presidency with a stop in York in 1992. In this photo the future president is shown after a jog through downtown York near the Yorktowne Hotel. Courtesy, The Schintz Studio

ACKNOWLEDGMENTS

Anyone who really knows the heritage and makeup of York County can understand how difficult it is to capture the large and diverse community in a few thousand words and a few hundred illustrations. It is crucial to pass on our heritage and reflect on our achievements, nevertheless, and this volume helps fulfill the task. Others already published, and still more to be published in the future, will help round out the rich story of York County and keep the spirit alive and accessible.

Many, many individuals and groups contributed knowledge, time, effort and skills to this updated version of the earlier *Setting Sun*. I risk omitting the names of important helpers by singling out some who assisted; nevertheless, it is my duty to emphasize this publication represents a team effort of large magnitude.

In the early stages of research for the revised, expanded book you are holding, I sent correspondence to a number of individuals I identified as specialists in certain areas of community life. It was the best decision I made and I am exceedingly grateful for the courtesies and the expression of enthusiasm that resulted. In my initial request I included a broadly sketched outline of the last twenty-some years and asked each correspondent to offer observations, opinions and facts. Everyone I wrote to responded and without exception they followed up with helpful information, opinions and referrals. Some contributors went to great lengths to provide information and I sincerely appreciate the help of everyone who responded. Included among those individuals are: Tom Donley, June Lloyd, Richard Brown, Lila Fourhman-Shaull, John C. Schmidt, Mary Stephenson, Gordon Freireich, David B. Carver, Fran Keller, Patrick Foltz, Ruthe F. Craley, Irvin Kittrell III, Joan Clippinger, Lamar Matthew, Jim Rudisill, Donna Shermeyer, Ellie Shoemaker and Dorrie Leader.

Numerous members of the York County Heritage Trust were indispensable advisors, researchers, and assistants, including June Lloyd, Lila Fourhman-Shaull, Justine Landis, Donna Shermeyer, Carol Himes, Carl Preate, Nancy Amspacher, Richard Banz and Dennis Kunkle. I enjoyed the warm support and assistance of staff members at the York County Chamber including Thomas E. Donley, an "advocate for York County, and at the same time for the City of York, the nation's revolutionary capital, city of firsts, city of champions!" My thanks also go to Loren H. Kroh, Vanessa DeLauder and Louise Heine. And a special salute to former Chamber president Carl Neu and my former employer Robert V. Iosue who conspired to get me involved in writing York history.

Others who made valuable contributions include Evelyn L. Knaub, Patricia A. Hershey, Mary Katherine Wynegar, Harry McLaughlin, Carol and Bill Schintz, Kerri J. Chiaramonte, Edward L. Bievenour, Pam White, Susan Kline, Jerry Sweitzer, Donnie Shaffer, Blair Seitz, Martha Frankenberry, Helen and Jack Gracey, Carter Hammond, Dan Barrick, Bucky Hill, Luther Sowers, Pam Hemzik and C. Warren Smith. My mentor in all things York County Historical is Virginia L. Kent who many years ago trained me to be a guide at the Golden Plough Tavern and instilled a sense of wonderment that continues today.

Finally, I would like to extend my deep appreciation to Heather Martin Zeug and her colleagues at the American Historical Press who made this a labor of love and a joy to experience.

Georg R. Sheets
Harrisburg, PA 2002

BIBLIOGRAPHY

_____, *The Italians in Pennsylvania*, Pamphlet No. 4, The Pennsylvania Historical and Museum Commission, Harrisburg, Pennsylvania, 1998.

Ames, Florence LaRose. *That Sovereign Knowledge: A History of the York Hospital and its Medical Staff*. York, Pennsylvania, York Hospital, 1990.

Bazelon, Bruce. *The Jews in Pennsylvania*. Pamphlet No. 2, The Pennsylvania Historical and Museum Commission, Harrisburg, Pennsylvania, 1986.

Beyer, George R., ed. *Guide to the State Historical Markers of Pennsylvania*. Commonwealth of Pennsylvania, The Historical and Museum Commission, Harrisburg, Pennsylvania, 1991.

Biddle, Gertrude Bosler, and Lowrie, Sarah Dickinson. *Notable Women of Pennsylvania*. Philadelphia, Pennsylvania: University of Pennsylvania, 1942.

Blockson, Charles L., *African Americans in Pennsylvania, Above Ground and Underground, An Illustrated Guide*. RB Books, Harrisburg, Pennsylvania, 2001.

Central Pennsylvania Business Journal, Harrisburg, Pennsylvania, various dates of publication.

Cadzow, Donald A. *Archaeological Studies of the Susquehannock Indians of Pennsylvania*. Harrisburg, Pennsylvania: Pennsylvania Historical Commission, 1936.

Carter, W.C., and Glossbrenner, A.J. *History of York County From Its Erection to the Present Time: 1729-1834*. Harrisburg, Pennsylvania: Aurand Press, 1930.

Clippinger, Joan S. *Wellsville, Remembrances for Tomorrow, 1892-1992*. Wellsville, Pennsylvania, Wellsville Centennial Commission.

Commager, Henry Steele. *Documents of American History*. New York, New York: Appleton-Century-Crofts, 1934.

Country Club of York. "History of the Country Club of York: 1899-1975." York, Pennsylvania: p.p., 1975.

Danner, Edwin R. *Pennsylvania Dutch Dictionary*. Dispatch Publishing Company, York, Pennsylvania, 1951.

Doutrich, Paul E. *The Evolution of an Early American Town: Yorktown, Pennsylvania, 1740-1790*. Dissertation, University of Kentucky, 1984.

Downer, Alan S. *The Memoirs of John Durang, American Actor 1785-1816*.

Pittsburgh, Pennsylvania, University of Pittsburgh Press for The Historical Society of York County, 1966.

Dudrear, Albert, Jr. *The Dudrear-Dodderer Family*. York, Pennsylvania: p.p., 1976.

Earnest Russell D. and Corinne P. *Papers for Birth Dayes: Guide to the Fraktur Artists and Scriveners, Vol. 1*. Second edition, Russell E. Earnest Associates, East Berlin, Pennsylvania, 1997.

Eberly, Phillip K. *Susquehanna Radio, the First Fifty Years*. Susquehanna Radio Corp., York, Pennyslvania, 1992.

Ebert, Catherine and John, Eds. *American Folk Art Painters*. Scribners, New York, New York, 1975.

Eichelberger, A.W. *Eichelberger Family Record: 1693-1900*. Hanover, Pennsylvania: Hanover Herald Print, 1901.

Engle, William H. *History of the Commonwealth of Pennsylvania*. Philadelphia, Pennsylvania: E.M. Gardner, 1883.

Farquhar, A.B. *The First Million—the Hardest: An Autobiography*. New York, New York: Doubleday, Page and Company, 1922.

First Presbyterian Church of York, Pennsylvania. *Two Hundred Years: 1762-1962*. York, Pennsylvania: p.p., 1962.

Fisher, George G. *Ordinances of the Borough and City of York*. York, Pennsylvania: Gazette Printing Company, 1896.

Fortenbaugh, Robert. *The Nine Capitals of the United States*. York, Pennsylvania: York Graphic Services, 1975.

Fortenbaugh, Robert T. and Tarman, H. James. *Pennsylvania: The Story of a Commonwealth*. The Pennsylvania Book Service, Harrisburg, Pennsylvania, 1940.

Freed, Theodore F., and Rosenmiller, W.F.O. "Pictorial History of Pleasure and Commercial Vehicles Manufactured in York County, Pennsylvania." York, Pennsylvania: 1977.

Friedman, Rabbi Moses N. "York Jewish Bicentennial." York, Pennsylvania: p.p., 1955.

Gazette and Daily. York, Pennsylvania: various dates of publication.

Gibson, John. *History of York County, Pennsylvania*. Chicago, Illinois: F.A. Bartley Publishing Company, 1886.

Glatfelter, Charles H. *York County Pennsylvania Lutherans*. State College, Pennsyl-

vania, Jostens Printing and Publishing Co., 1993.

Gordon, General John B. *Reminiscences of the Civil War*. New York, New York: Charles Scribners Sons, 1903.

Gotwalt, Helen Miller. *Crucible of a New Nation-First York County Court House, 1754-1841*. York Pennsylvania: York County Bicentennial Commission, p.p., 1976.

Greiman, Edward A. *Memoirs*. York, Pennsylvania: Graphic Services and White Rose Engravings Company, p.p., 1968.

Griffin, Benjamin T. *The Americanization of a Congregation*. Trinity United Church of Christ, York, Pennsylvania, 1984.

Groff, Betty. *Betty Groff's Pennsylvania Dutch Cookbook*. Macmillan Publishing Company, New York, New York.

Hall, Clifford J., and Lehr, John P. "York County and the World War." York, Pennsylvania: p.p., 1920.

Hardt, P. *The Self-Taught Conveyancer or Farmers' and Mechanics Guide*. Baltimore, Maryland: Shaffer and Maund, 1819.

Hartman, Terry. *The Folkculture of Pennsylvania Dutch Farmers' Market*. Washington, D.C.: National Endowment for the Humanities, n.p.,1978.

Hatch, Carl E., Hicks, Joseph B., and Kohler, Richard E. *York, Pa. in the Roaring Twenties*. York, Pennsylvania: Martin Library, p.p., 1973.

Hawkins, Charles A., and Landis, Housten E. *York and York County—A Sesqui-Centennial Memento*. York, Pennsylvania: York Daily Press, 1901.

Heisey, John W. *York County in the American Revolution*. York, Pennsylvania: The Historical Society of York County, 1971.

Hopkins, Leroy and Smith, Eric Ledell. *The African Americans in Pennsylvania*, Pamphlet No. 6, The Pennsylvania Historical and Museum Commission, Harrisburg, Pennsylvania, 1984.

Hubbert-Kemper, Ruthann, Clymer, Paul I., et al. *Preserving a Palace of Art: A Guide to the Projects of the Pennsylvania Capitol Preservation Committee*. Pennsylvania Capitol Preservation Committee, Harrisburg, Pennsylvania, 2000.

Hubley, Jim. *Off the Record.* York, Pennsylvania, 1994.

Hulan, Richard H. *The Swedes in Pennsylvania.* Pamphlet No. 5, The Pennsylvania Historical and Museum Commission, Harrisburg, Pennsylvania, 1994.

Jezierski, John Vincent. *Enterprising Images: The Goodridge Brothers, African American Photographers, 1847-1922.* Wayne State University, Detroit, Michigan, 2000.

Jones, Jeri L. *York County Pennsylvania Geologic Guide.* York, Pennsylvania: York Rock and Mineral Club, p.p., 1980.

Kain, Emily. *The Women's Club of York, Seventy-five Years.* York, Pennsylvania: p.p., 1975.

Kammer, Ruth L. *Inside Westside.* Memorial Hospital, 1986.

Kent, Barry C. *Discovering Pennsylvania's Archaeological Heritage.* Harrisburg, Pennsylvania: Pennsylvania Historical and Museum Commission, 1980.

_____. *Susquehanna's Indians.* Commonwealth of Pennsylvania and the Historical and Museum Commission, Harrisburg, Pennsylvania, 1984.

Kindig, Joseph III. *Architecture in York County.* York, Pennsylvania: The Historical Society of York County, p.p., 1979.

Klees, Fredric. *The Pennsylvania Dutch.* The Macmillan Company, New York, 1961.

Lafayette Club. *The Lafayette Club Murals.* York, Pennsylvania: p.p., 1962.

Latimer, Robert Cathcart. *Reminisces of York, 1891-1901.* N.p.

Lewis, Arthur H. *Hex.* New York, New York: Trident Press, 1969.

Lloyd, June Burk. *Faith and Family, Pennsylvania German Heritage in York County Area Fraktur,.* York County Heritage Trust, York, Pennsylvania, 2001.

Lutheran Social Services, South Region. *The Messenger.* York, Pennsylvania: n.p., n.d.

Magda, Matthew S. *The Welsh in Pennsylvania,* Pamphlet No. 1, The Pennsylvania Historical and Museum Commission, Harrisburg, Pennsylvania, 1998.

_____. *The Poles in Pennsylvania,* Pamphlet No. 3, The Pennsylvania Historical and Museum Commission, Harrisburg, Pennsylvania, 1986.

Martin, Jere, *Pennsylvania Almanac.* Stackpole Books, Mechanicsburg, Pennsylvania, 1997.

McClure, Jim. *Never to Be Forgotten.* York, Pennsylvania, *York Daily Record,* 1999.

Mellander , G.A., and Carl E. Hatch. *The Depression 1930s: The York Dispatch Index,* Strine Printing Company, York, Pennsylvania, 1973, 1999

Miller, Lewis. *Sketches and Chronicles.* York, Pennsylvania: The Historical Society of York County, p.p., 1966.

Moore, Frank, ed. *Diary of the American Revolution.* New York, New York: Charles Scribner, 1860.

Morning Journal. York, Pennsylvania: various dates of publication.

Nye, W.S., and Redman, John G. *Farthest East—Wrightsville, Pa.* York, Pennsylvania: p.p., 1963.

Olson, McKinley C. *J.W. Gitt's Sweet Land of Liberty.* New York, New York: Jerome S. Ozo, 1975.

Patriot News. Harrisburg, Pennsylvania: various dates of publication.

Peckham, Betty. T*he Story of a Dynamic Community—York, Pennsylvania.* York, Pennsylvania: York Area Chamber of Commerce, 1945.

_____. York, Pennsylvania: *A Dynamic Community Forges Ahead.* York, Pennsylvania: York Area Chamber of Commerce, 1957.

Pennsylvania Gazette. York, Pennsylvania: various dates of publication.

Prowell, George R. *History of York County, Volume I.* Chicago, Illinois: J.H. Beers and Company, 1907.

Rudisill, James. *York Since 1741.* York Graphic Services, York, Pennsylvania, 1991

Rupp, I. Daniel. *History of Lancaster County.* Lancaster, Gilbert Hills, 1844.

Schlegel, Philip J. *Recruits to Continentals: A History of the York County Rifle Company, June 1775-1777.* York, Pennsylvania: The Historical Society of York County, p.p., 1979.

Secor, Robert. *Pennsylvania, 1776.* College Park, Pennsylvania: Pennsylvania State University, 1976.

Small, Cassandra Morris. *Letters of '63.* Detroit, Michigan: Stair-JordanBaker, Inc., 1929.

Stetler, Polly. *Overnight Success: The Yorktowne Hotel at 70.* Colorgraphics, York, Pennsylvania, 1995.

Sunday News. Lancaster, Pennsylvania: various dates of publication.

Tassia, S.M. *Valencia 10th Anniversary, 1929-1939.* Valencia Ballroom, York, Pennsylvania, 1939.

Taub, Lynn Smolens. *Greater York in Action.* York, Pennsylvania: York Area Chamber of Commerce, 1968.

Thernstrom, Stephan, ed. *The Harvard Encyclopedia of American Ethnic Groups.* Harvard University Press, 1981.

Wentz, Abdel Ross. *The Beginnings of the German Element in York County.* Pennsylvania, New Era Printing, Lancaster, Pennsylvania, 1916.

Weiser, Frederick S., et al, eds. *Der Reggeboge (The Rainbow).* Pamphlet Newsletter, Quarterly of the Pennsylvania German Society, Brenigsville, Pennsylvania, Many issues, University of Pennsylvania, Philadelphia, Pennsylvania.

Whiffen, Marcus and Koeper, Frederick. *American Architecture, Vols. I and II.* The MIT Press, Cambridge, Massachusetts, 1981.

Yearbook of the Historical Society of York County For the Year 1941: Notes and Documents Concerning the Manorial History of the Town of York. York, Pennsylvania: The Historical Society of York County, p.p., 1941.

Yoder, Don, et al. *Pennsylvania Folklife,* Member Magazine, Pennsylvania Folklife Society, Lancaster, Pennsylvania, All issues, University of Pennsylvania, Philadelphia, Pennsylvania.

York City Fire Department. *History of the York Fire Department, 1776-1976.* Marceline, Missouri: Walsworth Publishing Company, p.p., 1976.

Zarfoss, Franklin W. *History of Churches, York County, Pennsylvania in Chronological Sequence 1700-1799,* 1988, n.p.

INDEX

CHRONICLES OF LEADERSHIP INDEX

Barton, Jno Z. 196-197
Bon-Ton Store, Inc., The 198-201
Bradley Lifting Corp. 202-204
Brown's Orchards & Farm Market 244-245
Drovers Bank, a Division of Fulton Bank 206-207
ESAB Welding & Cutting Products 246-247
Gent-L-Kleen Products, Inc. 248-249
Hamme Associates 250-251
Hoffmeyer & Semmelman 252-253
Horn & Company, D.E./Pennfield Corporation 208-209
JLS Automation 221
Martin Memorial Library 239
Memorial Hospital 254-255
Morex Corporation 210-212
Normandie Ridge Senior Living Community 214-215
Pediatric Health Associates, P.C. 216-217
Penn State York 218-220
Quigley Motor Co., Inc. 222-223
Readco Manufacturing, Inc. 256-257
Red Lion Antique Center 258-259
Red Lion Bus Company and Red Lion Tours & Travel 224-225
Seligman, Friedman & Company, P.C. 243
Sesame Personnel & Sesame Temps Inc. 226-227
Simms Machinery, Inc. 266
Stauffer Biscuit Company, Inc., D.F. 260-261
Susquehanna Pfaltzgraff Co. 228-229
Tighe Industries, Inc. 230-231
United Defense Ground Systems Division 232-233
Warners Moving & Storage 234-235
York Barbell Company 262-263
York County Chamber of Commerce 205
York County Herritage Trust 213
York Health Corporation 264-265
York Hospital/ Wellspan Health 236-238
York International Corporation 240-242

GENERAL INDEX

Italicized numbers indicate illustrations.

A

Abbottstown 85, 90, 118
Abolition Act 268
Acco Industries 98
AC Valve Corp. 187
Adams, John *64*, 65
Adams, Samuel *47*
Adams County 16, 57, 65, 66, 156, *177*, *178*, 268, 269
Adams-Hanover Counseling Services 182
Adas Israel Congregation 101, 270
Addagyjunkquagh (Indian) 13
Adlum, John 26
Adlum, Joseph 27
Agriculture 22, 24, 42-43, 56, *174*, *175*, *177*, 189
Agricultural and Industrial Museum 189, 191, 274
Air Transportation Authority 189
Albright, Anna Maria Ursula Duenckle 44

Albright, Philip 44
Alexander, Jane M. 273
Allen, Lillie B. 154, 273
Allis Chalmers Corporation 98; Hydro-Turbine Division 184
Almshouse 66, 67
Althaus, William 184, 274
American Chain Company 98
American Legion, York 150
American Red Cross, York County Chapter 147
Andrews, John 55, *56*
Anshe Hadas Congregation 101
Appell, Louis J., Jr. 137, 149
Armand, Charles (Marquis de la Rouerie) 57
Armand's Legion 57
American Hydro Corp. 186, 187
AMF 184, 186
AMP Inc. 191, 275
Anshe Hadas Congregation 270
Armor, Thomas 29, 36
Armstrong, John, Jr. 61
Army Hospital 269
Arnaux Electric Light Company 100
Asbury, Francis 58
Articles of Confederation 268
Aswan Dam 184
Automobile industry 114, 115, 121
Avalong 152

B

Bachtell, Dick 141
Bacon, Samuel 61
Back River Wastewater Treatment Plant 187
Baer, Jacob 97
Baer, John H. 97
Bailey, William 58
Bair, Robert C. 112
Bair Station *162*
Baltimore & Ohio Steam Railway Company 74, 76, 77
Baltimore Company 73
Bank of Hanover and Trust Co. 269
Baptiste, Ezekiel 83
Barnitz, Anna Barbara Spangler 25
Barnitz, Catherine Hay 25
Barnitz, Charles 25, 67, 76
Barnitz, David Grier 25
Barnitz, George 83
Barnitz, Jacob 83
Barnitz, John 25
Barnitz, John George Charles 25
Bartgis, Matthias 59
Barton, Jno Z. 196-197
Barton, Thomas 27, 29
Battle of Gettysburg 269
Battle of Hanover *165*
Battle of North Point 269
Batwell, Daniel 55
Bauer, Martin 18
Baugher, Frederick 78
Bauserman, C.F. 118
Bay, Andrew 29
Bear, Charles H. 121

Bear's Department Store 118, *119*, 132, *133*, 138, 155, 270, 274
Beaver, James A. 106
Beck, Charles 101
Beckner, William H. 145
Bedford 21
Beidinger, Nicholaus. *See* Bittinger, Nicolas
Bell Motor Car Company 115
Bennett, Isaac 111
Bennett, Joseph 16
Bentz, Matilda 66
Bentz, Sophia 66
Berghous, A. *90*
Berks 275
Bermudian (town) 43
Beth Israel Congregation 270
Better York Inc. 181
Beyer, Joseph 18
Biddle, Nicholas 76
Bike Nite *186*, *190*
Billmyer, George 69
Billmyer (York) House *169*
Bishop, John 22
Bittinger, Christian 36
Bittinger, John W. 112
Bittinger, Nicolas 23, 36
Bixler, Jacob 59
Black, Chauncey Forward 106, 107, 109
Black, Jeremiah S. 106
Black, Louise 109
Black, Mary Dawson 102, 107
Black Diamonds, The 140
Black Horse Inn and Tavern 21
Blair, A.R. 101, 102
Blue Moon Orchestra 140
Blunston, Samuel 15
Blymire, John 128, 129, 136
Boltz, Margaret 150
Bond, W.S. 121
Bonham, Elizabeth 108
Bonham, Horace *107*, 108, 110, 160, 163, *178*, 269
Bonham, Mary Lewis *162*, 163
Bonham House 110, 166, 167
Bon Ton (department stores) 48, 49, 111, 126, 183, 270
Bon-Ton Store, Inc., The 198-201
Borg-Warner Corporation, York Division of 98, 158, 185; complex *184*
Boston Marathon 184
Bott, Hermanus 22
Bottstown 22, 103
Boudinot, Elias 46
Braddock, Edward 28, 29
Bradford Pear Trees 184
Bradley, Margaret 66
Bradley Lifting Corp. 202-204
Breakfast Club, The (drawing) *168*
Brenner, John S. *191*, 192
Brethren in Christ 43, 44
Brillhart, Michael J. *191*
Broadbeck, A.R. 117
Brockie (mansion) 107
Brookside Park 109
Brown, Cassandra S. 137

Brown's Orchards & Farm Market 244-245
Bruce, D. Scott 111
Brule, Etienne 10, 11
Buchanan, James 106
Buchart-Horn Inc./Basco Associates 184, 187
Buehler's Hotel 73
Bulette, Warren C. 145
Bunker Hill 268
Buon, Jean *150*
Burgoyne, John 50
Burroughs, Thomas H. 81
Butler, Richard 71
Bush, Barbara *182*
Bush, George 186
Bush, George W. *187*

C
Calvert, Cecilius (Lord Baltimore) 12, 33
Calvert, Charles (fourth Lord Baltimore) 16
Campbell, Mr. and Mrs. Howard *270*
Campbell, John 58, 59, 63
Camp Scott *93*
Camp Security 41
Canadochly settlement 14
Canals 75-76
Cantler, David 61
Capitol City Airport 179
Capitol Theater *138*, 158
Carl, Jere S. 101
Carl, Michael 23
Carli, Othmar 160
Carlisle 21, 28, 45
Carlisle Market 113
Carlton, John *25*
Carroll Township 81
Carter, Jimmy 156, 157
Carter, W.C. 17, 70
Carver, David B. 187
Cass, Lewis 106
Cassatt, David 61, 67, 71
Cassatt Building 95
Caterpillar Tractor Company 158, 185, 190, 274
Cathcart, Robert 59, 63
Cathcart, Thomas 101,102
Cayuga Indians 11
Cazenove, Thomas 62
Central Market 104, 105, 110, 128, 158, *167*, 170, 171, 190,*191*, 270
Centre Square 22, 23, 24, 25, 26, 32, 40, 44, 46, 48, 52, 53, 58, 62, 63, 72, *77*, 81, 82, 84, 85, 87, 91, 92, *94*, 103, *104*, *105*, 111, 112, 113, 127, 131, *133*, *161*, *174*,187, 195, 197, 268, 269
Chalfont, Edward J. 84
Chalfont, James 75
Chamber of Commerce, York Area 111, 112, 121, 129, 147, 150, 156, 158, 160, *168*, 270
Chambersburg 90
Chanceford Township 81
Chandler, David 23, 31
Chapman, Mattie 274
Charles I (king of Great Britain) 12
Charles II (king of Great Britain) 12, 268

Chatman, Thomas 274
Cherry Lane *174*, 175
Cherry Lane Park *170*
Chesapeake Bay 181, 268
Chester County 16, 18, 90
Children's Home 97, 270
Christ Lutheran Church 18, 23, *24*, 31, 46, 55, 66, *85*, 104, 113, *173*
Churches and synagogues: Adas Israel Congregation, 101, 270; Anshe Hadas Congregation, 101, 270; Beth Israel Congregation, 270; Christ Lutheran Church, 18, 23, *24*, 31, 46, 55, 66, *85*, 104, 113, *173*; Church of the Brethren *43*; Cristo Salvador Hispanic Catholic Church, 158; First English Lutheran Church, 42, *58*, *59*; First Moravian Church, 27, 36, *37*, 55, 66; First Presbyterian Church, 39, 58, 59; First Reformed Church, 42; German Evangelical Lutheran Church, 23, *24*, *58*, *59*, 66; German Reformed Church, 24, 31, 53, 62, *63*, 67; Methodist Episcopal Church, 57, 58, 62, *63*; Ohev Sholom Synagogue, 101, *159*; St. John's Episcopal Church, *27*, 51, 55, 56, *58*, *59*, *115*, 142; St. John's German Lutheran Church, 95; St. Matthew's Lutheran Church, *24*; St. Patrick's Church, 43, *70*, *159*, 270; St. Paul's Lutheran Church, 95, 146; Second English Lutheran Church, *58*, *59*; Temple Beth Israel, 100, *102*, 147, 188; Temple of Justice, *193*; Trinity Reformed Church, 24; Trinity United Church, *173*; Union Lutheran Church, 131-132; Warrington Friends Meeting House, *28*; York Friends Meeting House, *30*, 98; Zion Reformed Church, 36, 46
Church of the Brethren *43*
City Council 183
City Hall 10, 146, 160, 191, 272
City Market 95, 100, 104
Civil War 89-93; Monument, 165
Claiborne, Loretta 184
Clark, Henry 26
Clark, John 44, 59, 63
Cleveland, Grover 103
Clinton, Bill 190, 274, *275*
Clinton, Hilary Rodham 190, *191*
Clockmaking industry 24
Clubs and organizations: American Legion, York, 150; American Red Cross, York County Chapter, 147; Chamber of Commerce, York Area, 111, 112, 121, 131, 147, 150, 156, 158, 160, *168*,187, 205, 270; Cosmopolitan Club, 159; Daughters of the American Revolution, York Town Chapter, 109, 110; Dutch Club, 138; Eagles, Order of, 115; Elks, Order of, 115; Girl's Club of York, 118; Historical Society of York County, The, 66, 68, 69, 108, 109, 110, 146, 151, 160, 163, 164, 166, 172, 191, 270, 274; Historic York County, Inc., 151; Junior League of York, *185*; Knights of Malta,

115; Knights of the Mystic Chain, 115; Lafayette Club, 111, 114; Manufacturers Association, 114, 145, 148; Merchant's Association of York, 111; Odd Fellows, Order of 115; Out Door Country Club, 109; Red Men, Order of, 115; Rotary Club, 147; Tall Cedars of Lebanon, 115; United Way, 147; Visiting Nurse Association, 114; Woman's Club of York, 114, 118; Women's Bureau, 150; YMCA, 97, 147, 270, 273; York Art Association, 114, 180, 182, 270; York Art Club, 114; York Association of the Deaf, 137; York Country Club, 111, 138, 150; York County Agricultural Society, 88; York County Colonization Society, 83; York County Medical Society, 129; York Music League, 138; York Twinning Association, 150; York Volunteers, 269; York Welfare Federation, 146; Young Woman's Club, 146; YWCA, 110. *See also* individual clubs and organizations
Coaler, Andrew 22
Cochran, Thomas E. 90
Codorus 181, 268, 270, 271, 272
Codorus (steamboat) *54*, 73, 269
Codorus Creek 10, 18, 21, 22, 24, 26, 44, 51, 55, 58, 61, 62, 68, 73, 76, *78*, 97, 103, 108, 139, 153, 155, 156; bike path, *160*
Codorus Frog-jumping Contest 152
Codorus Furnace 29, 30
Codorus Mills 99
Codorus Navigation Company 72, 73; seal of, *72*
Codorus Township 43
Cohen, Herbert B. 136, 137
Cold Springs Park 109
Colebrookdale 44
Coliseum Theater 124, 140, 271
Collins, Samuel 66
Colonial Courthouse 182, 275
Colonial Hotel 94, 113, 155, 274
Columbia 99
Columbia, Lancaster & Philadelphia Railroad 77
Commonwealth National Bank 46
Conestogoe Indians 13
Conewago Creek 24, 43, 131
Conewago Falls 73
Conewago Turnpike 66
Connolly, Frank P. 96
Conojehela Valley 14
Conrad, Hal 32
Continental Congress *172*
Continental Insurance Co. 187
Continental Square 21, 22, 95, 149, *165*, *166*, *189*, *193*
Conway, Thomas 50,51
Conway Cabal 49, 51, 52, 63, 268
Cookes House 52, *155*
Cookson, Thomas 21, 22, 59
Coolidge, Calvin 120
Cooperstown *179*
Cope, Gilbert 30

Cosmopolitan Club 159
Court House: (1754) 25, *25*, 26, 40, 41, 45, 46, 47, 48, 49, 52, 53, 65, 69; (1839) 62, *63*, *80*, 81, 84, 87, 88, 92, 118, *119*, 143, 149, 156, 164, *165*; reconstruction of Colonial, 22, *25*, 18, 156, *164*. *See also* Colonial Courthouse
County of York Business and Entrepreneurial Resource Center (CYBER) 186
"Cow Insurrection" 59
Cox, James M. 120
Cox, Thomas 25
Craley, N. Neiman 154
Craley 16
Cresap, Thomas 14
Crispus Attucks Association Center 143, *182*, 271
Cristo Salvador Hispanic Catholic Church 158
Croll, Christopher 22
Crown Cork and Seal 187
Cruise, Walter 36, 38
Cumberland County 28, 29, 106, 178, 186, 272, 275
Currier and Ives Gallery 159
Curry, John 128, 129

D

Dale, James A. 82
Dallastown 109, 152, *189*
Daughters of the American Revolution, York Town Chapter 109, 110
Dauphin 178, 275
Davis, Gardner and Webb foundry-machine shop 73
Davis, Jefferson *273*
Davis, John 141
Davis, Phineas 74, 76, 135, 269
Day, John 25
Deane, Silas 53
Deane, Simeon 52
Declaration of Independence 268, *268*
Delaplane, Helen V. 120, 139
Delaware River 10, 11
Delroy 14
Delta 16, 269
Dempwolf, Frederick 95, 146
Dempwolf, J.A. 95, 100, 103, 105, 112, 164, 169
Dempwolf, Reinhart 95
Dentist's Supply Company 112
Dentsply International 185
Depression, Great 135-140, 271
Devers, Jacob Loucks 145, *146*, 272
Dickens, Charles 85, *86*
Dick's Bloomery 29
Diehl, John Adam 18
Dietz, Gilbert A. 137
Dietz, Jacob 81
Digges, John 16
Digges Choice 16
Dill, James 44
Dill, John 36
Dill, Matthew 25, 39
Dillsburg 25, 36, 177
Dingee and Company, W.W. 88

Dispatch Publishing Co. 185
Distilling industry 24-25, 117
Distribution 178, 186
Dixon, Jeremiah 33, 268
Dobrosky, Tony 189
Domville, Paul 13
Donaldson, Joseph 36
Dongan, Thomas 13, 19
Dorcas Society 269
Dorney, Sheryl Ann 186, 274
Doudel, Jacob 31
Doudel, Michael 31, 36, 37, 38, 40, 61-62, 67, 73, 87
Douglas, Stephen 89
Dover Township 24, 86, 87
Drovers and Mechanics Bank 46
Drovers Bank, a Division of Fulton Bank 206-207
Doze, William C. 156
Duffield, George 46
Dunkards (German Baptists) 43, 44, 82
Dunn, Robert 71
Dunn, William 84
Durang, Ferdinand 70
Durang, Frederick 42
Durang, Jacob 41
Durang, John *40*, 41, 42, 70
Dutch Club 138
Dutch (German) Reformed Church 268
Dutch settlement 11

E

Eades, Benjamin 70
Eagles, Order of 115
Early, Jubal 90, 92
Eastern Baseball League 273
Eastern Market 103, 104, 189, 270
Easton 21, 107
East Prospect 14
Edgecomb (residence) 112
Edie, James 59
Edie, John 59
Edison Electric Light Company 103, 139, 270
Education 55-56, 58-61, 71, 81, 97-98, 148-149, 188. *See also* Schools and Colleges
Edwards, Evan 44
Eichelberger, Eli 153
Eichelberger, George 41
Eichelberger, Jacob 41, 73, 83
Eichelberger, Lydia Worley 41
Elchelberger, Martin 22, 23, 36, 41, 44
Eichelberger, Michael 22, 79
Eichelberger Performing Arts Center 180
87th Regimental Band, Pennsylvania Volunteers 89
Eisenhart, Charles A. 99
Eisenhower, Dwight D. 148
Elgar, John 54, 73, 76, 89, 269
Elizabeth Moore's Inn 46
Elks, Order of 115
Elm Beach *131*, *132*
Elm-spring farm 67
Elmwood 153
Elmwood Theater 137

Elmwood Mansion *181*
Emigsville 190, 274
Engel USA Co. 187
Engle, Jacob 43
English settlement 11, 12-14
Erie 99
ESAB Welding & Cutting Products 246-247
Etters 16
Etting, Elijah 100
Etting, Reuben 100
Etting, Shinah 100
Evangelical Zeitung, Die (newspaper) 79
Evans, Fitz James 95
Everett, Ron 273
Ewell, R.S. 90
Eyster, George 30
Eyster, Weiser and Company 78

F

Fahs, C.M. 117
Fairmount 103
Fairmount Park Road Race 114
Fairview Township 81
Falkler, Charlie 142
Falkler, William A. 160, 161
Family Service 182
Farmer's Market 97, 100, 104, 158, 170
Farquhar, A.B. 88, 89, 90, *91*, 93, 111
Farquhar, Elizabeth Jessop 89, 102
Farquhar, Francis 111, 112, 114
Farquhar Company, A.B. 88, 132, 136, 148; plant of, 115
Farquhar Park *130*, 131, 160, *166*
Fayfield 135
Feder, Jacob 101
Federal Fire Company 56
Feldman, Benjamin 101
Feldmann, W.H. 131
Fells, James Eugene *185*
Fields Department Store, J.W. 152
Fine, John S. 129
Fiorito, Joe 141
Fireside Terrace 150
First English Lutheran Church 42, *58*, 59
First Moravian Church 27
First Night York *190, 193*
First Pennsylvania Regiment 38
First Presbyterian Church 39, *58*, 59
First Reformed Church 42
Fisher, Charles 52, 53
Fisher, John 20, 24, 25, 52, 53, 63
Fisher, John S. 121
Fisher, William J. 145, 148
Fisher house 155
Floods: (1817) 71-72; (1933) 139, 271; (1972) 153-154
Fluhrer Building 95, *168*, 169
Fluhrer's Jewelry Store 103
Food processing 178, 185
Ford, Daniel 75
Ford, Gerald 156, *157*
Ford, Henry 270
Fort Duquesne 65
Foster, J.F. 137
Foust, Thomas M. 155

Franklin, Benjamin 28, *29*, 49, 52, 53
Franklin, William 28
Franklin County 39, 178
Freed, Mr. and Mrs. Theodore F. *270*
French and Indian War 28-29, 35, 36, 39, *189*
Frey, Tobias 89
Frey, William 89
Freystone 89, 103
Friedman, Moses *150*
Furnace Creek 268

G

Gage, Thomas 35
Galbreath, Albert 99
Galleria Mall 188
Gardner, John 83
Gardner, Martin 66
Gardner, Peter 17
Garfield, James A. 107
Gates, Horatio 36, *49*, 50, 51, 52, *164*
Gates House *23*, 51, *151*, 153, 155, *172*, 173
Geesy, C.A. 111
Geise, Frank 101
Gelwicks, Frederick 23
General Borough Law 106
General Gates House 273
General Telephone Company 107, 185
Gent-L-Kleen Products, Inc. 248-249
Gentzler, Waldo Emerson 60
George II (king of Great Britain) 21
George III (king of Great Britain) 35, 38, 55
Gerber, John L. 121
German Evangelical Lutheran Church *23, 24, 58, 59*, 66. *See also* St. Matthew's Lutheran Church
German Lutheran School 44, 55
German Reformed Church 24, 31, 53, 62, *63, 67*
German settlement 14-15, 18
Gettysburg 36, 61, 85, 91, 93, 141, 179, 270
Gettysburg College 60, 61
Gettysburg Pike 90
Gibbs, Mitch *160*
Gibson, John 25
Gibson, M.B. 112
Gichner Mobile 186
Gipe, Florence 102
Girl's Club of York 118
Gitt, J.W. 138, *139*, 154, 274
Glacken, Ed *149*
Glatfelter, Millard E. 60
Glatfelter, Samuel 121
Glatfelter Co., P.H. 185
Glatfelter Insurance Agency 181, 186
Glen Rock State Bank 270
Globe Inn 69, 72
Glossbrenner, A.J. 17, 70
Golden Lamb Tavern 42
Golden Plough Oyster Festival *190*
Golden Plough Tavern 22, *23*, 51, *151*, 153, 155, *172, 187*, 273
Golden Venture, The (ship) 190, 274
Goldsboro 16, 78, 156
Good, Bill 141
Good, Walter 141

Goode, Alexander D. *147, 179, 187*, 274
Goodling, George A. 154, 155
Goodling, William F. 155
Goodridge, Evalina 269
Goodridge, William C. 83, 84, 269, 270
Goodyear Tire & Rubber Company 191, 275
Gordon, John B. 90, *91*, 92, 269
Gore, Albert, Jr. 190, *191*
Gore, Tipper 190, *191*
Gotwad, Mary *124*
Gotwalt, Jacob 95
Gotwalt, Samuel A. 137
Governor's Mansion 121
Grafius, Abraham 66
Grant, Ulysses S. 89, 99
Graybill, Jacob (Crebill) 22
Greeley, Horace 99
Green, Marc 148
Green's Dairy 185
Grieger, Henry 67
Grier, David 44, 62
Griest, Amos 84
Griest, John 268
Griest, Margaret Garrettson 84
Griffith, W.H. 67
Grimek, John 141, *272*
Grist, John 14
Grist Creek 14
Groff, M. Valerie 138
Groll, Christian 18
Gross, John K. 99
Grove, Bruce 122
Grumbacher, Max *111*, 121
Grumbacher's dry-goods store 110
Guckes, Johannes (Cookes) 52, 155
Guinston 27
Gunmaking industry 30

H

Habitat for Humanity 186
Hahn, Michael 36
Hahn Home for Women *143*
Haines, Mahlon N. 121, 122, *272*; house of, 121, *122, 272*
Haines Acres 149, 273
Hall, Thomas 16
Hallam Furnace and Forge 29
Hamme Associates 250-251
Hanover Square *165*
Hallam Township 73, 81, *173*
Halloween Parade 270
Hamilton, Hance 25, 26, 29
Hamilton Bank annex 46
Hancock, John 45, *46*, 49
Hand, Edward 40
Hand-in-Hand Company 268
Hannah Penn Junior High School 271
Hanover Borough 23, 24, 36, 39, 43, 66, 81, 99, 100, 111, 139, 185, 189, 190, 268, 269, 270, 274
Hanover Brands 181, 186
Hanover United 190, 274
Hantz, Jacob 86
Harding, Warren G. 120
Harley-Davidson Company 184, 185, 186,

186, 271, 274; Rodney C. Gott Motorcycle Museum 185
Harnish, Samuel 81
Harrisburg 13, 59, 65, 66, 72, 73, 75, 77, 86, 87, 90, 96, 117, 123, 138, 139, 151, 178, 183, 273
Harrisburg International Airport 179
Harrison, Benjamin 103
Harrison, William Henry 79
Hartley, Catherine *45*
Hartley, Thomas 36, 44, *45*, 50, 57, 59, 62, 63, 65, 268
Hartman, Daniel 87
Hartmann, John 85
Hartmann Building *85*
Hatch, Carl E. 123, 124, 136
Hath, Robert Gamel 27
Haughy, Thomas 27
Hauptmann, Bruno Richard 136
Hay, George 89, 90
Hay, Jacob 67, 103
Hay, John 25, 70, 93
Hay, Julia Maul 25
Hay's Addition 70
Health care 101-102
Heiges, George 103
Helb, Theodore R. 117
Heller, Roger *150*
Hendricks, Henry 22
Hendricks, James 13, 14
Hendricks, John 13, 14
Hendrickson, Cornelius 10, 11
Henneisen, John 67
Henry, John Joseph 57
Henry, Patrick 50
Herrman, Amos W. 128
Hersh, G. Edward 67
Hersh, Grier 67, 111, 112, 118, 270
Hersh, Mrs. Grier 114
Hershey Foods Corporation 187, 274
Hespenheide, W.H. Jack 135
Hess, Wilbert 128, 129
Hetrich, Christian 66
Hex murder 127-129
Heyer, Valentine 17
Hicks, Joseph B. 123, 124
Highland Park 108, 109
Hill, Michael *185*
Hinsman, Joseph 22
Hippodrome Theater 124, *125*
Historical Society of York County, The 66, 68, 69, 108, 109, 110, 146, 151, 160, 163, 164, 166, 172, 191, 270, 274
Historic York County, Inc. 151
History of York County (book) 17
Hoffman, Bob 141, 142
Hoffmeyer & Semmelman 252-253
Hohman, John George 127
Hoke, Samuel (Hoake) 22
Holtzapple, George E. 102, 270
Home Furniture Company 132
Hooke, Frederick 59
Hoopes, Robert 44
Hoover, George W. 99
Hoover, Herbert 120

Hopewell Township 81
Horn & Company, D.E./Pennfield Corporation 208-209
Hotels, inns, and taverns: Black Horse Inn and Tavern, 21; Buehler's Hotel, 73; Colonial Hotel, *94, 113,* 155, 274; Elizabeth Moore's Inn, 46; Globe Inn, 69, 72; Golden Lamb Tavern, 42; Golden Plough Tavern, 22, *23,* 51, *151,* 153, 155, *172, 187,* 273; Penn Hotel, 138, 155; White Hall Hotel, 79, 86; Yorktowne Hotel, 121, 138, 141, 146, 156, 187, *188,* 190, 270, *275*
Howard University 180
Hub Store 88
Hudson, Henry 10
Hugentugler, Ephram S. 122, 126, *130,* 131
Humphrey, Hubert 154
Hunt, Levi Clarence 60
Hunter, Bill 142
Hurricane Agnes 153, 180; destruction caused by, *153*
Hurricane of 1933 139
Hurst, George 137

I

Indians 9-13, 19, 22, 28, 32-33, 268. *See also* individual tribes
Indian Steps 32
Indian Steps Museum 32, 33
Industries 177, 181, 186, 270
Influenza epidemic of 1918 118, 120, 270
Inman, Henry 12
Inners, Christian 81
Iosue, Robert V. 156, *157*
Iron industry 29-30, 86
Iroquois, Five Nations of the 11, 12, 13, 19
Irvine, William 45
Irwin, Elisabeth 26
Irwin, George 57
Internet 183, 187

J

Jackson, Stonewall *273*
Jackson Theater 124
Jacobs, Lorann *189*
Jacobus (town) 126, 274
Jail: (1756) 26; (1768) 26
Jameson, David 29
Jaroschy, Francois 137
Jefferson, Thomas 100
Jemison, Mary 268
Jessop, Edward 89
Jessop, Jonathan 24, 56, 73, 76, 84, 89
"Jewish Bill" 100
Jewish Community Center 188
Jewish residents 100-101
JLS Automation 221
Johnson, Lyndon B. *152*
Johnston, Samuel 27, 31, 33, 44
Johnston, William 58
Joice, John 71
Jones, Robert 26
Judicial Center *188,* 192, 275
Junior League of York *185*

K

Kahn, Solomon 100
Kain, George Hay, Jr. 137
Karenga, Maulana 273
Katz, David 101
Kay, Jack 159
Kean, John 36
Kean, Thomas 268
Keesey, Horace 111
Keesey, Tom 141
Keith, Governor 15
Keller, Alverta Herbst 137
Keller, H. Dietz 113, 114
Kennedy, John F. *151*
Kenny, James 44
Kerr, C.M. 131
Kerr, James W. 101
Key, Francis Scott 70
Keystone Brewing Company 117
Keystone Opportunity Zone (KOZ) 181, 275
Kindig, Joseph, II 135
Kindig, Joseph E., III 18
King, Adam 72
King's Dam 139
Kirk, Elisha 24
Kirk, Jacob 81
Kirkwood, Daniel 61, *81,* 82
Kleffel, J.V. 118
Klein, Jacob 26
Kline, John 73, 269
Klinefelter, Samuel 60
Kling Corp. 186
Knighton, Raymond F. 119
Knights of Malta 115
Knights of the Mystic Chain 115
Kohler, Richard E. 123, 124
Kohl's 191, 275
Koons, Jeff *169,* 180
Korean War 148, 149, 273
Kottcamp, Christian Charles 96
Kottcamp, Harry 96
Kraber, Ed 141
Kraut, Christoph 18
Kreutz Creek 14, 17, 268
Kreutz Creek settlement 14, 23
Kreutz Creek Valley 16, 17
Krout, John D. 158
Ku Klux Klan 124, 126-127, 136
Kurtz, George P. 61
Kurtz, John 46

L

Labor-Management Council 185
Lafayette, George Washington 72
Lafayette, Marquis de 49, 51, *52,* 57, *72,* 111, *164,* 193
Lafayette 193, 268, 269
Lafayette Club 111, 114
Lafean, D. H. 111
Laffe, Madame Annette *150*
Lake Williams 131
Lamarr, Hedy *146*
Lamberville, John de 11
Lancaster 32, 41, 45, 52, 65, 66, 135, 178, 179, 183, 185, 273, 275

Lancaster County 14, 16, 21, 25, 28, 29, 31, 43, 90, 128, 131, *174,* 268
Landys, Samuel 17
Langworthy, Edward 46
Lanius, Christian 87
Lanius, Henry 120
Lanius, W.H. 111
Latimer, Lissie 91
Latimer, Robert Cathcart 108, 109
Laub, Michael 22
Laucks, Israel Forry 97, 100
Laucks, Mrs. Israel 102
Laucks, S. Forry 114, 145
Lauer, Stewart E. 148
Lauman, Christian 62
Laurel Fire Company 49, 52, 56
Laurens, Henry 46, 48, *49,* 50
Lawmaster, Frederick 30
Lawrence, David L. 151
Leader, George M. 151, *272,* 273
Lebach, Joseph 100
Lebanon 178, 275
Leber, Guy 135
Lee, Arthur 38
Lee, Richard Henry 38, 48
Lee, Robert E. 90, 91, 93, 270, *273*
Lehmayer, Nathan 87
Lehmayer's 87, 155, 270, 274
Leibowitz, Michael 101
Leightner, Ignatius 30, 31
Lenhart, Godfrey 24, 47, 58
Lever, John 30
Levin, Sylvan 137
Lewis, Ellis 16
Lewis, James 67
Lewis, Samuel S. 120, 136, 271
Lewis State Park, Samuel S. *174*
Lewisberry 16, 156
Lewistown 137
Lincoln, Abraham 89, 93, 269, 270
Lindenberger, John 71
Lischy, Jacob 23, 24
LIVE (band) 180, 189, 274
Livingston, Philip *53*
Loeffler, George Lewis 62
Loganville 102, 155, 191, 274
Long, John Luther 111, 270; *Madame Butterfly,* 111, 270
Long Level 11, 12
Long Lost Friend, The (book) 127
Loucks, George 73
Louis XIV (king of France) 35
Lovell, James 46, 52
Lower Chanceford Township 32, 81
Lower Susquehanna Valley 153
Lutheran Social Services of South Central Pennsylvania 182
Lutheran Theological Seminary 61
Lyles, Victoria *150*

M

Maclay, William 62
Madison, James 69
Magni, Kerry *159*
Mahoney, John J. 147

Main Street York 181
Manchester Township 24, 59, 131
Mandell, Robert 137
Maneval, Charles H. 155
Manheim Township 268
Manufacturers Association 114, 145, 148, 270
Manufacturing 178, 181, 185, 186, 187, 189, 272
Maple Donuts *192*
Marcus Hook *273*
Marietta 128
Market Sheds 69, 104
Market Street Bridge *111*
Marshall, Elizabeth N. 159
Marsh Creek 36
Martin, Milton D. 103
Martin Carriage Company 115
Martin Memorial Library 103, *168*, 183, 193, 271, 239
Mary Ann Furnace *268*
Maryland & Pennsylvania Railroad 113
Marshall, Elizabeth N. 184, 274
Mason, Charles 33, *268*
Maternal Health Center 272
McAllister, Archibald 44
McAllister, Mary Dill 39
McAllister, Richard 25, 38-39, 44
McBlain, Walter 111
McClellan, W.H. 111
McClellan Heights 119
McFall, John T. 108
McFeeson, John 16
McKinley, William 93
McLaughlin, Harry J. *141, 168*
McLean, Alexander 111
McLean, Archibald 33, 46
Meyer, John 108, 110
Meyer, Lewis 79
Mayersville 108, 110
Meem, John 26, 47
Meier, Solomon 268
Meisenhelder, E.W. 102
Meisenhelder, Edward, Jr. 143
Meisky, A.B. 135
Mellander, G.A. 136
Memoir of John Durang (book) 41
Memorial Hospital *181*, 254-255
Memorial Osteopathic Hospital 143
Menges Mills 151
Merchant's Association of York 111
Merges, Henry R. 160
Methodist Episcopal Church 57, 58, 62, 63
Meyer, Solomon 65, 73
Michael, Joel 140
Mifflin, Thomas 50, 52
Millard, Addison 135
Miller, H.W. 118
Miller, Henry 31, 36, 37, 40, 44, 61, 62, 63
Miller, Henry, Jr. 61
Miller, Lewis 41, 56, *68*, 69, 70, 72, 89, 91, 93
Miller, Ray A. 152
Milligan, Lambdin P. 106
Milling industry 24, 78
Minshall, Thomas 27
Mitchell, Cameron 150, 151, 273

Mitchell, Robert 141
Mitzell, Charles M. 150
Mohawk Indians 11
Monaghan Township 81
Monocacy Road 18, 22, 24
Monoghan settlement 36. *See also*
    Dillsburg
Monroe, James 83
Moody, Ida Frances 137
Moore, Mary 46
Moravian residents 42
Morex Corporation 210-212
Morgan, Margaret 269
Morgernstern, Philip 42
Morris, Charles 57, 83
Morris, George S. 61
Morris, John Gottlieb 57
Morris, Robert Hunter 22
Morse, Otis B., IV 152
Mott, Lucretia 83
Moul, Charles E. 118
Moul, Clayton E. 136
Moul, Margaret E. 274; Home for the
    Handicapped 184
Mundorf, Peter 62
Mussano, Frank 152
Myers, Elizabeth B. 163; birth record
    of, *163*
Myers, Emory 138
Myers, Jacob N. 163; birth record of, *163*

N
Naill, M.W. 118
National Baseball Hall of Fame and
    Museum 179
Nearing the Issue at the Cockpit
    (painting) 107
Neu, Carl F. *168*
Neumann, John N. 269
Newberrytown 16
Newberry Township 16, 81, 84
New Cumberland Army Depot 186
New Cumberland Army Services Depot 272
New Eastern Market 158, 170
New Freedom 16
New Holland 66, 86
New Oxford 85
Newspapers: *Evangelical Zeitung, Die*, 79;
    *Pennsylvania Chronicle and York
    Weekly Advertiser*, 59; *Pennsylvania
    Gazette*, 49, 58; *Pennsylvania Herald
    and York General Advertiser*, 59;
    Pennsylvania Journal, 37; *People's
    Advocate*, 79, 81; *Republicanische
    Herald, Der*, 79; *Sunday News*, 152;
    Sunday Patriot News, 141; *True
    Democrat*, 99; *York Daily Record*, 73,
    81, 139, 140, 154, 185; *York Dispatch*,
    32, 99, 100, 103, 114, 117, 121, 122,
    123, 126, 128, 138, 139, 145, 150, 157,
    160, 186, 187, 274; *York Gazette, Die*,
    268; *York Gazette and Daily*, 65, 72, *73*,
    81, 82, 90, 139, 154, 274; *York High
    Weekly*, 141
New York Wire Cloth Company 148

New York Stock Exchange 186
Nine Hundred Block (book) 142
Nixon, Edward 151
Nixon, Richard 151, 154, 187, *274*
NixonCounty Park, Richard 187, *274*
Noel, Daniel K. *105*, 106, 270
Noel, Jacob 106
Noll, Nellie 128
Northern Central Railroad 78
Normandie Ridge Senior Living Commu-
    nity 214-215
North Hopewell Township 128
North Mall 152
North York Borough 108, 110
Noss' Sons, Inc., Herman 98

O
Odd Fellows, Order of 115
Odd Fellows Hall *88*
Ohev Sholom Synagogue 101, *159*, 188, 270
Old Smokestack Property 193, 275
Old St. Mary's Church 269
Olde York Street Fair *178, 190*
Oneida Indians 11, 19
One Man's Journey (short story) 142
Onondaga Fort 11
Onondaga Indians 11, 19
Onvesant, Matthias 22
Orpheum Theater 124, 138
Ottemiller Company, W.H. 115
Out Door Country Club 109

P
Padden, John H. 148
Paine, Thomas 52, *53*, 155
Palatines 42, 268
Panic of 1837-1839 79
Panic of 1893 108
Parker, Alton B. 114, 120
Parry Corporation, Martin 121
Peach Bottom atomic plant *152*, 153, 157, 273
Peach Bottom Township 16, 39, 62, 81
Pedersen, Trudy 154
Pediatric Health Associates, P.C. 216-217
Penn, Granville 25
Penn, John 19, 58
Penn, John, Jr. 58-59
Penn, Richard 19, 33
Penn, Thomas 19, 31, 33, 268
Penn, William *12, 13,* 14, 15, 18, 19, 25, 268
Penn Common 88, 92, 113, 114
Penn Hotel 138, 155
Penn State Agricultural Extension 189
Penn State York, 218-220. *See also*
    Pennsylvania State University, York
Pennington, James W.C. 84, 85
Pennsylvania Academy of Fine Arts 103
*Pennsylvania Chronicle and York Weekly
    Advertiser* (newspaper) 59
Pennsylvania Colonization Society 83
Pennsylvania Department of Transporta-
    tion 153
Pennsylvania Gas and Electric Company 131
Pennsylvania Gazette (newspaper) 49, 58
Pennsylvania (German) Dutch residents 82

Pennsylvania Herald and *York General Advertiser* (newspaper) 59
Pennsylvania Historical Commission 12
Pennsylvania Journal (newspaper) 37
Pennsylvania Railroad Company 136, 139; bridge of, 103
Pennsylvania State Arts Council 95
Pennsylvania State University, York 148, 273
Pennsylvania Telephone Company 99
Pennsylvania Turnpike 143, 179
Pentz, Mrs. D. 102
People's Advocate (newspaper) 79, 81
People's Drug Store 274
People's Electric Light Company 103
Peoples State Bank of East Berlin 270
Perry 178
Peters, Richards 52
Peters, William 31
Petroskey family, Dale *179*
Pfaltzgraff Company 187, 273
Pfohl, James C. 137
Philadelphia 21, 42, 65, 66, 75, 76, 84, 90, 95, 99, 101, 103, 107, 114, 129, 147, 153, 172, 178, 179, 180, 188, 268, 270
Philadelphia Millinery *96*
Phineas Davis School 135
Pickering, Timothy 47, 52
Pidgeon, Joseph 14
Pietists. *See* Dunkards
Pigeon Hills 14
Pigeon Hills settlement 16
Pinchot, Gifford 121, 138, 139
Pioneer (boat) 75
Piperberg, Jonas 101
Pistone, Bernard 158, 159
Pitt, James 27
Pittsburgh 65, 77
Pluck (oil painting) *269*
Polack, Rodney W. 119
Poorhouse Run flood-control project 153
Population figures 177, 178, 180, 183, 187, 188, 189, 191, 192, 269, 273, 274, 275: (1800) 65; (1820) 72; (1830) 75; (1850) 87-88; (1860) 89; (1880) 99; (1890) 108; (1914) 114; (1920) 120; (1940) 143; (1950) 148; (1960) 151; (1970) 154; (1980) 158, 177; (1990) 177, 188, 189; (2000) 178, 192
Post Office 143
Potomac River 23
Poulain, Denise *150*
Powell, Colin *185*
Prigg, Edward *269*
Printing industry 178
Privat, Charles *150*
Prohibition 122, 178; repeal of, 137
Prospect Hill Cemetery 53, 83
Protective Association 270
Prowell, George R. 29, 36, 47, 73, 79, 86, 98, 112, 114
Public Common 69, 88. *See also* Penn Common
Pulaski, Casimir 52, 53, 55
Pulaski's Legion 55
Pullman Company 115

Q
Queensgate Shopping Center 152
Quigley Motor Co., Inc. 222-223

R
Race riots of 1969 191, 275
Racial tensions 189, 273, 274
Railroads 74, 76-77, 85-86, 136, 179, 180, 189. *See also* Baltimore & Ohio Steam Railway Company; Columbia, Lancaster & Philadelphia Railroad; Maryland & Pennsylvania Railroad; Northern Central Railroad; Pennsylvania Railroad Company; Wrightsville & Gettysburg Railroad Company; York-Wrightsville Railroad
Railroad Station House 62, *63*
Rail Trail 179, *275*
Ramona Restaurant 24
Ramos, Israel 274
Rankin, John 16
Raudenbush, George K. 137
Rauhauser, John F., Jr. 156, *187*
Readco Manufacturing, Inc. 256-257
Reading 21, 44, 66, 127
Reagan, Ronald 156, 186, 274
Red Lion 147
Red Lion Antique Center 258-259
Red Lion Bus Company and Red Lion Tours & Travel 224-225
Red Men, Order of 115
Reed, William 69
Rehmeyer, Nelson 127, 128, 271; house of, *127*
Rehmeyer's Hollow 127, 128, 129
Reineberg, Edward C. 99
Reineberg, Lee 129
Reisinger, Ray 96
Reistertown 85
Religion 23-24, 27-28, 31, 43-44, 57-59, 71, 82, 100-101. *See also* Churches and synagogues
Reminiscences of the Civil War (book) 91
Republicanische Herald, Der (newspaper) 79
Rescue Fire Company 114
Reservoir Hill Park 175
Revolutionary War 35-41, 44-45, 50, 69-70, 273
Rice, C.P. 121
Richard M. Nixon County Park 187, *274*
Ridge Avenue School 148
Rivera, Delma 274
Roberts, T. 59
Robertson, Charlie 190, 191, *191*
Robinson, Andrew 67
Robinson, Penrose 78
Roland, William S. 101, 102
Rolling Stone Magazine 189, 274
Roosevelt, Franklin D. 120, 136, 141
Roosevelt, Theodore 93, 114, 120
Root, B.M. 112
Root Company, B.M. 112
Rosenau, Nathan 100
Rosenmiller, W.F.O. (Fred) *270*
Rossville *164*

Ross, George 44, *268*
Ross, James 39, 40
Rotary Club 147
Roth, John 36, 37, 41
Rousset, Mr. *150*
Rozelle, Mabel 124
Rudy, Charles 103, *273*
Rudy, George B. 99
Rudy, J. Horace 103, *273*
Rudy Company, J. Horace 103
Rush, Benjamin 52, *268*
Russel, William 44
Rust Belt 180
Ruth, Raymond 135
Rutter Bros. Dairy 185

S
Safe Harbor Dam 135
St. Clair, John 29
St. John's Episcopal Church 27, 51, 55, 56, 58, 59, *115*, 142
St. John's German Lutheran Church 95
St. Matthew's Lutheran Church 24
St. Patrick's Church 43, *70*, *159*, 270
St. Paul's Lutheran Church 95, 146
St. Regis Paper Co. 185
Saltzgiver, John Henry 114
Satz, Lorie *116*
Scenic Theater 124
Schaad, Henry C. 154, 273
Schall, James 75
Scherer, Jacob 18
Schintz, Bill *178*
Schlegel, Philip J. 36, 37
Schmeiser, Georg 18
Schmeiser, Mathias. *See* Smyser, Mathias
Schmidt, George S. 154
Schmidt, John C. 67, 72, 83, 98, 114, 118
Schmidt, Mrs. Henry D. 109
Schmidt and Ault Paper Company 110, 118
Schmidt and Company, H.S. 113
Schmucker, Samuel S. 61
Schools and colleges: German Lutheran School, 44, 55; Hannah Penn Junior High, 271; Pennsylvania Academy of Fine Arts, 103; Pennsylvania State University, York, 148, 273; Phineas Davis School, 135; Ridge Avenue School, 148; Shiloh Elementary School, 149; Smith Junior High School, Edgar Fahs, 153; Thompson Business College, 152; University of Pennsylvania, 55, 60, 61, *273*; West York High School, 151; William Penn Senior High School, 138, 189, 271, 273; York Academy of Arts, 148; York College of Pennsylvania, 25, 55, 56, 63, 112, 136, 149, 156; York Collegiate Institute, 61, 98, 102, 103, 124, 138, 139; York County Academy, 55, 56, 59, *60*, 61, 66, 71, 77, 81, 82, 84, 85, 97, 107, 137, 138; York High School, 118, 141; York Junior College, 152
Schultz, Clinton W. 118
Schultz, Heinrich 18
Shultz, Johann *172*

Schultz, John 81
Schultz, Valentine 18
Schwaab, Georg. *See* Swope, George
Schwaab, Michael. *See* Swope, Michael
Scotch-Irish settlement 15-16
Scott, Willard *192*
Sears 270, 273
Second Continental Congress 268
Second English Lutheran Church *58*, 59
Second Pennsylvania Regiment 38
Seitz, Roland F. 112
Seligman, Friedman & Company, P.C. 243
Seneca Indians 11, 19
Senft, Henry 137
Sesame Personnel & Sesame Temps Inc. 226-227
Sesquicentennial celebration 94, 112, 113, 127, 270
Seven Valleys *179*, 187
Shaffer, Addison 98
Shawnee Indians 32
Sheffer, Craig 180
Sheridan, Philip Henry 89
Shiloh Elementary School Building 149
Shipley, Thomas 114, 121
Shipley, William S. 145
Shipley, William W. 145
Shrewsbury Township 81, 112, 126, 150
Shugart, Zachariah 22
Shultz, Christina 16
Shultz, Johann 16; house of, *17*
Shultz, Martin 17; house of, *16*
Shultz, Samuel 100
Simms Machinery, Inc. 266
Simon, C.W. *271*
Simpson, Bobby *182*
Singer house 96
Sipe, Lester 135
Sirovich, Jacob 101
Sitler, Jacob 57
Slagle, Christopher (Schlegel, Christoffel) 23
Slavery 66, 83. *See also* Underground Railroad
Small, Alexander 87
Small, Anna Maria Ursula 44
Small, Cassandra Morris 91, 93
Small, David 90, 101; house of, *96*
Small, George 44, 73, 77, 103
Small, Isabel Cassatt 98
Small, Joseph 81
Small, Luther 103
Small, Peter 66
Small, Philip Albright 61, 77, 78, 90
Small, Samuel 61, 77, 78, 90, 95, *98*, 101, 102, 103
Small, Sarah Latimer 77
Small, W. Latimer 90, 91, 99, 103
Small and Smyser iron works 86
Small and Son, George 78
Small Athletic Field *170*
Small Company, P.A. and S. 44, 61, 78, 90, 95, 111
Small house 111
Smith, Beauchamp E. 148

Smith, Bert 150
Smith, Bruce B. 10
Smith, C. Elmer 121
Smith, Edgar Fahs 61
Smith, James 29, 30, 36, 38, *39*, 46, 59, 62
Smith, John 8, 10
Smith, John Allen 60, 61
Smith, Lucy 137
Smith, Matthew 39, 40
Smith, S. Fahs 111
Smith, Steven Morgan 98
Smith, C. Warren 189
Smith, James 268
Smith, John 268
Smith Company, S. Morgan *98*, 148
Smith Junior High School, Edgar Fahs 153
Smyser, Adam 87, 110
Smyser, Edward 110
Smyser, Henry 110
Smyser, Mathias 18, 110
Smyser, Michael 110
Smyser, Philip 110
Smyser, Roman 135
Smyser, Samuel 88, 110
Smyser-Roger Company 86
Smysertown 103, 110
Snow, Pearl 142
Snyder, John L. 154
Snyder, Simon 69, *70*
Somerset County 106
Southern Pennsylvania Telephone Company 99
Sova, Virgil 160, *168; The Gift of Knowledge* (painting) *168*
Spangler, Baltzar 21, 22, 24, 25, 31, 61
Spangler, Baltzar, Jr. 27, 61
Spangler, Daniel 67
Spangler, George *68*
Spangler, Jacob 72, 73
Spangler, Kaspar 24
Spangler, M.H. 72
Spangler, Michael 70
Spangler, Rudolph 24, 31
Spangler, S.H. 31
Sprenkle, Charles E. 118
Sprigg, George H. 67
Springdale 112, 129
Springettsbury Manor 13, 21, 25; map of, *15*
Springfield Township 81
Spring Garden Band 87, 89, 269
Spring Garden Township 107, 129
Spring Grove 14, 136, 181
Springdale 270
Springettsbury Manor 268
Springwood 109
Stair, Christopher 81
Stair, Robert 146
Stanko, Steve 141
Stanton, Edwin M. 93
Starbucks Coffee Company 190, 274
Stauffer, David F. 98
Stauffer Biscuit Company, Inc., D.F. 260-261
Stauffer/Meiji Biscuit Company 186
Stephenson, Mary F. 152

Steuben, von, Baron Friedrich Wilhelm Ludolf Gerhard Augustin 52
Stevens, Thaddeus 61, 71, 81, 84, 85
Stevenson, George 25, 26, 31, 33
Stephenson, Marion *167; From Farm to Market* (mural) *167*
Stevenson, Robert 88
Stewart Connectors 186
Stock, Joe "Nardie" 142
Stoddard, Benjamin 44, 51
Stoer, Christian 62
Stoer, Peter 67
Stone Mountain *273*
Stony Brook 14, 16, 17, *172*
Stover, "Hunk" 142
Strand-Capitol Performing Arts Center 138, 158, *171*, 180, 182
Strand Theatre 87, 103, 124, *138*, 155, 158, 274
Strayer, J. Calvin 111
Strine, Horace Frank 114
Strubinger, Lewis M. 114
Stuke, Arnold 22
Stuke, Nicholas 22
Sully, Thomas 56
Sunbury 21
Sunday News (newspaper) 152
Sunday Patriot News (newspaper) 141
Sun Fire Brigade 32, 49, 56. *See also* Laurel Company
Sun Fire Company 268
Sun Oil Seaman's Memorial *273*
Sununu, John 186, *187*
Susquehanna and TideWater Canal 75, 76
Susquehanna Broadcasting Company 153
Susquehanna Cable Company 273
Susquehanna Pfaltzgraff Co. 228-229
Susquehanna River 9, 10, 11, 12, 13, 14, 15, 16, 18, 21, 23, 24, 25, 29, 32, 33, 36, 43, 45, 53, 54, 59, 62, 63, 65, 66, 71, 72, 73, 75, 77, 87, 90, 131, 135, 156, *174*, 177, 181, 268
Susquehanna Trail 126
Susquehanna Valley 9, 10, 11, 19, 75, 177, 181, 187
Susquehannocks 8, 9, *10*, 11, 12, 13, 32, 33
Swallow, Silas C. 123
Swedish settlement 11
Swope, Eva 46
Swope, George 18, 22, 25
Swope, Michael 22, 38, 44, 46, 79

T
Tall Cedars of Lebanon (organization) 115
Tannenberg, David 66
Tanner, Jacob 44
Target (department stores) 191, 275
Tassia, Sadie *140*, 271
Taylor, Arthur Russell 142
Taylor, Katherine Haviland 142
Taylor, Zachary 87
Temple Beth Israel 100, *102*, 147, 188
Temple of Justice *193*
Terlazzo, Tony *141*, 272
Terpak, John 141
Tewel, Max 101

Theaters: Capitol Theater, *138*, 158;
    Coliseum Theater, 124, 140, 271;
    Elmwood Theater, 137; Hippodrome
    Theater, 124, *125*; Jackson Theater, 124;
    Orpheum Theater, 124, 138; Scenic
    Theater, 124; Strand Theater, 87, 103,
    124, *138*, 155, 158, 274; Wizard
    Theater, 124; York Theater, 138; York
    Little Theater, 180, 182
Thom McAn 274
Thomas, William 141
Thomasville 135
Thompson, William 39
Thompson Business College 152
Thompson's Battalion 39, 40
Three Mile Island atomic plant 156, 157,
    158, 274
Tighe Industries, Inc. 230-231
Tourism 179, 185, 186
Trattner, Abe 101
Trenwyth Industries 186
Trinity Reformed Church 24
Trinity United Church *173*
True Democrat (newspaper) 99
Trumbull, John 52
Turner, Robert P. 145, 148
Tuscurora Indians 19
250th Anniversary Party *167*, 191, *192*, 275

U

Underground Railroad 83-85
Union Fire Brigade 56. *See also* Vigilant
    Fire Company
Union Lutheran Church 131-132
United Defense Ground Systems Division
    232-233
United States Army Hospital *92*
U.S. Census Bureau 183
U.S. Conference of Mayors 274
U.S. Department of Defense 188
U.S. Immigration Service 190, 274
Underground railroad 269
Union Sunday School 269
United Auto Workers 185
United Way 147, 182
University of Pennsylvania 55, 60, 61;
    Seaman's Memorial, *273*; Smith Walk, *273*
Updegraff, Joseph 31

V

Valencia Ballroom 140, 141, 271
Valley View Park 138
Van Buren, Martin 79
Vandersloot, John Edward 32, 33
Variety Iron Works 86
Victorian Heritage Festival 160
Vietnam War 154
Vigilant Fire Company 56, 114, 120, 136
Visiting Nurse Association 114
Volstead Act 122
Vyner, Louis 137, *138*

W

Wagner, Daniel 36, 46, 59, 63
Wagner, Samuel 67

Wagner, William 2, 6, 67, 69, 70, 78, *161*
Wagonmaking industry 30
Walker, Andrew 44
Walker, Isador 100
Walker, Margaret Louise 154
Wallace, Evalina 269
Wal-Mart 191 275
Wanbaugh, William C. 137
Wanner, Atreus 123
War of 1812 61, 70, 106
Warners Moving & Storage 234-235
Warrington Friends Meeting House *28, 164*
Warrington Township 81
Wasbers, Henry, Sr. 108, 111
Washington, George 31, 36, 37, 38, 39, 40,
    44, 45, 49, 50, 51, 52, 57, 63, 65, 68,
    164, 268
Washington Borough 9, 10, 14
Washington Hall 88
Washington Township 43
Watson, Patrick 25
Watt, Andrew 96
Watt, Richard 95, 96
Watt and Brother 96
Watt Brothers and Company 112
Watts, A.I. 148
Wayne, Anthony 44, 45, 57
Weaver, Daniel 30
Weaver, J.O. 100
Weaver, Jacob E. 129, 135
Weaver Piano Company 100
Webster, James 96
Webster, Richard Watt 96
Weigel, Nathanial 95
Weightlifting Hall of Fame 142, 274
Weiser, Charles 87
Weiser, Jacob 98
Wellsville 177
Welsch, Jacob 22, 24
Welsch, Samuel 24
Welsh, Henry 67
Welshantz, Conrad 30
Welshantz, Joseph 30
West Chester 30
West Manchester Mall 185
West Manchester Township 88, 110, 129, 184
West Manheim Township 81
West Side Osteopathic Hospital 143
West Side Sanitarium 143, 270
West York Borough 141
West York High School 151
WGAL TV 273
Whisler, Ulrich 21
White, Thomas 90
White, William 46
White Hall Hotel 79, 86
White Rose (official symbol) *190, 271*
White Rose Baseball Team 270
White Supremacists *192, 275*
Widagh (Indian) 13
Wiest, John 101, 102
Wiest, Peter *86*, 87
Wiest's Department Store 86, 87, *113*, 155
Wilcocks, Henry 59
Wilkinson, James 40, 50, 51

Willem, Johannes 163; birth and baptismal
    record of, *163*
William Penn Museum 13
William Penn Senior High School 138, 189,
    271, 273
Williams, Israel 71
Williams, Lowell W. 114, 115
Williams, S. Barnitz 137
Williams, Samuel 101
Williams, Smyser 111
Willis, William 26, 83; house of, *83*
Willow Bridges 107
Wilmouth, Margaret 26
Wilson, Woodrow 117, 120
Winans, Ross 76
Winter, C.F. 97
Winter, John 97
Wise, John 81
Wizard Theater 124
WNOW Radio 273
Wolf, A. and E. 86
Wolf, E.I. 77, 78, 81
Wolf Supply Company 87
Woman's Club of York 114, 118
Women's Bureau 150
Woodyear, Thomas 67
WORK-radio 136, 271
World War I 114-115, 117-119, 272;
    Veterans monument *189*
World War II 145-148
Worth Infantry 269
WOYK-radio 136
Wright, James 22
Wright, John, Jr. 22, 25, 84
Wright, Phebe 85
Wright, William 84, 85
Wright's Ferry 36, 62. *See also* Wrightsville
Wrightsville 25, 62, 66, 71, 77, 84, 90, 91,
    92, 99, 118, 135, *170, 172*, 178, 270
Wrightsville & Gettysburg Railroad
    Company 85
Wrightsville-Columbia Bridge *90*
WSBA-radio 149, 272
WSBA-TV 149, 153, 273
WZIK-radio 136

Y

Yellow Soap (book) 142
YMCA 97, 147
Yocumtown 16
Yohe, Luther 151
"York" (locomotive) *74*, 76
York, Carlisle and York Springs Episcopal
    Church 29
York, Duke of 12
York Academy of Arts 148
York Airport 135
Yorkana 14
Yorkarts 180, 182
York Art Association 114, 180, 182
York Art Club 114
York Art Store 114
York Association of the Deaf 137
York Bancorp 183
York Bank 2, 6, 67, 79

York Bank and Trust Co. 183, 185
York Bar Bell Company 141, 142, 262-263
York Barrens 16
York Body Corporation 132
York Borough Centennial 106
York Brewing Company 117
York Bus Company 143
York Carriage Company 114, 270
York Catholic School 271
York Chamber of Commerce 187, 205. *See also* Chamber of Commerce, York area
York Charrette 273
York City Band 87
York City Market 270
York City Police *192*
York City Softball League 149
York College of Pennsylvania 25, 55, 56, 63, 112, 136, 149, 156
York Collegiate Institute 61, 98, 102, 103, 124, 138, 139, 270; basketball team of 1918-1919, *122*; class of 1895-1896, *109*; class of 1920-1921, 116; second building of, *103*
York Container Company 185
York Corporation 148
York Country Club 111, 138, 150
York County (map) *275*
York County Academy 55, 56, 59, *60*, 61, 66, 71, 77, 81, 82, 84, 85, 97, 107, 137, 138, 268
York County Agricultural Society 88
York County Bank 87
York County Chamber of Commerce 180, 205. *See also* Chamber of Commerce
York County Colonial Courthouse 186, *275*; *See also* Colonial Courthouse
York County Colonization Society 83
York County Courthouse 179, 187, *190*, *193*, 269, 274
York County Economic Development Agency 181
York County Gas Company 87
York County Heritage Trust 182, 191, 193, 213, 269, 275
York County Industrial Development Authority 185. *See also* York County Idustrial Development Corporation
York County Industrial Development Corporation 187; CYBER Center, 186
York County Interstate Fair 88, 92, 137, 148, 151
York County Jail 41
York County Medical Society 129
York County Planning Commission 181
York County Prison 269
York County Rifle Company 36
York County Shopping Center 149, 273
York County War and Welfare Fund 146
York Cultural Alliance 182
York Daily Record (newspaper) 73, 81, 139, 140, 154, 185, 274
York Depot 89
York Dispatch (newspaper) 32, 99, 100, 103, 114, 117, 121, 122, 123, 126, 128, 138, 139, 145, 150, 157, 160, 186, 187, 274

York Fair Grounds 109, 113, 118, 120, 143, 152, *165, 170, 172*
Yorkfest *190*
York Fire Department 56
York Flying Service 135
York Foundation 182
York Friends Meeting House *30*, 98
York Gas Company 118, 131
York Gazette, Die (newspaper) 268
York Gazette and Daily (newspaper) 65, 72, *73*, 81, 82, 90, 139, 154, 274
York Graphic Services 186
York Haven 16, 66, 87, 131, 136
York Haven Paper Company 118
York Haven turnpike 79
York Haven State Bank 270
York Health Corporation 264-265
York High School 118, 141
York High Weekly (newspaper) 141
York Hospital *102*, 103, 129, 270; association of, 101
York Hospital/ Wellspan Health 236-238
"York House" *178*
York Ice Company 145
York Imperial Apple 269
York International Corporation 186, 240-242
York Junior College 152
York Junior Symphony Orchestra 182
York Little Theater 137, 150, 151, 180, 182
York Mall 273
York Manufacturing Company *98*, 124
York Murals Program 274
York Music League 138
York National Bank 95, 118, 269
York Oil Burner Company 136, 141
York Opera House 106, *107*, 112, 138, 270
York Oratorio Society 270
York Ordnance Depot 272
York Paint and Hardware Company 86
York Peppermint Patties 181, 187, 274
York Plan 145, 148, 272
York Police Department 122
York Railways Company 108; streetcar, *108*
York Recreation Commission 137
York Riflemen 31, 268
York Rifles 89, 269
York Safe and Lock Company 100
York Sanitary Milk Co. *271*
York Spanish Council 274
York Spring Wagon Works 103
York Square 100, 118, *134*, 138
York Street Railway Company 103, 108, 143
York Symphony Association 180
York Symphony Orchestra 137, 138, *158*, 182, 272
York Telephone and Telegraph Company 99
York Telephone Company 99, 136
York Theater 138
Yorktown Paper Mill 185
Yorktowne Dance Theatre 159
Yorktowne Hotel 121, 138, 141, 146, 156, *168*, 187, *188*, 190, 270, *275*
York Trust Company 95
York Twinning Association 150
York Visiting Nurse Association 270

York Volunteers 269
York Wagon Gear Company 108, 113
York Wall Paper Company 109
York Wallcoverings 186
York Water Company 71, 77, 131, 136, 152, 154, *167*, 175, 269
York Welfare Federation 146
York White Roses (baseball team) 271
York-Wrightsville Railroad 85
York Youth Symphony Orchestra 182
Young, Edward 71
Young, Hiram 99
Young, Kim *274*
Young Family 186
Young Woman's Club 146
YWCA 110, 270, 273

Z
Zech, L.U. 129
Ziegle, Gottlieb 75
Ziegle, Thomas A. 89
Ziegler, Frank A. 99
Ziegler, Georg 18
Ziegler, J.T. 101
Ziegler, Jacob 18
Ziegler, Philip 18
Zimmerman, Georg Adam 18
Zinn, Jeannette 118
Zion Reformed Church 36, 46
Zollinger's 274
Zorger, Frederick 30